Contemporary Economic Problems

Deficits,
Taxes, and
Economic Adjustments

Contemporary Economic Problems

Deficits, Taxes, and Economic Adjustments

Phillip Cagan, editor
Eduardo Somensatto, associate editor

American Enterprise Institute
Washington, D.C.

880730

Distributed by arrangement with

UPA, Inc.
4720 Boston Way
Lanham, Md. 20706
3 Henrietta Street
London WC2E 8LU England

Library of Congress Cataloging-in-Publication Data

Contemporary economic problems.

(AEI studies ; 455)
1. United States—Economic conditions—
1981-   . 2. United States—Economic
policy—1981-   . 3. Budget—United
States.   4. Taxation—United States.
5. Balance of trade—United States.
I. Cagan, Phillip.   II. Somensatto, Eduardo.
III. Series.
HC106.8.C665   1987   330.973′0927   87-1395
ISBN 0-8447-3621-X (alk. paper)
ISBN 0-8447-3620-1 (pbk. : alk. paper)

1 3 5 7 9 10 8 6 4 2

ISSN 0892-3981
AEI Studies 455

Printed in the United States of America

CONTENTS

Introduction

Phillip Cagan
Eduardo Somensatto

After 1980 the rate of inflation in the U.S. economy fell sharply, and budget and trade deficits rose to record size. Directly or indirectly these developments figure in the major policy issues currently debated across the nation. Disinflation and the collapse of oil prices have invited proposals to alleviate the resulting strains on domestic industries and the financial system. The budget deficit has influenced the allocation of government expenditures and the nature of tax reform. Moreover, the foreign trade deficit has prompted proposals to moderate the swings in the dollar exchange rate and to protect against foreign competition.

The essays in this volume address these issues. Each essay is preceded by a summary, and this introduction provides a brief overview of the interrelated policies and developments.

An anxious U.S. public and Congress have focused on the trade deficit, raising questions about our international economic policy and our ability to compete in world markets. At first after 1980, the strengthening of the dollar exchange rate from a low level confirmed a return of confidence in the vitality of the economy. But later the magnitude of the dollar's appreciation and the worsening trade deficit came as a painful surprise. Traditional theories differed on the explanation for such a steep rise in the dollar, and none seemed fully adequate. Economists and the public found the dollar's behavior puzzling, and many questioned the desirability of allowing exchange rates to float without government intervention.

Fluctuations in the dollar highlight the need to distinguish between short-run volatility and longer-run movements in exchange rates. Recent short-run daily and monthly variations appear to be largely unpredictable, just as in past periods of floating rates. Longer-run movements, however, can usually be traced to trade and investment patterns and national policies—the so-called fundamentals. Yet our understanding of longer-run movements remains deficient, as dramatized by their recent lack of correspondence to traditional theories. Our present ability to manage exchange rates wisely, therefore, is clearly limited.

Notwithstanding the likely difficulties, the administration in 1985

1

moved from its previous policy of nonintervention to one of promoting coordination among nations to control exchange rates. The purpose was to moderate political pressures for protection by forcing the dollar down and thus reducing the trade deficit. The change in policy raised anew the issue of whether coordination of national economic policies and intervention to stabilize exchange rates can be effective or, considering the likely outcome, desirable. The new coordination has primarily meant prodding other countries to adopt stimulative demand policies, so far with meager results.

The huge trade deficit heightened fears that U.S. industry was losing out to foreign competition and declining. The use of trade quotas and tariffs gained adherents in Congress. Deterioration of the trade balance, however, can be traced in large part to the increase in the budget deficit and the resulting appreciation of the dollar. Long before the trade balance deteriorated, post–World War II trends in world trade indicated growing foreign competition for U.S. manufacturing. Yet apart from a few industries, U.S. manufacturing on the whole is not losing competitiveness or declining. The overall manufacturing share of GNP shows no tendency to decline, and productivity performance in manufacturing remains within historical norms. Impressions to the contrary reflect employment shifts from manufacturing to services. Experience with protectionist measures has shown that they are a costly and, in the long run, ineffective way to deal with the trade deficit.

Appreciation of the dollar and increased foreign competition did have an important benefit. They supported the reduction in inflation from 1980 to 1985. In reverse fashion the dollar depreciation since early 1985 could work to escalate inflation. Yet, because of continuing foreign competition and the sluggish pace of economic activity, little evidence of price escalation materialized through 1986.

Indeed, although the sluggish economy led the Federal Reserve to pursue a highly stimulative monetary policy, the stimulus was unexpectedly offset by an unusual decline in monetary velocity. The increased uncertainty over how monetary growth was affecting aggregate demand led to abandonment of the brief experiment with monetary targeting. The conduct of policy returned for short-run guidance largely to interest rates, which have often not been very reliable. Monetary policy now lacks a reliable guide and needs to be conducted with great caution to avoid the oft-repeated error of over-stimulating the economy and reviving inflationary pressures.

The recent success in reducing inflation produced and in part reflected a sharp decline in commodity prices, particularly the price of oil. The price fluctuations in oil raised again the issue of vulnerability to possible future shortages. The risk that future oil prices may at times be low can discourage the maintenance of domestic production and exploration. A case can be made for a government guarantee of some appropriate minimum price to eliminate such risk and thus to protect national security interests against future shortages. Such a case should be considered separately from the political issue of aiding the recent distress in the petroleum industry.

The distress in the petroleum and farming sectors added to strains in parts of the financial system as deregulation increased competition. An unusually large number of banks and thrifts are classified as problem institutions, and many face dissolution. The problems of depository institutions have raised questions about the stability of the entire financial sector and especially about the viability of the federal deposit insurance system. This system for protecting deposits needs reform. But reform should avoid the temptation to provide 100 percent protection to borrowing firms against failure and to depositors against losses. A vibrant and efficient financial system depends on a market in which losses as well as gains occur and where risks are accepted and properly managed.

The distress in some sectors and the long-run trend toward services in the economy are widely cited to explain the slow growth, almost stagnation, of real wages since the early 1970s. Another explanation is the expansion of youth and women in the labor force and the growing importance of fringe benefits not included in measured wages. In fact, however, these trends account for very little of the wage slowing, as shown by analysis of their effects. Moreover, recent concerns about increased dispersion of wages as a result of sectoral employment shifts are apparently misplaced in view of the decline in dispersion of wages for individual workers. Presumably the slower growth of wages reflects basic trends in productivity. Proposals to restructure industry or to eliminate foreign competition through protectionist measures would be self-defeating.

The federal budget deficit is the leading explanation for the large U.S. trade deficit. Efforts to bring the budget under control led to the Gramm-Rudman-Hollings legislation to force reductions, though with important exemptions of the main entitlement programs. So far, despite a significant containment of the growth of the budget, expenditure authorizations in 1986 for the new fiscal year satisfy the law's stated goals partly with the help of some legerdemain. Substantial further reductions in authorizations in subsequent years to meet the intention of the law appear highly questionable. The composition of the budget, however, has undergone major changes. Aside from defense and interest, the budget is increasingly composed of transfer

3

payments to the elderly and the poor, with some shift away from grants to state and local governments in reflection of the president's "New Federalism."

On the revenue side of the budget, the administration's desire to reform income taxes bore fruit with the passage of the Tax Reform Act of 1986. The steep reduction in tax rates and the broadening of the tax base equalized effective tax rates on different kinds of capital, which should improve the allocation of capital and reduce the influence of taxes on decision making. At the same time, the shift in tax revenues from individuals to corporations has raised fears of an adverse effect on investment. The overall increase in the cost of capital is not large, however, and the effect on investment remains uncertain.

Tax reform reflected the view that tax policy has adversely affected our competitive position in international trade. The disincentives to saving and investment hurt our ability to compete in world trade. The Japanese success in industrial progress and trade is thought to reflect a favorable tax system. Surprisingly, examination of Japanese taxes and comparison with the U.S. system show only minor differences in the taxation of capital; but the Japanese system provides substantial incentives for household saving, and investors benefit greatly from the long-time absence of major changes. Although increases in U.S. household saving may be difficult to achieve, stability of the tax system is a lesson from Japan worth learning.

In examining these policy issues, the authors of these ten essays have benefited from joint discussions of the common developments that bear on each topic. All of these issues will likely remain for some time central to the conduct of macroeconomic policies. They merit careful analysis and full discussion.

1

The Behavior of the Dollar: Causes and Consequences

Jacob S. Dreyer

Exchange rate flexibility has made a positive contribution to external payments adjustments and to the maintenance of an open trade and payments system in a period of massive external shocks. It is questionable whether any less flexible system would have survived the strains in the past decade.

GROUP OF TEN
June 21, 1985

The constant expansion of our economy requires . . . reliable exchange rates around the world. We must never again permit wild currency swings to cripple our farmer and other exporters.
PRESIDENT RONALD W. REAGAN
State of the Union Address
February 4, 1986

It is our view that the market will determine what the value of the U.S. dollar will be.
JAMES A. BAKER III
Secretary of the Treasury
February 4, 1987

Summary

In October 1986 Japan and the United States announced an agreement to fashion their policies in such a manner as to keep the exchange rate within an agreed upon range. The precise bounds of the range were not made public, nor were the specific mutual policy commitments.

The Tokyo-Washington agreement was one more step in a departure by the Reagan administration from its original policy toward exchange rate management. When the administration came into office in January 1981, the dollar had been on a six-month rebound from its nearly record low. The shift

5

by the Federal Reserve in October 1979 toward controlling monetary aggregates was beginning to lend credence to the resolve of its anti-inflationary stance. In addition, the sharp depreciation of the dollar in 1977–1978 raised U.S. competitiveness and, in conjunction with other factors, caused an improvement in the U.S. trade balance.

The election of Ronald Reagan was viewed by foreign exchange markets as favoring a strong U.S. currency, and the first several months of his administration witnessed a virtually uninterrupted appreciation of the dollar. One of the administration's first acts was to discontinue the massive intervention operations carried out by the Federal Reserve and the Treasury during the Carter years. The stated policy of the new administration was to let the dollar exchange rate be determined solely by market forces and to intervene only when the markets became disorderly

True to its stated policy, the administration did not interfere with the continuing appreciation of the dollar. It kept rising even throughout the recession of 1981–1982, as the adherence to tight money kept interest rates in the United States substantially higher than in other industrial countries, the recession-induced lower demand for imports postponed the widely expected deterioration of the trade deficit, fiscal policy rapidly became highly stimulative, the tax legislation of 1981 was very favorable for investment, Europe was following the United States into a recession, and the United States was increasingly perceived as providing the best political and business climate for international investors.

Even though these factors, especially when taken together, provide a plausible explanation of the dollar's early rise, formal models of exchange rate determination failed to predict the appreciation of the dollar or even adequately to explain it ex post. Many economists suspected that the structure of the relationships between the exchange rate and its theoretical determinants had been undergoing significant alteration. Their suspicion was reinforced by the behavior of the dollar after mid-1982.

In the summer of that year the Federal Reserve relaxed its iron grip on the money supply, and interest rates in the United States tumbled in relation to those abroad. The U.S. trade position began to deteriorate, and the onshore-offshore interest rate differential on dollar-denominated instruments— a proxy for a "safe haven" premium—shrank. In spite of these developments, which could have been expected to sap the strength of the dollar, its climb was interrupted in late 1982 for only about one quarter. It resumed its ascent in early 1983, especially against the European currencies.

As the dollar continued to appreciate in 1983 and 1984, its rise became ever more troubling to analysts, businessmen, and policy makers. Even though real growth in the United States in 1983 and until mid-1984 was higher than in the rest of the world and inflation-adjusted bond yields remained well above those in other industrial countries, other presumed determinants of the exchange rate, most conspicuously the money supply and the current account, behaved in a manner that should have weakened the dollar. Yet the dollar kept growing stronger and thus increasingly put many American industries at a competitive disadvantage.

Despite numerous calls from the adversely affected sectors of the economy for remedial policy action, mounting diplomatic pressure from some allied governments, and intensifying congressional criticism, throughout the long rise of the dollar the administration essentially abstained from intervening in the foreign exchange markets and, more broadly, from treating the exchange rate as an explicit policy target. Its spokesmen pointed out, correctly, that the strength of the dollar was a direct consequence of enormous net capital inflows attracted into the United States for a great variety of reasons. The gist of the argument was that with high domestic investment, enormous federal deficits, and low saving rates, discouraging capital imports would inevitably lead to higher real interest rates. To the admonitions from various quarters to smooth out short-term fluctuations in the dollar exchange rate, the administration spokesmen responded, again correctly, that there is no evidence that such fluctuations inflict harm on the economy or that anybody has sufficient insight to distinguish between exchange rate changes that reflect a bona fide adjustment and those that arise from speculative attacks on the currency.

From mid-1984 until March 1985 the advance of the dollar accelerated, even though virtually all theoretical exchange rate determinants had pointed for some time toward its imminent fall. This inexplicable behavior of the dollar led a number of analysts to advance postulates of market irrationality. At least equally plausible is the postulate that not nearly enough is known about the process governing the determination of asset prices in general and exchange rates in particular to be confident that the various explanations offered leave out no important determinants.

In the political arena James Baker, who succeeded Donald Regan as secretary of the Treasury at the beginning of 1985, inherited a near-record-high dollar, a manufacturing sector battered by import penetration and loss of foreign markets, and a rising protectionist sentiment in the Congress. Under the new leadership, the Treasury, in collaboration with the Federal Reserve (which complied with but never became enthusiastic about the nonintervention policy of the first Reagan administration), tried to counter the dollar's advance by intermittently intervening in the foreign exchange market.

The dollar crashed on its own and started a steep decline in March 1985. It kept declining through the summer even though the underlying theoretical fundamentals were not much different in mid-1985 from what they were a year before. But since the consensus was that the rise of the dollar through early 1985 had been unjustified, its subsequent decline was taken as entirely explicable by the fundamentals. A brief pause in the dollar's descent in the late summer of 1985 spurred or perhaps only advanced a switch in U.S. policy

toward exchange rate management. On September 22, 1986, the U.S. Trea-
sury engineered the Plaza Agreement, committing the five largest industrial
countries to coordinating their policies with the aim of bringing the dollar
down. The agreed upon course of action included joint intervention in foreign
exchange markets. Since then sizable intervention operations have frequently
been undertaken by U.S. authorities both unilaterally and in concert with
other countries.

The new attitude and policy of the administration toward exchange rates
were given the presidential seal of approval in the 1986 State of the Union
address and confirmed at the Tokyo summit in May 1986. The bilateral
Japanese-American agreement in October 1986 on the appropriate range for
the yen-dollar rate is the latest reflection of this policy.

Such a policy may succeed in reducing fluctuations in some bilateral
dollar exchange rates, but even this outcome is by no means assured, as the
experience of the late 1970s has shown. The policy of deliberate suppression of
exchange rate variations is bound, however, to shift elsewhere the burden of
adjustment to various unforeseeable shocks. Most likely, money and capital
markets would bear a heavier burden of adjustment, but a greater burden
would also be imposed on prices and on output produced and traded. For a
given set of domestic policies and an inherently unpredictable pattern of future
disturbances, the exchange rate policy now being put in place is not likely to be
effective in increasing economic stability or improving economic performance.
The opposite outcome is much more likely.

A floating exchange rate system has been the subject of lively
controversy since before the inception of floating rates in March 1973.
The debate, among national policy makers, business leaders, and
economists, has frequently revolved around the observed behavior of
exchange rates and its consequences. What some have viewed as wild
swings others have perceived as a highly beneficial absorption of real
and monetary shocks; what some have considered an unmitigated
calamity for exporters and importers, others have seen as part and
parcel of an adjustment of external payments positions.

There has been much more to the debate, of course, than emo-
tional characterizations of exchange rate movements and their effects.
The 1970s witnessed numerous trailblazing efforts to push theories of
exchange rate determination well beyond the inherited approaches
based on flow of payments. Creative marriages of economic and
modern finance theories gave birth to many sophisticated analyses of
foreign exchange markets. The role of liquidity creation and the
characteristics of reserve assets under a floating system have been
seriously explored both in academic literature and by policy makers.
Some progress has been made in developing gauges of the welfare

implications of alternative exchange rate regimes. Various modalities of a policy of official intervention in foreign exchange markets have been further explored, both theoretically and empirically. The issue of international harmonization of macroeconomic policies aimed at stabilizing exchange rates has been subjected to highly sophisticated game-theoretical and information-theoretical analyses. Yet the main focus of the debate has invariably been the issue of what causes exchange rates to move as they do and what are the economic consequences of their movements.

In recent years the debate has become even livelier. The dollar's dizzying rise from mid-1980 through early 1985, accompanied by rapidly rising U.S. trade and current account deficits, intermittent episodes of rapid monetary expansion, and (since 1982) the shrinkage of the interest rate differential between the United States and other major countries, has thrown theories of exchange rate determination of the 1970s into disrepute. Almost continuous turbulence in the foreign exchange market and rapid movements of not just nominal but also real (that is, inflation-adjusted) exchange rates contributed to the puzzlement of economists and practitioners alike. The precipitous plunge of the dollar against the yen and European currencies since March 1985, while not yet fully digested by exchange rate models, is virtually certain to deepen the disarray among those who seek to identify factors that predictably cause exchange rates to move.

Economists have responded to the fireworks in exchange markets over the past decade critically and quite candidly reassessing the exchange-rate-determination theories of the 1970s, by attempting to refine them further, and by proposing new explanations for the startling behavior of exchange rates, some of them departing radically from the received wisdom of earlier decades. The behavior of exchange rates in the 1980 –1986 period produced a discernible shift of sentiment among analysts away from freely floating rates and a stunning reversal in the stated position of the Reagan administration. In the first policy statement by the new administration on international monetary matters, in May 1981, the under secretary of the Treasury for monetary affairs repeatedly stressed the need to allow exchange rates to adjust to changing circumstances and shifting expectations. He interpreted the looming current account deficits in conjunction with a rising dollar as a reflection of the attractiveness of the American economy and strongly emphasized that "our exchange market policy can best be described as a 'return to fundamentals.'"[1] Some four years later the administration engineered a concerted multilateral intervention effort, started prodding other governments into global management of exchange rates, and declared exchange rate movements responsible for agricultural and industrial woes.

Although the turnabout of the Reagan administration can be and has been explained as a tactical move designed to give vent to mounting protectionist pressures in the Congress and congressional initiatives—so far unsuccessful—to legislate a fixed exchange rate system[2] or at least a much more active official involvement in exchange rate management[3], the growing disillusionment with the performance of floating rates is unmistakable. Three major swings in the real exchange rate of the dollar—the sharp depreciation between 1976 and 1980, the even sharper appreciation from mid-1980 to the first quarter of 1985, and the decline, steeper still, since March 1985—shattered the placid views of the floating-rate regime so prevalent in the mid-1970s. These large swings in real rates have come to be held increasingly responsible for persistent current account imbalances and for misallocation of productive resources among sectors and countries, both giving rise to an intensifying protectionist mood and fostering discord among the Western allies. Because these medium-term movements in real exchange rates cannot be easily or convincingly explained by traditional economic fundamentals, the view that they must be a result of rational or irrational speculation has been gaining credence.

Concomitantly, previous widespread beliefs that floating exchange rates promote payments adjustment, cushion real shocks and absorb monetary shocks, or contribute to international harmony by allowing individual countries to pursue autonomous monetary policies have been shaken. Moreover, since medium-term swings in real exchange rates have been accompanied by high variability of nominal exchange rates at higher frequencies—daily, weekly, and monthly— many have come to regard medium-term swings and short-term variations as interconnected. The latter have been interpreted as a manifestation of market inefficiency, resulting in false price signals and increasing foreign transaction costs. On both counts floating exchange rates have begun to be viewed by some analysts, and many more economic policy makers, as impeding international trade and lowering its efficiency.

Given all these and other perceived defects of the floating rates system, it is hardly surprising that proposals to change or modify it have attracted the interest of public policy analysts and the attention of decision makers.[4] The end of the lively controversy over the performance of floating exchange rates is not nearly in sight.

The primary purpose of this paper is to review the record of floating rates over the past decade, survey various explanations of their performance, and evaluate the accumulated evidence pertaining to their effects on the economy.[5] The paper focuses exclusively on the exchange rates of the dollar and the U.S. economy. It consists of four sections. The first section presents "facts," that is, various measures of the medium-term movements and short-term variability of the dollar exchange rates. The second, central section reviews various notions of exchange rate misalignment as well as explanations offered for its occurrence. The third section does the same for the volatility of exchange rates. The fourth section evaluates the evidence on the consequences of exchange rate volatility. Finally, the conclusion explores certain policy implications.

Movements in Dollar Exchange Rates

So much has been said in the past several years about the swings in the value of the dollar and its volatility that there appears little to be added. The "value" of the dollar is not, however, an unambiguous concept. Different measures of the value of the dollar—nominal or real, bilateral or multilateral rates—will give noticeably different pictures of its changes.

Medium-Term Movements. We may start with the record of medium-term swings in the value of the dollar, using for this purpose several alternative indexes. No attempt is made to evaluate the relative advantages and drawbacks of a particular index either as a gauge of the dollar's change against the generality of currencies or as a measure of U.S. international competitiveness. The purpose of this section is thus not to try to select the "best" indicator of the overall dollar movements but, quite the opposite, to demonstrate that no such single measure can be defined unambiguously.

Nominal exchange rates. Figure 1–1 presents quarterly averages of nominal dollar exchange rates against the currencies of Japan, West Germany, Switzerland, the United Kingdom, and Canada. After the turbulence in 1973–1974, thought to have been due first to the change of the exchange rate regime and then to the first oil shock, relative calm prevailed in the foreign exchange markets in 1975–1976. This period of calm (except for the sharp depreciation of the pound) led many to believe that the period of learning was over and from then on exchange rates would behave well. It was thought, in particular, that exchange rates would move so as largely to offset the differentials in national inflation rates and would thereby contribute to timely elimination of imbalances in international payments. As the figure illustrates, the calm ended in late 1976. From then on, bilateral nominal exchange rates of the dollar (except against the Canadian dollar) displayed pronounced swings from quarter to quarter and very large

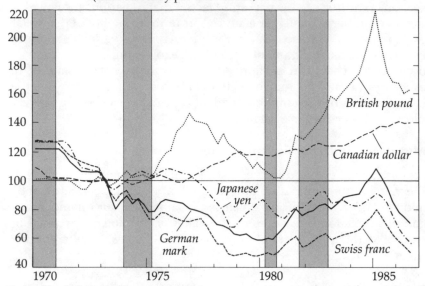

FIGURE 1–1

NOMINAL EXCHANGE RATES, 1970–1986
(local currency per U.S. dollar; 1973: I = 100)

NOTE: Shaded areas are recessions.
SOURCE: International Monetary Fund, *International Financial Statistics*.

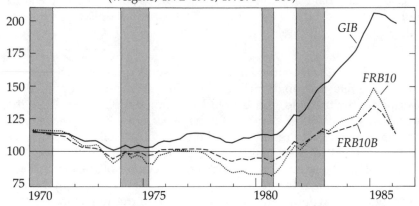

FIGURE 1–2

NOMINAL EXCHANGE RATE INDEXES, 1970–1986
(weights, 1972–1976; 1973: I = 100)

NOTE: Shaded areas are recessions. FRB10 is the Federal Reserve Board index of the dollar's value against the currencies of ten major industrial countries; FRB10B has the same currency coverage and base period. See text for differences in weights. GIB is a "global" index with bilateral rates.
SOURCE: International Monetary Fund, *International Financial Statistics* and *Direction of Trade Statistics*.

swings over a span of several years. A quarter-to-quarter change of 10 percent or more in the exchange rate has occurred several times in the past ten years against the pound, the yen, the German mark, or the Swiss franc, as has 50 percent cumulative change over periods of less than two to four years.

Figure 1–2 depicts movements in three indexes of nominal exchange rates. FRB10 is the Federal Reserve Board index of the dollar's value against the currencies of ten major industrial countries. The weights reflect the importance of the countries' foreign trade in the aggregate foreign trade of the group. FRB10B designates an index that has the same currency coverage and base period as FRB10 but whose weights are assigned in accordance with the countries' importance in bilateral trade with the United States. A comparison of changes in these two indexes reveals occasional sizable divergences between them, movements in the FRB10B being distinctly more muted.[6] It is not surprising, of course, that both indexes display less medium-term variability than the bilateral rates between the dollar and the currencies of Japan and Western Europe.

To appreciate fully the extent of arbitrariness in measuring changes in the composite nominal exchange rate of the dollar, consider movements of the GIB ("global" index, bilateral weights). This index includes, in addition to the currencies of industrial countries, currencies of a number of the most important U.S. trade partners among less-developed countries.[7] Since some of those countries effectively peg their currencies to the dollar, the medium-term variability of this measure of the international value of the dollar should be considerably smaller than that of FRB10B or FRB10, let alone than the variability displayed by the bilateral exchange rates depicted in figure 1–1. But this is demonstrably not so, simply because the group includes a few countries with very high inflation whose currencies' massive depreciation against the dollar (in conjunction with large weights based on their trade with the United States) has dominated changes in the overall index.[8]

The very uneven pace of the dollar's decline since March 1985 against different currencies has spurred a proliferation of exchange rate indexes. At least half a dozen alternative indexes have recently been constructed by official and private financial institutions. The search for "the best" or "the most representative" index is, however, largely futile in the absence of criteria for discrimination among them. In any event, although the amplitude of medium-term movements in the nominal value of the dollar in the past ten years has been very large by all past standards, the comparisons presented in figure 1–2 suggest that its magnitude depends largely on an essentially arbitrary choice of a particular index.

Real exchange rates. While the nominal exchange rates of the dollar—bilateral or composite—measure its value in terms of other currencies, real exchange rates purport to reflect its value in purchasing power over foreign goods and services. They are frequently taken as an approximate measure of America's competitive position and are most commonly expressed as an index relative to some base period.[9]

Figure 1–3 is a plot of real bilateral rates between the U.S. dollar and the yen, the deutsche mark, the pound, the Swiss franc, and the Canadian dollar. A comparison with figure 1–1 reveals great similarity in medium-term movements of the bilateral nominal and real rates, suggesting that changes in relative price levels play a limited role, at least in the medium run, in affecting these nations' competitiveness.

A few points are in order. First, a change in the index indicates real appreciation or depreciation of the dollar in relation to its value in the base period. A change tells us nothing about its overvaluation or undervaluation unless we assume that in the base period the dollar was "properly valued" and the criterion for such proper valuation is the purchasing power parity.

Second, it is by no means self-evident, even conceptually, which price indexes are appropriate deflators for nominal exchange rates. Are the changes in real rates supposed to measure the relative price shift between imports and domestic goods, between exports and foreign goods, or between domestic and foreign exports to third markets? In two-country trade models with the composite traded good common to both countries and nontraded goods specific to each country, the real exchange rate would be expressed as the ratio of traded to nontraded goods prices; in models with traded goods specific to each country but no interaction with nontraded goods, the real exchange rate would be the ratio of foreign to domestic traded goods prices, that is, (the reciprocal of) the terms of trade. Even a cursory glance at price series for U.S. exports and for services (as a proxy for nontraded goods) displays enormous differences in patterns, suggesting that the use of one or another price index would produce very different pictures of real exchange rates thus derived.[10]

The third, related point is that the most frequently used price indexes—the wholesale and consumer price indexes—are also the most inappropriate conceptually. But they are also the most readily available for a large number of countries, and the method of their construction is reasonably consistent among countries.

While real bilateral rates are supposed to reflect changes in the

FIGURE 1–3
REAL EXCHANGE RATES, 1970–1986
(local currency per U.S. dollar; 1973: I = 100)

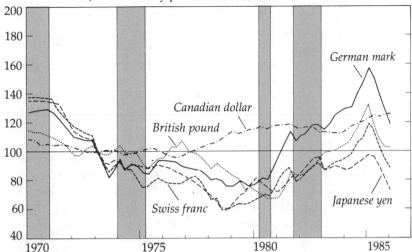

NOTE: Shaded areas are recessions.
SOURCE: Same as fig. 1–1.

FIGURE 1–4
REAL MULTILATERAL EXCHANGE RATE INDEXES, 1970–1986

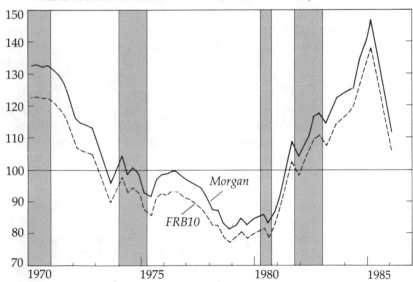

NOTE: Shaded areas are recessions. Indexes computed by the Morgan Guaranty Trust and by the Federal Reserve Board.
SOURCE: Same as fig. 1–1.

U.S. competitive position vis-à-vis a particular country, the overall competitiveness of U.S. goods in world markets is commonly taken to be proxied by the real effective exchange rate. The most frequently used indexes of such rates for the dollar are those computed by the Federal Reserve Board and the Morgan Guaranty Trust. Both are depicted in figure 1–4. The systematic differences between the two measures of effective rates arise from different coverage and weighting schemes as well as from different base periods.[11]

More generally, the selection of a particular exchange rate index should be governed by the purpose for which it is used. For example, the exchange rate as an indicator of compatibility between the macroeconomic policy of the United States and the rest of the industrialized world would call for the use of an index of nominal exchange rates of the currencies of a small number of major countries weighted by their gross national products. Indexes of real exchange rates based on U.S. bilateral trade shares would reflect changes in U.S. competitiveness in its domestic market and also in the markets of those countries whose currencies were represented in the basket. Indexes of real exchange rates based on countries' shares in global trade (the so-called multilateral weights) are purported to capture changes in U.S. competitiveness vis-à-vis the countries represented in the basket not only in bilateral trade but also in third markets.

Other things being equal, the broader the coverage of currencies in the index, the more accurate is supposed to be the measure of the change in the overall U.S. competitive position caused by movements of the dollar and the U.S. price level in relation to foreign currencies and foreign price levels, respectively. Figure 1–5 depicts movements in three measures of the dollar's composite real rate: the Federal Reserve Board basket of currencies, the Morgan Guaranty Trust basket, and the "global index," that is, a basket also including currencies of a number of less-developed countries (see footnote 7). All three indexes are based on relative weights derived from U.S. bilateral (rather than global) trade shares of each country in the basket, and all three indexes have the same base period.

An examination of these various measures leads to several observations. First, indexes of real rates differ substantially from one another, often by as much as 10–12 percent. Such indexes should be interpreted as quantitative gauges of the dollar misalignment only with great caution and ample caveats. This is especially important when the index is broad based and includes countries resorting to exchange controls, price controls, or widespread trade restrictions. Under such circumstances the index may be a highly distorted measure of the shift in effective relative prices. No matter which measure of

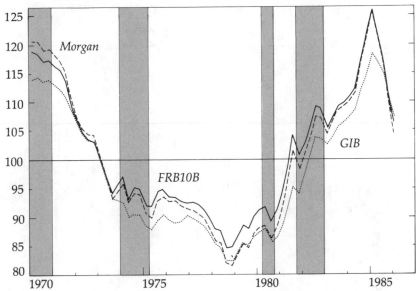

FIGURE 1–5
REAL BILATERAL EXCHANGE RATE INDEXES, 1970–1986

NOTE: Shaded areas are recessions. GIB is a "global" index with bilateral rates. Morgan and FRB10B are based on nominal indexes compiled by the Morgan Guaranty Trust and the Federal Reserve Board, respectively. All three indexes are adjusted for rates of inflation (CPIs).
SOURCE: Same as fig. 1–2.

the real effective exchange rate is used, however, the dollar has experienced several very large swings since 1970 in relation to other currencies.[12] Even though we do not know the exchange rate at which the dollar was "valued competively," such large swings suggest that U.S. producers of tradable goods may have experienced similarly large changes in their competitive positions vis-à-vis their foreign competitors. Second, the two largest medium-term swings in the real effective exchange rate occurred from early 1970 through early 1974 and from mid-1980 through early 1985, suggesting that such large swings need not necessarily be a unique characteristic of a floating rate regime.

Short-Term Volatility. Misalignments of a currency, that is, departures of its real exchange rate from a postulated equilibrium rate over a period of several years, have to be distinguished from volatility, that is, variability of exchange rates changes over much shorter periods. While the concept of misalignment is commonly employed to analyze a country's competitive position and its consequences, the concept of

FIGURE 1–6
Average Absolute Monthly Percentage Changes in Selected Bilateral Rates (Annualized), May 1970–November 1986

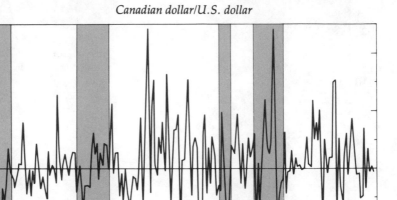

Canadian dollar/U.S. dollar

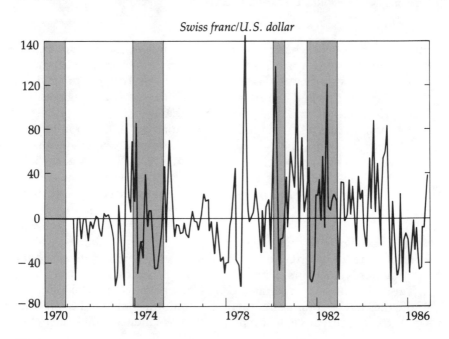

Swiss franc/U.S. dollar

FIGURE 1–6
(continued)

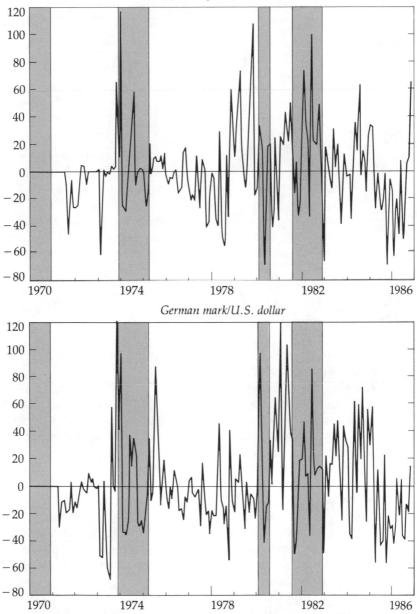

Japanese yen/U.S. dollar

German mark/U.S. dollar

(Figure continues)

19

FIGURE 1–6
(continued)

British pound/U.S. dollar

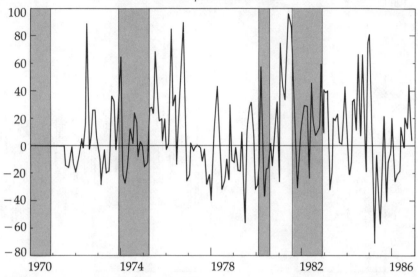

NOTE: Shaded areas are recessions.
SOURCE: Same as fig. 1–1.

volatility is used essentially to judge the extent of price uncertainty and its effects on output or trade.

Note that the dividing line between the two concepts is not a sharp one. First, there can be no single criterion for the appropriate frequency of examined changes in the exchange rate. For risk takers in financial markets (who influence the cost of hedging facing risk averters), the relevant time period may be a day or a week; for exporters and importers, a month or a quarter; for strategic planners at multinational corporations, from several quarters to several years. Needless to say, a given measure of volatility would vary substantially with the frequency chosen. Over a year or longer the concepts of misalignment and volatility converge. Second, if misalignment is caused by a shock of which the strength, duration, and effects are unknown, the uncertainty thus created will probably increase short-term volatility as well.[13]

Of greater importance is the choice of criteria for selecting a particular measure of volatility and of a benchmark for evaluating its severity. Frenkel and Mussa suggest that "the simplest measure of turbulence in foreign exchange markets is the average (absolute) percentage changes in exchange rates over some interval of time."[14] This measure of turbulence for five bilateral rates of the dollar based on monthly data is presented in figure 1–6. Except for the Canadian dollar, the measured volatility increased around 1978–1979 and has remained high, at least as compared with the mid-1970s. Apart, however, from allowing a comparison of changes in exchange rate volatility over time, this measure does not permit us to judge to what extent the observed volatility was justified by policies or other identifiable circumstances.

To ascertain whether the volatility of an exchange rate is justified (or, alternatively, whether it is excessive), we need some frame of reference. Concerns about exchange rate volatility arise primarily from its effect on the future domestic-currency value of international transactions. Therefore, measures of volatility should focus not so much on the magnitude of exchange rate changes as on their unpredictability. The variance or standard deviation of nominal exchange rate series of a given frequency (usually monthly) is perhaps the most commonly used gauge of the unpredictability of monthly exchange rate variation.[15] Table 1–1 contains such measures of variability of five bilateral dollar exchange rates for a number of three-year subperiods. What is interesting about these numbers is the difficulty of discerning any pattern of period-to-period changes in this measure that is common to all the bilateral rates examined. It is clear nonetheless that the last three-year subperiod (from mid-1983 through mid-1986), encompassing the last leg of the dollar's rise and its subsequent steep decline, is characterized by a much higher variability of bilateral exchange rates than any of the preceding subperiods.

A number of studies have shown that the time pattern of exchange rate volatility represented by standard deviations is roughly similar to the pattern revealed by average absolute percentage changes.[16] It should be pointed out, however, that either measure of unpredictability can be challenged. It is obvious that the appropriateness of this measure is contingent on a systematic connection between the variability (measured ex post) and uncertainty (experienced ex ante). It is quite conceivable to have high variability resulting from *expected* exchange rate changes and, vice versa, to have pegged exchange rates associated with great uncertainty about their future levels. It is not possible to say whether or to what extent a given measure of variability has underestimated or overestimated exchange rate uncertainty.[17]

These considerations aside, the question remains: What is the appropriate standard against which the variability of exchange rates should be judged? If any measure of exchange rate volatility is compared with the same measure of the volatility of price indexes, the conclusion is clear: for virtually every country, time period, frequency, index, or ratio of national price indexes, nominal exchange rates display substantially greater volatility than prices.[18] This result is not surprising and is fully consistent with the now widely accepted view of exchange rates as prices of assets. It can be argued, therefore, that a proper benchmark for gauging exchange rate volatility should be the observed volatility of prices of other financial assets. Such comparisons have been made over the past several years by a number of authors.[19] Their conclusions are that the measured volatility of prices of a wide array of financial assets (stock prices, short-term interest rates, long-term bond yields, actively traded commodity futures) has been consistently greater than the analogously measured volatility of exchange rates.

To sum up, while various indexes suggest that exchange rate volatility has been higher throughout the period of floating than the volatility of goods prices and, moreover, that exchange rate volatility has increased since 1979, the ambiguity of volatility measures (both absolute and relative) makes it very difficult to draw any policy conclusions without additional considerations. To these I turn in subsequent sections.

Misalignments of the Dollar

Figures and numbers presented in the previous section make clear that, whichever exchange rate index is chosen, the dollar has displayed very large swings in the past ten years against the generality of other currencies. Furthermore, the appreciation of the dollar between the summer of 1980 and the first quarter of 1985 (as well as its previous depreciation in 1977–1979, though to a lesser extent) was apparently out of line with such observed fundamentals theoretically determining the exchange rate as money supplies, price levels, interest rates, or income levels. This apparent divorce of the dollar exchange rates from their observed theoretical fundamentals brought to the fore once again the old concept of exchange rate disequilibrium or misalignment. In the context of the prolonged rise of the dollar, misalignment could only have meant its overvaluation.

It is a trivial observation that these concepts presuppose a notion of an equilibrium exchange rate. Without such a notion the concept of misalignment is vacuous.

22

The Meaning of Exchange Rate Equilibrium. Exercises in economic semantics attempting to clarify the meaning of exchange rate equilibrium have a long and venerable history.[20] Different definitions of equilibrium have been proposed over the years by different authors. In the present discussion it appears sensible to dispose at once of definitions of equilibrium that are irrelevant in examining medium-term movements of the dollar exchange rates and concentrate on those that may be applicable.

One such definition of equilibrium—clearing of foreign exchange markets—is quite irrelevant to the discussion of the dollar's misalignment. Apart from episodes of foreign exchange controls in the United Kingdom and France and a brief period in the mid-1970s when Germany and Switzerland imposed de facto negative interest rates on financial holdings by foreign residents, impediments to capital mobility have not in recent years prevented equilibration of supply and demand.

Another definition of equilibrium differentiates between private and official supplies of and demands for foreign exchange. In other words, if a particular exchange rate can prevail only because of official intervention, it is by definition a disequilibrium rate. This definition is also irrelevant for the discussion that follows. The most vocal critics of the dollar's misalignment in 1982–1984 suggested, in fact, that it was due in part to the lack of official intervention by the United States rather than to excessive official intervention.

With foreign exchange markets being cleared at all times, in what sense can we speak of exchange rate misalignment? Discussions of the past several years suggest that misalignment is to be taken alternatively as (1) a departure of the actual exchange rate from the rate compatible with its presumed fundamental determinants, (2) an exchange rate caused by aberrant behavior of the markets, or (3) exchange rates that produce macroeconomic or microeconomic outcomes inferior to those that could have been obtained had the exchange rates not been misaligned.

The Failure of Models of Exchange Rate Determination. The most common definition of misalignment is a divergence of the actual rate from its value as justified by the fundamental determinants, the latter being specified by a particular theory of exchange rate determination. If the exchange rate justified by such fundamental determinants could be known, calculating the extent of misalignment would be a simple matter.

Soon after generalized floating began in 1973, it became obvious that the flow models of exchange rate determination of the 1950s and

23

the simple monetary models of the early 1970s failed to explain the observed behavior of exchange rates adequately or to predict it with reasonable accuracy. Particularly troubling were an early demise of the hypothesis of real exchange rate neutrality—that is, that of roughly offsetting movements in nominal exchange rates and relative national price levels—and an apparent lack of correlation between changes in current accounts and exchange rate movements. In an attempt to take account of observed patterns of behavior, theorists began in the mid-1970s to construct dynamic models of exchange rate determination allowing for temporary departures of actual rates from their (variously defined) fundamental values. These temporary departures, labeled exchange rate overshooting, were modeled as a consequence of different speeds of adjustment between foreign exchange and goods markets.[21] Thus a concept of "momentary" or "current" exchange rate equilibrium was born. Such an equilibrium allows for a rational divergence of the exchange rate from its long-term fundamental equilibrium. It incorporates all relevant information, however, including full realization by market participants of the temporary nature of the factors responsible for overshooting.

With the emergence of dynamic exchange rate models, the task of correctly specifying fundamental determinants became paramount. All these models have a qualitatively common time path of adjustment to an unanticipated disturbance: a sharp change in the nominal exchange rate followed by its gradual convergence toward long-term equilibrium. Misspecification of the long-term equilibrium exchange rate would falsify the specification of its dynamic adjustment path as well.

Fundamental determinants of exchange rates are postulated by competing theories whose validity should be empirically verifiable. But empirically confirmable specification of long-term equilibrium exchange rates turned out to be an enormously frustrating task. Many theoretical models of exchange rate determination rely, directly or indirectly, on one or more parity conditions: purchasing power parity, nominal interest rate parity, or real interest rate parity. If the selected parity condition does not hold, neither does the postulated long-term equilibrium. In a well-known paper Cumby and Obstfeld, after performing a series of statistically sophisticated tests, decisively reject each of the parity relationships over recent years.[22] At the very least their findings suggest that the risk premium embedded in forward exchange rates may vary over time in a manner still to be discovered. At worst their results may be interpreted as a proof of misspecification of those theoretical exchange rate models that rely on the parity relationships examined.

One can argue that fundamentals of exchange rate determination are only as credible as their explanatory and predictive power of actual exchange rate behavior. Empirical verification of the predictive power of structural models of the late 1970s and early 1980s led to even more disappointing results than those obtained by Cumby and Obstfeld. In a series of influential studies, Meese and Rogoff found that a random walk model predicts future spot exchange rates better than structural models (or, for that matter, better than time series techniques and the forward discount) over any forecasting horizon up to one year.[23] Moreover, their forecasts were based on *actual* future values of the determining variables, and the model coefficients were permitted to vary with the forecasting horizon selected. Thus the forecasts Meese and Rogoff obtained by using structural models were much better than those obtainable when the determining factors themselves must be predicted.

These findings are supported by a multitude of other studies. Bilson, Frankel, and Frenkel suggest that the monetary model has lost its validity. Dornbusch and Frankel, among others, present evidence of a breakdown of the portfolio-balance approach.[24]

If the existing structural models are incapable of specifying empirically valid fundamental determinants of exchange rates and hence their long-term equilibrium values, the concept of exchange rate misalignment becomes fuzzy. For the concept of misalignment to have any meaning, the empirical failures of exchange rate models must be explained, and, if possible, new structural models that fit the experience with floating rates must be developed. Otherwise misalignment of a currency would have to be defined simply as a reflection of aberrant market behavior or an exchange rate different from some more or less subjectively postulated norm.

Why have the models failed? The empirical failures of exchange rate models have many possible explanations. The basic question is whether the poor forecasting performance of the models arises from theoretical misspecification or from inadequate estimation of the parameters of the model. Those who lean toward the misspecification hypothesis point out, for example, that models of exchange rate determination do not take into account unexpected shifts in demand for money or changes in inflationary or other expectations. This suggests that exchange rate theories may be deficient because our understanding of monetary economics or our grasp of the process of forming expectations is inadequate. Some analysts favoring the misspecification hypothesis also point out that properly specified exchange rate models are likely to differ among countries.

25

Some of those who emphasize estimation problems argue that the need for simplification often leads to estimation of structural models very different from those implied by the particular underlying theory of exchange rate determination.[25] Others, such as Meese and Rogoff, postulate that one likely explanation for the disappointing performance of structural models is the instability of parameters. They argue that the parameters of exchange rate models vary over time, in contrast to standard econometric practice. Shifts in trade patterns, supply shocks, or dramatic changes in monetary regimes and fiscal policies during the past decade may all have affected the relationships between exchange rates and their theoretical determining factors. In other words, the very nature of the process of exchange rate determination may be evolving.

Economic theory suggests, of course, that changes in economic relationships are to be expected, and the problem of structural instability of the relationships among economic variables has been addressed in the empirical literature in a more general context. The argument for such structural instability is even more compelling, however, when one of the variables is a speculative price.

Attempts at improving estimating methods (as by Meese and Rogoff) by relaxing the assumption of fixed coefficients failed to improve significantly the out-of-sample forecasting performance of structural exchange rate models. Neither a procedure updating the forecasting equations nor forecasts with the coefficients themselves following a random walk led to impressive results. Moreover, these experiments used actual future values of determining variables—money supplies, interest rates, and so on. This suggests that the unpredictability of such variables in real life is not the main explanation for the failure of structural models to forecast: knowing the future values of these variables would not have permitted improving on the current spot exchange rate as a predictor of the future spot exchange rate (at least at forecasting horizons up to approximately six quarters). Alternatively, these results strongly suggest that all historical information identified by the examined structural models as being relevant is already embedded in the current structure of exchange rates. Finally, and perhaps most important, these results imply that the dismal performance of structural exchange rate models is due not so much to inadequate estimating procedures as to our limited understanding of the process of exchange rate determination.

In what respect our understanding of this process may be deficient is a very controversial matter. We now understand that, even though exchange rates influence and are influenced by the prices of goods, they are determined largely by asset market considerations. As

26

a price of a financial asset, the current spot exchange rate incorporates the expected values of all future determining variables, discounted back to the present.[26] This and other asset characteristics of exchange rates have led to adoption of one version or another of capital asset pricing models in developing theories of exchange rate determination. At the same time, the exchange rate's role as a macroeconomic variable has led to reliance on macroeconomic models in developing exchange rate theories. It is clear that to achieve a reasonable approximation of the process of exchange rate determination the two sets of attributes of the exchange rate—that of a financial asset and that of a macroeconomic variable—must be combined in a model incorporating both macroeconomic relationships and an appropriate asset pricing mechanism.

The prospects for constructing such a model do not at present appear promising. Unlike in a standard capital asset pricing model, it would be unrealistic to mimic, say, a stock market paradigm by assuming a very large number of substitutable assets and a fixed supply of each asset. The number of currencies relevant from the point of view of a multicurrency portfolio manager is very small, and the supplies of those currencies are neither fixed nor predictable. Moreover, the supply of a particular currency may be influenced by the demand for it (for example, through official intervention in foreign exchange markets or targeting of interest rates by central banks), and the demand for a particular currency is always influenced by its expected supply. Furthermore, exchange rates qua assets respond mainly (some would say exclusively) to expectations, that is, to unobservable variables that are notoriously intractable in empirical work.

The early appreciation: mid-1980 through mid-1982. The unsatisfactory state of structural models of exchange rate determination became especially obvious after 1982. In fact, the first two years of the dollar's sustained rise, from mid-1980 to mid-1982, conformed tolerably well to a number of theories. During that period the expected values of all the main theoretical determinants moved more or less simultaneously in the "right" direction, that is, in a direction that could have been expected to strengthen the dollar. Expected inflation in the United States was falling in relation to expected inflation in other industrial countries; U.S. short-term and long-term interest rates—both nominal and real—rose in relation to those abroad; the tax cuts of 1981 increased the after-tax rate of return on new investments in the United States; the U.S. current account was strong while the current accounts of other large industrial countries, except for the United Kingdom, were deteriorating; and, arguably, safe haven considerations may

27

have augmented the demand for U.S. assets in preference to foreign assets.

All these factors contributed to the rise of the dollar in 1980–1982, although understandably, different studies produced different numerical estimates of the contribution of each factor to the appreciation. Much more substantial differences arise when analysts go to the source, namely, to the policies or events that affect the exchange rate directly or influence the factors mentioned—inflation or interest rates. Some analysts, like McKinnon, argue that the appreciation of the dollar was due solely to the very tight monetary policy in the United States.[27] Others stress the role of increased after-tax returns.[28] Many economists, like Feldstein, conclude that budget deficits, actual and anticipated, account for most of the dollar's rise.[29] Others, like Evans, find that the exchange rate of the dollar is not affected by changes in the budget deficit.[30] The professional consensus is nonetheless that the first leg of the dollar's long climb can be explained to a large extent by what has become known as the U.S. tight-money–easy-fiscal policy mix, with other factors playing secondary roles.

Although until the summer of 1982 the behavior of the dollar could have been explained by its theoretical fundamentals, even then many analysts considered the dollar grossly overvalued. Bergsten, for example, estimated the overvaluation at that time to be "at least 20 percent."[31] The prevalence of such views raises a question about the extent to which misalignment is a purely judgmental or normative concept. I return to this question later.

Sparkling bubbles: mid-1982 through mid-1984. The second leg of the dollar's appreciation, beginning in the second half of 1982, cannot be convincingly explained by changes in its theoretical fundamentals. In mid-1982 some of those fundamentals started moving against the dollar. Nominal short-term interest rates in the United States came down sharply as the Federal Reserve, concerned with the continuing contraction of real output, de facto abandoned the targeting of monetary aggregates. The difference between inflation-adjusted short-term interest rates in the United States and those abroad shrank to zero and even turned negative. The difference in long-term interest rates, though remaining in favor of the dollar, also shrank. The U.S. current account balance, despite a recession-induced fall in imports, turned negative in 1982 while the current account positions of Japan and Europe started to improve. The difference between the Eurodollar rate and the domestic U.S. interbank interest rate peaked in the late summer of 1982 and started to decline rapidly, suggesting an erosion of safe haven considerations.[32]

With so many fundamentals moving in the "wrong" direction and the international value of the dollar still going up, no model of exchange rate determination could explain the observed reality. The divergence between theory and reality became even more acute when the recovery in the United States, which started earlier and was initially stronger than in other industrial countries, contributed to such a rapid increase in the U.S. current account deficit that the prospect of a substantial net external debt accumulation for the United States in the next few years became a virtual certainty.

One way out of the quandary was a reliance on the growing federal deficit as the main culprit in the dollar's rise. One feature of conventional portfolio-balance models is that, in a world of high substitutability among assets denominated in different currencies, an increase in future government spending not matched by a future increase in revenues will, provided money is held constant, cause the currency to appreciate. If expectations are rational, this appreciation will be instantaneous. Thus any *observed* pattern of exchange rate appreciation can be explained by presuming a particular (unobservable) path of *expected* government spending.

Formal models relying on this mechanism were indeed constructed,[33] and in the public policy debate the rapidly growing U.S. budget deficit was increasingly cited as the factor primarily responsible for the dollar's surge. In 1983 and early 1984 this explanation might have been plausible. The recovery from the recession in the United States was robust, the government deficit as a share of GNP was growing, and economic sluggishness abroad might have made the supply of foreign capital to the United States very elastic with respect to expected returns. The money supply, however, was expanding rapidly without having any discernible dampening effect on the appreciation of the dollar. Moreover, by mid-1984 federal government spending and the deficit as a share of GNP were expected to stabilize in the years ahead.[34] Further appreciation should have been at least halted, and perhaps even reversed, by these factors immediately, but of course, it was not.

A hypothesis that the dollar was driven upward by rational speculation rather than by changes in fundamentals had been advanced well before the fundamentals moved decisively against the dollar. The possibility that factors irrelevant in theory might induce short-term departures of the exchange rate from its stable value was very much in the center of discussions in the mid-1970s, when a sizable body of empirical literature was aimed at confirming or refuting the existence and persistence of what were then called bandwagon effects. The debate was couched in terms of the possibility that destabilizing or insufficiently stabilizing speculation might *temporarily* drive the exchange rate from the level justified by fundamentals.[35]

The notion of a speculative bubble introduced into the finance literature in the late 1970s was different from that of a bandwagon of the mid-1970s in that the destabilizing speculation was self-fulfilling, driving the exchange rate ever further from the value dictated by the fundamentals.[36] In a speculative bubble the bidding for the dollar is caused by expectations of an *accelerating* rate of its appreciation. Rational market participants are aware that the explosive path of the exchange rate must eventually come to an end, that is, that the bubble must eventually burst. But, although the probability of the bubble's eventually bursting is one, the probability that it will burst in the week or month immediately ahead is relatively small. A certain interest rate differential together with some expected rate of appreciation over the coming week or month multiplied by the (relatively large) probability of the bubble's not bursting in the near future would induce many people to hold on to the appreciating currency despite the certainty of its collapse in the more remote future. The bubble actually bursts when the subjective probability of collapse in the very near term rises to the point at which the prevailing interest rate differential together with the expected rate of appreciation in the event of noncollapse is not sufficient to compensate for the possible large capital loss.

The bubble theory of exchange rate determination received a great deal of attention in the mid-1980s. This attention stands in sharp contrast to the mid-1970s, when the possibility of an explosive exchange rate path was ruled out by assumption in all standard models of exchange rate determination.[37]

A critical examination of the theory of speculative bubbles would take us too far afield. A few comments are nonetheless necessary. First, the process of currency appreciation described by bubbles does not require a definition of an equilibrium determined by fundamentals, not even for the purpose of computing the capital loss in the event of sudden collapse. If the currency appreciation is due to a speculative bubble, the currency is misaligned by definition. In other words, the theory implicitly postulates that some expectations are more fundamental than others.

Second, a bubble path of some duration, such as the dollar appreciation between the summer of 1982 and early 1985, is indistinguishable from a trend, and a bubble burst is indistinguishable from a trend reversal. The trend may be caused by unobservable factors, such as gradual unidirectional shifting in preferences. In empirical applications, therefore, the apparent detection of bubbles may simply be a result of omitting certain explanatory variables.[38] More generally, although a number of studies find explosive bubbles in exchange markets, these findings crucially depend on the validity of model specification and the characterization of the nature of market expectations.[39] Not surprisingly, other identifying assumptions about expectations and alternative underlying models lead to rejection of a rational speculative bubble hypothesis.[40]

A third and related point is that, if every prolonged movement of the exchange rate away from its specified equilibrium level is a speculative bubble (which could be shown to exist under a particular set of presumed expectations), the validity of the model purporting to depict this equilibrium level could neither be confirmed nor refuted. In a world of recurring long-lasting rational bubbles, models of exchange rate determination based on fundamentals have no empirical content. The specification of exchange rate equilibrium in such a world is therefore arbitrary, and so also must be the degree of exchange rate misalignment.

Mystifying bubbles: mid-1984 through March 1985. The continuing rise of the dollar from mid-1984 was especially astounding in light of the behavior displayed by other supposed fundamental factors of exchange rate determination. Economic growth in the United States slowed, short-term interest rates fell, long-term inflation-adjusted interest rate differentials favoring the dollar kept shrinking, and the U.S. trade deficit was exploding. The stage was set for acceptance of nonconventional models of exchange rate determination.

Exchange rate behavior described by rational bubbles, though a substantial departure from exchange rate determination theories of the 1970s, nonetheless implies economically rational behavior based on the perceived calculus of risk and reward. But throughout the summer of 1984 and beyond, as the dollar continued to appreciate, the rationality of such a calculus became increasingly suspect. The dollar bubble became so mystifying that a number of theorists felt compelled to abandon the heretofore sacrosanct assumption of market rationality.[41]

The crossing of the Rubicon into the land of presumed market irrationality was facilitated by numerous studies undermining the belief (widely held in the 1970s) that forward rates were unbiased.[42] If the forward discount or interest rate differential is in fact a biased predictor of the corresponding future spot rate, so that money can be made by betting against its prediction, the rationality of market expectations can indeed be questioned.[43]

One possible explanation of the bias is the so-called peso problem, a twin brother of the rational speculative bubble. A relatively

31

small probability of a sharp depreciation of a currency in, say, the next three months (as for the pegged Mexican peso in 1976 or the floating dollar in 1982–1984), should be reflected in the forward discount. If the test of bias is, however, based on a sample not encompassing the episode of the big currency decline (which presumably occurs later), the bias shown by the test would be invalid.

A more conventional explanation for the observed bias is the existence of an unobservable risk premium incorporated in the forward discount. The existence of a risk premium means that dollar and nondollar assets are less than perfect substitutes in investors' portfolios or, alternatively, that an element of incremental risk is attached to holding dollar assets. The greater the investors' risk aversion, the higher the risk premium. Portfolio theory stipulates theoretical determinants of the risk premium, but its empirical measurement is extremely difficult and imprecise. While an argument can be made that the risk premium associated with holding dollar assets rose marginally with expectations of rapid accumulation of net external debt by the United States, the very consistency and large size of prediction errors of forward discounts undermine the plausibility of arguments that the errors were predominantly caused by the risk premium factor.

The shortage of good explanations for the bias in forward rates opened the door for explanations of the dollar's behavior based on market irrationality. In an analysis using a simplified version of the well-known framework for analyzing the dynamics of government deficits and debt, Krugman finds that the need to service the growing external debt of the United States must force the dollar down to a much greater extent than is reflected in the forward discount or long-term interest rate differentials. The paper, written in the early summer of 1985, states that the market "has failed to realize that its expectations about continued dollar strength are not feasible."[44] The only question was how fast the dollar would fall, that is, in terms used by Marris in his book centered on the same argument, Would the landing be hard or soft?[45]

The core of these arguments was that the dollar exchange rate must ultimately return to a level compatible with a steady state, for example, in Krugman's formulation, a stable ratio of external debt to GNP. This implied substantial depreciation of the dollar from its early 1985 level. Krugman thought that "the market has not done its arithmetic." This is quite doubtful. While there was substantial agreement in early 1985 that the dollar must eventually come down to help reverse the deterioration of the U.S. current account deficit, there was demonstrably no agreement on when the decline would start, what would trigger it, how far the dollar would fall, or at what pace. As Krugman correctly points out, the value of the stable debt-to-GNP ratio, the number of years needed to reach it, and the time path of debt accumulation cannot be known in advance. The dollar exchange rate in early 1985 is perfectly compatible, for example, with a rapid accumulation of external debt in the next few years and a very gradual deceleration of its growth in later years. Models of debt-deficit dynamics can be simulated for any set of postulated parameters, yielding a particular path toward the steady state. The path of decline of the dollar shown by a particular simulation might suggest that the market "has not done its arithmetic" even for the short run. But even so the case for rejection of market rationality as it came to be understood would be exceedingly weak.

Bursting bubbles: March 1985 through late 1986. The dollar reached its peak in March 1985 and in the subsequent six quarters registered a decline comparable in steepness to that of its depreciation in the early 1970s. Since the decline was widely expected, it was also easy to explain as it got under way: rates of money growth in the United States (as measured by M1) were stuck in a double-digit range; legislative action in the summer of 1985 apparently reversed earlier expectations of rising federal deficits;[46] economic growth in the United States in 1985 remained subdued while prospects for growth in Europe began to look brighter; the Plaza Agreement of September 1985, signaling resistance of the G-5 group to an appreciation of the dollar in the future, may have skewed the probability distribution of its expected exchange rates; the sharp fall in oil prices at the very beginning of 1986, while improving the U.S. overall terms of trade, was even more beneficial for Japan, Germany, and other countries relying on petroleum imports more heavily than the United States; the U.S. trade and current account deficits were ballooning; and in late 1985 the expectations, subsequently fulfilled, were that the Federal Reserve would aggressively try to push short-term interest rates down.

Since virtually all fundamentals were in concordance with the dollar's decline, its behavior since March 1985 can ostensibly be taken as a reaffirmation of traditional exchange rate theories.[47] Comforting as it may be, this reaffirmation does not wipe out their previous record of failure.

As to the theories invoking bubbles, the decline of the dollar validates them axiomatically. Rational bubble theories predict that the currency will start to decline when the *subjective* probability of its collapse in the period immediately ahead rises above some critical threshold. Since a subjective probability distribution cannot be mea-

33

sured, such a critical level is reached whenever the rational bubble bursts, by virtue of the underlying theoretical construct. Irrational bubbles are even more blatantly self-validating. Since irrationality is taken to reflect the component of an exchange rate level unexplainable by the theory, a drop toward the range of rationality, that is, the range supported by the theory, automatically validates the claim of previously irrational overvaluation. In commenting on Krugman's paper, Mussa characterized an irrational bubble as "a theory that can rationalize virtually everything and be contradicted by virtually nothing . . . . It must be rejected not because it is wrong, but because it is incapable of being wrong."[48]

The puzzle of the strong dollar from 1982 to early 1985 remains unresolved.[49] It was nonetheless a sobering and educational experience. We have learned, among other things, these lessons:

• Monthly and quarterly changes in exchange rates are large and entirely unpredictable.

• Such changes in nominal and real rates are highly correlated.

• Forward and spot rates move together, implying a close correlation between changes in actual spot rates and expected future spot rates.

• Movements in nominal and real exchange rates are only weakly related to changes in theoretical fundamentals, such as current account imbalances, differential rates of monetary expansion, or even interest rate differentials.

• Movements in exchange rates are apparently determined by expectations, whose formation we understand poorly and are incapable so far of modeling satisfactorily.

One conclusion from these lessons is that the concept (let alone the measure) of a fundamental value or equilibrium level toward which rational markets are supposed to nudge a straying exchange rate has become vague and diffuse. Since we are not really certain what is to be included in the set of fundamental determinants or how to characterize market rationality, we cannot operationally define "misalignment," except in a normative sense.

Normative Benchmarks. One class of notions of misalignment bypasses some of the numerous conceptual problems and some of the empirical difficulties discussed above. Implicit in such notions are certain postulated levels of exchange rates that produce economic outcomes superior to those achievable at alternative levels of exchange rates. In this framework misalignment or overvaluation of the dollar in the first half of the 1980s amounts to a subjective assessment of the actual exchange rate in relation to the chosen benchmark.

A good example of such a benchmark is the fundamental equilibrium exchange rate (FEER) introduced by John Williamson.[50] He defines the FEER as a real exchange rate that would probably produce a current account balance offsetting the underlying capital account over the business cycle while at the same time maintaining internal balance. One could easily argue that the FEER would minimize unnecessary adjustment costs in the economy and perhaps even smooth the path of output growth. It is easy to see, however, that calculating *the* FEER, as Williamson readily acknowledges, is subject to a substantial margin of error and so, consequently, is the derived measure of misalignment.

Much more troubling than the measurement problems is the proposition that the FEER is *the* appropriate normative benchmark. The same reservation applies to any other definition using the current account equilibrium as the norm. Barring default on its debt, a country cannot accumulate current account deficits indefinitely, but it can do so for a very long time.[51] Whether it should or should not do so would, from the point of view of economic optimality, depend on myriad factors, such as demographic trends, physical factor endowments, opportunities for investment (with tax incentives taken into account), saving preferences, use of borrowed funds, rate of productivity growth, and so on. It is possible within a very wide range to specify very different sustainable or desirable paths of cumulative current account deficits. They would generally yield very different values for the FEER and, again, very different measures of misalignment.

Another normative benchmark frequently used in calculating currency misalignment invokes the notion of underlying competitiveness. Bergsten's calculations of the dollar misalignment cited earlier are an example. Although his calculations appear to rely on the old and by now largely discredited purchasing power parity relationship, in principle there need be no connection between the proposition that purchasing parity is what determines the equilibrium exchange rate and the claim that the appropriate actual exchange rates should approximately equalize production costs among various countries (if that is what maintaining "underlying competitive position" really means).

This particular benchmark, like all other benchmarks in the same class, is haunted by computational and conceptual difficulties too numerous to discuss here. It is fairly obvious that alternative specifications of production costs (average or cycle adjusted, current or expected, for goods only or for goods and services, with or without tax incentives, for traded, tradable, or all goods and services) would yield dramatic differences in the calculated benchmark exchange rate and so also in the derived measure of misalignment. The fundamental objection to the norm, however, is that even in a framework of managed exchange rates one could advocate, on economic efficiency or welfare grounds, a number of exchange rates different from that at which the underlying competitive positions are equalized.

In sum, notwithstanding the widespread perception of the dollar's excessive strength from 1982 through early 1985, the concepts of misalignment or overevaluation remain more diffuse than ever. Empirical failures of traditional models of exchange rate determination undermine the credence of misalignment measures as proxies for divergences between actual exchange rates and their equilibrium values based on fundamentals. Bubble theories suffer from a lack of sufficient empirical content for their testing. Concepts of misalignment in relation to a normative benchmark are valid only to the extent that the validity of the norm itself is accepted. And since we still cannot convincingly explain why the dollar rose by early 1985 as much as it did, we cannot assess how far misaligned it was or may remain.

Volatility of the Dollar

In the section presenting the factual record of movements of the dollar exchange rate, I mentioned that the volatility of exchange rate changes over short periods of time must be distinguished from longer-term movements, such as those discussed in the preceding section. I noted at the same time that, as the time span over which the variability of the exchange rate is defined lengthens, the concepts of volatility and misalignment converge. Finally, I cited findings that suggest an interconnection between large exchange rate swings in the medium term and increased variability over the short run.

I now review various evaluations of exchange rate volatility and explanations for its occurrence. In what follows, volatility is to be understood as the variability of monthly or more frequent changes in exchange rates.

Standards for Assessing Exchange Rate Volatility. In the 1980s the issue of volatility has been overshadowed by concerns about the dollar's misalignment. Nonetheless, references to "excessive turbulence" in foreign exchange markets have become a staple of many official pronouncements and have found their way into academic writings as well. Furthermore, while the issue of volatility has been treated with relative equanimity in the United States, short-term variability of exchange rates proved considerably more vexing to the Europeans.[52]

Goods prices and asset prices. The exchange rate undoubtedly turned out to be incomparably more volatile than proponents of floating rates in the 1950s or 1960s thought likely. One—possibly the main—reason for this manifest lack of foresight is that the debates of earlier decades, especially of the 1950s, took place in a world in which international trade in assets was small in relation to the trade in goods and services. It was thought then, with some justification, that changes in the supply of foreign assets denominated in different currencies and in the demand for them would mirror changes in trade-related flows of payments and credit.

All this changed with the restoration of currency convertibility in major foreign countries in the late 1950s and the emergence of off-shore markets in the early 1960s. As the volume of international trade in assets grew many times faster than the volume of trade in goods and services, the asset characteristics of exchange rates gradually became dominant. Economists are now in general agreement that in the short run exchange rates are determined in much the same way as the prices of other financial assets.

In spite of this agreement, short-term exchange rate variability is frequently gauged against the variability of price indexes. As discussed at some length in previous sections, by this criterion the dollar exchange rate has been very volatile indeed. The justification for comparing the short-term variability of exchange rates and that of price indexes is, however, dubious.

Consider an unanticipated shock to the economy. Goods markets would converge to the new equilibrium through both price and quantity adjustments. Generally, the initial adjustment would be borne by inventory corrections, changes in the level of production and employment, and so on, allowing price adjustments to the unanticipated economic shock to be delayed and weakened. On the aggregate level this adjustment process would manifest itself as a sluggish change in price indexes.

By contrast, foreign exchange markets subjected to an economic shock react to it by instantaneously and fully adjusting prices to whatever level the market considers the new short-term equilibrium. Moreover, like other financial asset prices, exchange rates are determined not only by present values of determining factors but also by their expected future values. An unanticipated shock, such as a policy change thought to have an influence on the future value of monetary factors, would cause current spot exchange rates to change instantaneously—in contrast to current prices of goods, which would remain temporarily unchanged even when their expected future prices were affected by the same policy change. Moreover, in a world of highly integrated financial markets, exchange rates are determined simultaneously with prices of other financial assets (including prices of commodity futures). Thus, in principle at least, an unanticipated disturbance affecting the expected future value of any financial asset would cause an exchange rate change as well. Since the variability of exchange rates is due to unanticipated changes in the underlying economic factors, the frequency and magnitude of such changes can be expected to determine the degree of exchange rate variability.

These considerations suggest that neither objective measures of variability, such as those presented in figure 1–6 and table 1–1, nor measures of exchange rate variability relative to that of goods prices allow a meaningful evaluation of exchange rate behavior. In fact, in view of the sluggish adjustment of prices in goods (and labor) markets, a high degree of exchange rate variability probably indicates the efficiency of foreign exchange markets in dissipating the effects of economic shocks. A severe policy disturbance that induced wealth holders to reshuffle their portfolios, for example, would cause substantial changes in exchange rates (and in prices of other financial assets) well before prices of goods began to adjust to the new environment. Were it not for the absorption of the initial shock by assets markets (and its corollary, abrupt changes in asset prices), such an unanticipated policy change would necessitate much faster adjustments in goods and labor markets, in both prices and quantities, causing greater dislocations.

A more meaningful criterion for assessing the volatility of the exchange rate is to compare measures of its variability with analogous measures of variability of other asset prices. The markets for financial assets—stocks, bonds, commodity futures—are auction markets and thus disperse unanticipated shocks as foreign exchange markets do, that is, by allowing instantaneous and, if necessary, large price changes. Indeed, the volatility of exchange rates is generally lower than that of other financial asset prices, which suggests that foreign exchange markets are no less informationally efficient, broad, deep, or resilient than other asset markets.[53]

Relevant and irrelevant information. The conclusion above does not mean that the observed exchange rate variability is justified in some absolute sense. It is frequently suggested, in fact, that exchange rates should be considered excessively volatile if changes in them substantially and persistently react to information that should be irrelevant to

TABLE 1-1

STANDARD DEVIATION OF MONTHLY PERCENTAGE CHANGES IN BILATERAL EXCHANGE RATES, 1970–1986

	1970–1972	1973–1975	1976–1978	1979–1981	1982–1984	1983:7–1986:7	1970–1986:7
Canadian dollar/U.S. dollar	0.855	0.627	1.177	1.000	0.932	0.897	0.970
Swiss franc/U.S. dollar	1.209	3.487	2.839	3.266	2.539	3.368	3.013
Japanese yen/U.S. dollar	1.116	2.392	2.389	2.989	2.737	2.922	2.635
deutsche mark/U.S. dollar	0.782	3.698	1.762	2.853	2.528	3.227	2.710
British pound/U.S. dollar	1.167	1.922	2.250	2.760	1.936	3.101	2.330

SOURCE: Author

39

exchange rate determination. The question is, in other words, Do exchange rates change in response to extraneous factors?

There are two steps in attempting to answer this question. The first is to ascertain that exchange rates are systematically moved in the short run by theoretically relevant economic news. The second is to identify factors responsible for the residual variance after exchange rate changes attributable to relevant economic news are accounted for.

Movements in asset prices in response to relevant news have received considerable attention in the economic literature in recent years. A typical test consists of examining changes in, say, bond price movements in response to the weekly announcement of a change in the money supply (at a time when the Federal Reserve is perceived as targeting monetary aggregates). The difference between the expected change and the announced change in the money supply is taken as a measure of a surprise affecting expectations about the future supply of money, which therefore instantaneously affects bond prices. Similar tests have been performed for exchange rates.[54] These tests suggest that exchange rates do respond to identifiable surprises—relevant factors—in a manner that can be justified on theoretical grounds, but the explanatory power of such surprises is extremely low, about 10 percent.

Since relevant factors have such a low explanatory power, one possible inference is that short-term exchange rate movements are influenced mostly by extraneous factors.[55] If this inference is correct, the exchange markets transmit price signals distorting the allocation of resources. Studies of domestic asset markets by Shiller and others find that asset prices are indeed moved by extraneous information, that is, their fluctuations are excessive in light of changes in the underlying factors determining their present value.[56] If this view is accepted, excessive volatility of stock or bond prices would imply excessive volatility of exchange rates as well, because of intermarket links.

Other, at least equally plausible explanations for these findings also exist. First is the perennial problem of omitted variables. Some variables are omitted by assumption, as risk premiums are in Shiller's work. Other variables, such as changing preferences, are omitted because they are unobservable and virtually impossible to proxy adequately in econometric work. Second, if stable relationships between medium-term exchange rate movements and their theoretical determinants are difficult to detect, there is reason to believe that the relationships between such determinants and short-term fluctuations are even more unstable.

More fundamentally, it makes a crucial difference whether the observed short-term variability of exchange rates reflects a constantly changing short-term equilibrium or, alternatively, is due to fluctuations around short-term equilibrium values. In the former case, fluctuations in actual exchange rates may be presumed to result from rapidly shifting asset preferences of international wealth holders. Clearly, shifts in asset preferences, especially if they are abrupt, are less likely to occur if changes in key economic variables are more stable or predictable. But any such changes affect expectations and thus entail shifts in asset preferences that take place virtually simultaneously with changes in the economic variables generating them. If these expectations are not properly taken into account, the effect on exchange rates of changes in underlying economic factors may appear magnified.

If the actual exchange rates fluctuate around their short-term equilibrium values, however, the presumptiom is that exchange rates somehow change under their own momentum. This is, in fact, a claim made by those who interpret persistent fluctuations of exchange rates around their short-term trends as evidence of "bandwagon" effects or as evidence of a "badly behaved" speculation in the foreign exchange market. A corollary of this assertion is the claim that foreign exchange markets are inefficient.

The efficiency of foreign exchange markets. By one of the most frequently used criteria, a market is said to be inefficient when systematic opportunities for above-normal risk-adjusted profits remain unexploited.[57] Such opportunities arise when the market fails to incorporate economic information fully or rapidly enough. Market inefficiency occurs, for example, when the information contained in the past price series can be used to predict future prices. If a certain pattern of exchange rate fluctuations is apparent, an astute speculator could use it to earn supernormal profits. Specifically, if bandwagons were a systematic feature of exchange rate behavior, those able to detect them could reap an advantage by going long in the currency when its rate begins to rise and going short in it when its rate begins to fall. Conversely, if such a bandwagon effect is an isolated incident or occurs randomly, so that past experience is not helpful in either predicting or identifying it, no supernormal profits can be earned by studying past price performance.

A number of studies have tested for efficiency of foreign exchange markets. Some tests rely on a comparison between observed changes in exchange rates in different periods of time; a systematic correlation between such changes, that is, predictability of future price changes on the basis of past price changes, would create a presumption of market inefficiency. In another group of tests, a given trading rule is consistently applied ex post to see whether it would yield returns over and above those that a buy-and-hold strategy would yield.

Studies employing these tests report with increasing frequency that even after adjusting for transaction costs (including the interest cost of carrying a currency position), substantial profits could have been made by following very simple trading rules.[58] But none of these methods for testing for market efficiency are foolproof. Bandwagons and (convergent) speculative bubbles may, of course, indeed be part and parcel of asset-market dynamics resulting from insufficiency of stabilizing speculation that would otherwise prevent the bandwagons from occurring. It is equally possible, however, that, if we could properly adjust "normal" profit for the considerable risk incurred by short-term currency speculation, reported filter-rule profits would simply reflect compensation for bearing this risk.[59]

As with medium-term exchange rate movements, there is no single criterion for judging whether or to what extent short-term fluctuations have been excessive. Neither is there a widely agreed upon set of factors thought to cause them. The question of the economic consequences of exchange rate movements at various frequencies and their possible implications for public policy remains. To this subject I turn next.

Consequences of the Dollar's Variability

Concern about harmful consequences of exchange rate fluctuations has been voiced since the very advent of the floating exchange rate regime. One strand of criticism of floating rates focused on the influence of their flexibility on the political aspects of economic decision making. Critics pointed out, for example, that the disappearance of the balance-of-payments constraint, that is, effectively of the official reserves constraint, will make it easier for countries in deficit to inflate their currencies. Conversely, in the absence of any obligation by monetary authorities to absorb capital inflows, flexible exchange rates are supposedly diluting the incentives surplus countries would otherwise have to adjust their payments positions. In other words, many observers believe that fixed exchange rates impose greater discipline on myopic or profligate politicians than flexible rates do.

Empirical evaluation of these arguments does not appear possible. First, it is now generally understood that while flexible exchange rates permit individual countries to choose their own long-run inflation trend, they do not provide the policy autonomy and the degree of insulation from external shocks that was hoped for or dreaded, as the case may be, before the era of generalized floating. Interdependence under flexible rates is clearly greater than had been expected, but its corollary is a lesser dilution of discipline than had been feared. Second, even if it were self-evident that economic policies since 1973 had been less responsible than before, many factors other than exchange rate flexibility could have been the more proximate cause of the deteriorating quality of economic policy. Interactions between economic policy decisions and an exchange rate regime, explored by Gottfried Haberler in his contribution to this volume, are complex and subtle. At any rate, charges that flexible exchange rates make the conduct of unsound economic policies easier are directed at flexible exchange rates qua the international monetary arrangement rather than at the exchange rate variability made possible by such an arrangement.

The second strand of criticism of flexible exchange rates has a narrower and more direct focus. The accusation is made that exchange rate oscillations cause variations in other economic variables —aggregate and sectoral output, price level, volume of international trade, foreign investment flows, and others—thus burdening the society with efficiency and welfare losses. The empirical literature examining such effects has been expanding rapidly in recent years. It is varied in the relationships explored, the methods used, and the results obtained. Because of its volume and diversity it cannot be surveyed here. Interested readers may consult three recent surveys of the literature dealing with this subject.[60] It is useful nonetheless to take up the most crucial conceptual issues and summarize some empirical results.

The period since generalized floating began has been characterized by an economic performance inferior to that recorded before 1973. Inflation in the industrialized countries, including the United States, has been more rapid; output growth has slowed and productivity growth has slowed even more; the growth of international trade volume has also slowed both absolutely and relatively to aggregate output; and structural unemployment has risen. More to the point, the past twelve years have witnessed an increase in variability of virtually all important economic aggregates and, arguably, widening divergences among the performances of particular sectors. Since, as I have shown, exchange rates also fluctuated a great deal, it is legitimate to inquire whether and to what extent variability in a number of economic aggregates can be attributed to exchange rate fluctuations and what therefore the imputed costs are of exchange rate variability.

The costs of variations in economic variables induced by exchange rate fluctuations fall into two categories: adjustment costs and uncertainty costs.[61] Adjustment costs arise because temporary changes in relative prices engendered by exchange rate fluctuations tend to shift resources alternately toward and away from tradable goods industries. Such reversible shifts of resources in response to temporary price incentives are inherently wasteful.

Uncertainty costs arise from exchange rate–induced fluctuations in profits (in domestic currency) on international transactions. Risk-averse economic agents would tend to shun foreign trade and investment. At the very least they would have to devote additional resources to hedging their profits against exchange rate fluctuations or perhaps attempt to raise the prices of their products.

It is usually not too difficult to detect a correlation between a particular measure of exchange rate variability and fluctuations of a selected economic aggregate. Even though this correlation tells nothing about causality, let alone the cost of such variability relative to that of relevant alternatives, it is frequently and very misleadingly invoked as evidence of deleterious effects of exchange rate fluctuations. This is not to deny, of course, that the behavior of exchange rates, including their variability, does affect other economic variables. But meaningful analysis of its effects must first come to grips with and incorporate a few crucial attributes of exchange rates that are germane to this issue.

Some Interrelated Concepts. Exchange rate movements, over both the short and the medium term, can be explained to some extent by underlying determinants. To this extent, assuming that the relevant underlying determinants are identifiable or predictable, exchange rate movements can be said to be systematic. The portion of the movement that cannot be explained by the underlying factors corresponds to the residual variability, which can be interpreted as the proxy for uncertainty.

What kind of variability? As discussed at some length earlier, the unsatisfactory state of exchange rate–determination theory allows for a confident explanation of only a small portion of medium-term exchange rate movements and virtually no explanation of short-term fluctuations.

The distinction between the explicable and inexplicable components is important for a number of reasons. First, assume for simplicity no correlation between the inexplicable component but perfect correlation between the explicable component of medium-term exchange rate movements and the movements in another variable of interest, say, export volume. In this case, by the very way the experiment is constructed, fluctuations in exports (and in the exchange rate) are caused by the variability of the underlying determining factors. Exchange rate variability has no separate effect on export volume.

Second, assume by contrast no correlation between the explicable component but perfect correlation between the inexplicable one and, as before, the volume of exports. In this case, export volume volatility can be said to be caused by exchange rate volatility only if we are confident that the inexplicable portion of exchange rate movements is not a result of model misspecification—for example, an omission of relevant variables. Otherwise variability in exports would be mistakenly attributed to exchange rate fluctuations, when in reality it is caused by another factor.

Third, the distinction between the explicable and inexplicable components of measured variability is important because it is the uncertainty engendered by fluctuating exchange rates that is the source of their harmful effects on the economy. Since changes in the underlying factors are not always predictable, exchange rate movements explicable ex post need not be foreseeable. But this source of uncertainty is not peculiar to any particular exchange rate regime.

Fourth, an argument that exchange rates fluctuate autonomously rather than in response to fundamentals (as reflected, for example, in irrational bubbles) can be applied only to the inexplicable portion of fluctuations. Whether our inability to explain more than a small part of exchange rate movements is a sufficient rather than simply a necessary condition for establishing autonomous fluctuations is a matter discussed in preceding sections. But to the extent that only such autonomous fluctuations are destabilizing (that is, add to the variability of economic aggregates), using a measure of variability without distinguishing between its explicable and inexplicable components is theoretically unjustifiable.

Another criterion for dissecting exchange rate variability into its components is the distinction between the movements of the fundamental or current equilibrium exchange rate and fluctuations of actual rates around such equilibrium levels. Of course, if the equilibrium exchange rate were strictly determined by the observed underlying fundamentals, this distinction would be perfectly equivalent to the one discussed above. The movements of the equilibrium exchange rate not only are not harmful but are a necessary adjustment to the evolution of the economic structure, shifts in policies, and other fundamentals. Only the fluctuations around equilibrium levels can be harmful. Once again, our ability to distinguish between the two components of observed exchange rate movements is rudimentary at best. Consequently, any empirically established relationship between

45

exchange rate fluctuations around their equilibrium levels and the variability of a particular economic variable is tainted by the imprecision inherent in culling out the former from the observed exchange rate movements.

The matter of exchange rate endogeneity. Even if the explicable component of exchange rate movements could be unambiguously identified, inferences about causality drawn from an established correlation between the variability of the remaining inexplicable portion and the variability of other economic variables would still be open to challenge. The reason for this is that the exchange rate is an endogenous variable in a macroeconomic structure—one that both influences and is influenced by other variables in the system, for example, the volume of exports. Exchange rate fluctuations cannot be simply assumed to be exogenous, put on the right-hand side of the regression equation, and declared a causal factor. Not even the unexplained residual can be treated as exogenous. In a structural characterization of the economy, all endogenous variables are shocked by external disturbances simultaneously. In the reduced-form solution of such a structural model this simultaneity of reactions to a shock would be manifested in a large covariation of error terms. In a single reduced-form equation, the equivalent of such a large covariation would be a high correlation coefficient between the inexplicable component of exchange rate movements and the portion of, say, export variability that cannot be accounted for otherwise. Thus an erroneous conclusion about the effect of exchange rate fluctuations would be reached even when the true reason for measured correlation is a perturbation inflicted on the economy by an identified external disturbance. Naturally, if actual exchange rate fluctuations (rather than their inexplicable part) were treated as if they were an exogenous variable, most consequences of changes in exogenous variables would be mistakenly attributed to exchange rate fluctuations.

Effects of Exchange Rate Variability: Empirical Results. Most empirical studies on exchange rate variability fail to distinguish adequately between the explicable and inexplicable components of exchange rate movements. Methodological objections aside, using one or another measure of *total* exchange rate variability as the causal factor would tend to exaggerate the measured effect. In spite of this measurement bias, there is very scant empirical evidence of directly measurable adverse effects of exchange rate fluctuations on such important variables as international trade and investment, output, or the rate of inflation.

Effects on international trade and investment. For understandable reasons the effects of exchange rate variability on trade have received considerable attention in the empirical literature. Two categories of effects have been examined: the effects on the overall volume of trade and the effects on trade patterns. Attempts have also been made to estimate the incremental costs of engaging in foreign trade activity that are due to exchange rate fluctuations.[62]

Generally speaking, the results are inconclusive. This was certainly true of studies using the data sample extending only through approximately 1981. No significant negative effects of exchange rate variability either on the volume of trade or on its patterns could be detected.

Since this outcome is counterintuitive, various explanations have been offered. The research staff of the International Monetary Fund recognizes the inadequacy of statistical techniques yet doubts that "more intensive or sophisticated tests would show a greatly different result."[63] Balassa points out the possibility that reducing exchange rate risk is frequently reduced through hedging in forward markets.[64] McCulloch suggests that exchange rate risk may be small when compared with risk originating from other sources, both economy-wide and firm-specific.[65] Furthermore, she points out, it is generally easier to diversify and hedge against exchange rate risk than against risk emanating from other sources.

Future studies encompassing the more recent years of high exchange rate variability may, of course, be able to demonstrate a more significant effect on trade. So far, however, such a convincing demonstration is lacking.

The only empirical study of international investment flows of some note is that by Cushman. Using a bilateral investment flow model and data through 1978, he achieves mixed results of exchange rate variability on direct investment—in concordance with his theoretical hypothesis.[66]

The results summarized above suggest that adjustment costs caused by exchange rate variability should not be substantial. Studies by Thursby, who in fact derives her measure of adjustment costs from export variability, confirm the hypothesis that these costs are no higher under fluctuating exchange rates than they would have been under fixed rates.

Effects on inflation and on output. Exchange rate fluctuations would be inflationary if the pass-through of exchange rate changes to import prices and then on to the general price level were asymmetrical— more rapid and complete when the domestic currency is depreciating than when it is appreciating. Such an assumption lies at the core of the so-called ratchet effect—a fairly prevalent notion in the mid-1970s—based on the presumed downward inflexibility of prices. The plausibility of this presumption largely hinges on the validity of the hypothesis that monetary policy systematically accommodates increases but is more or less unresponsive to decreases in import prices.

The existence of a ratchet effect was extensively tested by Goldstein for the period 1958–1973.[67] The results of his tests failed to confirm the existence of a ratchet effect. Repeated testing over the more recent period also failed to confirm the asymmetry in the effects of exchange rate fluctuations on the price level.[68] Virtually no empirical evidence supports the ratchet hypothesis. Moreover, anti-inflationary policies and the observed behavior of commodity prices in the 1980s have further weakened its plausibility.

Some analysts point out that only direct effects of exchange rate changes on the price level were tested. They posit that in addition to the direct effects, there may be another, indirect channel of asymmetrical transmission of exchange rate changes to the price level—through wage behavior.[69] The argument would be valid if wages were formally indexed or behaviorally linked to changes in import prices rather than to the overall price index. This does not appear to be the case, certainly not in the United States.

It may be noticed that the lack of asymmetry in the effect of exchange rate changes on import prices (and, as a corollary, the lack of evidence of an inflationary bias imparted by exchange rate variability) does not preclude the possibility that exchange rate fluctuations magnify (symmetrical) fluctuations of price level and thus increase the variability of inflation. Given the endogeneity of exchange rates and the price level, however—the similarity of their responses to many of the same exogenous factors and their strong influence on each other —it is difficult to imagine an empirical test that would yield a convincing result. Indirect evidence can be obtained by studying the behavior of the firm as it pertains to its pricing practices in response to exchange rate volatility. It ought to be emphasized once again that what matters in this context is not the overall variability of exchange rates but the inexplicable part of exchange rate fluctuations—a proxy for exchange rate uncertainty. Systematic exchange rate movements may also affect the firm's pricing behavior, but this would be a reflection of its informed reaction to predictable changes in its future competitive environment rather than of uncertainty.

Existing studies, both theoretical and empirical, present a wide array of possible responses of a firm to exchange rate uncertainty. At best the results of these studies with respect to the firm's pricing behavior should be characterized as ambiguous.[70] More recent evidence suggests that the response of tradable goods prices to exchange rate changes has become, if anything, more sluggish.[71] But even if tradable goods prices responded to exchange rate changes rapidly and even if the response could be attributed entirely to exchange rate uncertainty, for the exchange rate fluctuations to have a discernible effect on the price level variability, the pass-throughs of import price changes to the overall price level would also have to be rapid. All available evidence suggests that they are not. The lags are, in fact, so long that short-term exchange rate fluctuations (those that reverse themselves within one quarter) have no discernible effect on the aggregate domestic price level.

The effect of exchange rate volatility on output has received much more attention from editorial writers and politicians than from research economists. Apart from charts demonstrating that increased exchange rate variability since 1973 has coincided with lower growth rates in real output in the United States and elsewhere, no evidence exists that exchange rate variability has had an adverse effect on output.

It is not clear how to go about testing for an independent effect of exchange rate fluctuations on output. One line of attack would be to relate exchange rate uncertainty to the level of each component of gross domestic product separately. If it could be shown that each is negatively affected by residual exchange rate fluctuations, a legitimate inference would be that they adversely affect overall production. No such evidence exists. If, however, there is only scant and inconclusive evidence of the negative effect of exchange rate variability on the volume of trade—presumably the most exchange rate–sensitive component of GDP—the effect on other GDP components must be even more difficult to detect.

Another line of attack would be to add up the deadweight losses of adjustment costs across sectors. This approach applied to the export sector did not yield robust results, and there is no reason to expect that it would fare any better when applied to other sectors.

One could also attempt to measure the effect of exchange rate uncertainty on the domestic investment. If a pervasive negative effect could be found, the conclusion could be drawn that residual exchange rate uncertainty, by reducing the rate of capital formation, hampers economic growth. As far as I can discover, the literature contains no such findings.[72]

The Choice of Benchmark. The continuing debate about the effects of exchange rate volatility on other economic variables is part of a broader debate about the optimality of alternative exchange rate arrangements. Even though most recent proposals call for officially managed rates rather than fixed parities, by tradition and for analytical convenience, when consequences of alternative regimes are being examined, fixed rates are customarily juxtaposed with flexible rates.

The most simplistic analyses, by assuming no fluctuations in nominal exchange rates, simply suppress the allegedly correlated fluctuations in other economic variables. Such a procedure guarantees the unsurprising result that, for a given set of circumstances, fixed exchange rates are associated with less variability in macroeconomic aggregates than flexible ones.

More sophisticated analyses attempt to postulate policies that would be necessary to ensure exchange rate fixity. Such counterfactual simulations are one way of creating a frame of reference for an evaluation of the relative merits of alternative exchange rate arrangements. A typical experiment would replicate some disturbance that has actually caused exchange rates to move—say, the dollar to go up—and postulate a policy response, such as an increase in bank reserves or a discount rate cut by the Federal Reserve, that would have prevented such a move. Would the response of short-term interest rates, bond yields, or commodity or equity prices be more or less subdued in the counterfactual situation than they were in reality? In particular, would the uncertainty about future movements in interest rates, prices, and so on, be greater or less than under freely adjustable rates?

Such counterfactual simulations are valid mental experiments. Unfortunately, their empirical implementation is extremely difficult. As the earlier discussion indicated, our ability to model exchange rate changes quantitatively is utterly inadequate. In a simulation such as that sketched out above we would know neither by how much a given disturbance had moved the dollar in the absence of a policy action nor how much of a monetary stimulus would have been required to prevent it from moving. As the experience of recent years has abundantly shown, neither do we know with any precision what the effect of the required monetary stimulus would be on the variation in the rate of inflation or on aggregate output. Despite these difficulties, without having a correctly specified fixed–exchange rate benchmark in mind, no meaningful assessment of the consequences of exchange rate fluctuations is possible.[73]

In light of the earlier discussion, if the economy is shocked by a (policy or nonpolicy) disturbance and the adjustment of exchange rates is deliberately prevented, other channels are bound to carry a greater adjustment burden. It would be difficult to construct a noncontrived macroeconomic dynamic system where a reduction in the number of adjustment channels is beneficial to the economy. As Willett forcefully argues, what is relevant is not the correlation between exchange rate volatility and some measure of instability in macroeconomic variables but the extent, if any, to which exchange rate fluctuations increase the instability of those variables.[74] He points out that for such an incremental contribution to the instability of the economic system either the exchange rate would have to fluctuate on its own or its fluctuations would have to magnify the variability in economic aggregates due to other reasons.

The first mechanism (convergent bubbles, or bandwagons, or destabilizing speculation) has been discussed at length in previous sections. The evidence of its existence and pervasiveness is weak, certainly too weak for drawing strong policy conclusions. As to the second mechanism, with the demise of vicious and virtuous circles in the 1980s, there is absolutely no evidence that exchange rate variability magnifies fluctuation in other economic variables. The case for a policy aimed at smoothing out exchange rate fluctuations is yet to be established.

Some Cautionary Implications for Policy

The record of floating exchange rates over the past decade has been characterized by very large medium-term swings and substantial short-term volatility. Three times during this period the cumulative changes in the exchange rate of the dollar against any of the indexes of currencies of other industrial countries exceeded 30 percent. Against individual currencies the medium-term dollar movements have been much sharper.

These massive changes of the dollar exchange rate have not been offset to any great extent by opposite movements in national price levels. As a result, prices and costs in the United States in relation to those of its trading partners have fluctuated much more than could be justified by productivity changes, profit-margin adjustments, cyclical fluctuations in capacity utilization, and other real economic factors. Distortions in the relative price and cost structure were especially flagrant at the peak of the dollar's strength in the second half of 1984 and early 1985.

The described behavior of the dollar contributed to a sense of growing dissatisfaction with the system of floating exchange rates. It has been recognized for some time that floating rates do not, as the textbook exposition claims, hermetically insulate countries from monetary shocks originating abroad or quickly reverse trade imbalances. The gyrations of the dollar in recent years have intensified and broadened the scope of criticism of the performance of floating rates.

In contradistinction to the period of early floating in 1973–1975, when the attention of economists and practitioners alike was focused on short-term exchange rate volatility, recent years have witnessed a shift of attention toward medium-term oscillations. One reason for this shift was the quick adaptation of markets to short-term volatility, which was accomplished mainly by a proliferation of financial instruments and techniques enabling wider dispersion of risk of short-term exchange rate changes. Another reason for the shift is that extensive empirical research failed to uncover discernible adverse effects of short-term volatility on output, prices, employment, volume of trade, or other important variables.

Some empirical evidence has begun to emerge that medium-term cycles may have some adverse effect on the volume of trade. But the evidence so far is suggestive rather than conclusive. There is no convincing evidence that such movements impart inflationary bias to the price level or have an adverse effect on aggregate output and total investment. But there is convincing evidence that medium-term exchange rate cycles tend to aggravate imbalances among sectors of the economy. Furthermore, it is now recognized that large exchange rate changes can destabilize existing trade arrangements and patterns and thereby give a spur to protectionism.

In response to these drawbacks of floating exchange rates, numerous proposals have been advanced and limited measures undertaken with the stated purpose of reducing exchange rate movements. Some of these proposals and initiatives aim at institutionalizing the coordination of macroeconomic policies among major industrial countries. Others advocate establishing "target zones" for exchange rates and directing policies at enforcing them.

Given what we do and do not know about the interactions between the exchange rate and other economic variables, proposals to attempt to fix or otherwise manipulate the exchange rate seem to be misguided. What we do know is that exchange rates, like prices of other assets, absorb and disperse an unending stream of unanticipated shocks. For a given degree of price rigidity in goods and labor markets and no particular pattern in the origin and nature of the various shocks, preventing exchange rates from adjusting freely would mean that adjustments would have to take place elsewhere—in money, debt, equity, commodity, and labor markets. Whether such a shift of the adjustment burden from foreign exchange to other markets is desirable would depend on the comparison of the welfare costs of different degrees of exchange rate flexibility. Some analysts find that the welfare costs of freely floating rates are generally lower than those of fixed rates.[75] Only if these findings could be successfully challenged would a case for fixing or managing the exchange rate be valid.

Furthermore, we now know that assets denominated in major currencies are sufficiently close substitutes to make sterilized intervention in foreign exchange markets ineffective, except perhaps in the very short run. One consequence is that there is no "cheap" way to influence exchange rates. To do so, appropriate policies would have to be specifically adopted for this purpose, and, as a corollary, some other policy target would have to be abandoned. Any assessment of the desirability of exchange rate targeting would have to evaluate the consequences of substituting the exchange rate for another policy target.

What we do not know about the interactions between exchange rates and other economic variables makes the argument in favor of active exchange rate management even weaker. As the discussion in this paper suggests, our understanding of the process of exchange rate determination is exceedingly limited, and our ability to explain quantitatively, let alone to predict, exchange rates—which is ultimately indispensable for intelligent policy formulation—is virtually nonexistent. It would be only fortuitous, therefore, if the exchange rate were fixed by the authorities at a level, or defended within a range, that would be credible, sustainable, and most beneficial (by criteria yet to be defined and agreed upon) to the operation of the economy. If, because of our ignorance of what the appropriate rate is, the target exchange rate were set at the "wrong" level, policies would be unwittingly directed at promoting prolonged price distortions and, consequently, efficiency losses. Moreover, even if the target exchange rate were initially set at a "proper" level, continuous structural changes or a discrete event such as an oil price collapse would make the initial target inappropriate and thus subject to revision, that is, to another guess. These difficulties in managing exchange rates would remain true even with perfect international coordination of monetary and fiscal policies aimed at validating a set of mutually agreed upon exchange rates.

Does all this mean that no case for fixing an exchange rate can ever be made? No, but such a case can be made only under very restrictive assumptions. If, for example, exchange rate pressures were always (or predominantly) a result of changes in the demand for money and the main policy goal was stabilization of output, resisting an incipient exchange rate change would be an appropriate policy, though not necessarily the only appropriate one. Similarly, if exchange rate pressures were caused mostly by autonomous speculation, that is, by unjustifiable expectations, and the authorities knew what expectations were justifiable, a policy designed to prevent exchange rate changes would be both desirable and profitable. Needless to say, these conditions do not prevail in the real world.

In the real world, unanticipated shocks of all kinds batter the markets continuously. We cannot always identify the shocks even ex post, seldom isolate their effects even as they occur, and (by definition) never predict their onslaught. Shock absorbers to cushion random and inevitable shocks are necessary to shield the economy from unnecessarily abrupt disruptions and dislocations. Flexible exchange rates, and asset markets in general, perform the vital function of such shock absorbers. Any attempt to prevent exchange rates from performing this function will probably send the economy along a bumpier road.

Notes

1. Statement of the Honorable Beryl W. Sprinkel before the Joint Economic Committee of the U.S. Congress, May 4, 1981.

2. These initiatives are embedded in various legislative proposals to return to some form of an internationally negotiated gold standard.

3. For example, "Competitive Exchange Rate Act of 1985"—an amendment to House Resolution 3498 offered by Representative John LaFalce (Democrat, New York) and an amendment offered by Senators Bill Bradley (Democrat, New Jersey) and Alan Dixon (Democrat, Illinois) calling for action in the foreign exchange market to depress the value of the dollar—*New York Times*, May 16, 1985. More recently the Senate Banking Committee voted out a bill, dated August 14, 1986, stating in Title I, subtitle A, section 1, paragraph 3, that "the United States and the other Summit countries should coordinate the participation by central banks in international currency markets, with the objective of reducing severe fluctuations in the values of the currencies of the major industrialized countries, deterring currency speculation, and promoting orderly adjustment of exchange rates to reflect changed economic fundamentals."

4. See, for example, John Williamson, *The Exchange Rate System*, Policy Analyses in International Economics no. 5 (Washington, D.C.: Institute for International Economics, 1983); or Morris Goldstein, "The Exchange Rate System: Lessons of the Past and Options for the Future," Occasional Paper 30 (Washington, D.C.: International Monetary Fund, 1984).

5. Among recent analyses of the floating rate experience, see Jeffrey R. Shafer and Bonnie E. Loopesko, "Floating Exchange Rates after Ten Years," *Brookings Papers on Economic Activity*, no. 1 (1983); or Maurice Obstfeld, "Floating Exchange Rates: Experience and Prospects," *Brookings Papers on Economic Activity*, no. 2 (1985).

6. The main reason that changes in FRB10B are more muted than those in FRB10 is Canada's much larger bilateral than multilateral weight in conjunction with the relative stability of the bilateral rate between the Canadian and U.S. dollars.

7. The FRB10 index includes the currencies of ten countries whose relative importance is given by each country's share (all exports plus imports) in the total trade of the group in the 1972–1976 period. The FRB10B index uses the same ten currencies but uses each country's share in the total trade of the group with the United States (rather than with the rest of the world) in the 1972–1976 period. The following list of the ten countries gives their relative weights (in percentage) in global trade shares and bilateral trade shares with the United States as the first and second numbers, respectively:

Belgium (6.4, 3.4); Canada (9.1, 40.1); France (13.1, 4.8); Germany (20.8, 10.1); Italy (9.0, 4.8); Japan (13.6, 20.8); the Netherlands (8.3, 4.6); Sweden (4.2, 1.6); Switzerland (3.6, 1.9); the United Kingdom (11.9, 7.9).

The Morgan Guaranty Trust index (not shown in the figure) includes, in addition to the ten countries in the FRB10 index, Australia, Austria, Denmark, Norway, and Spain. The weights are based on bilateral trade with the United States in 1980.

The "global index" depicted in figure 1–2 includes, in addition to the currencies of the fifteen countries in the Morgan Guaranty Trust index, the currencies of eighteen more countries: Algeria, Brazil, China (People's Republic), Egypt, Hong Kong, India, Indonesia, Israel, Malaysia, Mexico, Nigeria, the Philippines, Saudi Arabia, Singapore, South Africa, South Korea, Taiwan, and Venezuela. The index uses weights based on each country's bilateral trade flows with the United States in the 1972–1976 period.

All indexes are set equal to 100 in the first quarter of 1973. The FRB10 index displayed here is slightly different from the series published by the Federal Reserve Board, which is set equal to 100 in March 1973.

8. For the purpose of assessing the effects of changes in the value of the dollar on the U.S. competitive position in the world, global trade weights are conceptually preferable to bilateral trade weights, and a broader coverage is preferable to a narrower one. Unfortunately, the trade statistics for many developing countries that are needed to construct a broadly based index weighted by global trade shares are not readily available.

9. The real exchange rate at time t, S_t, is a product of

$$(S_t/S_0) \times (P_0^*/P_0)/(P_t^*/P_t),$$

where S denotes the nominal exchange rate in foreign currency units per dollar; P and P^* denote foreign and U.S. price level indexes, respectively; and the subscript zero indicates the base period.

If differential changes in foreign and U.S. price indexes are exactly offset by changes in the nominal exchange rate, the real exchange rate stays constant. Setting all values in the base period equal to one reduces the formula for the real exchange rate to $\overline{S}_t = S_t(P_t/P_t^*)$. Values of S_t greater than one indicate real appreciation of the dollar; less than one, real depreciation.

10. For an extensive analysis of time series properties of various price indexes and exchange rates, see Louka T. Katseli, "Real Exchange Rates in the 1970s," in John F.O. Bilson and Richard C. Marston, eds., *Exchange Rate Theory and Practice* (Chicago and London: University of Chicago Press, 1984).

11. Deflators used to compute real rates are all consumer price indexes (CPIs). The FRB10 index is described in note 7. The Morgan Guaranty Trust index depicted in figure 1–4 uses weights based on each country's trade share in the total trade of the group, *not* on its trade share in U.S. bilateral trade with the group. Trade shares used in constructing the FRB10 index are based on 1972–1976 trade statistics, those for the Morgan Guaranty Trust index on 1980 trade statistics.

More generally, it is important to notice that formulas for real effective exchange rates differ from commonly used price indexes in that the former are geometric averages and the latter arithmetic averages. More precisely, a real effective exchange rate index, I, is expressed as

$$I_t = \prod_{i=1}^{n} (S_i/P_i)w_i$$

where $I_0 \equiv 100$, S_i is the bilateral nominal exchange rate of currency i in period t in relation to the base period, P_i is the ratio of the price level in country i to the U.S. price level in period t in relation to the ratio in the base period, and w_i is the weight of currency i in the basket of n currencies.

This formulation allows for an investigation of separate effects of each country's relative price changes and nominal exchange rate changes on the real effective exchange rate. A more commonly used fixed-weight index formula, however, namely,

$$\hat{I}_t = \sum_{i=1}^{n} (S_i/P_i)w_i$$

may trace a noticeably different time path of the composite real exchange rate than that given by I.

12. For a comprehensive analysis of changes in the real value of the dollar (and other currencies) under different exchange rate regimes, see Michael L. Mussa, "Nominal Exchange Rate Regimes and the Behavior of Real Exchange Rates: Evidence and Implications" (Paper prepared for the Carnegie-Rochester Conference Series on Public Policy, November 22–23, 1985).

13. More on various connections between misalignment and volatility can be found in Shafer and Loopesko, "Floating Exchange Rates."

14. Jacob A. Frenkel and Michael L. Mussa, "The Efficiency of Foreign Exchange Markets and Measures of Turbulence," *American Economic Review*, vol. 70, no. 2 (May 1980).

15. For a discussion of advantages and disadvantages of this and other measures of exchange rate unpredictability, see the analysis of variability of many exchange rates by Anthony Lanyi and Esther C. Suss, "Exchange Rate Variability: Alternative Measures and Interpretation," *IMF Staff Papers*, vol. 29, no. 4 (December 1982).

16. Ibid.; see also Jeffrey H. Bergstrand, "Is Exchange Rate Volatility 'Excessive'?" *New England Economic Review* (Federal Reserve Bank of Boston), (September–October 1983); and Bonnie E. Loopesko, "Notes on Exchange Rate Variability," Board of Governors of the Federal Reserve System, June 1985.

17. For a different view and further discussion of the relationship between the exchange rate variability and its uncertainty, see M. A. Akhtar and R. Spence Hilton, "Exchange Rate Uncertainty and International Trade: Some Conceptual Issues and New Estimates for Germany and the United States," Federal Reserve Bank of New York, Research Paper no. 8403, May 1984.

18. See Bergstrand, "Is Volatility 'Excessive'?"; Obstfeld, "Floating Exchange Rates"; and the references cited therein.

19. See especially Bergstrand, "Is Volatility 'Excessive'?" pp. 11–13; and Loopesko, "Exchange Rate Variability."

20. A classic example is Fritz Machlup, *Essays in Economic Semantics* (Englewood Cliffs, N.J.: Prentice-Hall, 1963). For a more recent analysis, see Jeffrey A. Frankel, "Six Meanings of 'Overvaluation': The 1981–85 Dollar," *Essays in International*

Finance, no. 159 (December 1985) (International Finance Section, Princeton University, Princeton, N.J.).

21. The best known exposition of exchange rate overshooting is that by Rudiger Dornbusch, "Expectations and Exchange Rate Dynamics," *Journal of Political Economy*, no. 84 (December 1976). In his model overshooting is caused by stickiness of goods prices. But any model in which one of the variables is not permitted to adjust instantaneously to an unanticipated shock can be made to produce overshooting, that is, an initial response of the exchange rate in excess of its long-run expected value. In the portfolio-balance model, for example, overshooting would be produced by a gradual rather than an instantaneous change in the current account.

22. Robert Cumby and Maurice Obstfeld, "International Interest Rates and Price Level Linkages under Flexible Exchange Rates: A Review of Recent Evidence," in Bilson and Marston, *Exchange Rate Theory and Practice*.

23. Richard Meese and Ken Rogoff, "Empirical Exchange Rate Models of the Seventies: Do They Fit Out of Sample?" *Journal of International Economics*, no. 14 (1983); Richard Meese and Ken Rogoff, "The Out-of-Sample Failure of Empirical Exchange Rate Models: Sampling Error or Misspecification?" in Jacob A. Frenkel, ed., *Exchange Rates and International Macroeconomics* (Chicago: University of Chicago Press, 1983); and Richard Meese and Ken Rogoff, "Was It Real? The Exchange Rate–Interest Differential Relation, 1973–1984," *International Finance Discussion Papers*, Federal Reserve Board of Governors, 1985.

24. The studies referred to in the text are John F. O. Bilson, "A Monetary Approach to the Exchange Rate; Some Empirical Evidence," *IMF Staff Papers*, no. 25 (1978); Rudiger Dornbusch, "Exchange Rate Economics: Where Do We Stand?," *Brookings Papers on Economic Activity*, no. 1 (1980); Jeffrey Frankel, "On the Mark: A Theory of Floating Exchange Rates Based on Real Interest Differentials," *American Economic Review*, no. 69 (1979); Jeffrey Frankel, "Monetary and Portfolio-Balance Models of Exchange Rate Determination," in J. Bhandari, ed., *Economic Interdependence and Flexible Exchange Rates* (Cambridge, Mass.: MIT Press, 1982); Jeffrey Frankel, "Testing of Monetary and Portfolio Balance Models of Exchange Rate Determination," in Bilson and Marston, *Exchange Rate Theory and Practice*; and Jacob Frenkel, "The Collapse of Purchasing Power Parities during the 1970s," *European Economic Review*, no. 16 (1981), pp. 145–65.

25. See, for example, Jacques Melitz, "How Much Simplification Is Wise in Modeling Exchange Rates?" in Paul DeGrauwe and Theo Peters, eds, *Exchange Rates in Multicountry Econometric Models* (New York: St. Martin's Press, 1983).

26. See Michael Mussa, "The Theory of Exchange Rate Determination," in Bilson and Marston, *Exchange Rate Theory and Practice*, for a formalization of this view.

27. Ronald McKinnon, *An International Standard for Monetary Stabilization*, Policy Analyses in International Economics no. 8 (Washington, D.C.: Institute for International Economics, 1984).

28. See, for example, *The Economic Report of the President for 1985* (Washington, D.C., 1986).

29. See, for example, *The Economic Report of the President for 1984*, (Washington, D.C., 1985); and Martin Feldstein, *The Budget Deficit and the Dollar*, National Bureau of Economic Research, Working Paper no. 1898. April 1986.

30. Paul Evans, "Do Large Deficits Produce High Interest Rates?" *American Economic Review* (March 1985), and "Is the Dollar High because of Large Budget Deficits?" unpublished manuscript, September 1985.

31. C. Fred Bergsten, in *From Rambouillet to Versailles: A Symposium*, Essays in International Finance no. 149 (Princeton, N.J.: Princeton University, 1982).

32. For calculations see Jeffrey A. Frankel and Kenneth A. Froot, "The Dollar as a Speculative Bubble: The Tale of Fundamentalists and Chartists," National Bureau of Economic Research Working Paper no. 1854, March 1986.

33. A good example is William H. Branson, "Causes of Appreciation and Volatility of the Dollar," in *The U.S. Dollar—Recent Developments, Outlook, and Policy Options* (Symposium sponsored by the Federal Reserve Bank of Kansas City, Jackson Hole, Wyoming, August 21–23, 1985).

34. See Congressional Budget Office, *The Economic and Budget Outlook: An Update*, August 1984.

35. Bandwagons should be distinguished from residual variance caused by unobservable variables, such as continuous changes in expectations.

36. For a comprehensive exposition of the bubble theory, see Olivier J. Blanchard and Mark W. Watson, "Bubbles, Rational Expectations, and Financial Markets" in Paul Wachtel, ed., *Crises in Economic and Financial Structure* (Lexington, Mass.: Lexington Books, 1982).

37. Dornbusch, among others, in 1976 ruled out the possibility of an explosive solution in his famous article "Expectations and Exchange Rate Dynamics." In 1982, however, he adopted the concept of rational bubbles of the early 1980s in his paper "Equilibrium and Disequilibrium Exchange Rates," *Zeitschrift für Wirtschafts und Sozialwissenschaften*, no. 102 (1982).

38. A good discussion of empirical issues can be found in Robert P. Flood and Peter M. Garber, "Market Fundamentals versus Price-Level Bubbles: The First Tests," *Journal of Political Economy*, vol. 88 (August 1980).

39. Best known among these studies are Wing T. Woo, "Speculative Bubbles in Foreign Exchange Markets," *Brookings Discussion Papers in International Economics*, no. 13 (March 1984); and Richard A. Meese, "Testing for Bubbles in Exchange Markets: A Case of Sparkling Rates," *Journal of Political Economy* (1985).

40. See, for example, Frankel, "Six Meanings of 'Overvaluation,'" app.; Frankel concludes that "the appreciation of the dollar has gone on for too long to represent a single rational bubble."

41. Paul Krugman expressed this view most eloquently in his paper "Is the Strong Dollar Sustainable?" in *The U.S. Dollar—Recent Developments, Outlook, and Policy Options*, (Symposium sponsored by the Federal Reserve Bank of Kansas City, Jackson Hole, Wyoming, August 21–23, 1985).

42. Cumby and Obstfeld, "International Interest Rates," is one of many recent studies confirming that the forward rate is a very biased (and occasionally perverse) predictor of the future spot rate.

43. For roughly four years, between early 1981 and early 1985, the forward discount on the dollar consistently underpredicted the extent of the subsequently realized appreciation of the dollar over the corresponding period.

44. Krugman, "Is the Strong Dollar Sustainable?" p. 131.

45. Stephen Marris, *Deficits and the Dollar: The World Economy at Risk*, Policy Analyses in International Economics, no. 14 (Washington, D.C.: Institute for International Economics, 1985).

46. See Congressional Budget Office, *The Economic and Budget Outlook: An Update*, August 1985.

47. The decline of the dollar is too recent and the time span of the decline too brief so far to allow for testing which of the competing exchange rate models would have predicted its path of decline most accurately.

48. Michael L. Mussa, "Commentary on 'Is the Strong Dollar Sustainable?'" in *The U.S. Dollar—Recent Developments, Outlook, and Policy Options* (Symposium sponsored by the Federal Reserve Bank of Kansas City, Jackson Hole, Wyoming, August 21–23, 1985).

49. In a recent very ingenious attempt to model the behavior of the dollar exchange rate, Frankel and Froot, "Dollar as a Speculative Bubble," depict it as a result of weighted forecasts of "fundamentalists" and "chartists," with weights determined by the relative accuracy of recent forecasts by the two groups. With the (unobservable) parameters they choose, their model fits the observed movements in exchange rates rather well, and their tale is probably a fair approximation of the behavior of portfolio managers, that is, the principal agents in foreign exchange markets. They do not, however, address the crucial question of the strong dollar puzzle, namely, why for such a long time chartists' forecasts based on a simple random walk performed so much better than fundamentalists' forecasts based on economic theory.

50. Williamson (*The Exchange Rate System*), in addition to the FEER, defines two other, positive concepts of equilibrium: market equilibrium, when the exchange rate equilibrates private supply and demand; and current equilibrium, when information about temporary factors (such as the divergence between the actual and the desired currency composition of portfolios) leads to a rational divergence of the actual exchange rate from the FEER.

51. A related concept of an equilibrium exchange rate discernible in academic work and public policy pronouncements relies on the notion of sustainability of policies. If a set of policies is deemed unsustainable, the exchange rate accompanying those policies is a disequilibrium rate. Thus, to the extent that U.S. policies of the 1980–1985 period were unsustainable, so was the strong dollar. It is worth pointing out, however, that a judgment about the unsustainability of a given set of policies need not (at least in principle) be equivalent to an assessment of their inferiority.

52. Of all people, Alexandre Lamfalussy, former chief economist of the Bank for International Settlements, wondered, "What possible good can result from daily, even hourly, ups and downs in the exchange rates?" (Address to the Atlantic Institute for International Affairs, "A Plan for An International Commitment to Exchange Rate Stability," Brussels, October 22, 1981).

53. The variability of exchange rates in relation to that of other asset prices varies substantially among countries. It is much greater for Japan than for the European currencies participating in the European Monetary System arrangement. It is also noticeably influenced by the extent to which national monetary authorities attempt at various times to dampen movements in short-term interest rates.

54. For a series of tests linking exchange rate movements to previous day releases of a number of economic indicators, see Gikas Hardouvelis, "Economic News, Exchange Rates, and Interest Rates," Department of Economics, Barnard College, Columbia University, February 1985.

55. See, for example, Krugman, "Is the Strong Dollar Sustainable?" A similar conclusion is drawn by Rudiger Dornbusch, "Flexible Exchange Rates and Interdependence," *IMF Staff Papers* (March 1983).

56. Robert J. Shiller, "Do Stock Prices Move Too Much to Be Justified by Subsequent Changes in Dividends?" *American Economic Review* (June 1981).

57. There are many variations of this definition of market efficiency in the very rich literature on the subject. For an excellent survey of this literature see Richard

M. Levich, "Empirical Studies of Exchange Rates: Price Behavior, Rate Determination, and Market Efficiency," in Ronald Jones and Peter Kenen, eds., *Handbook of International Economics* (Amsterdam: North-Holland, 1984).

58. See, for example, Michael P. Dooley and Jeffrey R. Shafer, "Analysis of Short-Run Exchange Rate Behavior: March 1973 to November 1981," Research Memorandum, International Monetary Fund, April 1982.

59. Filter-rule trading means taking an unhedged long position in a currency whenever it appreciates a given small amount from its recent low and a short position whenever it depreciates from its recent high. If the short-term interest differential exactly equals expected exchange rate change or if exchange rate changes are not serially correlated, no filter rule should result in systematic profits over a buy-and-hold strategy.

60. Victoria S. Farrell with Dean A. ReRosa and T. Ashby McCown, "Effects of Exchange Rate Variability on International Trade and Other Economic Variables: A Review of the Literature," Board of Governors of the Federal Reserve System, Staff Studies, no. 130, December 1983; International Monetary Fund, Research Department, "Exchange Rate Volatility and World Trade," Occasional Paper, no. 28, July 1984; and Robert Solomon, "The Consequences of Exchange Rate Variability," Brookings Discussion Papers in International Economics, no. 24, December 1984.

61. Prolonged departures of real exchange rates from their (perhaps unknown) equilibrium levels entail another kind of costs: efficiency costs. Distortion of the structure of relative prices caused by such prolonged divergences results in a suboptimal pattern of deployment of productive resources yielding less than maximum output for a given level of resource availability. Efficiency costs of this kind are not, however, a consequence of exchange rate variability per se and, in fact, are more likely to arise when the exchange rate is fixed by the authorities.

62. See Marie C. Thursby, "The Resource Reallocation Costs of Fixed and Flexible Exchange Rates: A Counterexample," *Journal of International Economics*, vol. 10 (February 1980).

63. International Monetary Fund, "Exchange Rate Volatility," p. 33.

64. Bela Balassa, "Flexible Exchange Rates and International Trade," in John S. Chipman and Charles P. Kindleberger, eds., *Flexible Exchange Rates and the Balance of Payments* (Amsterdam: North-Holland, 1980).

65. Rachel McCulloch, "Unexpected Real Consequences of Floating Exchange Rates," *Essays in International Finance*, No. 153 (International Finance Section, Princeton University, August 1983).

66. As reported in Farrell et al., "Effects of Exchange Rate Variability." Cushman finds statistically significant negative effects of real exchange rate variability on bilateral trade flows. The IMF Research Staff in "Exchange Rate Volatility" applied Cushman's model to a data sample extended through 1981 and could not confirm his results regarding the effects on trade.

67. Morris Goldstein, "Downward Price Inflexibility, Ratchet Effects, and the Inflationary Effects of Import Price Changes: Some Empirical Evidence," *IMF Staff Papers*, vol. 24 (November 1977).

68. See, for example, International Monetary Fund, "Exchange Rate Volatility," app. 3.

69. Solomon, "Consequences of Exchange Rate Variability," pp. 18–19.

70. A comprehensive discussion of these issues can be found in Richard M. Levich and Clas G. Wilborg, *Exchange Risk and Exposure* (Lexington, Mass.: D.C. Heath, 1980).

71. See, for example, Catharine L. Mann, "Prices, Profit Margins, and Exchange Rates," *Federal Reserve Bulletin* (June 1986).

72. Farrell et al., "Effects of Exchange Rate Variability," reports a memorandum prepared by Peter Kenen for the U.S. Treasury Department in 1979 in which a significant negative effect of exchange rate variability on real gross fixed-capital formation was established. Kenen takes gross domestic investment in 1976 in relation to that in three previous years and regresses it on mean monthly changes in nominal and real bilateral rates over the 1974–1976 period. The established correlation merely confirms that the 1973–1974 period witnessed more frequent and stronger disturbances (the tail end of the commodity boom, the change in the exchange rate regime, the oil stock, a severe recession, Watergate) than the comparatively placid year of economic recovery 1975.

73. The discussion here abstracts from the possibility that exchange rate fluctuations could be suppressed around a nonequilibrium level (however defined). In this case, efficiency losses caused by relative price distortions will not be captured by a standard macroeconomic structure used for counterfactual simulations of the kind described.

Moreover, the fixed exchange rate is assumed to be credible to the market. If the market doubts the authorities' ability or resolve to defend the rate at its current fixed level, the resulting uncertainty would manifest itself in greater fluctuations in various economic variables, such as international interest differentials, long-term bond yields, and leads and lags in trade-related payments.

74. Thomas D. Willett, "The Causes and Effects of Exchange Rate Volatility," in Jacob S. Dreyer, Gottfried Haberler, and Thomas D. Willett, eds., *The International Monetary System: A Time of Turbulence* (Washington, D.C.: American Enterprise Institute, 1982).

75. For a very careful analysis of these issues, see Allan H. Meltzer, "Variability of Prices, Output, and Money under Fixed and Fluctuating Exchange Rates: An Empirical Study of Monetary Regimes in Japan and the United States," February 1985.

2

The International Monetary System and Proposals for International Policy Coordination

Gottfried Haberler

Prologue as an Epilogue

Some dramatic developments came too late to be considered in the text below. The outstanding one is the sharply increased volatility of exchange rates. On October 31, 1986, Secretary Baker and his Japanese counterpart Mr. Miyazawa declared the dollar/yen exchange rate "broadly consistent with the underlying fundamentals." Yet two months later the dollar slumped. On January 21, 1987, Baker and Miyazawa held an emergency meeting. The dollar plunged again. Two typical news headlines: "If the Dollar Cracks" (The Economist, February 7, 1987); "Dollar Battered in Hectic Day" (New York Times, February 10, 1987).

Whatever the outcome, a lengthy period of uncertainty and turmoil is not the best way to set exchange rates. U.S. policy of pressuring Germany and Japan to expand suffers from two serious weaknesses. First, the United States still needs foreign capital to finance budget deficits. Second, even a large noninflationary expansion of the German and Japanese economies would have only a minor effect on U.S. trade deficits. All this supports the principal conclusions of the present paper: Large U.S. budget deficits are the main cause of the trade deficit. Governments do a poor job setting exchange rates. Markets, too, make mistakes, but if left alone markets do much better than governments. Ergo, the system of floating exchange rates should continue.

Summary

After James Baker became secretary of the Treasury in February 1985, the Reagan administration's balance-of-payments policy took a sharp turn from a passive, laissez-faire, benign-neglect approach to an activist, interventionist one. Under Baker's predecessor market forces were allowed to set the exchange value of the dollar. Under Baker the policy was first to talk the dollar down and

63

then to push it down by internationally concerted interventions in the foreign exchange market.

The reason for the switch is well known. From 1980 to February 1985 the dollar appreciated sharply relative to all foreign currencies. The strong dollar stimulated imports and discouraged exports, producing huge trade deficits causing unemployment in export and import competing industries, which triggered strong protectionist pressures in Congress. True, the market had turned around and in March 1985 the dollar started on a lengthy decline. But that was not immediately clear. So Secretary Baker organized the surprise meeting of the Group of Five (the United States, England, France, Germany, and Japan) at the Plaza Hotel in New York, where it was decided to bring the dollar further down by concerted interventions in the foreign exchange market.

Parallel with the initiative on the monetary front, the United States has been pushing for "international policy coordination." This theme was taken up by the Tokyo Economic Summit in May 1986. The heads of state of seven nations (the Group of Five plus Canada and Italy) instructed their seven ministers of finance to meet at least once a year to check the "mutual compatibility" of their policies. The ministers conducted "their first exercise of multilateral surveillance" in September 1986 and issued a bland statement, a collection of generalities: the ministers agreed to continue to promote noninflationary growth, to continue to remove structural rigidities, to resist protectionist pressures, and so on.

In practice, the vaunted international policy coordination has boiled down to the increasingly urgent and impatient demand by the United States that Germany and Japan stimulate their economies in order to reduce their trade surpluses and U.S. deficits, threatening them with a further decline of the dollar and with a protectionist explosion in the U.S. Congress. The United States and Japan, dubbed the Group of Two, have reached an agreement. On October 31, 1986, after a secret meeting, Mr. Baker and the Japanese Minister of Finance Kiichi Miyazawa issued a "Statement on Economic Cooperation." Apart from the usual phrases about "the importance of continuing cooperative action" and the like, the substantive content is: The Bank of Japan reduced the discount rate from 3½ percent to 3 percent, and the Japanese government promised to submit to the Diet a fiscal package of 3.6 trillion yen (about $22 billion) in additional expenditures spread over several years and a sizable reduction of marginal tax rates. Actually, these reforms had been announced earlier. The United States promised to "remain fully committed" to reducing the budget deficit and, most important, agreed that the dollar-yen rate is "now broadly consistent with the present underlying fundamentals." In plain English, the United States will, for the time being, not ask for any further appreciation of the yen. But the agreement is not a return to fixed exchange rates. Nothing has been said about defending the exchange rate or about what should be done when the fundamentals change.

The U.S.-Japanese agreement demonstrates the superiority of quiet diplomacy. It was easier for the United States to reach an agreement with Japan than with Germany because Prime Minister Nakasone, unlike German Chancellor Helmut Kohl, was not confronted with an early election. But the American policy of pressuring the Germans and the Japanese to get rid of their trade surpluses suffers from two serious weaknesses: First, the United States still needs foreign capital to finance its huge budget deficits and, second, several econometric studies—by the IMF, the Federal Reserve Board, and private analysts—indicate that even a substantial increase of the German and Japanese GNP growth will have only a small effect on the U.S. trade deficit. The correction of the U.S. external deficit must go hand in hand with the reduction of the budget deficit, which reflects the insufficiency of domestic savings to finance both private-sector investment and public-sector borrowing. The United States cannot go on indefinitely importing capital on a large scale. First, sooner or later investors will get nervous and there may develop a stampede out of the dollar; second, the rapidly mounting service charge on the foreign debt will make it necessary to reduce the trade deficit and turn it into a surplus. These changes will make it necessary to devote a growing portion of output to exports and import substitution, implying a squeeze on consumption and investment—in other words, a reduction in the living standard, which with rigid wages would pose a serious problem.

No modern government relishes unemployment and all want growth. Much of the high European unemployment is structural, not Keynesian. The conclusion that I draw from all this is that each country should make its own judgment. Criticism and advice of other countries should be given quietly through institutions such as the OECD, BIS, and the IMF. Public criticism, echoed by the media in cruder form, is internationally counterproductive.

The U.S. switch to an activist balance-of-payments policy reflects a fairly widespread disenchantment with floating exchange rates. Floating was forced on most reluctant policy makers by the breakdown of the Bretton Woods system in the late 1960s and 1970s. But it was never fully accepted. It was blamed for the wide swings of the dollar and the huge U.S. trade deficits.

It is easy to see that we were lucky to have entered the 1980s with floating exchange rates. If the world had been on fixed exchange rates when capital flowed into the United States on a large scale, Europe would have suffered a massive loss of international reserves and intense deflationary pressure. The fixed-rate system would have broken down, which would have caused a severe recession. Thanks to floating, this did not happen.

The strong dollar and large U.S. trade deficits were not a gigantic market failure. On the contrary, up to a point they were highly beneficial and pulled *the world economy out of the recession. I say up to a point, because with the benefit of hindsight we can say that in 1984 the market did overshoot. But the market corrected itself and the dollar started to decline in March 1985, well before the U.S. policy changed.*

The budget deficits, too, were a blessing up to a point; they pulled the U.S. economy out of the recession. But unlike the markets, a reversal of government policy is not yet in sight, although there is now almost universal agreement that deficit spending has gone much too far. It is in the nature of the political process that governments are slow to admit mistakes and that the legislative machinery delays corrective action.

The determination of exchange rates should therefore be left to the markets; in other words, the system of floating exchange rates should continue. Jacob Dreyer argues convincingly in this volume that economists simply do not know enough about the determination of exchange rates to identify the "correct" rate. This is strikingly demonstrated by the fact that there is no agreement among experts on whether the dollar has declined far enough to eliminate or sharply reduce the U.S. trade deficit, let alone on how much it should decline. There is even no agreement on how much the dollar has already declined overall. We know, of course, how much it has declined against individual currencies; there exist many sharply divergent indexes of the overall decline, but there is none that is generally accepted as the best of the lot, let alone the correct one.

From all this it follows that a return to some sort of fixed exchange rate is out of the question. It is hardly necessary to explain at length that a return to the gold standard is also out of the question. Who would want to entrust the international monetary system to the mercies of South Africa and the Soviet Union, the two by far most important producers of gold? A Bretton Woods type of fixed but adjustable exchange rate is very vulnerable to destabilizing speculation. If the members of the Group of Five are unable to agree on the pattern of exchange rates of their currencies, how could it be done in a wider circle?

Early in 1987, the European Monetary System (EMS) was shaken by an acute crisis. The French franc was very weak because of widespread strikes in France. The German mark was strong. Prime Minister Jacques Chirac insisted that this was "a mark crisis, not a franc crisis" and called on the German authorities to "do what is necessary:" either upvalue the mark or reduce interest rates and stimulate the economy—in plain English, create a little inflation. After hectic negotiation, the ministers of finance papered over the cracks in the system with a token 3 percent appreciation of the mark and the Dutch guilder and a 2 percent appreciation of the Belgian franc against the other European currencies. The situation has been made more troublesome by a sharp slide of the dollar against the mark and the yen despite the Baker-

Miyazawa agreement. According to press reports, that is what the U.S. administration wants in order to keep the pressure on Germany to expand. It is true that sufficient inflation in the surplus countries, Germany and Japan, would let the deficit countries, the United States and France, off the hook. But it would be like infecting the healthy instead of curing the sick. Worldwide inflation is not a sound basis for the world economy. All this provides a classic demonstration of the dangers of politicization of exchange rates. Markets do a better job than governments in setting exchange rates.

Introduction

Since the breakdown of the Bretton Woods system of stable but adjustable exchange rates early in the 1970s, the international monetary system and its reform have been under almost continuous discussion. The system of floating exchange rates instituted in 1973 has never been fully accepted. In the past two or three years the criticism of floating has sharply increased and the call for monetary reform become more and more intense. The wide swings of the dollar, rising from June 1980 to February 1985 by 19 percent against the Japanese yen and 89 percent against the German mark, and then declining rapidly from February 1985 to September 1986 by 41 percent against the yen and 39 percent against the German mark; the huge trade and current-account deficits; and the resulting protectionist pressure have been most disturbing events. All had been blamed on the system of floating exchange rates.

Before continuing the story it must be pointed out that, while the appreciation and depreciation of the dollar in terms of single currencies is clear-cut, measuring the overall appreciation or depreciation of the dollar presents very difficult index number problems. I confine myself to some general remarks. Interested readers should consult the preceding chapter by Jacob Dreyer and the literature cited there.

There exist many indexes of the value of the dollar; in fact, the number has sharply increased in the past year. These indexes are weighted averages of the changes of the value of the dollar relative to individual currencies, the weights being the volume of trade—trade-weighted indexes. The various indexes differ with respect to the currencies covered, the system of weighting, and some other characteristics. The indexes are either bilaterally weighted, using as weights each country's volume of trade with the United States, or multilaterally weighted, using as weights each country's total trade or some more sophisticated system. The indexes yield divergent measures for the overall change of the dollar's value, the divergence being much greater for the decline of the dollar since 1985 than for the preceding appreciation. The reason for this asymmetry is that from 1980 to 1985 the dollar rose with respect to all currencies. After February 1985 the dollar did not decline against all currencies. The currencies of Taiwan, South Korea, and Hong Kong, for example, did not rise against the dollar, and the currencies of inflationary countries in Latin America and elsewhere declined.

Until recently the most widely used indexes were the Federal Reserve Board index (ten countries, multilateral weights), the Morgan Guaranty Trust index (fifteen countries, bilateral weights), the International Monetary Fund index (seventeen countries, sophisticated multilateral weighting system), and the U.S. Department of the Treasury index (twenty-two countries, bilateral weights). The four indexes cover the countries of the Organization for Economic Cooperation and Development (OECD), Western Europe, Japan, and Canada (the Treasury index adds Finland, Greece, Iceland, Ireland, and Turkey). All four indexes leave out South Korea, Taiwan, Hong Kong, Singapore, and the rest of the world. Thus they give an exaggerated impression of the magnitude of the decline of the dollar since February 1985.

Several attempts have been made to broaden the coverage of the indexes. I mention three. The first was presented by Michael Cox, "A New Alternative Trade-Weighted Dollar Exchange Rate Index."[1] This index covers all 131 U.S. trading partners and uses bilateral weights, reaching the conclusion that "only about a 6 percent depreciation of the dollar has occurred" from January 1980 to May 1986. This probably understates the decline of the dollar because the index is (as the author points out) in purely *nominal* terms and does not allow for inflation. Specifically, the inclusion of the highly inflationary Latin American countries vitiates the outcome. It is true that the four indexes mentioned above, too, are formally in nominal terms. But in the OECD countries inflation rates did not diverge very much during the 1980s, so that these indexes can be regarded as a close approximation to a real—that is, to an inflation-corrected—index.

The second comprehensive index, "Why Our Trade Gap Persists," was presented by Irwin L. Kellner.[2] According to this index the dollar has hardly declined since March 1985. Since the index is in nominal terms (not corrected for inflation), it probably understates the decline of the dollar. But according to the author, preliminary calculations suggest that adjustment for inflation changes the result only marginally.

The third attempt to broaden the geographic base of the index has been presented by Jeffrey A. Rosensweig, "A New Dollar Index: Capturing A More Global Perspective."[3] This index includes the Asian countries of Taiwan, South Korea, Hong Kong, and Singapore. It excludes the Latin American countries because of their high inflation rate. This index yields a depreciation of the dollar by about 20 percent.

Each of the existing indexes has its strong and weak points, and I believe that there is no good reason to single out one of them as the best of the lot or the correct one. This is unfortunate, because it means that we simply do not know by how much the dollar has declined overall since February 1985. It is true that attempts are under way in several places to construct a comprehensive inflation-corrected index. I doubt, however, that this will settle the question of how much the dollar has declined overall. The difficulties of such an inflation-corrected index are formidable because, for example, most of the highly inflationary countries have exchange controls and multiple rates. Mexico, the third largest trade partner of the United States, is a striking example.

An important implication of this conclusion is the following: policy makers and their economic advisers are confronted with the question whether the dollar has already declined sufficiently to eliminate the balance-of-payments deficit. The answer depends partly on how much the dollar actually has declined. The uncertainty about this has important implications for economic policy. More on this later.

The changed outlook on the balance of payments and exchange rates is highlighted by the sharp reversal of the Reagan administration's policy since the arrival of James Baker at the Treasury Department in February 1986. Under Baker's predecessor, the team of Donald Regan and Beryl Sprinkel in the Treasury, U.S. policy was one of laissez-faire, hands-off benign neglect of the balance of payments.[4] It opposed official interventions in the foreign exchange markets. The policy of benign neglect, also called a "passive" policy with respect to the balance of payments and exchange rates, was well stated in the Economic Report of the President for 1984:

> In the 1950s and 1960s central banks were committed to maintaining their countries' exchange rates at fixed levels. This effort became increasingly difficult over time, due particularly to divergent inflation rates among countries. By 1971 the dollar had become unsustainably overvalued in the sense that the supply of dollars greatly exceeded the private demand for dollars. Central banks made up the difference, buying unwanted dollars in exchange for foreign currencies. The effort was abandoned in 1973 and the major currencies moved on to a system of floating, i.e., market-determined, exchange rates. When exchange rates float, there is no such thing as undervaluation or evaluation, in the sense of excess

market supply or demand for currencies. The value of the currency is whatever the market dictates that it should be.

It is nearly impossible to imagine the world economy going through the past 10 years in the straightjacket of fixed exchange rates. Given the events of this period, notably the large changes in oil prices and the divergent macroeconomic policies among the industrialized countries, floating exchange rates have performed well.[5]

In spring 1985, under the James Baker–Richard Darman team in the Treasury, the stance of U.S. policy turned sharply from a passive–laissez-faire approach to an active-interventionist one. The reasons for the change are not hard to find; they are the understandable concern about the strong dollar, the huge trade and current-account deficits that in a few years have made the United States the world's largest debtor and, above all, the fear of a protectionist explosion. That this fear is not groundless has been demonstrated by the Democratic omnibus trade bill that was passed by the House of Representatives with a large bipartisan majority.[6]

The first big success of the new policy was the agreement of the Group of Five at the surprise meeting in the Plaza Hotel, New York City, September 22, 1985. The five members agreed that "some further orderly appreciation of the main non-dollar currencies against the dollar is desirable,"—in other words, that the dollar should be pushed down by internationally concerted interventions in the foreign exchange markets. The decision of the Group of Five was endorsed by the Economic Summit in Tokyo in May 1986.

In his State of the Union Message in February 1986 President Reagan went a step further. He said:

> The constant expansion of our economy and exports requires a sound and stable dollar at home and reliable exchange rates around the world. We must never again permit wild currency swings to cripple our farmers and other exporters. . . . We've begun coordinating economic and monetary policy among our major trading partners. But there's more to do, and tonight I am directing Treasury Secretary Jim Baker to determine if the nations of the world should convene to discuss the role and relationship of our currencies.

This seems to say that it may be possible to organize a Bretton Woods type international conference to negotiate a return to some sort of fixed exchanges. A brief reflection leads to the conclusion that this is practically out of the question. It is, therefore, not surprising that Secretary Baker changed his mind after talking things over with his European colleagues. On December 11, 1986, he said there was no need at that time for the United States to call an international monetary conference to consider changing the present floating exchange rate system.

How Floating Was Forced on Reluctant Policy Makers

Since the memories of most policy makers are so short, it is well to recall once again, very briefly, how floating was forced on most reluctant policy makers.

During the first fifteen to seventeen years after World War II the value of the dollar was unquestioned, the dollar was convertible into gold, and the Bretton Woods system of stable but adjustable exchange rates had practically become a dollar standard: "The dollar is better than gold" was the slogan. True, in 1958 and 1959 the U.S. balance of payments developed deficits of $3.4 and $3.9 billion, which was then regarded as alarming.[7] The Eisenhower administration promptly took anti-inflationary measures, which caused a mild recession in April 1960–February 1961, the balance of payments improved, and prices remained stable until 1965.

Thereafter the picture changed when President Johnson, ignoring the advice of his economic advisers, financed the escalating cost of the war in Vietnam and of the equally expensive domestic Great Society programs with inflationary bank credit rather than with higher taxes. True, the rising inflation (less than 10 percent) was not very high compared with what came ten years later. But the international situation had changed. There had been a fairly drastic realignment of currencies: in 1949 the British pound and numerous other currencies in the sterling area were devalued, and in 1958 the French franc was sharply devalued. Even more important, the war-ravaged countries in Europe and Asia had recovered. Especially in Germany and Japan what Keynes called the "classical medicine" of sound money and sound public finance (which he said should be given a chance) had produced the German and Japanese economic "miracles." So the dollar lost its unique position; it was no longer as good as gold. The crucial fact was that the U.S. inflation rate was higher than the three strong-currency countries—Germany, Japan, and Switzerland—were ready to accept. The balance of payments weakened, and the gold reserve declined.

The policy response of successive administrations was to impose increasingly severe restrictions and controls. Duty-free allowances for returning U.S. tourists were reduced from $500 to $100, for example; American foreign aid that used to be granted "un-tied" was tied to purchases in the United States—a sort of "buy American" policy. Similarly, to reduce foreign exchange costs of military expenditures

71

abroad, shipments from the United States were substituted for foreign supplies, although this policy involved a sharp increase in real cost. These measures were described in the literature as a de facto depreciation of the "foreign aid dollar," "the tourist dollar," etc. Unsurprisingly, these measures and "voluntary" restraints on capital exports (direct investments as well as bank lending) were ineffective. In the fourth quarter of 1967 confidence in the dollar was shaken by the devaluation of the British pound and by a large balance-of-payments deficit.

So on January 1, 1968, President Johnson dramatically announced a sweeping seven-point "program of action" which, if it had been fully enacted, would have put the United States under full-fledged exchange control. To indicate the flavor of the official thinking at that time I mention a few of the points. Mandatory tight capital export controls, based on the Trading with the Enemy Act of 1917, were put into effect by executive order. (It came as a surprise to most Americans that they had been living under a state of "national emergency" ever since President Truman had proclaimed it during the Korean War December 19, 1950.) Border taxes on all imports and similar refunds (subsidies) for exports were imposed to offset U.S. indirect taxes. A "tourist tax," graduated according to the amount spent per day, was proposed to be levied on American tourists traveling outside the Western Hemisphere. This tax was supposed to reduce the "tourist deficit" in the balance of payments by $500 million. Fortunately, this proposal was rejected by Congress.

Late in 1969 and 1970 the pressure on the dollar was alleviated a little by the 9.3 percent "upvaluation" of the German mark in September–October 1969 and by the U.S. recession of December 1969–November 1970, which brought down the rate of inflation from 5.7 percent in 1969 to 3.1 percent in 1972. Despite all that, to hold the line foreign central banks, especially the German Bundesbank, were forced to intervene massively in foreign exchange markets by buying many billions of dollars until February 1973 when floating started.

On August 15, 1971, President Nixon declared the dollar inconvertible into gold for foreign central banks, imposed a surcharge of 10 percent on all imports, and introduced wage and price controls in the United States to force a realignment of exchange rates. This was accomplished at the Smithsonian Conference in December 1971. The devaluation of the dollar was about 8 percent against most major currencies.

President Nixon called the Smithsonian Agreement "the most significant monetary agreement in the history of the world." Unfortunately, it did not last very long. In June 1972 the British pound was set afloat, taking with it many currencies in the sterling area. The pressure on the dollar rose again sharply. Investors (speculators) all over the world had learned their lesson: under fixed but adjustable exchange rates a currency under pressure can only go down, not up, and the chances are that it will be devalued sharply because the authorities want to be sure that they will not have to repeat the painful operation in the near future. This situation is ideal for the speculator: if he has guessed right, he makes a large profit; if he has guessed wrong, he loses only the cost of the transaction. Under floating, speculation obviously is a much more risky business.

To make a long story short, the pressure on the dollar continued, and foreign central banks had to buy billions of dollars to hold the line. The end came early in 1973. On January 23, 1973, the Swiss National Bank stopped buying dollars and let the franc float up. So a flood of dollars swept into Germany. In four days (February 5–9, 1973) the Bundesbank bought $5 billion to hold the line. That was the last gasp of the system of "stable but adjustable" exchange rates under Bretton Woods.

The Floating Dollar in the 1970s

Since 1973 the international monetary system, or nonsystem, as some critics call it, has been one of widespread floating; all major currencies and many others float. There are, of course, areas of stable exchange rates; according to IMF statistics some thirty-four countries peg their currencies to the dollar, others to the D-mark, the yen, and the French franc; and the European monetary system (EMS) maintains a precarious stability among the members of the European Community (EC), minus Britain. But "two thirds to four fifths of world trade is conducted at floating rates."[8]

Central banks were slow to get used to floating rates. While the Bretton Woods system was disintegrating, a prestigious IMF committee, the Committee of Twenty, was working on monetary reform. Right to the end it stuck to the position that "the reformed system should be based on stable but adjustable par values."[9]

But in January 1974, on the occasion of the first oil shock, J.H. Witteveen, then managing director of the IMF, said in a major policy speech: "In the present situation, a large measure of floating is unavoidable and indeed desirable."[10] Otmar Emminger added, "I think this is still valid today, after the second oil shock." It is safe to say that no system other than widespread floating could have coped with the turbulent period of the 1970s and early 1980s. The oil shocks certainly were highly disturbing, but their importance has been greatly exaggerated. The fact is that the two oil shocks were preceded and accompanied by highly inflationary cyclical booms, which, in turn, were superimposed on an inflationary groundswell that had started in the middle 1960s.[11]

The dollar was weak through the 1970s because inflation was high. In June 1974 the annual rate of inflation in the United States reached 12 percent, the highest ever in peacetime. Inflation was world-wide; even Switzerland had an inflation rate of 10 percent. Although anti-inflationary measures and the severe recession of November 1973–March 1975 brought U.S. inflation down to about 5 percent in 1976, inflation reaccelerated when the Carter administration switched from fighting inflation to expansion, reaching a peak of close to 20 percent in 1980. The strong-currency countries, Germany, Japan, and Switzerland, however, continued the fight against inflation. Switzerland applied monetary shock treatment, bringing the rate of inflation down abruptly to zero, and accepting a short but severe recession (a GNP drop of 7 percent) as the cost of price stability.[12] The German reaction was essentially the same, though a little less drastic than the Swiss.

No wonder that the dollar was weak all those years. In the fall of 1978 a "dollar rescue operation" was organized, with the United States, in effect, borrowing about $30 billion in foreign currencies to hold the line. The pressure on the dollar eased, but there was no lasting improvement because there was no sustained tightening of monetary policy. In 1979 the situation deteriorated rapidly, inducing President Carter to appoint Paul Volcker chairman of the Federal Reserve System. At the annual meeting of the IMF in Belgrade Volcker was told by foreign central bankers that they would stop supporting the dollar unless the United States took credible measures to curb inflation. Volcker stepped on the monetary brake, a real turning point. But a price had to be paid for stability: the severe twin recessions of the early 1980s (January 1980–July 1980 and July 1981–November 1982).

In the 1970s every spell of weakness of the dollar gave rise to an outburst of criticism of floating. Floating and excessive volatility of exchange rates, it was said, were responsible for the high inflation. Actually, the opposite is true. Inflation forced floating on reluctant policy makers. High inflation is incompatible with fixed exchanges for the following reason: Under fixed exchanges all participating countries must have approximately the same rate of inflation. It is, however, impossible for sovereign countries to agree on an inflation rate of, say, 6, 7, or more percent. There will always be some who will find it excessive and let their currencies appreciate. The same is true of deflation.

There are many examples. In the 1970s Germany, Japan, Switzerland, and some other countries did not accept the rate of inflation that a fixed exchange rate with the dollar would have imposed on them. In other words, floating protected them from imported inflation. Similarly, in the 1930s floating (or at that time devaluation of currencies against gold and the dollar) enabled many countries to extricate themselves from the deflation that raged in the United States.

All this disproves another argument against floating. It has been said and is still said that floating has not provided countries the freedom, which advocates of floating had promised, to pursue the macroeconomic policy they want; in other words, floating rates do not protect countries from disturbances from abroad.[13]

Floating protects a country from purely monetary disturbances from abroad; no country can be forced to inflate its economy or to deflate it, as they have been forced under fixed exchanges. But floating does not protect against *real* disturbances from abroad. Real disturbances are not merely exogenous events, such as oil shocks or protectionist measures abroad, but also real changes caused by monetary forces. Deflation, for instance, causes unemployment, which in turn leads to a decline of the deflating country's *real* demand for the exports of its trade partners.

But contrary to what critics often say, floating has an anti-inflationary disciplinary effect. Central bankers know that if they yield to inflationary pressures they risk a run on the currency, with painful real effects. Unfortunately, floating does not provide full protection against inflation, for a strong inducement to resist inflationary pressure can be overwhelmed by an even stronger propensity to inflate. Examples are not hard to find.

The Strong Dollar: 1980 to February 1985

The dollar's spectacular ascent started late in 1980. It reached its high point in February 1985 and was followed by a rapid decline. The causes of the strong dollar are still being debated. The late Otmar Emminger, former president of the German Bundesbank, called the persistent strength of the dollar "the most over-explained—and maybe least understood—economic event of our time."[14] With the benefit of hindsight it is possible, I submit, to identify the most important factors and to explain certain baffling features that make the strong dollar almost a unique event.

The rise in interest rates and growing confidence that under the chairmanship of Paul Volcker the Federal Reserve would bring inflation down certainly was an important factor explaining the upturn of the dollar late in 1980, two years before the U.S. economy turned up from the recession. But it is difficult to avoid the conclusion that the dollar's rise also had something to do with the election of Ronald Reagan, that it was a vote of confidence of the market for the incoming conservative administration. This view is perfectly compatible with the widely accepted proposition that triple-digit budget deficits caused by the tax cuts of 1981 produced the strong dollar by driving up interest rates, which led to a huge net capital inflow. The strong dollar, in turn, stimulates imports and restrains exports; in other words, it creates a trade deficit. There is still another way in which the government deficit increased the trade deficit. The budget deficits resulting from tax cuts in 1981 and 1982 undoubtedly had a stimulating effect on the U.S. economy. The vigorous cyclical recovery of the U.S. economy, which started in November 1982 in conjunction with the sluggishness of Western Europe and the weak market for U.S. exports in debt-ridden Latin America, would have worsened the trade balance even if high interest rates had not attracted foreign capital and the dollar had not gone up. But there can be no doubt that the strong dollar was by far the most important cause of the trade deficit.

The U.S. economy from 1980 to 1985 has two baffling features. First, it is paradoxical that huge budget deficits—and trade deficits—should accompany strong currency. In innumerable cases, both in this country and elsewhere, in developed and developing countries, large budget deficits have been associated with inflation, flight of capital, and a more or less rapid decline of the currency in the foreign exchange market. Why was it different in the United States? The main reason surely is that the Federal Reserve managed to contain inflation in a period of vigorous cyclical expansion. Sound monetary policy and the credibility of the Fed's policy to hold the line against inflation were and are essential to maintain the confidence of foreign (and domestic) investors in the dollar. If the policy changed or the credibility of the Fed to stick to it eroded, the picture would change rapidly.

A second baffling feature of the period is that inflation declined. Business cycle upswings are usually associated with rising rates of inflation. Why was it different in the 1980s? The strong dollar certainly was important, because it reduced prices of imported goods and put a damper on export prices. Later, the collapse of the oil price was an anti-inflationary factor. Perhaps some credit should also be given to structural reforms and deregulation of industries, such as airlines and trucking.

These developments were influenced, as noted, by the strong performance of the U.S. economy in the 1980s, which contrasted with the sluggishness of Western Europe. The U.S. economy has created many millions of new jobs while employment in Europe has been stagnant. Unemployment is now much higher in most European countries than in the United States—9 percent in Germany, 13 percent in Britain, 15 percent in the Netherlands. All this has received much attention on both sides of the Atlantic.[15]

Analysis of the stagnation and high unemployment of the European economies has produced two alternative interpretations or explanations—a macroeconomic-Keynesian one and a microeconomic classical one. The Keynesian one attributes the high unemployment to a deficiency of aggregate demand and assumes that it is widespread. The obvious cure is increasing aggregate demand by monetary-fiscal expansion.[16] The Keynesian interpretation seems to underlie the administration's policy of asking the Europeans to stimulate growth by expansionary measures.[17]

The microeconomic-classical interpretation regards the high European unemployment as structural and spotty due to inflexibilities, rigidities, and immobilities, especially in the labor market; concretely, it is attributable to overregulation of industries, overgenerous welfare programs, high unemployment benefits, a vast "social safety net" protecting workers and firms from losses caused by changes in demand and supply. As a consequence, the strength of the labor unions in Europe is much greater than in the United States. The result is that in nationally and (despite the Common Market) internationally fragmented labor markets, wages are too high for full employment. The high cost of these policies has led to oppressively high taxes in general and to extremely high marginal tax rates in particular.

All this is compounded by the fact that the regulations and restrictions differ from country to country, which sharply limits the scope of the Common Market. The United States enjoys the immense advantage of a real free-trade area of continental size with free mobility of capital and entrepreneurship and considerable mobility of labor. Europe cannot match that despite the Common Market. The European handicap is all the more serious because transportation, communications, electric power, airlines, railroads, telephones, and telegraph are operated by government enterprises that often are inefficient, but in any case are impervious to competition. In the United States airlines compete with each other and with railroads, buses, and trucks throughout the country.

In the two papers cited earlier, Arthur Burns and Herbert Giersch describe the contrast between the United States and Europe in great detail, and Giersch shows that in Germany the situation has sharply deteriorated over the past fifteen or twenty years. This can be expressed by saying that in Europe the level of "natural" unemployment has sharply risen in the past fifteen to twenty years and is now much higher than in the United States.

Some counterfactual theorizing will be useful. Suppose that in 1980 the international monetary system had been one of fixed exchanges. Even more capital would have flowed into the United States than under floating because there would have been no exchange risk if the fixed rates were credible (gold standard), or if the exchange rates were "fixed but adjustable" (Bretton Woods): the investors would have known that the currency of a country that loses reserves is likely to be devalued and that the currency of a country that gains reserves is likely to be upvalued. Europe would have lost reserves and would have experienced intense deflationary pressure. The United States would have gained reserves and suffered inflation if it followed the rule of the game. The outcome surely would have been a breakdown of the system of fixed exchange rates, probably after fruitless attempts to stop the capital flow by more-or-less tight controls. Such a breakdown would have been a most disturbing event; the consequence would have been a sharp slowdown of the economy or a full-blown recession.

The outcome would have been the same if in 1980 a system of target zones had been in operation. The dollar would have hit the upper limit of the zone. Market participants would have known that the dollar could only go up, and speculators would have had a field day. The authorities would have no choice but to shift the zone and perhaps to widen it, demonstrating that this approach is no better than the parvalue (Bretton Woods) system.[18]

My conclusion is that we were lucky to enter the 1980s with floating exchange rates.

The sharp rise of the dollar is now often portrayed as a gigantic market failure. Some critics have gone so far as to say that the grossly overvalued dollar has cost the U.S. economy millions of jobs and has cut the growth rate in half. This is an enormous exaggeration. Some jobs have been lost in manufacturing, but over the whole period millions of jobs have been added.

Up to a point in 1984 when the market did overshoot, the package of a strong dollar, capital inflow, and trade deficits was an indispensable prop for U.S. prosperity. But contrary to what supply siders had promised, tax cuts did not generate sufficient savings to finance both government deficits and private investments. If the dollar had not gone up, say because investors lacked confidence in the dollar, interest rates would have gone much higher, and government borrowing would have crowded out private investment, which would have aborted the expansion.

To avoid being misunderstood, let me say that I did not then and do not now object to the tax cuts or to the budget deficits in the early 1980s. On the contrary, I think they were part of a very good policy designed to get the United States out of the severe recession. I would suggest only that there can be too much of a good thing.[19]

My overall conclusion is that the strong dollar was a good thing for the United States until some time in 1984. Furthermore, there can be no doubt that the U.S. trade deficit has been highly beneficial for the rest of the world, developed as well as less developed, for the U.S. economy was the locomotive that pulled the world economy out of the recession.

The Declining Dollar—March 1985 to . . .

We have seen that the sharp appreciation of the dollar after 1980 was a rational and highly beneficial response to the serious problem posed by the huge budget deficits. But with the benefit of hindsight a case can be made for the proposition that the appreciation of the dollar went too far in 1984; in other words, the market overshot in 1984.

The dollar reached its high point in February 1985. Then it declined rapidly. What caused the decline? There were, I believe, no powerful external shocks that would explain the turnaround of the dollar in February–March 1985. The shift in administration policy came later, and there was no sharp decline in the volume of capital inflow. It is true that there were large interventions by central banks, by the Federal Reserve, and by the central banks of other Group of Ten countries. Between January 21 and March 1, 1985, about $10 billion were sold against D-marks, yen, and some other currencies. This sum is not negligible, but it is difficult to believe that the interventions by themselves would have brought about the downturn of the dollar. This becomes clear if we apply the modern asset-theoretic approach, also called the "portfolio adjustment" approach, to the determination of exchange rates—a stock theory rather than a flow theory, which formerly was popular. The relevant stock is that of internationally traded financial assets denominated in U.S. dollars and other major currencies.

For details of the theory see the chapter in this volume by Jacob Dreyer. I confine myself to two remarks. First, in today's highly developed international capital markets—Eurodollar and Euroyen markets, which developed after most important currencies became convertible in the 1950s, with thousands of sophisticated market participants, banks, corporate treasurers, and speculators of different kinds—in this environment the asset-theoretic approach surely is the right one. Second, whatever the precise definition of the relevant types of assets, the size of the stock undoubtedly is enormous, amounting to trillions of dollars. Compared with this, $10 billion sold by central banks is insignificant, unless these sales are part of a clear and explicit shift in policy, as happened later on in 1985.

A pronounced shift in the general outlook for the U.S. economy seems to have caused the market to change. Up to February 1985 the general outlook was optimistic. Then in March a more pessimistic reassessment of the outlook took place. The economy seemed to be slowing down and interest rates began to decline.

Discounting the importance of the interventions for the explanation of the downturn of the dollar in early 1985 does not mean that interventions in the foreign exchange market never have much effect. If the authorities make it clear that the interventions are part of a basic shift in policy, the situation is different. That is precisely what happened later in 1985 when the Treasury team of James Baker and Richard Darman abandoned the passive, laissez-faire balance-of-payments or exchange rate policy of their predecessors and developed an increasingly activist, not to say aggressive, interventionist policy of talking the dollar down and later pushing it down by interventions in the foreign exchange market.

The major motive of the change in policy was the fear of a protectionist explosion. That this fear is not groundless was demonstrated by the Democratic trade bill passed in 1986 by a large bipartisan majority in the House—an unmitigated monstrosity that President Reagan accurately described as an antitrade bill.

The first result of the new balance-of-payments policy was, as we have seen, the September 1985 decision of the Group of Five to push the dollar down by internationally concerted interventions in the foreign exchange market. The decision was unexpected and caused considerable turbulence in the market. The announcement itself pushed the dollar down sharply, before any of the central banks intervened. Private demand for dollars has fluctuated greatly since then because the new activist policy has forced market participants to speculate not only about the prospects of the economy and possible changes in domestic monetary and fiscal policy, but also about the intentions of the authorities concerning interventions.

A vivid description of the interaction of these various forces and the resulting shifts in the foreign exchange market can be found in the periodic reports of the Federal Reserve Bank of New York on Treasury and Federal Reserve foreign exchange operations. Intervention sales of dollars by the Federal Reserve and foreign central banks amounted to over $10 billion during the first two or three months after the September meeting of the Group of Five. According to the latest reports there seem to have been hardly any interventions in the first quarter of 1986.

Parallel with its drive to reform the international monetary system through concerted interventions in the foreign exchange market, the administration has stepped up its push for international coordination of "economic and monetary policies." The purpose is to avoid or minimize the emergence of international imbalances such as the large U.S. trade deficits and the Japanese and German surpluses. The reduction of the discount rate by the Federal Reserve and the German and Japanese central banks in March and April 1986 has been hailed as the "first step to international coordination."

It was generally assumed that at the Tokyo Summit in May 1986 international monetary reform and concrete proposals for coordination of policy would be the main economic topics. If they were, the official Tokyo Economic Declaration does not reveal anything about it. The seven-page Declaration is long on generalities and short on specifics. The summiteers congratulate themselves on what has been achieved since the last economic summit but recognize that "they would still face a number of difficult challenges," that "noninflationary growth is the biggest" objective, and that it "must be reinforced by policies which encourage job creation. . . . It is important that there should be close and continuous coordination of policy among the seven Summit countries." The Group of Seven is the Group of Five plus Canada and Italy. The heads of state "welcome" the recent decision of the Group of Five "to change the pattern of exchange rates and to lower interest rates," but "agree that additional measures should be taken to ensure that procedures for effective coordination of international economic policy are strengthened further." What these additional measures might be is not stated, but "the Heads of State agree to form a new Group of Seven Finance Ministers" and the Group of Five is "requested" to include Canada and Italy in its meetings whenever "the international monetary system or related measures are discussed." The ministers of finance of the Group of Seven are requested "to review their economic objectives and forecasts at least once a year . . . to ensure their mutual compatibility . . . taking into account indicators such as GNP growth rates, inflation rates, interest rates," and several other generally used economic variables. The heads of state "reaffirm the undertaking at the 1982 Versailles Summit to cooperate with the International Monetary Fund in strengthening multilateral surveillance . . . and invite Finance Ministers and Central Banks to focus first and foremost on underlying policy fundamentals, while reaffirming the 1983 Williamsburg commitment to intervene in exchange markets when to do so would be helpful."

The heads of state warned against the dangers of "persistent protectionism" and made the usual pious pleas for "opening the international trading and investment system." Then they went home and did the opposite. The United States, for example, imposed a stiff import duty (35 percent) on Canadian cedar shingles. This step did, however, have a beneficial side effect: it gave the Canadian government an opportunity to teach our congressional protectionists a lesson by retaliating promptly and forcefully, slapping a stiff tariff on American computer parts, Christmas trees, tea bags, periodicals, and several other items.

Given that the IMF has for a long time been engaged in multilateral surveillance, that ministers of finance and central bankers frequently meet in the IMF, OECD, BIS (Bank for International Settlements), in the Group of Five, and Ten, and on other occasions—given all that, the creation of still another overlapping group can hardly be regarded as a great achievement.

In the light of recent developments, what are the prospects for reform of the international monetary system? As noted above, President Reagan in his State of the Union message in February 1986 asked Secretary Baker "to determine if the nations of the world should convene to discuss the role and relationship of our currencies. We must never again permit wild currency swings to cripple our farmers and other exporters."

This was widely interpreted to mean that it may be possible and desirable to hold another Bretton Woods type of international conference for the purpose of returning to some sort of fixed exchange rates. Such a proposal has been made by the French government.

The Bretton Woods conference was held in 1944 during the War. It was run by the United States and Britain. Today the power structure is entirely different. There is what may be called the Group of Three (the United States, Japan, and Western Germany); the Group of Five (the Group of Three plus Britain and France); the Group of Seven (the Group of Five plus Canada and Italy); and the Group of Ten (the Group of Seven plus Holland, Belgium, Sweden, and Switzerland). In addition, there are the less-developed countries organized in the Group of Twenty-four.

It is not surprising that Secretary Baker said he does not think that at this time "the United States needs to call an international monetary conference to consider changing the present floating exchange-rate system; instead an attempt should be made to 'refine' the international economic policy-coordinating machinery that they agreed upon at the Tokyo economic summit in May." He also said that the "finance ministers still hadn't agreed on what they might want in any new monetary system,"[20] to which I would add that they are unlikely to agree in the foreseeable future—for the following reason.

It is hardly necessary to explain at great length why a restoration of the gold standard is impossible. Who would want to entrust the future of the international monetary system to the mercies of South Africa and the Soviet Union, the two largest gold producers? Stable but adjustable exchange rates à la Bretton Woods is, as we have seen, very vulnerable to destabilizing speculation. The basic difficulty of any fixed-rate system is that it requires a high degree of mutual policy adjustment or international policy coordination, which in the present-day world can be achieved only in exceptional cases. The vaunted European monetary system (EMS) is no exception. It is a Bretton Woods–type system of stable but adjustable exchange rates, very vulnerable to disruptive capital flows. Frequent realignments of exchange rates are preceded and accompanied by destabilizing speculation, which requires tight exchange control in some participating countries—in France, for example.

Early this year, the EMS was shaken by a severe crisis, which underscores the conclusion that markets do a better job than governments in setting exchange rates. The row between two members of the EMS, France and West Germany, has provided a striking example of the dangers of politicizing exchange rates and of the unworkability of a Bretton Woods–type international monetary system.

It was not surprising that the French franc came under intense pressure after Prime Minister Jacques Chirac capitulated to student demonstrations, thereby effectively telling trade unions and other pressure groups that street demonstrations and violence pay. When the franc fell, Chirac attacked the German authorities. "This is a mark crisis," he said, "not a franc crisis. Let the German authorities do what is necessary."[21] What is regarded as necessary is a realignment of exchange rates and a little inflation in Germany. The realignment was achieved after hectic negotiations and a thirteen-hour emergency meeting of the ministers of finance on January 11, 1987. The value of the German mark and the Dutch guilder increased by 3 percent and that of the Belgian franc by 2 percent against the other members of the EMS. This can only be described as a token realignment, which will make hardly a dent in the underlying disequilibrium.

The other requirement, a little inflation in Germany, was called for in an editorial of the *Wall Street Journal*, "Waiting for Bonn:" "What

Germany needs is strong, domestic-led growth, which it's not going to get until it stops fixating on its inflation rate—near zero—and starts feeding some marks to its economy and advancing its tax cuts."[22] The German Socialist party, the left-wing opposition to Chancellor Helmut Kohl's conservative government, ought to be grateful for the support it gets from conservative governments and newspapers abroad.

All this caused confusion and much turbulence in the foreign exchange markets. The dollar depreciated sharply against the mark and the yen despite the Baker-Miyazawa agreement. Foreign central banks bought many billion dollars to hold the line. According to rumors and press reports (which gained credibility through belated and half-hearted official denials), the administration wanted the dollar to decline in order to bring pressure on Germany and Japan to stimulate their economies. It is true that sufficient inflation in the strong currency surplus countries, especially Germany and Japan, would let the deficit countries, the United States and France, off the hook. But it would be like infecting the healthy instead of curing the sick. Worldwide inflation is not a sound basis for the world economy.

It is instructive to reflect for a moment on why we never hear about balance-of-payments problems of different regions of large countries, say the United States, despite the occurrence from time to time of serious regional disturbances. The most important reason is that monetary policy is the same throughout the United States, ruling out the significant differential inflation that often occurs between sovereign states. Also very important are perfect mobility of capital and much higher interregional mobility of labor than can be found between sovereign states anywhere in the world, even in the European Common Market. Still another factor, which has been mentioned in the literature, is the common fiscal system. If a region in the United States is experiencing a serious disturbance, it automatically gets some relief from the reduction of its tax liabilities to the federal government and possibly some contribution from the government through unemployment benefits and the like.

I conclude from all this that floating should continue, and I am convinced that it will, for the following reason: a return to fixed exchange rates would require international agreement on the rates that should be fixed. It is not inconceivable, but it is practically impossible that a meaningful agreement on the pattern of exchange rates could be reached in the Group of Seven or even in the Group of Five. By "meaningful," I mean a set of exchange rates that the participants undertake to defend.

Consider the simplest but most important case: the exchange

value of the dollar relative to a few major currencies. There is no agreement among policy makers and experts on whether the dollar has declined sufficiently to eliminate or sharply reduce the current imbalances—U.S. deficits and German and Japanese surpluses. The Germans and Japanese think it has declined sufficiently. Federal Reserve chairman Volcker agrees. Other experts, inside and outside the administration, believe that it has to decline more. Moreover, we have seen that no agreement exists even on the question of how much the dollar has already declined overall.

Specific exchange rates should not be discussed in the glare of widely advertised meetings of the Groups of Five, Seven, Ten, the economic summits, or the annual meetings of the IMF and the World Bank. Exchange rates can be quietly discussed in the OECD, the IMF, the BIS, or in bilateral meetings.

A good example is the famous agreement between the United States and Japan, the Group of Two as it was dubbed in October 1986. After a secret meeting in San Francisco, Secretary of the Treasury Baker and the Japanese Minister of Finance Kiichi Miyazawa announced the terms of the agreement: The Bank of Japan reduced the discount rate from 3½ percent to 3 percent, and the Japanese government would submit to the Diet a "supplementary budget" providing 3.6 trillion yen (about $22 billion at the rate of 160 yen per dollar) additional expenditures spread over several years, and a proposal to reduce marginal tax rates for personal and corporate income to stimulate investment. These reforms are parts of the "Miyazawa Plan" that had been proposed in 1986. Mr. Baker stated that "for its part the United States remains fully committed" to reducing the budget deficit and to resisting protectionist pressures. Most important, the ministers agreed that "the dollar-yen rate is now broadly consistent with the underlying fundamentals." For the time being, therefore, the United States will not press Japan to let the yen go still higher. But the dollar-yen rate has not yet been fixed; the current relative stability cannot even be regarded as a big step toward a fixed rate. The agreement is that the rate *now* is consistent with the fundamentals. There is no indication that an agreement exists on precisely what the fundamentals are. Whatever they are, they are bound to change over time. To settle on a fixed rate, there would have to be an agreement on how to determine a change in the fundamentals and a commitment to defend the rate by interventions in the foreign exchange market. But the usual sterilized interventions that leave the money supply unchanged would not do. It would require stronger medicine: nonsterilized interventions. It is a long way to a fixed rate!

I repeat therefore: Floating should and will continue. For the

85

foreseeable future a return to fixed rates is impossible. If the United States and Japan cannot agree on a fixed rate, how can an agreement be reached in a wide circle? Free markets do a better job than governments in setting exchange rates. True, markets do make mistakes. But in competitive markets mistakes are quickly corrected. It is in the nature of the political process that governments are slow to admit a mistake and that they delay reversing themselves, which makes the correction when it finally must be made all the more painful.

International Policy Coordination

In the past two years international policy coordination has once again been all the rage, with the United States in the driver's seat. In practice the principal concrete manifestation of the new drive for policy coordination has been the increasingly urgent and impatient American demand that Germany and Japan stimulate their economies in order to reduce their trade surpluses and the U.S. trade deficits. More on that presently. First it will be well to review very briefly the historical roots of international policy coordination or cooperation—the two terms are often used interchangeably.

Barry Eichengreen recently reminded us that early in the interwar period—not to go further back—proposals were made to improve the working of the international monetary system by policy coordination.[23] One of the resolutions of the Genoa Conference (1922) says, for example: "Measures of currency reform will be facilitated if the practice of continuous cooperation among central banks . . . can be developed. Such cooperation of central banks . . . would provide opportunities of coordinating their policy, without hampering the freedom of the several banks."[24]

Later in the 1920s the Bank for International Settlements (BIS) was established in Basle, Switzerland. Its original purpose was to manage the transfer of German reparations to the victors in World War I. It survived the Great Depression of the 1930s and even the Second World War—a monument to the staying power of international bureaucracies. It developed into an international institution for consultation, cooperation, and coordination of monetary policy. Formally it is a European institution, the club of the major European central banks, but its monthly meetings are regularly attended by a governor of the Federal Reserve System and by a high official of the Bank of Japan.

After the end of World War II, European economic cooperation and coordination received a strong push from the Marshall Plan. A large international bureaucracy was set up in Paris. This, too, managed to enlarge and to perpetuate itself. After several metamorphoses it became the OECD (Organization of Economic Cooperation and Development), representing the industrial countries, including the United States, Canada, and Japan.

It would lead too far to discuss all the other international agencies that are directly or tangentially involved in policy coordination; they include the International Monetary Fund, the United Nations and its numerous offshoots, the European Economic Commission, the Economic Commission for Latin America (ECLA), the United Nations Conference on Trade and Development (UNCTAD), etc.

The drive for international coordination of policies again went into high gear with the Tokyo economic summit of May 1986. As mentioned, the heads of state instructed the ministers of finance of the Group of Seven to meet "at least once a year" to review "the mutual compatibility" of their policy objectives and forecasts, "taking into account indicators such as GNP growth rates, inflation rates, interest rates, unemployment rates, fiscal deficit ratios, current account and trade balances, monetary growth rates, reserves, and exchange rates."

The ball has been picked up by the Interim Committee of the IMF. The April 1986 Interim Committee communiqué refers to "the possible usefulness of indicators in implementing Fund surveillance" (paragraph 6). The committee asked the executive board to explore "the formulation of a set of objective indicators related to policy actions and economic performance, which might help to identify a need for discussion of countries' policies."[25]

On September 27, 1986, just before the annual meeting of the IMF and the World Bank, the ministers of finance of the Group of Seven met in Washington, D.C. "to conduct the first exercise of multilateral surveillance pursuant to the Tokyo Economic Summit Declaration of the heads of State of May 6, 1986."[26] The one-page statement is a bland document, evidently a compromise which, according to press reports, was reached after spirited and somewhat acrimonious discussions:

> The Ministers reviewed recent economic objectives and forecasts collectively, using a range of economic indicators, with a particular view to examining their mutual compatibility. The Ministers noted that progress had been made in promoting steady, noninflationary growth. The Ministers also noted, however, that the present scale of some current-account imbalances cannot be sustained. The exchange rate changes since last year are making an important contribution toward redressing these imbalances. The Ministers agreed that cooperative efforts need to be intensified in order to reduce the imbalances in the context of an open, growing

world economy. They noted, in this connection, that economic growth in surplus countries was improving, but that such growth will need to be sustained. Countries with major deficits must follow policies that will foster significant reductions in their external deficits; those countries committed themselves, among other things, to make further progress in reducing their budget deficits in order to free resources to the external sector. The Ministers agreed that the policies of all countries would be formulated with the following objectives in mind: To follow sound monetary policies supporting non-inflationary growth; to continue the process of removing structural rigidities in order to increase the long-term production potential of their economies; and to continue efforts to resist protectionist pressures.

The vagueness of this statement underscores what was said above—that so far the only concrete attempt at international policy coordination has been the insistent U.S. pressure on Germany and Japan to stimulate their economies.

The current drive for international policy coordination, including U.S. pressure on Germany and Japan, is a replay of what happened in the late 1970s. The surrounding circumstances were somewhat different, but then as now the United States had what were considered enormous and intolerable trade deficits—$31 billion in 1977, $34 billion in 1978—and the policy response was the same: The surplus countries, mainly Germany and Japan, were urged by the United States to stimulate their economies. This was called the "locomotive theory," which was later expanded to the "convoy theory," a proposal for coordinated fiscal-monetary expansion in a large number of countries.[27] In an extreme form this approach was put forward by H. J. Witteveen.[28] This scenario called for real growth in the United States to average 4 percent a year from 1978 to 1980, compared with 4.5 percent in 1978; 7.5 percent real growth a year in Japan from 1978 to 1980, compared with 5.7 percent in 1978; and 4.5 percent in Germany from 1978 to 1980, compared with 3.1 percent in 1978. The consequence of these changes in the relative growth rates of the three countries, and of other changes of similar magnitude for other industrial countries, would have been to reduce the U.S. trade deficit by $1.8 billion, the Japanese surplus by $5.7 billion, and the German surplus by $4.8 billion. Herbert Stein very aptly called this approach "international fine tuning." It is not surprising that it was not implemented. I will, therefore, confine myself to a dicscussion of the special case—U.S. pressure on Germany and Japan to stimulate their economies.

In one important respect the economic situation in the late 1970s was very different from what it is in the 1980s. It will be recalled that an inflationary boom escalated consumer price increases from about 5 percent per year in 1976 to almost 20 percent in 1980, because the Carter administration immediately embarked on an expansionary policy. No wonder that the dollar was weak despite large interventions in the foreign exchange market. Under these circumstances if Germany and Japan had acceded to American demands for stimulation of their economies by monetary fiscal expansion, the result would have been more rapid worldwide inflation followed by a more severe worldwide recession.

In the 1980s the U.S. economy took a different course. After the stabilization crisis of 1981–1982 the economy took off on a vigorous expansion, which passed its fourth anniversary in November 1986. Unlike earlier cyclical expansions, the current one has been marked by declining rather than rising rates of inflation. But the huge trade deficits still dominate the scene, and the United States continues to press Germany and Japan to stimulate their economies. Addressing the annual meeting of the IMF and the World Bank on September 30, 1986, in Washington, President Reagan said faster growth "is the key" to the major problems of the world economy. The United States has done its part. U.S. economic recovery has pulled the world out of the recession; now "other industrial nations must also contribute their share for world recovery and adopt more growth oriented policies." Secretary Baker still insists that there are only two solutions to the global trade imbalance. Either the other industrial countries must grow faster or the dollar has to decline further to make U.S. industries competitive. Since the famous U.S.-Japanese agreement in the Baker-Miyazawa accord of October 31, 1986, U.S. criticism is now addressed mainly to Germany. The official criticism has been echoed in sharper forms in the media. Anthony M. Solomon, former president of the New York Federal Reserve Bank, wrote in early 1986,

> Now that exchange rates are on a more reasonable course and oil prices are declining, there is every likelihood the inflation rate in Germany will be negative in 1986. Clearly, that ought to offer immense opportunity for German authorities to provide stimulus to lower the current-account surplus, to lower unemployment and to contribute to a better balance in the world economy without threatening any outbreak of inflation. Instead, from German officials we get stonewalling because the economic thinking that pervades is every bit as ideological, every bit as divorced from the realities of the time, as we have seen on occasions in the United

89

States in the past five years. That ideology is constructing a seemingly impenetrable intellectual roadblock to the execution of necessary policy changes.[29]

All this is hardly convincing. The conservative German government of Helmut Kohl would like nothing better than to approach the 1987 election with rising output and employment—all the more so since they are criticized by the left-wing opposition and the labor unions with the same largely Keynesian arguments that the conservative U.S. administration uses. They are afraid, however, of giving the impression that they have caved in to American pressures.

The American policy suffers from two weaknesses: first, reproaching Germany and Japan for their large export surpluses ignores the fact that the U.S. external deficits represent an inflow of foreign capital, which the U.S. economy still needs because domestic savings are insufficient to finance both private investments and huge budget deficits. Second, several econometric studies have concluded that the effects of even a substantial increase in the rate of growth in Germany and Japan on the U.S. external deficit would be minimal. The *IMF World Economic Outlook* concludes:

> Unfortunately, the effects on the U.S. current account of shifts in growth rates abroad appear to be relatively small. It is unlikely that a 1 percentage point increase in domestic growth in Japan and the Federal Republic of Germany (maintained over a three-year period and with allowance for induced effects on growth in other countries) would alter the U.S. trade balance by more than $5–10 billion.[30]

Note that the study makes allowance for indirect effects and that a rise of real growth by one percentage point, say from 3½ to 4½ percent, over three years is quite substantial.

This does not deny that faster noninflationary growth would be desirable or that in the short run pressure on the United States would be alleviated if the Germans and Japanese embarked on a highly inflationary expansion. What it does mean is that in order to bring down the external deficit the U.S. budget deficit must be reduced. This is an American responsibility, which cannot be shifted to other countries.

Now let us assume that the dollar has declined far enough to shrink the external deficit sharply; or assume that expansion abroad has reduced the U.S. deficit, which implies that capital inflow from abroad has stopped. Interest rates will rise and, if the budget deficit has not been sharply reduced and domestic savings have not increased, public sector borrowing will crowd out private sector investment. This underscores the decisive importance of the budget deficits. The September 1986 statement of the Group of Seven put it succinctly: "Countries with major deficits committed themselves to make further progress in reducing their budget deficits, *in order to free resources to the external sector.*" Of course, how to reduce the budget deficit sufficiently fast without causing a recession is a difficult problem.

There is another aspect of the dollar problem that also underscores the importance of speedy action on the budget deficit. The U.S. economy is in its fifth year of expansion—one of the longest in the history of business cycles. Naturally, it shows signs of slowing down. The Federal Reserve has been under increasing pressure to reduce interest rates to prevent a slide into a recession. The Fed has insisted that it cannot go much further unless Germany and Japan go along, because there is danger that when the interest differential between the United States on the one hand, and Germany and Japan on the other, shrinks, capital inflow will stop or a net outflow will develop, causing a sharp decline of the dollar.

I think that the possibility of such a development canot be excluded. But I still believe that an irrational stampede of investors at home and abroad out of dollars, as some experts have been predicting for the past three years, is unlikely, because the market understands that in such a case central banks, the Fed, and foreign central banks would intervene, organizing a dollar rescue operation as they did in 1978. It surely would be better, however, not to let it come to that, but to attack the evil at its root by reducing the budget deficit. For two reasons, the United States cannot go on forever importing capital from abroad: first, sooner or later investors at home and abroad will become nervous if they see no change in policy, and a run on the dollar may develop; second, the service charge on the foreign debt rises rapidly. The economy will have to do without new capital from abroad and will have to develop an export surplus to service the foreign debt, implying a sizable squeeze on what is called "domestic absorption"—that is, on consumption and investment. In other words, the standard of living will be reduced below what it otherwise would be. If the trade deficit and the associated inflow of foreign capital continue for, say, two or three more years, it has been estimated that the service charge on the foreign debt may near 1 percent of GNP. This surely would not be a crushing burden, but in a sluggish economy could well trigger a recession.

Some Policy Conclusions

No modern government is indifferent to unemployment—all of them want full employment and rapid growth. Germany and Japan are no exception. But it is also true that tolerance and fear of inflation vary somewhat from country to country. Germany, for example, with its history of destructive inflation, hyperinflation after World War I, and equally damaging repressed inflation after World War II, is more fearful of inflation than the United States is.

If this is granted, it follows, I believe, that all countries should be allowed to pursue their policies as well as they can, provided they observe the rules of the game as laid down by the IMF and the GATT. Currencies should be freely convertible at fixed or flexible exchange rates; there should be no manipulation of exchange rates, no import restrictions on balance-of-payments grounds, and the like. Let the Europeans struggle with their structural unemployment; if the Germans, the Dutch, or the Belgians think that they need two-digit unemployment to keep inflation at bay, it is their problem, not ours.

This does not mean, however, that countries should never criticize each other or should refrain from giving advice. Far from it. All governments make mistakes, all can learn from the failures and successes of others, and they should welcome friendly criticism and advice. But this is best done quietly in organizations such as the OECD, the IMF, and the BIS, or in bilateral negotiations. The superiority of quiet diplomacy has been strikingly demonstrated by the famous U.S.-Japanese agreement reached by Secretary Baker and Japanese Minister of Finance Miyazawa.

This approach is surely much better than criticizing each other publicly. Threatening other countries with a further decline of the dollar—"using the dollar as a weapon," as it was put in the press—may serve domestic political objectives but is internationally counterproductive, because no country likes doing things under pressure from abroad. The politicization of exchange rates is a dangerous game. It has caused much turbulence in the foreign exchange markets. Free markets do a better job of setting exchange rates than governments do.

Notes

An abbreviated version of the first part of this chapter appeared in *The AEI Economist*, "The International Monetary System," American Enterprise Institute, Washington, D.C. July 1986.

1. *Economic Review*, Federal Reserve Bank of Dallas, September 1986.
2. *Economic Report*, Manufacturers Hanover Trust, September 1986.
3. *Economic Review*, Federal Reserve Bank of Atlanta, June/July 1986.
4. The phrase "benign neglect" was first used by Gottfried Haberler and Thomas Willett, *A Strategy for U.S. Balance of Payments Policy* (Washington, D.C.:

American Enterprise Institute, 1971), p. 15. Although the meaning was carefully explained, it was often misunderstood as neglecting or excusing the cause of the balance-of-payments troubles, namely high inflation. On that issue, see Gottfried Haberler, *U.S. Balance of Payments Policy and the International Monetary System*, AEI Reprint No. 9, American Enterprise Institute, Washington, D.C. 1973.

5. Economic Report of the President (Washington, D.C., 1984), p. 50. It is interesting that the Report for neither 1985 nor 1986 has any discussion of the exchange rate problem.

6. The product of protectionist pressure in the 99th Congress was the omnibus trade bill, H.R. 4800. Briefly summarizing its 450 pages is difficult, but the following examples indicate the flavor. Any country with a bilateral nonpetroleum trade surplus of more than $3 billion would have to cut trade by 10 percent each year. Additional industry-specific sanctions deal with a host of products including, among others, knitting needles, bicycle speedometers, steel, coal, agriculture, plums, and services. The current discretion of the executive branch in dealing with unfair trading cases referred by the International Trade Commission would also be removed. Overall, H.R. 4800 would strike a devastating blow to world trade and economic liberalism.

Another protectionist effort was the Textile and Apparel Trade Enforcement Act (1985), which includes copper, shoes, artificial fibers, dolls and, for good measure, fishing tackles to attract votes in Congress. It passed both houses of Congress with a large bipartisan majority, but the House of Representatives failed by a few votes to override the presidential veto. The act would have cut back textile imports from most countries to 1 percent of the growth of the U.S. market.

7. Measured on the so-called liquidity basis, which was then widely used. For details, see Gottfried Haberler and Thomas D. Willett, *U.S. Balance-of-Payments Policies and International Monetary Reform: A Critical Analysis* (Washington, D.C.: American Enterprise Institute, 1968), and Gottfried Haberler and Thomas D. Willett, *A Strategy for U.S. Balance of Payments Policy,* (Washington, D.C.: American Enterprise Institute, 1971).

8. See Morris Goldstein, "The Exchange Rate System: Lessons of the Past and Options for the Future," Occasional Paper 30, International Monetary Fund, Washington, D.C., July 1984, pp. 3–4.

9. *International Monetary Reform: Documents of the Committee of Twenty*, International Monetary Fund, Washington, D.C., 1974, p. 8.

10. Quoted by Otmar Emminger, then president of the German Bundesbank. See *The International Monetary System under Stress. What Can We Learn from the Past?*, AEI Reprint No. 112, Washington, D.C., May 1980, also appears in the conference volume *The International Monetary System: A Time of Turbulence*, in Jacob Dreyer, Gottfried Haberler, and Thomas Willett, eds. (Washington, D.C.: American Enterprise Institute, 1982).

11. See my paper, "Oil, Inflation, Recession and the International Monetary System," *Journal of Energy and Development* 1, no. 2 (Spring 1976), pp. 177–90, reprinted in *Selected Essays of Gottfried Haberler*, Anthony Y.C. Koo, ed. (Cambridge, Mass.: MIT Press, 1985).

12. In Switzerland the pains of disinflation were alleviated by the buffer of "guest workers" from abroad. But this is only a part of the explanation.

13. All these arguments against floating have been used by the socialist government of France of President Francois Mitterrand, which has proposed a Bretton Woods type of conference to return to some sort of fixed exchanges. It is not clear yet whether the conservative government of Jacques Chirac has changed the French position.

14. See his widely quoted paper *The Dollar's Borrowed Strength*, Group of Thirty, Occasional Papers, No. 19, 1985, p. 3.

15. See, for example, Erich Grundlach and Klaus-Dieter Schmidt, "Das amerikanische Beschäftigungswunder: Was sich daraus lernen lässt" ("The American Employment Miracle: What Can We Learn from It?") Kiel Discussion Paper No. 109, Institut für Weltwirtschaft an der Universität Kiel, West Germany, July 1985; Stephen Marris, "Why Europe's Recovery is Lagging?" in *Europe Magazine of the European Community*, March–April 1984; Herbert Giersch, "Eurosclerosis," Kiel Institute of World Economics, Discussion Paper No. 112, University of Kiel, West Germany, October 1985; and Arthur Burns, "The Economic Sluggishness of Western Europe" in *The United States and Germany: A Vital Partnership* (New York: Council on Foreign Relations, 1986).

16. Some analysts would say that what is needed is a change in the monetary-fiscal mix. In my opinion this has been greatly overdone. At any rate it complicates matters greatly and makes the problem unsuitable for international coordination. Concretely, it is one thing to tell the Europeans to stimulate growth by monetary-fiscal expansion and an entirely different thing to tell them to change their monetary-fiscal mix. This would immediately lead to the further question of whether the fiscal stimulus should be brought about by lowering taxes or by increasing expenditures.

17. It is true that some officials (not to mention supply siders outside the government) sometimes urge Europeans to follow the U.S. example—to reduce taxes, deregulate industry, etc. This is good advice, but it does not lend itself to being laid down in international agreements.

18. As far as I know, "reference rates" and "reference zones" were first proposed by Wilfred Ethier and Arthur L. Bloomfield in their pamphlet, *Managing the Managed Float*, Essays in International Finance No. 112, Princeton, N.J.: 1975. The authors claim that the reference zone system is superior to the parvalue system. In my paper, "The International Monetary System after Jamaica and Manila," in William Fellner, ed., *Contemporary Economic Problems* (Washington, D.C.: American Enterprise Institute, 1977), pp. 262–264, I gave reasons why I cannot accept that claim. The theory of target zones has been further developed by John Williamson in several important papers. See especially John Williamson, "The Exchange Rate System," *Policy Analyses in International Economics* No. 5 (Washington, D.C.: 1983), Institute for International Economics, and "Exchange Rate Flexibility, Target Zones, and Policy Coordination," *World Development*, October 1986. The latest refinement is that the zones should have "soft buffers," that is to say, that the authorities are not obligated to intervene when the exchange rate leaves the zone. That brings the target zone approach close to free floating.

19. This problem cannot be further pursued in this paper. Nor is this the place to go into the question whether the recession was entirely the fault of monetary mismanagement by the Fed, as extreme monetarists and extreme supply siders assert—strange bedfellows like two scorpions in a bottle who kill each other, leaving the intended victim unscathed!

20. *The Wall Street Journal*, December 12, 1986.

21. The *Financial Times*, London, January 7, 1987. The recent row between France and Germany is reminiscent of what happened in 1968 and 1969. Then, as now, France was shaken by violent student demonstrations and strikes, the French franc was weak, and the German mark strong. President de Gaulle's minister of finance declared, "This is not, properly speaking, a French crisis. It is an international crisis," and President de Gaulle said devaluation "would be the

worst form of absurdity." The Germans were equally adamant. "An official spokesman told a news conference that the decision not to upvalue the mark was 'final, unequivocal and for eternity.' " The impasse dragged on until after de Gaulle's resignation on April 28, 1969; his successor then devalued the franc by 11.1 percent on August 8, 1969. For further details see Robert Solomon, *The International Monetary System 1945–1981* (Harper & Row, New York, 1982).

22. The *Wall Street Journal*, January 7, 1987. The editorial argues that in the past year or two Germany has had negative inflation, which permits noninflationary expansion. This argument is, however, unconvincing for two reasons: First, although it is true that the price index has slightly declined, that was due to the collapse of the oil price and a price decline of some other commodities. This anti-inflationary factor has spent its force. Second, and even more important, a monetary expansion that merely restores price stability would have an insignificant effect on the global trade imbalance. Econometric studies have shown that even a sharp increase of real GNP growth in Germany and Japan would have only a minor effect on the U.S. trade deficit. The conclusion is that expansion in Germany would have to be highly inflationary to take the heat off the dollar.

23. See Barry Eichengreen, "International Policy Coordination in Historic Perspective: A View from the Interwar Years," in Willem H. Buiter and Richard C. Marston, eds., *International Economic Policy Coordination* (Cambridge, England: Cambridge University Press, for the National Bureau of Economic Research, 1985), pp. 139–83.

24. From Resolution 3 of the Report of the Financial Commission of the Genoa Conference, 1922.

25. The proposed use of "indicators" has been hailed as a new approach and a major advance of policy making in general and of international coordination of policies in particular. In my opinion there is nothing new in this "approach"; not even the term "indicators" is new. In 1973 a report for the Committee of Twenty on Reform of the International Monetary System and Related Issues by "The Technical Group on Indicators" (under the chairmanship of Robert Solomon) discussed the use of indicators in the adjustment process (see *International Monetary Reform*, IMF, Washington, D.C., 1974), pp. 51–76. Any discussion of the state, performance, and prospects of a particular economy cannot help using economic variables

26. Quotations from the official statement of the meeting.

27. This episode was discussed in my chapter, "Reflections on the U.S. Trade Deficit and the Floating Dollar," in William Fellner, Project Director, *Contemporary Economic Problems, 1978* (American Enterprise Institute, Washington, D.C., 1978). See especially pp. 227–30 and the Postcript, pp. 240–43. See also Herbert Stein's trenchant analysis of the whole approach in "International Coordination of Domestic Economic Policies," *The AEI Economist*, June 1978, American Enterprise Institute, Washington, D.C.

28. H.J. Witteveen, "Scenario for Coordinated Growth and Payments Adjustment," presented at the IMF meeting in Mexico, May 24, 1978.

29. Anthony M. Solomon, "Germany Puts Savings Over Jobs," *Wall Street Journal*, March 24, 1986.

30. *IMF World Economic Outlook* (Washington, D.C.: International Monetary Fund, October 1986), p. 24. Several other econometric studies, too, have reached the conclusion that faster growth in Germany and Japan has little effect on the U.S. current account. See, for example, unpublished studies by the staff of the Federal Reserve Board. See also Filles Oudiz and Jeffrey Sachs, "Macroeconomic Policy Coordination among the Industrial Economies," *Brookings Papers on Economic Activ-*

ity 1, William C. Brainard and George L. Perry, eds., The Brookings Institution, Washington, D.C., 1984; and Jeffrey A. Frankel, "The Sources of Disagreement among the International Macro Models and Implications for Policy Coordination," Working Paper No. 1925, National Bureau of Economic Research, Cambridge, Massachusetts, May 1986.

3

Changes in Industrial Structure and Foreign Competition— The Policy Arguments

Kenneth M. Brown

Summary

Huge trade deficits in recent years have been viewed as a major problem for U.S. industry, and many policy proposals have been advanced to deal with the situation. But how serious is the trade deficit, and what are its causes? Because our current trade policies are extremely costly to the economy, before we enlarge their scope we must be clear on causes and effects.

This nation's increased dependence on international trade is a long-term trend. From 1950 to 1979, imports rose from 4.5 percent of GNP to 11.1 percent; in 1985 that figure reached 13.1 percent. Exports kept pace until the past several years, when the trade deficit reached unprecedented heights. Although it is natural to assume that the trade deficit has hurt manufacturing (which is more export-intensive than services), the data clearly show that manufacturing output as a percentage of gross national product has been stable for many years. Most new jobs are in the service sector, not in manufacturing, but in terms of output the economy is not "deindustrializing."

The trade deficit has its roots in the federal budget deficit, since foreigners must export to the United States to acquire the dollars needed to support the net inflow of capital to finance this debt. It does not follow that U.S. manufacturing would have been better off had we balanced the budget. On the contrary, some of the budget-balancing policies advocated—such as tax increases—might have been quite harmful to manufacturing output.

Whatever the nature of the trade "problem," there is no shortage of proposed solutions, many of which may be characterized as protectionist. It has long been recognized that trade barriers owe much to our political system, which favors policies that confer large benefits on few people and impose small costs on many. In addition, a system has evolved that requires a large bureaucracy to guide the ever more complex negotiations over more and more

97

commodities. Examples abound of special protection for particular goods and special arrangements with particular countries. Public choice theory explains why the bureaucracy prefers such labor-intensive policies over multilateral agreements (such as GATT) that would move us to simpler, freer, and less costly trade policies.

Some of the current policies are tied to fears that the United States is becoming less competitive, in the sense that our products are falling behind in quality, innovation, and efficiency of production. (Recent speeches by members of the Cabinet have scolded U.S. business for such shortcomings.) Can trade policies be devised to spur business into making needed changes? Should temporary trade barriers be offered in return for promises to innovate? In a word, no. Such policies would certainly increase the already huge costs of protection and would incur added costs were the government to try its (inept) hand at decisions best left to the free market.

Other policies have been advanced for the purpose of reducing special protection—the ad hoc barriers erected to help certain industries, bearing no relation to any coherent trade policy. This is an important objective, as special protection is estimated to cost consumers more than $50 billion a year. Unfortunately, strengthening existing trade-relief institutions, such as the International Trade Commission, would probably serve only to increase protection obtained through such channels without reducing special protection. Still other proposals offer additional ideas for fine tuning trade policy, but most of them would do little to reduce the costs of trade barriers, for they underestimate the ability of protectionist interests to adapt to new rules of the game.

Two principles should govern our trade policies. First, we should revive GATT procedures for reducing trade barriers all around. Second, we should recognize that our trade policy does not need new gimmicks for micromanaging trade barriers. Rather, we need institutional restraints on the ability of the government to interfere in international markets.

Introduction

The mammoth trade deficit of the past several years has been viewed as a major problem for U.S. industry. Foreign competition, it has been argued, has led to "deindustrialization" of the U.S. economy and hence deserves a major policy response to deal with the alleged cause (foreign competition) and the effect (depressed conditions in manufacturing). Such policy responses can have a major effect on the economy. Trade barriers are among the most costly regulations now extant; modifications of our trade policy now debated could be more costly still, even though many of these proposals call for actions more subtle than tariffs and quotas.

This chapter deals with both the alleged problems and a variety of proposed solutions. Its purpose is to examine changes in the structure of U.S. industry, particularly as they are related to international trade, and to analyze the trade policies adopted and currently preferred. The chapter concentrates on the more direct forms of trade regulation (quotas, tariffs, etc.) rather than on international monetary policy.

Deindustrialization or Schumpeterian Change?

The United States is becoming more dependent on world trade. This is a long-term trend, not a sudden quirk of the 1980s. From 1950 to 1979, imports rose from 4.5 percent of gross national product to 11.1 percent (1982 dollars, NIPA basis). In 1985 imports equaled 13.1 percent of GNP. This trend is indicative of an increasing global interdependence, as almost every country is engaging in trade more intensively. Exports followed about the same growth path as imports for many years but reached only 10.1 percent of GNP in 1985, as the trade deficit soared.

Allegations of Deindustrialization. In economic policy, it can be disastrous for the government to buck a long-term trend in the belief that it is a mere aberration. In current trade policy, the question is whether the recent divergence of exports from imports is temporary and self-correcting or whether it is so entrenched that it deserves a concerted policy response. A related question concerns the state of our manufacturing sector. Is trade deindustrializing America? Are we becoming a nation of service industries, having to import more and more manufactured goods, unable to compete in world markets? If so, does this change require a drastically different domestic policy and a more aggressive trade policy to improve our competitiveness? Or can we be confident that the free market will eventually generate the best outcome for which we can realistically hope?

Much of this ground has been covered in the debate over industrial policy that began in the late 1970s and that by now has, for all practical purposes, dropped out of view. Various economists, notably Charles Schultze[1] and Richard McKenzie,[2] have argued persuasively that deindustrialization is a myth and that governmental actions under the rubric of industrial policy would be highly inefficient and ineffectual. Nevertheless, some of the same arguments made to justify industrial policies are now being advanced as justifications of interventionist trade policies, and so they are worthwhile to examine afresh.

The question "Is trade deindustrializing America?" can be approached by determining whether we are in fact undergoing a process of deindustrialization. If we are not, then of course trade cannot be blamed for something that is not happening.

Deindustrialization presumably means a decline in a nation's manufacturing sector. But the evidence strongly implies that our manufacturing sector is holding its own and will continue to do so. The best statistic with which to measure this is manufacturing's share of total output, expressed in constant dollars. As figure 3–1 shows, this share has displayed no downward trend during the past several decades.

FIGURE 3–1
MANUFACTURING OUTPUT AS PERCENT OF GNP, 1948–1985

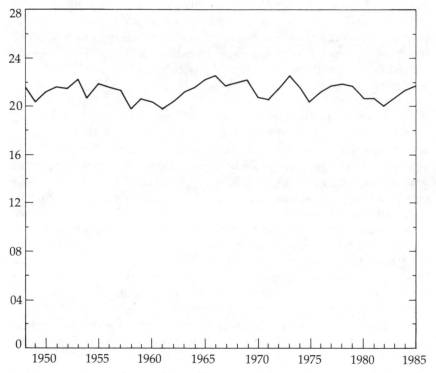

SOURCE: U.S. Department of Commerce, Bureau of Economic Analysis.
NOTE: 1982 dollars.

Those who wish to prove that deindustrialization is a problem typically use some other measure. Sometimes the share of output held by the "goods-producing sector" is presented. This indeed has de-creased somewhat since the 1950s, owing to declines in agriculture, mining, and construction (the three industries that are added to manufacturing to get goods production). A decline in the share of goods production is characteristic of all advanced economies—including the much-admired Japanese economy—and policies that would attempt to reverse such a basic trend are particularly unpromising.

Another means of exaggerating the problem (if there is one) is to express manufacturing and total output in *current* dollars. Since the prices of manufactured goods have risen less rapidly than other prices, the manufacturing share has declined from 28 percent in 1960 to 21 percent in 1984. But since the growth in manufacturing productivity that made this result possible is all to the good, one would not propose policies to cure this "problem" either.

Still another way to misstate the situation is to measure the trend in manufacturing's share from a peak year, such as 1979, to a recessionary trough, such as 1982. Since manufacturing output varies more over the business cycle than does total output, measuring from peak to trough is sure to show a declining share for manufacturing. This method of measurement was used by industrial-policy advocates before the latest recovery had progressed very far.

Some have worried about the declining share of employment in manufacturing and, comparing 1986 with the peak year of 1979, about the absolute decline (8.5 percent) in manufacturing jobs. This is indeed a political concern and will be discussed later in this section. But the decline in share of manufacturing jobs owes much to the relatively rapid growth in productivity in manufacturing. Moreover, U.S. manufacturing employment has been quite robust in comparison with that of other industrialized countries.

The stability of manufacturing's share of output has been recognized by others, notably Robert Z. Lawrence in his 1984 book, *Can America Compete?*[3] He concluded, just as I have, that America is not deindustrializing and, at least through 1982 (the year of the most recent data available to him), growth in manufacturing was not impeded by trade. He points out, for example, that despite the popular perception that imports were wrecking the auto industry, most of the decline in U.S. auto sales in the early 1980s was caused by the domestic decline in demand for autos, not by incursions of imports.

Since Lawrence's period of analysis predates much of the dollar's appreciation, it is reasonable to wonder whether his conclusions are still valid.

The rise of the dollar during the 1980s coincided with a surge of manufactured imports and virtually no growth of exports. Between 1980 and 1985, imports of manufactured goods increased by 97 percent while exports increased by just 1 percent (both in current dollars). In light of such figures, how could anyone possibly doubt that the rise of the dollar severely damaged U.S. manufacturing? Any U.S.

manufacturing executive would testify under oath that he could have sold more of his product, both here and abroad, if the dollar had been lower. While it is therefore tempting to blame the dollar, deeper analysis is called for.

First, we can strengthen the evidence that U.S. manufacturing has done remarkably well in recent years. (As will be discussed later, some individual industries have faltered, but here we will deal with manufacturing in the aggregate.)

If trade had been deindustrializing the United States, then manufacturing would have shifted abroad. But between 1980 and 1984, manufacturing output grew much faster in the United States than in any industrialized OECD country except Japan. Those who believe that our industry is stagnating should be aware that Europe's industry is doing measurably worse.

As noted earlier, maufacturing output bears a clear relationship to gross national product. A regression of the form:

$$\Delta \text{ (log manufacturing output)} = a + b\,\Delta \text{ (log GNP)}$$

gives a close fit. John Tatom finds that such an equation, estimated with data from the third quarter of 1947 through the third quarter of 1980, fits the data quite well ($\bar{R}^2 = 0.66$).[4] This should not be taken to imply a causal relationship, but only that GNP and manufacturing output move together fairly closely (though manufacturing fluctuates more widely around its trend). More important, Tatom finds that the equation *under*predicts the growth of manufacturing from the fourth quarter of 1980 through 1985. In other words, manufacturing output grew faster during a period of rapid dollar appreciation than would be predicted on the basis of its historical pattern linked to overall economic growth. Either the dollar had no effect, or some offsetting forces were more important.

Effects of the Rise in the Dollar. The simultaneous occurrence of a rise in the dollar and a stronger maufacturing sector should not be viewed as a paradox. With elementary supply-and-demand analysis, we can see that they could easily coexist.

A good case can be made that the main cause of the 1980–1984 strengthening of the dollar was an increased demand to invest in the United States rather than to purchase our goods. Between 1980 and 1985, a great change took place in investment flows, with foreign investment in the United States growing substantially and net U.S. investment abroad shrinking to nothing.

Several forces were at work. The Economic Recovery Tax Act of 1981 (though modified a year later) eased depreciation rules and extended the investment tax credit, thereby enhancing investment incentives for domestic and foreign investors alike. In addition, the huge borrowings by the federal government have resulted in a larger stock of debt, higher interest rates, and hence an increased demand for dollars by foreigners who wish to acquire U.S. debt. Some have argued the "safe haven" hypothesis, that the United States was believed to be the world's safest place for investment, owing to our political stability, the low probability of the government's confiscating foreign investment, and our security from armed threats.[5] Moreover, the sheer strength of the U.S. economy after 1982 was a magnet for capital.

All of the above points also apply to U.S. investors who, as was noted, markedly avoided foreign investment. If this analysis is correct, then the situation was one in which the dollar was driven up largely for investment reasons, not because of a drop in demand for U.S. goods.

Some have argued that the key event in the market for U.S. goods was an exogenous decline in the demand for U.S. exports, owing to changes in tastes, slow growth in foreign income, and an increase in the supply of competing goods—in other words, a decline in competitiveness. If this were the case, then U.S. exports would certainly have declined, but so too would the value of the dollar. Since the dollar rose significantly between 1980 and 1984, it means either that there was no decline in competitiveness (in the above sense) or if there was it was swamped by the increased demand for investment in the United States.

Still one can ask: If the dollar had been lower during this period, wouldn't our exports have been stronger and, therefore, wouldn't our manufacturing sector have done better? In answering this, we cannot simply assume a lower dollar and figure higher industry sales according to price elasticities of demand. Rather, we must posit a reason *why* the dollar could have been lower and consider all of the economic effects that this reason implies.

Had a lower budget deficit been accomplished by means of lower federal spending, it is possible that we could have achieved a situation with higher exports and a healthier economy overall. This, I believe, is the only scenario under which it can accurately be said that a lower dollar would have brought greater strength to U.S. industry, but it was, and remains, the least likely of all the possibilities for lowering the dollar.

Other possibilities for a lower dollar can be examined. Suppose the dollar had been lower because the demand for U.S. investment had been lower, owing to less confidence in the United States as a safe haven. What reasons could one offer for this reduced confidence? Fears of runaway inflation? Higher taxes on business and investment? Lower aggregate demand for goods produced in the United States? Inept economic policy in general? Any of these possibilities would have been harmful to U.S, industry, quite probably harmful enough to offset any positive effects of a lower-valued dollar.

Suppose we view the federal budget deficit as the main cause of the high dollar. Two possibilities need to be considered. First, a high federal deficit financed without foreign lending. Would U.S. industry have been as healthy if it were subject to the intense domestic crowding-out effects that this would have entailed? Second, a much lower federal deficit. Had this been accomplished by raising taxes and without reducing spending, I find it hard to believe that the economy could have rebounded from the 1982 recession with the strength that it did. Perhaps a big tax increase would have reduced the trade deficit, but it would have hurt industrial output at least as severely as has the actual trade situation, particularly if the brunt of the tax hike had fallen on business. U.S. industry would have felt the harmful impact of cyclical effects that would have far outweighed any possible price effect of a lower dollar. This cyclical effect would have included negative macroeconomic effects on our trading partners.

Thus, I question simple assertions that a strong dollar harmed industry. Had the dollar been weaker, the causes of this weakness might well have been even more harmful to industry.

Structural Change and Jobs. If the share of manufacturing has been fairly stable for many years, is it not still possible that within the economy there has been an increasing degree of turmoil or, in the current parlance, "structural change?" That is, has the share of manufacturing stayed constant with so much interindustry or interregional migration of resources as to impose heavy costs on labor and business?

A Commerce Department study examined this question in terms of a sixty-five–industry classification of the entire economy.[6] For ten peak-to-peak periods from 1948 to 1984, the study calculated the sum of the percentage-point changes in share of total output for these industries. Signs of the changes were ignored, so that an increase in share for an industry would contribute as much to the measure of change as would a decline. Totals were adjusted for the number of years in the period.

The latest period studied, 1979–1985, experienced virtually the same degree of structural change as the average for the ten periods. The least structural change occurred during the period of fastest growth, 1960–1966. The most structural change occurred during the two periods that included the two wars since 1948.

The analysis was repeated using numbers of full-time equivalent employees instead of output. The measure of structural change for the latest period, 1979–1985, was just slightly greater than the average for all periods.

According to these measures, structural change is not accelerating. Why then is there a popular conception that the contrary is true? To answer this, the Commerce study introduced one more measure of structural change—job losses. For each of the same periods and the same industries, it added up job losses, ignoring job gains. (This is not strictly speaking a measure of job losses, as it assumes that if an industry's employment grew then no one lost his job.) This measure expresses the idea that what people really worry about is losing jobs. By this measure, the latest period (1979–1985) exhibited average annual structural change much greater than during 1973–1979 and also significantly above the average for 1948–1985. This analysis suggests that two sources of political concern are masked by aggregate figures on manufacturing output—changes in employment and the decline in specific industries in a growing economy.

Unlike its share of output, manufacturing's share of employment has been declining steadily for some time. In 1960 30.1 percent of private sector nonagricultural workers were engaged in manufacturing, but by 1986 that share had fallen to 23.4 percent. This percentage varies with the business cycle but, as table 3–1 shows, the trend is downward.

Some have decried the shift of labor to the service sector, believing it to be the cause for lower growth of productivity and wages. While it is true that measured productivity growth is much slower in services than in manufacturing, a few qualifications are in order. First, productivity measurement in the service industries is difficult because of the difficulty in measuring the product itself. The implicit assumption is often made that output is proportional to labor inputs, thus assuming away the possibility of productivity growth. More fundamentally, it is fallacious to conclude that the movement of a worker from a high-productivity industry to one with lower productivity results in lower productivity in the aggregate. The industry productivity figures are always averages for the industry's entire work force; at the margin, it is quite possible that the worker who moves is of lower-than-average productivity and is going to a job where his productivity will be increased, even though it remains below the average in his original industry. In fact, it is very likely, since this would be the natural market result. It is not even accurate to depict

TABLE 3–1
DISTRIBUTION OF U.S. EMPLOYMENT, 1959–1990
(percent)

Industry	1959	1969	1979	1985	Projected 1990
Total (thousands) [a]	67,784	81,508	101,471	109,489	116,865
Agriculture[b]	8.2	4.4	3.3	2.9	2.7
Goods-producing	31.8	31.1	27.6	24.2	23.8
Mining	0.9	0.6	0.7	0.6	0.6
Construction	5.8	5.4	5.8	5.7	5.3
Manufacturing	25.1	25.1	21.1	17.9	17.9
Durable	14.1	14.8	12.8	10.7	11.0
Nondurable	11.0	10.3	8.3	7.2	6.9
Service-producing	60.0	64.5	69.1	72.9	73.5
Transportation, communication, and public utilities	6.3	5.7	5.3	5.1	5.1
Trade	19.9	20.5	22.0	22.8	23.2
Finance, insurance, and real estate	4.4	4.7	5.4	6.0	6.0
Services[c]	17.5	18.6	20.7	24.0	25.1
Government	11.9	15.0	15.7	15.0	14.2

a. Includes wage and salary jobs and self-employed, as tabulated by Personick.
b. The projections are the U.S. Bureau of Labor Statistics moderate growth figures.
c. Includes private households.
SOURCE: Valerie A. Personick, "A Second Look at Industry Output and Employment Trends through 1995," *Monthly Labor Review* (November 1985), table 1. Updates provided by Personick.

the service industries as being significantly lower paying than manufacturing. Among full-time workers in 1984, men in service industry jobs had annual earnings slightly higher than men in manufacturing. The same is true for women if we exclude those in "personal services," that is, those who work in certain low-paid occupations in households and lodging places.[7]

There are, moreover, reasons to suspect that the actual decline is exaggerated by the figures cited in table 3–1. As Richard McKenzie and Stephen Smith point out, the trend toward contracting out has artificially reduced the count of production workers in manufacturing while inflating the number of workers ostensibly in the service sector.[8] Data necessary to measure this effect precisely are not available, but McKenzie and Smith note that the total number of production workers in manufacturing and service-producing sectors remains unchanged at three-fourths of the private labor force between 1965 and 1985. They also observe a downward trend in the ratio of value added to manufacturing shipments, the magnitude of which implies a nominal shift of more than a million workers to the service sector.

Another statistical refinement is based on the realization that part-time work is much more common in the services than in manufacturing. This means that worker-hours are better than employment as a measure of shifts of labor resources from manufacturing to the services. Between 1959 and 1984, manufacturing lost 6.6 percentage points of its share of employment but only 5.0 points of its share of worker hours. Likewise, the service-producing sector gained 12.3 percentage points in its share of employment, but just 10.8 points in its share of worker hours.

Considerations such as these do not falsify the proposition that manufacturing's share of total jobs is declining, but they should lessen concerns about the abruptness of this shift of resources.

As suggested by the above discussion, much of the problem of job loss and output decline has been concentrated in just a few industries. During the 1982 recession, which magnified the problems of industry, by far the most "troubled" industries were motor vehicles, iron and steel, textiles, shoes and leather, knitting, and apparel. In 1977, these industries accounted for only 4.5 percent of total employment, 5.6 percent of total output, and about 20 percent of manufacturing output. But by 1982 their combined employment had dropped by 16 percent and their output by 14 percent in constant dollars—enough to blight the aggregate economic statistics quite significantly. Each of these industries has sought, and obtained, special protection from foreign competition during the 1980s.

The other four-fifths of manufacturing, however, *grew* rapidly even as the economy headed into recession; constant dollar output gained 14 percent, and employment grew 6 percent.

This concentration of poor performance in just a few industries has continued. According to a recent Labor Department study, the industrial sector as a whole is healthy, but a few manufacturing industries are in deep trouble.[9] Tobacco manufactures, iron and steel foundries, leather products, special industrial machinery, and basic steel have declined fairly steadily since the late 1960s, and the Labor Department study expects the declines in employment and output in these industries to continue. Nevertheless, of the fifteen industries projected to have the fastest growth rates between now and 1995, eleven are in manufacturing.[10] Like so many others, this study concludes that the U.S. economy is not deindustrializing. Unfortunately, the publicity given to the relatively few troubled industries has contributed to the perception that all of manufacturing is obsolete and uncompetitive.

Industry requests for protection appear to be closely related to job losses (whatever the cause). Taking as a sample the thirteen industries that filed a total of fifty-one cases with the International Trade Commission between 1975 and 1984, I correlated filings per thousand workers and growth rates of employment between 1975 and 1984. The relation was negative and significant ($\bar{R}^2 = .47$, t = $- 3.43$) which implies that the slower an industry's employment was growing the more likely an industry would file for protection. Employment growth was uncorrelated with findings of injury, however, and it did not predict which industries ultimately were granted relief, decisions that have to be based on injury caused by imports, not just on declines in employment.

Structural change in the economy—that is, changes in the relative sizes of industries—has ebbed and flowed but has never come to a halt. Schumpeter termed the process "creative destruction" because he considered it necessary for economic progress.[11] Let us conclude this section with a discussion of the nature of current structural changes.

We have already discussed the relationship between the major sectors of the economy. For many years, various service industries (particularly health care, financial services, and telecommunications) have been growing rapidly. The shift to services is nothing new; the United States has been predominantly a service economy for at least fifty years.[12] Agriculture has been shrinking in output share and in employment for decades. These trends are characteristic of every advanced economy.

In what way is the United States unique? How is our comparative advantage changing? If we cannot export steel, cars, or petrochemicals, what will we sell to pay our import bill?

This country's comparative advantage is shifting to the production of high-technology goods. There is no universally accepted definition of what is or is not a high-tech product or company. Studies of the subject define high-tech industries as those with relatively high expenditures on research and development or those whose work forces have relatively high proportions of scientists and engineers. Although any such definition is arbitrary, the classifications are fairly consistent from study to study, and the conclusions are, in my judgment, robust with respect to the definition of "high-tech industry."

Results reported by the Federal Reserve Board are typical.[13] High-tech industries, defined by the Fed to be office and computing machines, copiers and related equipment, electronic communications, electronic components, and medical instruments, went from 6.1 percent of the FRB Index of Industrial Production in 1977 to 12.9 percent by the end of 1984. In these seven years, the index of production for all of industry went from 100 to 121.8, but the index for the high-tech sector topped 250. Employment has grown relatively rapidly in high-tech industries, according to a Labor Department study.[14] This study uses three definitions of high tech; in its narrowest definition, the highest of the high-tech industries are drugs, computers, communications equipment, electronic components, aircraft, and guided missiles and space vehicles.

High-tech products are selling better in world markets too. According to a Commerce Department study, "High-tech products have been increasing as a share of U.S. manufactures trade, accounting for 43 percent of exports and 25 percent of imports in 1984."[15] The report goes on to note with dismay that trade surpluses in high-tech products declined after 1980, but this was caused by a rapid increase in imports (mainly consumer electronics not produced domestically), neither surprising nor worrisome during a period of healthy technological progress worldwide. High-tech exports grew faster than other exports, an indication that our comparative advantage remains in high-tech goods.

Over the years, various theories have been produced to explain this country's relative specialization in technologically advanced products. According to the factor-endowments approach, it is entirely natural for us to so specialize when we have devoted by far the most resources to scientific and technological education and to research and development activities, both private and governmental.

According to the product-cycle approach, it is natural for new industries to originate in advanced countries and then, as these industries become mature and amenable to mass-production techniques, to migrate to nations with low-cost labor. In this model, our comparative advantage in a particular industry is only temporary; our real comparative advantage is in developing industries.[16]

Sven Arndt's empirical work is illustrative.[17] He defines three types of products: product-cycle goods (making heavy use of R&D and human capital), Ricardo goods (intense in the use of natural resources), and Heckscher-Ohlin goods (standardized in design and production technology). Abstracting from the effects of the dollar's decline, he finds that the trade balance in Ricardo goods has been negative and on a modest secular decline. In Heckscher-Ohlin goods, the trade balance has also deteriorated. In contrast, the trade balance in product-cycle goods "has shown a strong and rising trend." Apart from international trade, product-cycle goods have claimed a rising share of U.S. production.

Given this view of our comparative advantage, it is natural for our mature industries—such as metals and automobiles—to migrate to nations with cheaper labor. We are on the frontiers of Schumpeter's creative destruction.

What implications has this for trade policy? An economist's instinct is to say, "Don't buck the trend. It is pointless to shore up declining industries, for their decline is inevitable. Jobs aplenty will be found in the rising industries." This approach requires more patience than some policy makers possess, but it would be inaccurate to depict the Congress as a bastion of support for dying industries. The necessity of structural change is widely understood. There is, however, the opposite extreme of trying to accelerate the process of change by stimulating the high-tech sector. A good case can be made for governmental support of research and development, but the trade policies suggested for the nourishment of our high-tech sector often amount to nothing more than protectionism, with all of its well-known defects.

Policy makers are easily tempted to make support for research and development much more specific and direct than, say, tax credits that apply to all R&D. Improved technology is not a cure-all for trade problems, because in some cases no feasible technological improvements can overcome foreign cost advantages. This being the case, it is best left to the market to decide where technical progress is worth the investment. Further, the results of goverment-funded technology and industrial policy are extremely hard to predict. In the late 1970s, when the debate over industrial policy was at its height, it was sometimes said that the goverment need not "pick winners," for it could *create* winning industries by means of sufficient R&D support and other attentions. Ironically, agriculture (which had benefited from decades of technological help) and not manufacturing was often cited as the prime example of governmental success in creating an internationally competitive industry.

This process of developing new industries while shedding the old is chancy and nerve-wracking. Now, for example, we may well wonder if we are losing our knack for such development in semiconductors, as Japan seems not only to have become the low-cost producer of standard products, like 64K and 256K RAM chips, but also to have taken the lead in custom designs too. Being on the Schumpeterian frontier is no particular honor for those watching their jobs disappear, and it is hard for policy makers to view such proceedings from the sidelines.

Recent Trade Policy and Proposals for Change

Since the days when the Smoot-Hawley Tariff reigned, tariffs have declined fairly steadily. The average tariff on dutiable imports is now only about 5 percent, compared with 13 percent in 1950 and more than 50 percent in the early 1930s. Over the past several decades, the General Agreement on Tariffs and Trade (GATT) has played a major role in steering multilateral negotiations in the direction of zero tariffs.

But many industries still enjoy significant trade barriers. Such industries as glassware, ceramic tiles, textiles, carbon steel, orange juice, benzenoid chemicals, sugar, dairy products, peanuts, and others have managed either to preserve their Smoot-Hawley benefits or to obtain protection more recently. These barriers are known as "special protection," since they are significant exceptions to the generally moderate trade barriers that prevail. According to studies cited later in this section, special protection costs U.S. consumers upwards of $50 billion, with efficiency losses to the entire economy of well over $10 billion. (Much of the consumers' loss is the producers' gain, so the net cost is less than the cost to consumers.)

Current issues in domestic trade policy (that is, policies of the United States, as distinct from international agreements such as GATT) deal mainly either with new proposals for special protection for industries that do not already have it or with proposals to reform the trade policy process so that special protection will be easier to obtain, more difficult to obtain, or more efficient from the point of view of benefits and costs. In this chapter I will deal with the policy process rather than with debates over protection of specific industries. First, however, let us consider the general nature of the battle between free trade and protection.

The Supply and Demand for Protection. Economists are untiring in their defense of free trade; their stamina is essential because the forces for protection are even more enduring and persistent. Before examining some of the current issues in trade policy, it is useful to set out a framework, or terms of reference, for the analysis. As a first approximation, one might view current debate over specific proposals to be a contest between the forces of free trade and those of protectionism. But how do people come to be free traders or protectionists? Some degree of understanding is obtained from a theory of rational economic behavior.

Mercantilist economist doctrines, which flourished from the sixteenth century to the eighteenth century, equated specie with wealth and saw regulation of trade as the means to accumulate specie. Some scholars interpreted mercantilism according to a paradigm that certain regulatory policies follow from the objective of balance-of-trade surpluses and the accumulation of specie. Adam Smith took a different view, reversing the direction of causation. The balance-of-trade objective is seen as resulting from the demand for regulatory rents by the domestic producers of goods. Mercantilism, in other words, was an intellectual smoke screen for those who wished to turn the power of the state to their own material benefit.

Modern-day protectionists rarely repeat the old mercantilist slogans, but they sometimes invoke the balance of trade as an end in itself, one that justifies barriers against imports. More frequently, they assert the need to save jobs, the costs of adjustment owing to increase in imports, and the need to give domestic firms the chance to modernize. I will discuss some of these issues at their face value, leavng the reader to determine whether such proposals are intended to camouflage self-interest.

The concept of "rent seeking" is particularly useful in the understanding of current trade policy. Rent seeking is the pursuit, involving the expenditure of resources, of transfer payments or monopoly franchises from the government. This concept involves more than just giving a name to those who try to get protection from foreign competition; it also helps to predict how proposed trade policies will affect the amount of protection produced.

As with any economic activity, rent seeking will be pursued more vigorously the higher its expected rate of return. If trade laws are changed in a way that lowers the cost of obtaining a given amount of protection, then more resources will be devoted to the process of obtaining protection and more protection will be supplied. In other words, there is a market for protection, with suppliers and consumers. If the rate of return of alternative resource uses (such as the production of goods) falls, then more of a firm's resources may be allocated to rent seeking. Thus we would expect to observe more pleas for protection during economic recessions, even if the level of foreign competition is unchanged.

There are parties to trade policy other than the firms and workers in a given industry. There are also the people who produce the policy—legislators, lawyers, government workers, lobbyists, and the like. The rent-seeking behavior of this group is an important determinant of the character (and to a lesser extent of the amount) of the trade policy that is supplied. The trade bureaucracy consists primarily of the thousands of government workers who formulate and carry out trade policies. Using figures from the 1987 *Budget of the United States Government*, I estimate that there are at least 6,200 such people in the executive branch. A much smaller but still powerful group works in the legislative branch. According to Bruce Yandle, the trade bureaucracy is one of the fastest growing segments of Washington's regulatory apparatus.[18] Counterparts in the private sector include trade lawyers and lobbyists, their consultants, representatives of foreign firms and foreign governments, and the employees of the firms and labor unions involved with trade whose job it is to formulate their organizations' policies. This group also numbers in the thousands.

Since bureaucracies wish to perpetuate themselves and to extend their power, it is predictable that they will favor trade policies that require much bureaucratic labor in order to work. Free trade would be the worst possible policy, since it would superannuate the trade bureaucracy completely. Far better to adopt policies that require huge bureaucracies and the specialized knowledge that they have accumulated. The ideal set of policies would:

• require long and detailed negotiations with as many countries as possible. Thus, we see a recent trend to bilateral negotiations, such as those with Canada, Mexico, Israel, and the Soviet Union, in addition to multilateral negotiations. That bilateral agreements require complex modifications of the multilateral pacts is all to the good from the viewpoint of the trade establishment.

• establish as many classifications as possible for traded goods. Indeed, our tariff regulations distinguish among thousands and thousands of goods, and only experts can tell what's what.

• encourage costly litigation over allegedly unfair trade practices. As Lawrence B. Krause has observed, ". . .The legal industry in the United States is using unfair trade charges to harass imports in order to earn legal fees from both American import-competing firms and foreign exporters to the United States."[19]

• connect trade to many other aspects of public policy, so as to make negotiations even more complex and frequent. Thus, trade has become a tool of foreign policy, with embargos of both exports and imports frequently being used to punish other nations for actions unrelated to trade. When in August 1986 it was decided to subsidize grain sales to the Soviet Union, Australia quickly considered linking that unwanted decision (it would cost them grain sales) to the renewal of their defense agreements with the United States. Domestically,

113

trade policy comprises questions of worker retraining, industrial re-structuring, tax policy, etc.

Indeed, activity in trade diplomacy has become so frenetic that it is difficult to detect any overall direction. Soon after the United States and Canada had agreed to negotiate a free trade agreement, for example, the United States imposed a tariff on certain Canadian wood products, to which Canada responded with a tariff on computers (on which a tariff reduction had recently been negotiated) and other products. Are we moving toward or away from free trade overall? Perhaps we have reached a kind of steady-state equilibrium, like a bathtub into which the faucet's inflow is equaled by the drain's outflow. Every time a trade barrier is removed a new one takes its place. The situation resembles that of a stockbroker who works on commission and churns his clients' portfolios, continually buying and selling at no profit for his client. This, at any rate, is the logical consequence of having a very large trade establishment that has all the well-known incentives to pursue its own interests.

Costs of Trade Barriers. That trade barriers are costly to the economy is axiomatic in trade theory; the proposition goes back to the earliest days of economics. Only recently, however, have the costs of protection been quantified with any degree of precision. Many studies have been published, some being partial equilibrium analyses of individual industries and others being attempts to determine the total costs of protection or, alternatively, the benefits of removing all tariffs. The findings of such studies are sufficiently impressive to deserve summary here.

The basic method for estimating the cost of restricting the import of a certain good comes straight out of price theory texts. Restricting quantity results in higher prices. The cost to consumers consists of (1) the greater number of dollars that they have to pay for the quantity that they still purchase plus (2) the loss of welfare they suffer by not consuming as much of the good as they did previously. Producers benefit because they charge higher prices for the restricted good. For the country as a whole, this benefit must be subtracted from the consumers' loss to get a net figure. The consumers' loss, however, *always* exceeds the producers' gain, and the net amount is known as the "dead-weight loss" to the economy.

Foreign producers may lose or gain from the trade restrictions, depending upon whether the higher price they charge (particularly when quotas are used instead of tariffs) outweighs the loss they suffer from selling less of their product. The U.S. government may recover some of the gains from foreign producers if it auctions quotas or charges a tariff; if so, this gain offsets some (but, in practice, never all) of the net loss to the U.S. economy.

The magnitude of such cost estimates depends critically upon the elasticities of demand and supply that are assumed, and various refinements of analysis cause these estimates to vary slightly from study to study. The only methodological controversy of importance comes from those who argue that the traditional analysis understates the true costs of protection.

Jan Tumlir surveyed recent literature on the "dynamic" costs of protection, meaning the costs (over and above the traditional measures) that reduce the economy's long-term growth.[20] The most important cost appears to be the tendency of protection to reduce competition and efficiency in the protected industries. With less competition, protected firms may extract monopoly rents. They may neglect opportunities for innovation that reduces costs or spawns new products. If any of the costs of protection tend to reduce the rate of growth of income, then the costs of protection will grow over time. Sometimes clumsy methods of protection can increase costs by inducing inefficiencies in the provisions of imports. This can happen when the most efficient supplying country is denied access to markets and is replaced by a higher-cost foreign supplier, or when the exporting country is allowed to form a cartel that gives shares of the market to its least efficient firms.

Gordon Tullock also argues that traditional methods of analysis understate the costs of protection.[21] In addition to the dead-weight loss measured traditionally, Tullock would count a significant part of the transfers as dead-weight loss because of rent seeking, the resources that interested parties spend to persuade the goverment to increase or decrease barriers. Tullock argues that since the rewards of winning protection are so great, the resources that can be usefully spent on obtaining it are significant. Tullock also questions the implicit assumption that the government efficiently spends the proceeds from tariffs.

In light of these considerations, the estimates cited below should be viewed as lower limits on the costs of protection.

The "voluntary export restraints" placed upon Japanese automobile exports to the United States in 1981 provided fodder for a number of studies. Under this arrangement, the Japanese agreed to limit their exports of automobiles to the United States to 1.68 million units per year. This limit was raised to 1.85 million units per year for April 1, 1982, through March 31, 1985. David Tarr and Morris Morkre estimated that the annual losses to the U.S. economy were just under $1 billion a year—$994 million in 1983 dollars.[22] This figure represented the total of consumers' losses ($1.109 billion) net of U.S producers' gains ($115 million). The big winner in the deal, according to Tarr and Morkre, was the Japanese auto industry, which garnered $824 million in annual quota rents derived from higher auto prices.

Robert Crandall found that the price of U.S. cars had been elevated by about $400 per car in 1983 and by $750 per car in 1984.[23] The prices of Japanese cars were estimated to have been $1,500 higher than they would have been without the quotas. His estimate of the welfare costs to the United States was $2 billion a year. Gary C. Hufbauer estimated that welfare costs to the United States were $3.1 billion in 1984.[24] The International Trade Commission estimated that prices of Japanese cars were $831 higher in 1983 because of the restraints.[25] This figure would yield a somewhat lower estimate of welfare costs than the other studies cited. These estimates translate into figures of the annual cost per job saved by the auto-import restraints, ranging from $133,000 (Hufbauer) to $241,000 (Tarr and Morkre).

Sugar quotas produce annual costs to consumers almost as high as the Japanese auto restraints, since the barriers cause U.S. sugar prices to exceed world prices by several orders of magnitude. Sugar was protected by quotas in effect from the 1930s through 1974 and then by duties and fees on foreign-produced sugar. A new quota went into effect in 1982. Unlike the auto quotas, sugar quotas are still in full force and may remain so for many years.

According to Tarr and Morkre, the annual cost to consumers is $735 million (1983 dollars).[26] The net cost to the economy is estimated at $252 million. Unlike the auto restraints, sugar quotas are so restrictive that most of producers' gains go to U.S. producers rather than to foreigners.

The cost of restrictions on textiles and apparel are extremely difficult to estimate because the restrictions themselves are so complex. The restrictions apply to thousands of individual goods, and there are numerous methods of partially evading them. But in this case the market itself has come to the aid of economic scholars—because textile quotas are openly traded in Hong Kong, the gap between import prices and costs can easily be inferred.

In 1980, those who wished to import textiles from Hong Kong had to pay "quota rents" of $218 million, according to Tarr and Morkre. Further analysis, taking into account the distortionary effects on consumption and the labor adjustment costs in the United States, yielded estimates of the net benefits to the U.S. economy of removing import quotas on Hong Kong textiles. For 1983, these benefits fell in the range from $372 million to $590 million. These are *annual* benefits; removing the barriers would have a present value of well over $1 billion. Since other countries—for example, South Korea and Taiwan —also face quotas on textiles, it is clear that these estimated benefits are just a fraction of the total that can be realized by removing all such barriers.

What about the total costs of protection? Tarr and Morkre use a modified version of a methodology devised by Brown and Whalley to estimate the benefits of removing all tariffs multilaterally.[27] Their estimate of benefits to the United States is about $10.5 billion for 1983. This covers only tariffs, and apparently no one has attempted to estimate the benefits of removing all other trade barriers too. If, however, we add the $2.4 billion cost of quotas in the four industries studied by Tarr and Morkre (steel, autos, sugar, and some textiles) and net out a terms-of-trade welfare loss of $200 million, we get a total of $12.7 billion—the benefits from eliminating all tariffs and four of the most important quotas.[28] The most recent estimate of the total cost of special protection by Hufbauer and Rosen put the cost to consumers in 1984 at $53 billion and the efficiency loss to the economy at $8 billion.[29] As mentioned earlier, all of these figures are undoubtedly too low.

Trade restrictions, then, may be the most costly form of regulations in this country. Environmental, health, and safety regulations also have huge costs although many of them have large offsetting benefits as well. The trade-barrier cost figures presented here, remember, are net of benefits to the producers of protected goods, so they ignore transfers of wealth that are much larger than the net costs.

Current Trade Policy. The Reagan administration espouses free-trade principles. The 1986 *Economic Report of the President* begins its chapter on trade by paraphrasing Adam Smith and goes on to state that the administration has rejected new calls for protectionism and placed primary emphasis on reducing barriers that restrict U.S. exports.

"Rejected new calls for protectionism" may describe the policy recommendations of the Council of Economic Advisers, but it is too strong a term for what actually happened in many cases. More accurately, the administration has frequently watered down protectionist proposals, but it has not moved all the way to the free-trade end of the policy spectrum. The voluntary export restraints that the Japanese were induced to accept are one such example; probably they prevented Congress from imposing potentially worse restrictions, but that is hard to prove. Steel is another example. The president rejected an International Trade Commission recommendation for relief and instead negotiated voluntary export restraints with sixteen countries. In textiles, the administration's actions have kept very costly trade barriers from becoming even larger.

The U.S. trade representative has been quite active in trying to reduce foreign barriers to our exports. This is clearly a cornerstone of any policy based upon free-trade principles. Getting rid of barriers is, however, an excruciatingly slow process, not only for the bureaucratic reasons discussed earlier, but because other nations employ stalling tactics. Should the United States complain of another country's barriers to U.S. widgets, for example, then the other country would insist on a two-year study of the situation, beginning with long delays owing to disputes over the proper definition of a widget. It would then be explained that the barriers to U.S. widgets are "cultural" and will take two or three generations to erase. Meanwhile, the U.S. widget industry would shrink to the point at which it could no longer afford to fight costly legal battles for relief.

Successes in negotiation have been few and, in value terms, tiny in relation to the trade deficit. Moreover, too often the emphasis seems to shift from opening markets to negotiating voluntary restrictions on exports to the United States. The U.S. semiconductor industry, for example, has long complained about barriers to selling in Japanese markets. After long discussions, the Japanese agreed to let the United States have a greater share of its market, though to date there is no evidence that much has changed. (The Japanese argued that the quality of U.S. chips was inferior.) But in the course of negotiations the scene shifted to allegations of Japanese dumping (selling semiconductors in the United States at less than their Japanese production costs). The Japanese did not admit this, but they did agree to raise the price of their semiconductors. This was hailed in the United States as "a new era of cooperation" with the Japanese.

The primary results of this diplomatically created cartel became apparent within weeks of its creation. The price of microchips skyrocketed in the United States, from $2 to $8 for 256K RAM chips, to the detriment of consumers and user-industries such as autos, electronics, and robotics. Firms in Korea and Singapore will be ready to step in and undercut the U.S.-Japanese cartel. This will push the Japanese toward production of more advanced custom chips (just as the auto restrictions pushed them into the production of larger, more expensive cars), and the enhanced profits that result from higher prices will help provide the required investment.

Potential benefits (except the immediate profits to U.S. semiconductor firms) will take longer to become noticeable. They include enhanced long-term health of the U.S. semiconductor industry and the innovation it generates. These benefits are rather speculative, as they depend upon the argument that high-tech industries are "strategic" and therefore offer the economy greater side benefits than do traditional industries. U.S. semiconductor firms, however, will feel less competitive pressure; whether they will make use of their newly acquired "breathing room" to advance technology remains to be seen. Defenders of the agreement argue that the only issue was dumping and that the law prohibiting it must be upheld, regardless of short-term price increases.

The Current Menu of Trade Policy Ideas. The costs of protection being so enormous, it is natural for policy makers to search for approaches that would provide the putative benefits of protection but at far less cost. Clearly, there are choices between efficient and inefficient means of protecting domestic industries, but the most efficient of these will still be costly. Several major trade bills have been introduced in recent years, and there are more to come. Instead of dealing with specific pieces of legislation, however, I will briefly discuss some of the major proposals that come up again and again.

Require firms to become more competitive in exchange for protection. One of the classic excuses for protection was the "infant industry" argument, which asserted that certain newly established industries eventually would be able to lower their average costs significantly if only they were given temporary shelter from imports. The latest, more active version of this policy is to *require* firms receiving protection to take actions that would make them more competitive—for example, investing in modern cost-cutting equipment.

A good example of this kind of policy is contained in the Trade and Tariff Act of 1984, which gave the steel industry relief from imports, in the form of voluntary restraint agreements (VRAs) with several steel-supplying nations. In return, the major steel companies listed in the legislation were supposed to reinvest substantially all of their net cash flow from carbon and alloy steel to modernize their factories.

On the face of it, this approach seems absurd. Why should a firm have to be cajoled into doing something that is in its own best interest? If there is an above-market rate of return to investment in new plant and equipment, then firms will make this investment without being pressured to do so.

Some of this impulse to dictate management may stem from the bureaucratic nature of the trade establishment; to carry out a program of mandated modernization would require resources to plan and

119

monitor industry actions. But most such proposals seem to have originated in Congress, which does not have a direct interest in expanding the trade bureaucracy. Perhaps some support for such proposals stems simply from the belief that government knows best. Most likely, however, the motivation is based in the desire to save jobs. Earlier I concluded that the loss of jobs appears to be the most important galvanizer of political concern. My reading of the forced-modernization proposals suggests that saving jobs, not efficiency, is paramount. (Conceivably even this objective could be defeated if the modernizing investment turned out to be labor saving and if output failed to increase enough to cause an increase in the demand for labor.)

The danger of giving protection in exchange for promised modernization lies not just in its inherent inefficiency. Possibly worse is the legitimacy it seems to confer upon protection. By implying that protection will be a net benefit, protection is made more palatable and thus more likely to be accepted by consumers and voters.

Ease antitrust laws as a form of trade policy. Two different proposals have been made in this regard. First, it has been argued that when the Justice Department considers proposed mergers, it should consider foreign competition. That is, when defining the market share of the firms that intend to merge, the imports of foreign firms should be included as part of the market. Otherwise, the measured market share of the would-be mergers would be too large, and this would weigh improperly against approval of the merger.

Including foreign imports is quite obviously the correct procedure. The Justice Department's 1982 merger guidelines stated for the first time that foreign competition frequently plays a role in merger analysis, and the 1984 guidelines went into more detail. The Herfindahl index (a measure of an industry's concentration) is now supposed to be calculated including the market shares of foreign competitors.

The second proposal is more controversial. Should relaxation of antitrust restrictions be granted as relief from harmful imports? The argument is that firms under heavy pressure from imports should be given greater leeway to merge, as this would allow cost reductions that would enhance competitiveness. It is hard to believe that this policy would be useful in many cases. Antitrust is supposed to balance gains from scale economies against losses from restraint of trade. When the potential losses are less than the gains, the merger should be allowed, irrespective of foreign competition. If the potential losses are significant, why should the public prefer this type of burden to the costs of more conventional protection?

Furthermore, it is doubtful that making firms merge would increase their competitiveness. In many industries, steel for example, it is the *smaller* firms that have demonstrated the necessary ability to improve quality and develop new products to fit market niches, not the largest firms. By blindly assuming the existence of scale economies where none exist, and then granting import relief as an inducement to merge, this approach to trade policy could make matters worse.

Another version of this idea would grant firms exemptions from antitrust rules so that they could negotiate freely with each other in the process of setting up adjustment plans. Clearly, overly rigid antitrust rules can hinder efficiency and hence international competitiveness. But as Robert Lawrence and Robert Litan point out, such exemptions would magnify the legal complications of existing antitrust law;[30] how, in years to come, could the Justice Department decide how much of an industry's anticompetitive behavior was allowable, owing to the exemption, and how much was prosecutable?

Engage in strategic trade policy. In theory, it should be possible to use threats of tariffs and quotas to persuade other nations to remove their trade barriers. In practice, it is difficult to find many examples of success, as it is hard to tell which threat was effective or whether foreign barriers were set up as bargaining chips. Moreover, our trade policy makers often seem to lose sight of the truly harmful trade barriers and to concentrate instead on ephemera or narrow interests. A farm-state congressman asserts that farm prices can be raised without harming exports, as we can use threats of trade sanctions to force other nations to buy our grain. Recent trade bills called for retaliation against nations that have "excessive" trade surpluses with the United States (as if there were some reason why exports should equal imports for every pair of trading partners). One bill would impose trade sanctions on countries that do not pay their workers adequate wages or protect them with adequate health and safety regulations (with "adequate" presumedly to be defined by the United States). These, of course, are merely subterfuges for outright protectionism. My point is that, while strategic trade policy may be attractive in the abstract, it is questionable whether our negotiators would be able to carry out the policy efficiently. More likely, they would wind up trading market access for worthless concessions. Worse, they might start a trade war reminiscent of Smoot-Hawley days.

Promote Exports. In trade theory, an exogenous increase in demand for the goods in which a country specializes results in an improvement in welfare of that country. If some policy could achieve

121

such an increase at sufficiently low cost, it would appear attractive. This is precisely what our wide array of export promotion activities tries to accomplish, with concessionary interest rates to foreign buyers, trade expositions, trade information, and various other encouragements to domestic firms and foreign buyers.

One problem with these programs is that they can be neutralized by similar incentives offered by other countries. Furthermore, it is hard to determine how cost-effective these programs are; studies by the General Accounting Office of several export-assistance programs have been inconclusive.[31] Export promotion is not the centerpiece of current trade policy, but more activist administrations could easily expand such programs beyond their sensible limits. It is but a short step from trade promotion, whereby the government serves as a free advertising agency, to industrial policy, whereby the government provides many other services, including finance and management, to private industry.

All of the policies discussed above have been advanced by people who consider themselves hardheaded realists and who dismiss the free-trade objections of economists as impractical, ivory-tower theories. "We must deal with the world the way it is," they say, "and not with some unrealistic model on a blackboard." Some even quote Adam Smith's exceptions to free trade, which were protecting industries vital to defense, retaliation for foreign trade barriers, a second-best argument, and the mitigation of adjustment costs. In my view, however, it is the free traders who are pragmatic and the interventionists who ignore important realities. All of the policies mentioned here, plus the Smithian exceptions, would require a degree of precision, knowledge, and lack of self-interest that is far beyond the abilities of our political and bureaucratic institutions. Anyone who thinks we can manage these activist policies well enough to generate net benefits has a highly idealized and abstract notion of how government works. Economists who understand this and therefore favor nonintervention are the true realists.

Free-Trade Pragmatism. Although many economists are unequivocal free traders, some have taken a position that is meant to be more pragmatic. They believe that political pressures will ensure that some degree of protection is inevitable. Moreover, they believe that the government should provide some level of trade adjustment assistance. Their pragmatism is to accept a certain amount of protection provided that it, along with trade adjustment assistance, take the most efficient form that can be devised.

I agree that the current level and mode of protection are grossly inefficient, but I question whether the proposed changes could in fact be made to work as they are intended. In effect, I claim to be even more pragmatic than the pragmatists.

The most specific analyses and proposals have been produced by Lawrence and Litan[32] and by Hufbauer and Rosen.[33] Their proposals have much in common, though perhaps Lawrence and Litan are more cautious about proposing changes that could lead to a greater role for government.

Both pairs of writers recognize the tremendous costs of our current methods of protection. Moreover, they recognize that the current level of protection could be provided at much less cost by substituting tariffs for quotas. One trouble with quotas is that they allow foreign producers to seize some of the monopoly rents resulting from reduced supplies to U.S. consumers (as in the case of textiles mentioned earlier). Tariffs divert some of the benefits to the U.S. Treasury. Further, the costs of quotas are hard to detect, while those of a tariff are clearer and, it is argued, therefore harder to perpetuate. Quotas remove more competitive pressure from domestic industries than tariffs do.

Another central problem with current policy is that most of the major forms of protection now in place did not go through any organized process of evaluation but rather were obtained by special efforts of the protected firms and workers. This has led to many anomalies and, worse, to a breakdown of the principals of multilateral free trade espoused by GATT. So-called voluntary restraints on imports violate, in spirit, free-trade agreements that injured U.S. interests are quick to invoke when it suits them. Like Lawrence and Litan, Hufbauer and Rosen condemn special protection as exceedingly costly, inequitable, and a blockade to initiatives for trade liberalization.

Both pairs of analysts would like to improve existing procedures for obtaining relief from import competition, in hopes of undercutting new attempts to obtain special protection. Both propose means of giving trade adjustment assistance to workers more efficiently.

Clearly, tariffs are more efficient than quotas (as discussed earlier in the section on the costs of protection), and the colossal costs of special protection are scandalous. But institutional changes meant to achieve greater efficiency must recognize the complexity of those institutions.

Consider first the matter of quotas versus tariffs. Without question, a nation could reduce the domestic costs of providing a given amount of protection to one of its industries by substituting a tariff of sufficient size or by auctioning quotas. The exporting country would be unable to seize the profit from restricting supply. But exporting countries are not oblivious to this; one of the attractions of quotas—particularly in the form of voluntary export restraints—is that it is relatively easy to persuade exporting countries to comply with them. As mentioned earlier, the Japanese auto industry profited greatly by having the United States cajole them into their voluntary restraints. Had we then tried to seize the billions of dollars in rents that thus accrued to the Japanese, it is certain that violent objections would have been lodged. Had we persisted, the Japanese no doubt would have retaliated.

Quotas should not be viewed as an inferior policy instrument adopted by governments ignorant of trade theory. Quotas are a means of securing the cooperation of the exporting country, albeit at additional expense to the consumers and taxpayers of the importing country. As such, they cannot be dispensed with so easily.

Lawrence and Litan, in a section entitled "Discouraging VRAs," suggest the erection of roadblocks that would deter the executive branch from requesting other nations to establish export restrictions. Congress, they say, should "direct the Customs Service to use no monies to monitor or assist in enforcing other nations' attempts to impose VRAs."[34] They also suggest extending the reach of the Sherman Antitrust Act to cover foreign participants in export cartels. These ideas appear to be based on the highly questionable assumption that our current voluntary restraints have been set up against the will of the Congress. In my view, if the existing VRAs are not what Congress wanted, they are the next thing to it. The auto VRAs were, according to the administration's explanation, put into place to dissuade Congress from mandating local-content requirements or some other trade barrier even more costly than the VRA.

Hufbauer and Rosen, in their effort to reduce the incidence of special protection, would put greater reliance on escape clause relief. Section 201 of the Trade Act of 1974 says that industries can petition the International Trade Commission for relief. They have to prove that they have been "seriously injured" or "threatened" with serious injury, and that increased imports are the most important cause. If the ITC agrees, it recommends some form of relief, usually tariffs, and the president, if he agrees, can grant that relief. Of the fifty-three import relief cases brought to the ITC between 1975 and 1984, the ITC recommended relief in twenty-eight and the president granted relief in thirteen. Section 201 relief now covers several billion dollars of imports, but its overall effect is far less than the totality of special protection.

Hufbauer and Rosen recommend lowering the threshold for escape clause relief. This could be done by lowering the import-causation test from "substantial cause" of injury to "contributed importantly" to injury. They would also give the ITC the sole power to grant or deny relief (though the president could decide on the form of that relief). Hufbauer and Rosen say that this ease of obtaining Section 201 relief would "decidedly subtract from trade relief granted through other means of special protection," though they concede that their changes in eligibility criteria would add to the frequency and volume of escape clause relief.

By my reading of the situation, however, 201 relief would increase—perhaps quiet considerably—and special protection would not decrease at all. The situation would resemble that of an overweight man who is put on a diet of salads and so consumes three salads a day *in addition to* his usual 12,000 calories. An industry that could do better by going for Section 201 would do so. But why would an industry that is ineligible even for the liberalized Section 201 relief be any less industrious in its quest for special protection? In other words, the demand for protection would be the same, and the Hufbauer and Rosen proposals would increase the supply. Since there is no reason to suppose that the Congress or the administration would reduce the supply of protection, it follows that the quantity of protection granted would increase.

In summary, if the pragmatists' proposals, particularly those of Lawrence and Litan, could be enacted and would operate as they envision, trade policy would be greatly improved in that costs would increase. But consideration of the reactions of the interested parties—firms seeking protection, politicians seeking to please their constituents, and foreign governments quick to protect their own interests—suggest that reform of trade policy is more difficult than the pragmatists depict it as being. In my view, a straightforward defense of free trade is likely to be more effective, however "unpragmatic" it may be.

Conclusion

U.S. industry is doing remarkably well, given the recent experience with the highly valued dollar. We are not deindustrializing, but we are undergoing change, just as we have for many decades. As the effects of a depreciating dollar are felt on imports and exports, the value of the many cost-cutting moves that U.S. firms have made in recent years will become even more apparent. Should trade policy become more protectionist, however, the resulting domestic costs and foreign retaliation will cancel many of the benefits from this future resurgence.

Unfortunately, the direction of trade policy practiced by a worried, quick-to-intervene Congress, inconsistent free-trade administrations, and a growing trade bureaucracy seems to be leaning toward more intervention in international trade.

Two general principles should govern our trade policy. First, we must work harder to receive the GATT procedures for reducing trade barriers all around. Second, we should recognize that our trade policy does not need a lot of gimmicks for fine tuning the granting and withdrawing of protection. Rather, we need institutional *restraints* on the ability of the government to interfere in international markets.

Notes

1. Charles Schultze, "Industrial Policy: A Dissent," *Brookings Review* (October 1983).

2. Richard B. McKenzie, *Competing Visions* (Washington, D.C.: Cato Institute, 1985).

3. Robert Z. Lawrence, *Can America Compete?* (Washington, D.C.: Brookings Institution, 1984).

4. John A. Tatom, "Domestic vs. International Explanations of Recent U.S. Manufacturing Developments," *Review*, Federal Reserve Bank of St. Louis, April 1986, pp. 5–18. Tatom's equation is based on data from the third quarter of 1947 through the third quarter of 1980. It is:

$$400 \, \Delta \ln XM_t = -4.128 + 1.745(400\Delta\ln X_t) + 0.485(400\Delta\ln X_{t-1})$$
$$(-5.60) \quad (13.40) \quad\quad\quad (3.72)$$
$$SE = 6.37 \quad \bar{R}^2 = 0.66 \quad DW = 1.92$$

XM_t is manufacturing output and X_t is real GNP. Growth rates are measured as 400 times the difference in the logarithm of the output series, which gives continuously compounded growth rates. SE is the standard error, and DW is the Durbin-Watson statistic. Manipulation of the estimated coefficients yields the following: When GNP growth equals its long-term average of 3.4 percent, then about the same growth rate is predicted for manufacturing output. In other words, the share of manufacturing in total output is constant, which is also evident in figure 3–1. In addition, manufacturing growth is strongly cyclical, with each 1 percent change in GNP associated with over twice (2.23, the sum of the coefficients) the change in manufacturing output.

5. On the last point, some have argued that the U.S. defense buildup was quite good for the economy because it strengthened the safe-haven effect.

6. John E. Cremeans, "Three Measures of Structural Change," in *The Service Economy: Opportunity, Threat, or Myth?* (Washington, D.C.: U.S. Department of Commerce, 1985). Updated statistics provided by the author.

7. Lynn E. Browne, "Taking in Each Other's Laundry—The Service Economy," *New England Economic Review* (July/August 1986), p. 23. The source for Browne's

data is U.S. Bureau of the Census, *Current Population Survey*, March 1985, computer tape. The data pertain to average annual earnings for year-round full-time workers.

8. Richard B. McKenzie and Stephen D. Smith, *The Good News about U.S. Production and Jobs* (St. Louis: Center for the Study of American Business, Washington University, 1986).

9. Ronald E. Kutscher and Valerie A. Personick, "Deindustrialization and the Shift to the Services," *Monthly Labor Review* (June 1986), pp. 3–13.

10. The eleven industries are: computers peripheral equipment; electronic components and accessories; telephone and telegraph apparatus; complete guided missiles and space vehicles; materials handling equipment; radio and communication equipment; scientific and controlling instruments; medical intruments and supplies; drugs; optical equipment and supplies; and plastics products.

11. Joseph A. Schumpeter, *Capitalism, Socialism and Democracy* (London: George Allen & Unwin, 1943), pp. 82–83. It is ironic that Schumpeter used U.S. Steel as an example of the successful *culmination* of a process of creative destruction. Today business analysts use the company's diversification and divestiture, as well as the success of its smaller new rivals, as examples of modern-day creative destruction.

12. Kenneth M. Brown, "The Service Sector of the Future," in *Statistics about Service Industries* (Washington: National Research Council, National Academy Press, 1986), pp. 37–59.

13. *Federal Reserve Bulletin*, July 1985, p. 489.

14. Richard W. Riche and others, "High Technology Today and Tomorrow: Small Slice of Employment," *Monthly Labor Review* (November 1985), pp. 50–58.

15. U.S. Department of Commerce, *United States Trade: Performance in 1984 and Outlook*, p. 14. This study defines high tech on a product basis rather than on an industry basis. Its high-tech products are: communication equipment and electronic components; aircraft, engines, and parts; professional and scientific instruments; office and ADP machines; engines, turbines, and parts; drugs and medicines; guided missiles, spacecraft, and parts; industrial inorganic chemicals; ordance and accessories; and plastic materials, synthetic resins, rubber, and fibers.

16. See David Dollar, "Technological Innovation, Capital Mobility, and the Product Cycle in North-South Trade," *American Economic Review* 76 (March 1986), pp. 177–90; and R.D. Norton, "Industrial Policy and American Renewal," *The Journal of Economic Literature* 24 (March 1986), pp. 1–40.

17. Sven W. Arndt, "Government Policy and the Decline in U.S. Trade Competitiveness," in Phillip Cagan, ed., *Essays in Contemporary Economic Problems, 1986* (Washington, D.C.: American Enterprise Institute, 1986), pp. 307–24.

18. Bruce Yandle, "The Evolution of Regulatory Activities in the 1970s and 1980s," in Cagan, *Essays*, pp. 132–33.

19. Lawrence B. Krause, testimony before the Joint Economic Committee, December 11, 1986.

20. Jan Tumlir, *Protectionism: Trade Policy in Democratic Societies* (Washington, D.C.: American Enterprise Institute for Public Policy Research, 1985), pp. 5–10.

21. Gordon Tullock, "The Welfare Costs of Tariffs, Monopolies, and Theft," in James M. Buchanan, Robert D. Tollison, and Gordon Tullock, *Toward a Theory of the Rent-Seeking Society* (College Station, Tex.: Texas A&M University Press, 1980), pp. 39–50.

22. David G. Tarr and Morris E. Morkre, *Aggregate Costs to the United States of Tariffs and Quotas on Imports: General Tariff Cuts and Removal of Quotas on Automobiles, Steel, Sugar, and Textiles* (Washington, D.C.: Federal Trade Commission, 1984), p. 8.

23. Robert W. Crandall, "Import Quotas and the Automobile Industry: The Costs of Protectionism," *Brookings Review* 2 (Summer 1984), pp. 8–16.

24. Gary Clyde Hufbauer and Howard F. Rosen, *Trade Policy for Troubled Industries* (Washington, D.C.: Institute for International Economics, 1986), p. 26.

25. U.S. International Trade Commission 1648.

26. Tarr and Morkre, *Aggregate Costs*, p. 91.

27. Fred Brown and John Whalley, "General Equilibrium Evaluations of Tariff-Cutting Proposals in the Tokyo Round and Comparisons with More Extensive Liberalizations of World Trade," *Economic Journal* 90 (December 1980), pp. 838–66.

28. Tarr and Morkre, *Aggregate Costs*, p. 2.

29. Hufbauer and Rosen, *Trade Policy*, p. 26.

30. Robert Z. Lawrence and Robert E. Litan, *Saving Free Trade: A Pragmatic Approach* (Washington, D.C.: The Brookings Institution, 1986), p. 93–94.

31. U.S. General Accounting Office, "Export Promotion: Activities of the Commerce Department's District Offices," (GAO/NS/AD-86-43), February 1986. "Export Promotion: Implementation of the Export Trading Company Act of 1982," (GAO/NS/AD-86-42), February 1986.

32. Lawrence and Litan, *Saving Free Trade*.

33. Hufbauer and Rosen, *Trade Policy*.

34. Lawrence and Litan, *Saving Free Trade*, p. 101.

4

Disinflation, the Dollar, and Velocity

Phillip Cagan

Summary

The rate of inflation, which contracted sharply from 1980 to 1982, declined even further in the ensuing business recovery. The further decline largely reflected gluts in grains and other basic commodities as well as the 1985 collapse of oil prices. The underlying rate as indicated by general labor costs stabilized around 4 percent per year and then in 1986 averaged 3 percent. Although that was still high by any peacetime standard except for the rampant inflation of the 1970s, the failure to escalate in four years of business expansion through 1986 was uncharacteristic of past cyclical fluctuations in inflation. Compared with earlier unsuccessful efforts to contain inflation, the 1980s seemed to exhibit special disinflationary influences.

An obvious special influence was the appreciation of the dollar, which reduced import prices and held down many other prices through intensified foreign competition. The strong dollar could be attributed to a fiscal deficit of unusual magnitude, which attracted a foreign demand for dollars to invest in Treasury securities. When the dollar finally began to depreciate in 1985, many feared prices would rise further as import prices reflected the exchange rate with a lag. Yet during 1985 and 1986 the effect of the dollar depreciation on inflation appeared minor.

The effect of the rise and decline of the dollar on inflation is shown by an index of prices constructed here for industries subject to foreign competition. These are four-digit SIC manufacturing industries in which imports plus exports constitute a quarter or more of the market and for which selling prices were available. The price index rose only about 7 percent less than did an index for all manufacturing prices from 1979 to 1985. This small difference during a half-decade of substantial dollar appreciation clearly provided very limited help in reducing inflation. Moreover, in the subsequent year and a half of dollar depreciation the index showed no impetus toward an escalation of inflation. Although import prices accelerated from mid-1985 to mid-1986, little passed

Kenneth Couch assisted with the statistical work of this study.

through to selling prices. A wage index constructed for these foreign-competing industries rose at the same rate as an index for all manufacturing over the entire period. Apparently profit margins absorbed most of the rise and decline in the dollar. Further dollar depreciation alone appears unlikely to revive inflationary pressures.

The containment of inflation has depended mainly on restrained economic growth and ample productive capacity. The wage give-backs that foreign competition forced in certain unionized industries have no doubt indirectly subdued inflationary expectations in other sectors. Nevertheless, unlike previous business expansions following recessions, aggregate demand in the first half of the 1980s did not subject the economy to inflationary pressures.

Yet monetary policy did not withhold stimulus but sought to revive economic activity and reduce interest rates. Monetary growth returned after the 1981–1982 recession to the inflation-generating rates of the 1970s. The monetary growth was offset, however, by an unusual slowing of velocity growth. An analysis of the public's demand for money balances reveals a substantial increase after 1974 as well as after 1980 compared with behavior implied by prior experience. New financial developments altered the payments system and disturbed the historical relationship between money and aggregate expenditures.

Since 1980 the sizable decline in short-term interest rates and the advent of interest payments on new checking deposits in good part account for the increase in money demand and decline in monetary velocity. But the inability of standard money demand equations or adjustments to the definition of money to account for the change in behavior in the second half of the 1970s leaves any prediction of money demand seriously open to question, until the reliability of a new equation can be established. The interference of financial developments with the previous relationship between money and aggregate expenditures underlies the Federal Reserve's abandonment of monetary targeting.

Monetary policy succeeded in subduing inflation in spite of severe economic costs, which, though less than were widely predicted, still afflict some sectors of the economy. With inflation now less in the public's attention, policy faces strong pressures to lower interest rates and stimulate economic activity. The difficulties of monetary targeting leave policy without reliable short-run indicators for guidance and heighten the uncertainty over the purpose and outcome of policy actions. Continuing high bond yields reflect a lingering uncertainty that inflation will stay down. Until a reliable new relationship between money and aggregate expenditures can be established, containment of inflation requires a cautious monetary policy that avoids overstimulation of the economy. Bond yields will continue to register the degree of market uncertainty over the Federal Reserve's commitment to a noninflationary economy.

This chapter traces the recent path of inflation and, in the first section, examines the effect on inflation of the appreciation and subsequent depreciation of the dollar. Price and wage indexes constructed for industries subject to foreign competition show the effect of the dollar on selling prices and profit margins. In the second section the absorption since 1980 of high monetary growth by unusually large increases in the public's demand for real money balances is examined with simulations of conventional demand equations. The failure of these equations to fit recent behavior lies behind the abandonment of monetary targeting and sets the conditions for its possible future reinstatement to help ensure a noninflationary monetary policy.

The Atypical Nonescalation of Inflation

Figure 4–1 depicts the recent decline of inflation. The consumer price index (CPI) in the top panel, covering all items, decelerated from an annual rate of 15 percent in 1980 to almost zero at the end of the 1981–1982 business recession, stabilized at a 4 percent rate in 1983–1985, and fell lower in 1986. Although inflation typically revives in business expansions, during the four years of expansion it declined further. The further decline occurred among commodity prices, and not only in fuels and food. In contrast service prices showed no deceleration after the recession. The second panel shows the commodity component of the CPI and a subcomponent excluding fuels and food. The decline in oil prices accounts for the decline in the first half of 1986. The inflation rate of services in the third panel has held steady at 4 to 5 percent.

The bottom panel of figure 4–1 shows the employment cost index, the best available series on wage compensation. Wages generally lag behind prices, and here too the deceleration of wages started later and continued longer. Wages decelerated to an annual rate of 5 percent by the final stage of the recession at the end of 1982 and worked down during 1985 and 1986 to 3 percent, suggesting that expectations of inflation, which are added into wage increases, gradually subsided. With an annual growth of labor productivity averaging 1 percent since mid-1979, increases in labor costs per unit of output have decelerated from 4 percent per year at the end of 1982 to 2 percent in 1986. These cost increases set a floor to the average rate of price inflation over the near term. A 3 percent rate of seemingly chronic inflation caused great concern in the 1950s. The recent decline has eradicated inflation dramatically compared with the 1970s and impressively compared with the 1950s, if the rate can remain below 3 percent.

FIGURE 4–1
INFLATION OF PRICES AND WAGES,
Quarterly, 1979–1986

Percent per year

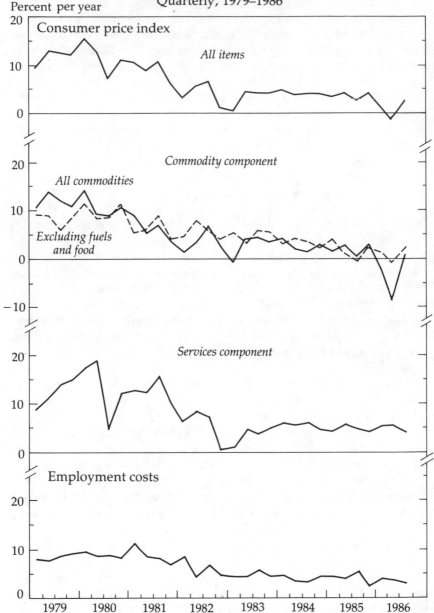

NOTE: Quarterly changes at annual rate of CPI-U version and employment cost index, compensation of all private workers.
SOURCE: Bureau of Labor Statistics.

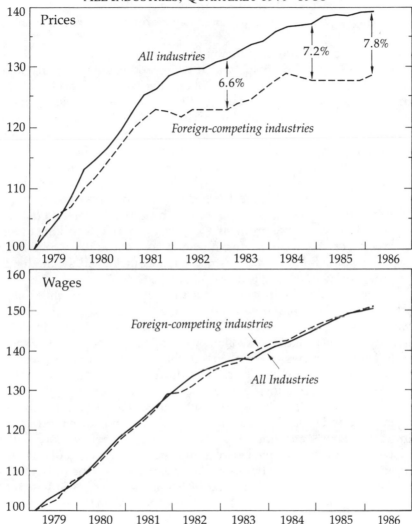

FIGURE 4–2
PRICE AND WAGE INDEX OF FOREIGN-COMPETING AND
ALL INDUSTRIES, QUARTERLY 1979–1986

NOTE: Top panel: Unweighted price index for thirty-four to seventy-four four-digit SIC industries in manufacturing with imports and exports 25 percent or more of domestic supply and producer price index of commodities excluding fuel and power. Indicated differences are percentage by which the foreign-competing industry index falls short of PPI.

Bottom panel: Unweighted wage index for 107 four-digit SIC industries in manufacturing with imports and exports 25 percent or more of domestic supply and unadjusted average hourly earnings index for manufacturing.

First quarter 1979´= 100.
SOURCE: Bureau of Labor Statistics.

In the long run inflation is controlled by monetary growth. In the short run, however, fluctuations in velocity affect the inflation rate, while the slow adjustment of prices causes output to absorb changes in expenditures.

The recent decline in inflation can be attributed to the two recessions of 1980 and 1981–1982, which were produced in part and reinforced by a restrictive monetary policy.[1] Recessions typically cut the underlying inflation rate in half. And here too, the underlying rate as measured by wages declined by half from 1980 to 1982. Also typical is a revival of the rate in the ensuing business cycle. This time, however, monetary policy helped avoid a cyclical revival of the rate, which declined further. The outcome resembled the early 1960s when the inflation of the 1950s finally expired and did not revive. The overall moderate pace of the cyclical expansion in business activity helps explain the two episodes, in both of which aggregate demand did not expand beyond normal productive capacity. There is a striking difference between the two episodes, however, in that the 1980s subdued a high and rising inflation that seemed out of control. Did the moderate pace of activity in the 1980s do the job alone?

Some obvious help came from the appreciation of the dollar, which intensified competition from foreign trade and exerted downward pressure on many commodity prices in 1983–1985, reinforced later by the collapse of world oil prices. While the relative depreciation of foreign currencies raised their internal prices, the main pressure from foreign trade on U.S. prices was downward.

We can look at industries subject to strong foreign competition for evidence of the effect of the dollar exchange rate. Figure 4–2 shows aggregated indexes of prices and wages of manufacturing industries in which exports and imports in 1984 were a quarter or more of the market.[2] This dividing line between industries that do and do not face foreign competition is arbitrary but serves to indicate the price effects of the exchange rate. The Bureau of Labor Statistics (BLS) has published price indexes for a number of these industries, though many of the indexes begin only in recent years. The top panel links the individual indexes into the aggregate index on the date each begins, starting with thirty-six industries in 1979 and expanding to seventy-four by the end of the period. The individual indexes are equally weighted in this limited sample to avoid the chance of dominance by a few large industries. This weighting treats each industry as equally representative of the behavior of all industries. (The inclusion of one petroleum industry has virtually no effect on the aggregate.) The companion series shown for comparison is the producer price index for all commodities, excluding fuel and power. The wage index in the bottom panel pertains to average hourly earnings for 107 industries (again unweighted for comparison with the top panel) that met the 25 percent export-import threshold. They account for a quarter of the total value of manufacturing shipments. The series shown for comparison is the average hourly earnings index for all manufacturing industries.

Foreign competition held down price increases moderately. In figure 4–2 prices of the foreign-competing industries rose 6½ percentage points less from 1979 to the first quarter of 1983, while the exchange rate appreciated considerably. Although the dollar subsequently appreciated much further to a peak in early 1985, the price difference of the foreign-competing industries widened to only 7 percentage points by the fourth quarter of 1984 and to 8 points by 1986. Since the foreign-competing industries are included in the aggregate index, the price difference between these and all other industries is somewhat greater than shown by figure 4–2. As of mid-1986, by some measures the dollar had fallen back to the level of mid-1982 and by well over half its original rise, but the price differential had yet to begin narrowing.[3]

Wages in the foreign-competing industries show no overall departure from the behavior in all manufacturing. The absence of a wage effect from foreign competition is perhaps surprising given the wide attention to the cost advantage of imports produced abroad with cheap labor. Apparently the interrelations of the U.S. labor market preclude much disparity in wage behavior among domestic industries. In any event, the similarity of wage changes suggests that the disparity in prices fell on profit margins and that the recent decline in the dollar need not lead to readjustments of wage differentials.

Although foreign competition from the stronger dollar reduced price increases to some extent in these industries, most of the effect came during the business recession. Since little further effect appeared in the ensuing business recovery, the strong dollar does not explain the absence of a cyclical revival of inflation.

To be sure, the dollar appreciation reduced the prices of imports to all industries. For the period from the fourth quarter of 1981 to the fourth quarter of 1984 before the collapse of oil prices, the BLS index of import prices fell 5 percent, while the deflator for GNP rose 13 percent, a price difference of 18 percent. This difference is less than half the concurrent rise in the Federal Reserve trade-weighted exchange rate index of 40 percent but, allowing for lags, corresponds roughly to the effect to be expected from past experience. A Federal Reserve study estimates that nonoil import prices usually reflect 60 percent of changes in the exchange rate over a period of two years.[4]

135

The price response appeared smaller in the appreciation of the 1980s, in part, no doubt, because the latter Federal Reserve index overstates the appreciation of the dollar vis-à-vis all countries and in real terms (that is, adjusted for relative inflation rates). Given that total imports are about 11 percent of GNP, the lower relative input cost of imports of 18 percent, even if fully passed through, helped shave the average price increase by only 2 percentage points. Spread over four years, this effect made only a minor difference.

Similarly, the depreciation of the dollar since early 1985 has yet to raise domestic prices significantly. While BLS import prices excluding fuels rose 7½ percent from mid-1985 to mid-1986, up from less than 2 percent the preceding twelve months (still far from reflecting the full decline in the dollar), the commodity component of the CPI excluding fuels continued decelerating (figure 4–1). Of course, falling oil prices partly explain why inflation declined in spite of the rise in other import prices. Import prices including fuels fell 10½ percent in the year ending in mid-1986, which reduced input costs throughout the economy. Furthermore, as implied by figure 4–2, lags presumably have delayed a reversal of the price effects in foreign-competing industries from the earlier appreciation of the dollar.

A slow response to exchange-rate fluctuations shows up as well in the continuing large U.S. trade deficit in 1986 in spite of the sizable decline in the dollar. In addition to the usual lag in response of international trade flows to price changes, as of mid-1986 import prices as noted reflect only part of the dollar depreciation, and the BLS index of dollar export prices declined less than 1 percent over the previous year. Apparently, profit margins have absorbed a good part of changes in the exchange rate.

Given the limited effect of the dollar exchange rate on prices in general, the absence of a revival of inflation after 1982 appears to reflect instead slow economic growth here and abroad. Low use of productive capacity forced down basic commodity prices and countered any upward pressure on aggregate prices. The continuation of a low inflation rate produced in turn a gradual unwinding of the inflationary premium built into wages, thus reinforcing the disinflation.

The success in bringing down the raging inflation attests to the effectiveness of a restrictive aggregate demand policy if pursued over an extended period. Although the administration had argued that its announced commitment to an anti-inflationary policy would enhance credibility in disinflation and speed its achievement with less than the usual repercussions on output, the credibility of the policy as such had little initial effect. The degree of disinflation in 1980–1982 was no more than could be expected from the decline in aggregate demand

and output.[5] When inflation subsequently failed to revive with the business recovery in 1983 and after, however, the successful outcome of the anti-inflationary policy gave it a credibility that the announced intentions lacked and that reinforced the disinflation.

The policy of the 1980s contrasted with attempts to arrest inflation over the previous decade and a half—in 1966, 1969, and 1973, each time reversed too soon to be effective for long. The successful maintenance of disinflation in the 1980s is all the more surprising in view of the vigorous attempts by the Federal Reserve to stimulate the economy, first in mid-1982 to end the recession and several times thereafter as the business recovery lagged. From the end of 1982 to the end of 1985 growth of M1 averaged 9 percent per year and escalated to 14 percent in 1986. Declines in monetary velocity offset the high monetary growth that would otherwise have rekindled inflation.

The Unpredicted Behavior of Velocity

Growth of the money supply became an announced target of monetary policy during the 1970s, at first reluctantly under congressional insistence but later more seriously as the tradition of guiding policy by interest rates proved inadequate in the inflationary turbulence of the 1970s. The escalation of inflation in the 1970s buttressed monetarist arguments that policy should rely on the historical relationship between money and aggregate expenditures and use monetary targets as a reliable guide.

Beginning in 1979 the Federal Reserve adhered to the announced monetary targets more closely than before, which helped achieve an effective anti-inflationary policy. At the same time, however, the relationship between money and aggregate expenditures changed radically. This change led the Federal Reserve first to demote M1 as a target in favor of other monetary aggregates and then, as all the aggregates began to behave unpredictably, to attach less importance to all monetary targets. The Federal Reserve has returned to being guided by interest rates and general economic conditions in spite of their limitations. The resulting lack of an acknowledged specific target increases the uncertainty over what course monetary policy will take.

What explains the developments that led to the abandonment of monetary targeting? Figure 4–3 shows the velocity of M1 (the ratio of GNP to the sum of currency and checking deposits in banks and thrift institutions), which is the traditional measure of the public's use of money. It tells us that in 1986 the average dollar transacted about $6.25 of annual expenditures on final goods and services. M1 velocity has generally been rising since World War II. It rose from the

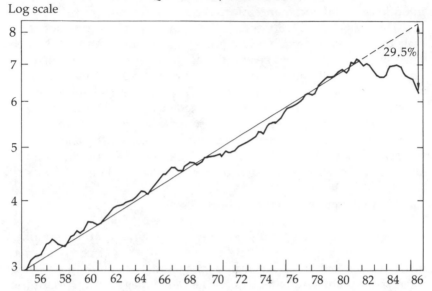

FIGURE 4–3
VELOCITY OF M1,
QUARTERLY, 1955–1986

Log scale

NOTE: Ratio of GNP to M1. Trend line of 3.26 percent per year from the first quarter of 1955 to the fourth quarter of 1981.
SOURCE: Bureau of Economic Analysis and Federal Reserve Board of Governors.

mid-1950s through the 1970s at an average rate of 3¼ percent per year. Most of the smaller deviations from this upward path reflected predictable responses to cyclical fluctuations in aggregate expenditures and interest rates. Major unpredicted deviations occurred in the 1970s and 1980s, however, when regression equations derived to predict the demand for money balances went far off track.

The first of these discrepancies is generally dated in mid-1974, when measured M1 began rising slower and its velocity faster than the equations predicted—which created the famous "case of missing money."[6] (Standard equations can predict the decline relative to the trend line in figure 4–3 from 1966 to 1974, but not the rise back to this trend line in the second half of the 1970s, as is detailed below.) In a search for omitted money the Federal Reserve added automatic transfer services (ATS) and negotiable orders of withdrawal (NOW accounts) to the definition,[7] but these failed to account for all the missing money. The new definition is used in figure 4–3. Under the old definition these discrepancies were even larger. In the major deviation of the 1980s, velocity of the new M1 fell increasingly below the extended trend line, by nearly 30 percent as of 1986, as is dramatically apparent in figure 4–3. The movements in the 1970s and 1980s depart radically from past behavior. They are plausibly attributed to new financial developments, particularly the introduction of attractive substitutes for money and interest payments on checking accounts. The effect of the new developments on the demand for money balances and the explanation of changes in the demand remain unclear. Regression equations derived to predict velocity have proven incapable of allowing for all the changes in behavior.

A partial explanation for the change in behavior of velocity and the difficulty of establishing a full explanation can be described with simulations of money demand regressions. The period from 1955 to 1974 is taken as the normal behavior of money demand. By fitting a standard form of the money demand equation to this period and then simulating the equation forward with various modifications, we can see how far the simulated values account for the subsequent change in behavior.

The standard form relates real money balances to real GNP and two interest rates on money substitutes (one rate relevant to individuals and another to businesses). The regression for M1 estimated here[8] departs from the standard form only in using real final sales for real GNP[9] and a revised deposit interest rate to cover new substitutes for money. The period of fit begins with 1955 after the Federal Reserve abandoned wartime interest-rate pegging and ends with mid-1974, just as the equation goes off track, as documented by numerous studies.[10]

Figure 4–4 presents a set of graphs based on the predicted and actual values of real money balances. The graphs begin with the third quarter of 1974 immediately following the period fitted by the regressions and end with the latest quarter of available data. The predicted values are dynamic simulations of the regressions (dynamic in the sense that the lagged dependent variable is the predicted value of each preceding quarter), which avoids the bias toward a good fit if the lagged *actual* value were used. Separate regressions were run for the different specifications of the variables in each panel, although these changes affect mainly the simulations and affect the earlier period fitted by the regressions hardly at all. The predicted and actual values of real money balances are presented in the familiar form of velocities, where the predicted and actual real balances are the denominator of a ratio with actual real domestic sales as the numerator. The period after 1974 was one in which velocity rose faster than its 3¼ percent average

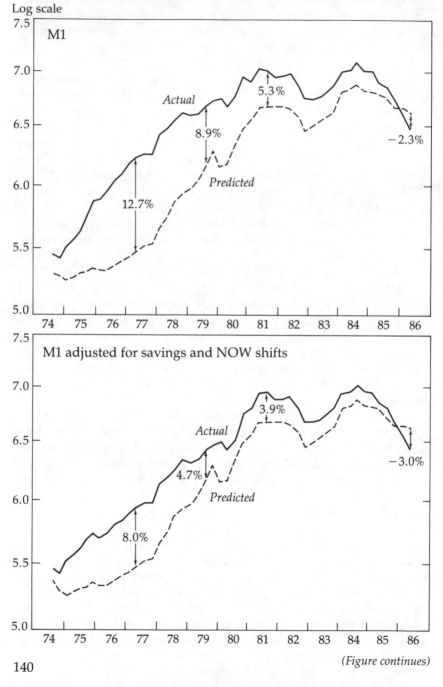

FIGURE 4–4
PREDICTED AND ACTUAL MONETARY VELOCITIES,
QUARTERLY, THIRD QUARTER OF 1974 TO THIRD QUARTER OF 1986

(Figure continues)

FIGURE 4–4
(continued)

Log scale

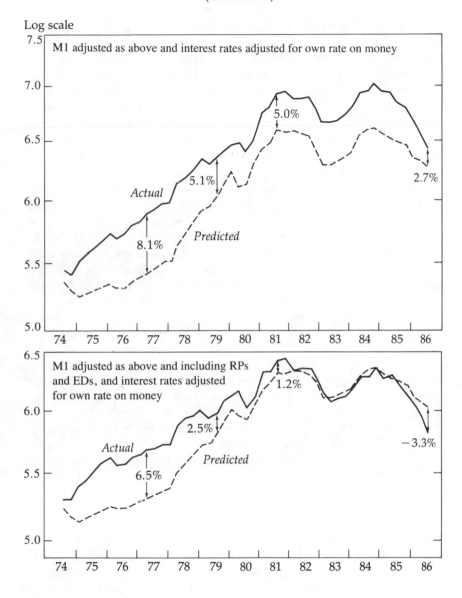

SOURCE: Ratio of real final sales to predicted and actual real money balances. Predicted balances are from regressions fitted to the first quarter 1955 to the second quarter 1974 as described in text. Marked differences are the logarithmic difference between the actual and the predicted series.

141

rate (see figure 4–3). The equations do not initially predict this more rapid growth, and hence the simulations in figure 4–4 start out well below the actual values.

The denoted vertical distances give the percentage difference between the two series. The largest difference occurs in the second quarter of 1977. Other differences denoted in the figure are for the third quarter of 1979 preceding the Federal Reserve's October change in operating procedure, the third quarter of 1981 at the start of the recession, and the latest quarter available. A predicted velocity below the actual velocity means that real money balances are overpredicted. It should be emphasized that the discrepancy shows the error in prediction of real money balances, and not of velocity, for which a prediction of real sales in the numerator would be required as well. Accurate prediction of real money balances is nevertheless an important step in guiding monetary policy toward the goals for output and inflation.

The top panel of figure 4–4 is based on the Federal Reserve's 1980 revision of M1 (still the official version) incorporating the new ATS, NOW, and super-NOW checking deposits, which seemed to be the money missing after 1974. Nevertheless, as the top panel shows, a substantial discrepancy still appears after 1974, which reaches a maximum of over 12 percent overprediction of money balances before it diminishes. The discrepancy far exceeds the expected range implied by the standard error of the regression fit, which is ½ percent. Twice the standard error gives a range of plus or minus 1 percent within which 95 percent of deviations are expected to fall. The persistence of the deviations in the same direction indicates a major change in behavior or in the data. No complete explanation for the discrepancy has yet been confirmed, although some additional adjustments presented below may account for part of it.

Whatever the explanation for the widening and then narrowing of the discrepancy in the 1970s, the equation predicts much better for a while after 1980. As shown in the top panel, the discrepancy narrows very gradually from 1981 to 1985, indicating that the movements and trend of the predicted series follow those of the actual series fairly closely despite the difference in level. Then in 1985 and 1986 the discrepancy narrows rapidly, and actual velocity falls below the predicted value. According to the equation, the reduction of growth in velocity after 1980 can be attributed to the lower growth of real sales and the steep fall in interest rates from the high levels of 1980. The disinflation accounts for the fall in interest rates, which contributed to an unprecedented decline in velocity compared with its strong growth during the previous period of generally rising interest rates.[11]

Modifications in the data described below reduce the discrepancy further, suggesting partial explanations for the missing money of the 1970s and the decline in growth of the 1980s. To be sure, a reduction in the discrepancy can be manufactured by many modifications and does not prove their validity without further independent confirmation, which is not yet available. The modifications below are plausible, though, and point toward the main reasons for the change in monetary behavior.

The second panel of figure 4–4 is based on two further adjustments of M1. One makes allowance for a permanent shift from demand to savings deposits by state and local government agencies from 1975 to 1977 as a result of a change in banking regulations permitting these agencies to own savings deposits. The Federal Reserve estimated the amounts of the resulting shift;[12] the adjustment pretends that they never left the money stock and restores them. The second adjustment reverses a one-time shift from savings deposits to NOW accounts when these became available nationwide in 1981. The amount of the shift estimated by the Federal Reserve is deducted from other checking deposits (OCDs) in the revised money stock.[13] The money demand equation cannot account for such shifts that stem from a change in regulations (apart from inserting ad hoc dummy variables). An adjustment of the data is required.

The adjustments covered by the second panel reduce the discrepancy between the predicted and the actual series. The maximum discrepancy is reduced to 8 percent compared with over 12 percent in the top panel. Although the discrepancy remains lower for the 1980s as well, the trends of the two series in the later period still differ. Predicted velocity rises about 7 percent more than actual velocity from the second quarter of 1981 to the third quarter of 1986 (an average of 1.3 percent per year).

A widely noted development to help explain the decline in velocity growth in the 1980s is the payment of interest on OCDs. The standard equation incorporates the steep fall in interest rates on money substitutes but not the advent of interest payments on money. There is no adequate way to take account of interest payments on only part of money balances in a one-equation model, however.[14] The proper treatment of interest- and non-interest-bearing components of money requires separate equations but is precluded here because of the difficulty of identifying substitutions between them. To continue with the traditional approach, we may retain a single equation and incorporate interest payments on money by subtracting the *average* rate paid on all money balances from the rates on substitutes. This is admittedly a rough approximation, since it ignores the difference in opportunity cost between interest- and non-interest-bearing money balances.

The third panel of figure 4–4 is based on the same adjusted money stock as in the second panel but adjusts for the average interest rate paid on money.[15] This adjustment of the interest rates has a negligible effect until NOW accounts spread nationwide in 1981.[16] The predicted series accounts for most of the decline in velocity growth in the 1980s. From the second quarter of 1981 to the first quarter of 1986 the decline in the predicted series differs from that in the actual series by only 2.3 (5.0-2.7) percent or 0.4 percent per year.

The bottom panel of figure 4–4 provides a further attempt to account for the discrepancy of the 1970s by including overnight repurchase agreements (RPs) and Caribbean Eurodollars (EDs). (The average interest rate on money balances was reconstructed to reflect this inclusion.) These assets became very close substitutes for corporate demand deposits during the 1970s. By transferring unneeded demand deposits into these components overnight, corporations could earn interest without losing much flexibility in the use of the deposits. Also, in response to high interest rates in the 1970s, tighter cash management techniques developed that reduced holdings of non-interest-bearing demand deposits.[17] The effect of these techniques cannot be readily measured, however, and in any event may be largely captured by the interest rates in the equation.

Inclusion of overnight RPs and EDs in money balances in the bottom panel eliminates nearly all the discrepancy from 1981 to 1985 but reduces it only slightly in the 1970s. This equation appears to predict money demand accurately in the 1980s until 1986 despite the remaining sizable discrepancy in the 1970s. But the increased discrepancy in 1986 aside (attributable to relatively attractive rates paid on super-NOW accounts not adequately represented by the average rate on money), little confidence can be placed in a forecasting equation that is unable to predict a good part of the 1970s. Adding the period after 1974 to the regression, moreover, does not improve the equation. In fact, with this extension of the period of fit, the regression deteriorates: the coefficients of the explanatory variables (sales and interest rates) lose importance, and the coefficient of the lagged dependent variable becomes implausibly large—all indicative of an unsatisfactory equation. In the deteriorated regression the independent explanatory variables explain little of the behavior of real money balances. Our inability to explain behavior in the second half of the

1970s results in the failure of regressions that include that period. The existence of the discrepancies in figure 4–4 for that period indicates that the corresponding increase in money demand has been overpredicted (the increase in velocity underpredicted), and the above adjustments are partly acting as proxies for some as yet unidentified developments.

A major source of the structural change in money demand has been the removal of prohibitions on the payment of interest on part of the money stock. Long advocated by proponents of less banking regulation, the introduction of explicit interest payments has disturbed the historical relationship between money and aggregate expenditures. The turnover of OCDs, as indicated by the ratio of debits to average balances on the order of fifteen per year, is significantly higher than the turnover of savings deposits, but far below the turnover of regular demand deposits. In the 1980s velocity reflected an increase in turnover rates of demand deposits offset by a growth in OCDs, which are widely held for savings as well as for checking. The traditional money demand equation cannot adequately allow for these developments simply by incorporating the average interest paid on all money balances.

The low turnover of OCDs compared with demand deposits seems to suggest that the narrow definition of money (M1A), which excludes OCDs, may do a better job of preserving the traditional relationship between money and aggregate expenditures. Indeed, the velocity measure of M1A shows a rather sharp increase in growth in the 1980s instead of the sharp decline as in figure 4–3 for M1.[18] In simulations (not shown) comparable to figure 4–4, however, M1A demand equations do poorly. The simulation errors far exceed those for the various versions of M1 in figure 4–4. Excluding OCDs does not eliminate the effects of structural changes in the payments system on the relationship between money and expenditures.

An alternative handling of these developments weights the various components of the money stock by their turnover rates, which is an old idea recently put into practice by the Federal Reserve staff.[19] The rates indicate how frequently each dollar transacts a purchase of goods and services. By giving low-frequency components less weight in a reconstructed monetary aggregate, the technique theoretically tightens the quantitative relationship between the weighted money stock and aggregate expenditures. The empirical results of this technique, while promising, have not helped explain the discrepancies in the predictions of the standard equation. A serious problem is the difficulty of estimating turnover rates only for purchases of final goods and services when the available data are debits covering all kinds of transactions and of estimating currency turnover from very limited data. In addition, analysis is handicapped because available estimates of the money stock weighted by turnover cover the period since 1970 only, making it impossible to test behavioral conformity with the 1950s and 1960s.

We may nevertheless examine the effect of using the Federal Reserve's estimated money series in which the components are weighted by their turnover rates. Assuming the weighting is less important for the period before the series begins in 1970, we may link the weighted series to the regular M1 as of 1970. The linked series covers the period 1955 to the present and can be used in the same regression form reported in note 8. The regression coefficients (not shown) are little different, and the actual and predicted velocities for the post-1974 period are shown in figure 4–5.

The actual velocity of the weighted money series, compared with the other velocities in figure 4–4, displays less decline in growth in the 1980s. This gives the weighted series the appearance of consistency with earlier behavior. The corresponding predicted velocity derived from the standard regression form, however, shows the same sizable discrepancy in the later 1970s and an *increasing* discrepancy during the 1980s. The weighted series, therefore, does not help explain the "missing money" of the 1970s and is not predicted by the standard explanatory variables in the 1980s. Whether this weighted money series can give rise to a new predictable money demand relationship requires a longer period of experience with it and remains to be seen.

The simulations in figures 4–4 and 4–5 clearly imply that an unidentified structural change occurred in money demand in the mid-1970s. If this change reflected developments that are ending, the passage of time will allow estimation of a new money demand equation that once again gives reliable predictions. Since it is too soon to tell when and if such developments have ended, the monetary authorities continue to give low priority to monetary targets.

Conclusion: The Problems of Preserving the Disinflation of the 1980s

Having brought down a raging inflation at considerable costs, monetary policy has the clear objective of avoiding any future need to repeat them. These costs differed from earlier predictions of the consequences of disinflation. Previous studies of the relation between price and output changes exaggerated the direct output losses of reducing inflation and largely overlooked the economic distortions produced by years of high inflation. Thus the 1981–1982 recession accompanying the main part of the disinflation fell far short of the loss

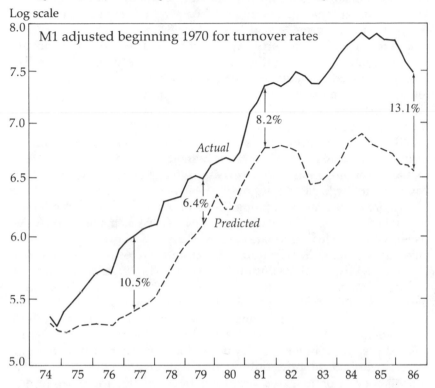

SOURCE: Ratio of real final sales to predicted and actual real money balances. Predicted balances are from regression fitted from 1955QI to 1974QII as described in text. Money series is Federal Reserve MQ series linked to M1 before 1970. Marked differences are the logarithmic difference between the actual and the predicted series.

in output and workdays that studies of previous experience predicted would be necessary.[20] Although these studies assumed that the escalating cycles of inflation in the 1970s and earlier with their brief periods of retrenchment could be used to predict the path of a sustained disinflation as was later pursued in the 1980s, they proved inapplicable and overpredicted the loss in output. The pessimistic predictions unfortunately reinforced the public's skepticism in 1979–1980 that monetary policy would persevere with disinflation and be successful.

Unforeseen indirect costs came later as the economy worked

through a protracted ordeal, still not completed, of undoing the previous adjustments to high inflation. These later indirect consequences of disinflation caught businesses, farms, and entire countries in a web of burdensome overindebtedness previously incurred when escalating inflation made real interest rates appear attractively low. Real capital gains on property values, which had been bid up to obtain hedges against runaway inflation, turned into losses under disinflation and proved inadequate to continue serving as collateral for no-longer-profitable loans. Basic commodities on which many indebted U.S. farms and foreign countries depended for export earnings felt the double sting of declining prices from the highs produced by inflationary overspeculation and of sluggish world trade. Finally, disinflation created turmoil in labor markets and trauma for workers in many troubled industries as excessive wage increases of the 1970s gave way to the hard realities of the 1980s.

In preserving and extending the gains against inflation, monetary policy faces some of the usual problems as well as a special one. As usual, when the fear of inflation subsides, political pressure builds to stimulate economic activity and reduce interest rates, especially urged in the mid-1980s as the solution for distressed industries and for the U.S. farm and Latin American overindebtedness, which is also endangering the solvency of many banks. In an unusual addition to these problems, monetary policy must operate through a financial system more volatile and less predictable than it used to be. The change in velocity behavior reflects innovations in financial instruments and technologies affecting the public's use of money. Unfortunately, the monetary laxity of the 1970s permitting high inflation increased incentives to find substitutes for non-interest-bearing money that now threaten the effectiveness of policies to stabilize its value.

The unpredicted decline in the growth of velocity since 1980, which absorbed a highly stimulative monetary policy and helped avert new inflationary pressures, nevertheless undermined reliance on monetary targeting. The decline in growth of velocity of M1 reflected a general decline in the velocities of all the monetary aggregates and nonfinancial debt. Part of the growth of financial assets in relation to GNP since 1980 can be attributed to a reversal of the shift to tangible wealth (real assets such as property and commodities) during the 1970s originally taken to protect against inflation. The reversal of this shift does not explain the decline in the growth of velocity, however. While the ratio of financial to tangible assets has returned approximately to its level of the early 1960s, the ratio of GNP to financial assets remains well below the mid-1960s norm.[21] This recent widely noted expansion of household and corporate debt may well reflect fundamental changes in financial behavior, but that it also relates to the public's willingness to hold more money in relation to GNP than formerly—and therefore helps to explain the decline in M1 velocity growth—is doubtful.

Although the preceding analysis of money demand equations finds that interest-rate effects can account for much of the recent behavior of M1 velocity, a reliable equation to predict ahead eludes estimation because of discrepancies that emerged in the second half of the 1970s. The discrepancies probably reflect a variety of financial developments, but no doubt mainly the growth of interest-bearing checking deposits that also serve as savings accounts. Weighting components of the money stock by turnover rates faces difficulties but may help, and only time will tell whether a new stable relation between money and the usual explanatory variables will develop.

Economic analysis can offer little guidance to the conduct of monetary policy so long as velocity behaves unpredictably. One response to this predicament is a spate of proposals to eliminate discretion in monetary policy altogether by various schemes that would operate automatically to preserve the value of money over the long run.[22] These proposals are far removed from the current conduct of monetary policy and have no influence on it.

In the present situation the long-run objective of stable prices and growth of output lacks short-run guides for its attainment. The authorities can watch the available arsenal of statistics, including monetary and financial aggregates, interest rates, and economic activity and prices, but none of these gives a reliable prediction of the path that a given monetary policy will produce two or three quarters ahead. The foreign exchange rate of the dollar, which has recently received new emphasis as a guide for monetary policy, is also an ambiguous indicator of inflationary pressures because of extraneous changes in the pattern of trade. Without reliable guides policy can keep inflation under control only by avoiding overstimulation of the economy, which means not pushing too close to peak levels of output and employment. Whether policy can maintain such a commitment to a noninflationary economy is far from ensured.

Notes

1. Discussed in Phillip Cagan, "Monetary Policy and Subduing Inflation," in William Fellner, ed., *Essays in Contemporary Economic Problems: Disinflation* (Washington, D.C.: American Enterprise Institute, 1984), esp. pp. 32–34.

2. That is, four-digit SIC manufacturing industries for which the sum of the ratios of exports to shipments and of imports to domestic supply equaled 25 percent or more, based on 1984 (and extrapolated 1983) data of the Department of Commerce and industry price indexes and average hourly earnings of the Bureau of Labor Statistics.

3. Different measures of the exchange rate all show a decline since early 1985 but by varying amounts. See chapter 1 by Jacob Dreyer in this volume.

4. See Catherine L. Mann, "Prices, Profit Margins, and Exchange Rates," *Federal Reserve Bulletin,* June 1986, 366–79. Another study finds a two-to-three-year lag in the export response of machinery and transport equipment (see Dennis M. Bushe, Irving B. Kravis, and Robert E. Lipsey, "Prices, Activity, and Machinery Exports: An Analysis Based on New Price Data," *The Review of Economics and Statistics* 68 (May 1986), pp. 248–55). For a review of other studies, see Charles Pigott and Vincent Reinhart, "The Strong Dollar and U.S. Inflation," Federal Reserve Bank of New York, *Quarterly Review* 10, no. 3 (Autumn 1985), pp. 23–29.

5. A credibility effect can be defined as a change in the expected rate of inflation that is not predicted by preceding price behavior but that influences future price changes. On the timing and magnitude of the credibility effect in 1980–1983, see Phillip Cagan, "Continuing Inflation" in Phillip Cagan, ed., *Contemporary Economic Problems: The Impact of the Reagan Program* (Washington, D.C.: American Enterprise Institute, 1986), esp. pp. 259–71.

6. Stephen M. Goldfeld, "The Case of the Missing Money," *Brookings Papers on Economic Activity* no. 3, 1976, pp. 683–730; and Gillian Garcia and Simon Pak, "Some Clues in the Case of the Missing Money," *American Economic Review* 69 (May 1979), pp. 330–34.

7. Thomas D. Simpson, "The Redefined Monetary Aggregates," *Federal Reserve Bulletin,* February 1980, pp. 97–114.

8. $\log (M1/P) = .82 + .14 \log(\text{real sales}) - .05 \log(\text{deposit interest rate})$
      (2.8)   (4.0)   (2.6)
$- .02 \log (\text{commercial paper rate}) + .71 \log (M1/P)_{-1}$
(4.1)   (8.4)

fitted quarterly for the first quarter of 1955 to the second quarter of 1974 by the Cochrane-Orcutt method ($rho = .34$ with t of 2.5), which allows for serial correlation of residuals. The standard error of the regression is 0.49 percent and the Durbin-Watson statistic is 1.95. Absolute values of t statistics are shown in parentheses.

The regression is representative of the standard equation estimated for this period. See note 10 for references. The lagged dependent variable on the right-hand side allows for partial adjustment of the actual to the desired money balances. P is the GNP deflator. Real sales are described in note 9. The deposit interest rate is constructed from data supplied by the Federal Reserve in Washington and is a weighted average of rates paid on small time and savings deposits, money market mutual funds, and (beginning with the fourth quarter of 1982 for simulations) money market deposit accounts. (For descriptions of these rates, see Helen T. Farr and Deborah Johnson, "Revisions in the Monetary Services (Divisia) Indexes of the Monetary Aggregates," Federal Reserve Staff Study, December 1985, pp. 7–16.) The commercial paper rate is for four-to-six-month paper before 1983 and four-month paper after.

9. Real final (domestic) sales are GNP excluding net exports and changes in business inventories, and deflated. Sales are superior to GNP as a proxy for total final transactions but not for national income. It is unclear whether the more appropriate explanatory variable for money holdings is income or transactions.

Perhaps both are appropriate, but multicollinearity precludes their joint inclusion. The domestic sales variable produces less decline in velocity than GNP does in recent years, when net exports had an unusually large decline, and is used here for that reason.

10. See Goldfeld, "The Case of the Missing Money"; John P. Judd and John L. Scadding, "The Search for a Stable Money Demand Function: A Survey of the Post 1973 Literature," *Journal of Economic Literature* 20 (September 1982), pp. 993–1023; and Cagan, "Monetary Policy and Subduing Inflation," esp. pp. 36–44.

11. Based on the money demand regression in note 8, the trend of velocity could in the future depend only on growth in aggregate expenditures should interest rates remain constant. The long-run elasticity of money demand with respect to aggregate expenditures is 48 percent, given by the regression coefficient divided by the complement of the coefficient for the lagged dependent variable, that is, $.14/(1 - .71)$. The long-run growth rate of velocity is therefore the change in log (real sales) $-$ log $(M1/P)$, which is $(1 - .48) = 52$ percent of growth in real sales. With economic growth of 3 percent, the trend would be 1½ percent per year, much below the previous growth trend.

12. Annual estimates interpolated quarterly from "A Proposal for Redefining the Monetary Aggregates," *Federal Reserve Bulletin*, January 1979, pp. 13–42, table 2.

13. From John A. Tatom, "Recent Financial Innovations: Have They Distorted the Meaning of M1?" *Federal Reserve Bank of St. Louis Review* 64 (April 1982), pp. 23–35, table 1.

14. If we make the unconfirmed assumption that the interest elasticity of the regression in note 8 applies as well to the new interest-bearing checking accounts, we can estimate the increase in demand for these accounts. From the fourth quarter of 1980 to the first quarter of 1986 the deposit rate fell from 10.5 to 7.3 percent. For NOW accounts introduced in 1981 and paying 5¼ percent in 1986, the rate differential fell from 10.5 percent to 2.0 percent. The long-run interest elasticity of .17, which is estimated by $.05/(1 - .71)$, when multiplied by the interest rate differential of $(\log_e 10.5 - \log_e 2.0)$, is 28 percent. This implies an increase in demand for money balances by households, which held $264 billion at the end of 1980, of $74 billion. From the end of 1980 to the first quarter of 1986, the GNP deflator rose 32 percent, and the effect of growth in real sales of 16½ percent added

$(.165 \times \dfrac{.14}{1 - .71} =)$ 8 percent. Hence, the increase in demand for real money

balances as of 1986 was $74 billion times 1.32 times 1.08 or $105 billion. The actual increase in other checking deposits was $156 billion.

This therefore implies that almost three-fourths of the actual increase in OCDs is explained by the regression. The remainder presumably reflects unexplained shifts from demand and savings deposits to OCDs, which we cannot identify. (On the effect of minimum balance requirements see note 16.)

15. A weighted average of rates paid on ATS, NOW, and super-NOW accounts and on RPs and EDs when these intruments are included (and zero rate for currency and demand deposits), calculated from data compiled by the Federal Reserve in Washington.

16. Minimum balance requirements have changed to affect money demand. NOW accounts had required minimums prescribed by regulations until eliminated in 1986. For this reason and also because of their attraction as savings, the average size of interest-bearing accounts in 1984 was $6,000 and excluding super-NOWs almost $5,000 in a survey of commercial banks outside New England, compared

151

with $2,000–3,000 for regular demand deposits as reported by the Functional Cost Analysis survey of the Federal Reserve.

These differences, though significant, are not sufficient to explain the prediction errors in the top panel of figure 4.

17. Richard D. Porter, Thomas D. Simpson, and Eileen Mauskopf, "Financial Innovation and the Monetary Aggregates," *Brookings Papers on Economic Activity* no. 1, 1979, pp. 213–29.

18. See, for example, John D. Paulus, "Monetarism: If It Ain't Broke Don't Fix It," *Economic Perspectives*, Morgan Stanley, New York City, May 7, 1986.

Similarly, the use of M2 in the regression simulations avoids part of the discrepancy of the 1970s but does not improve the predictions of the 1980s and generally fits the data with larger residual errors. Also, M2 is theoretically unappealing as a monetary aggregate because its dividing line with M3 is arbitrary and hard to distinguish.

19. Paul A. Spindt, "Money Is What Money Does: Monetary Aggregation and the Equation of Exchange," *Journal of Political Economy* 93 (February 1985), pp. 175–204; and David E. Lindsey and Paul A. Spindt, "An Evaluation of Monetary Indexes," Board of Governors of the Federal Reserve System Special Studies Paper 195, March 1986.

20. For a reconsideration of the output costs of disinflation, see Cagan, "Containing Inflation," esp. pp. 254–58.

21. In the following table financial assets held by private nonfinancial sectors fell relative to total tangible (physical) assets in the 1970s but recovered by 1985 to the relative level of the 1960s. At the same time the GNP velocities of financial as well as tangible assets declined.

Ratios	1965	1970	1975	1980	1985
Financial to tangible assets	.38	.36	.32	.28	.36
GNP to:					
Financial assets	1.12	1.15	1.12	1.16	0.99
Tangible assets	0.42	0.41	0.36	0.32	0.36

NOTE: Total private domestic tangible assets at replacement cost exclude consumer durables. Financial assets comprise holdings of deposits and credit market instruments of households, farms, and nonfarm noncorporate businesses, and liquid assets of nonfinancial corporations. End of year data for assets and calendar year data for dollar GNP.

SOURCE: Board of Governors of the Federal Reserve System, *Balance Sheets for the U.S. Economy 1945–85*, April 1986.

22. For a review see Milton Friedman and Anna J. Schwartz, "Has Goverment Any Role in Money?" *Journal of Monetary Economics* 17 (January 1986), pp. 37–62.

5

The Ups and Downs of Oil

Hendrik S. Houthakker

Summary

The sharp fall in oil prices during late 1985 an early 1986 came as a surprise only to those who believed that oil, as a supposedly essential commodity, is somehow exempt from the laws of supply and demand. Actually, fluctuations in oil prices can be explained by market forces, both within and without the industry. In the 1950s and 1960s the world price had a declining trend resulting from massive discoveries in many parts of the world. When demand, stimulated by a worldwide boom, caught up with supply, the trend was reversed. In the early 1970s the inflationary pressures released by the breakdown of the Bretton Woods system of fixed exchange rates in due course had their impact on the world oil market. The United States, whose oil reserves had been prematurely exhausted by the import quota system, became dependent on the Persian Gulf countries, already the main suppliers of Europe and Japan.

The leading oil exporters had already organized themselves into a potential cartel, and in late 1973 OPEC seized the opportunity provided by the Arab-Israeli war to impose its price. Acting with due regard to long-run prospects, OPEC was able to maintain its price in real terms until the fall of the shah of Iran. Saudi Arabia, the cartel's leader, could have offset the ensuing loss of production but chose not to do so for apparently political reasons. OPEC abandoned its prudent long-term strategy, focusing instead on short-term profits. High oil prices strengthened production and weakened consumption outside the cartel, thus causing OPEC to lose control of the world market; its market share fell from over 50 percent in 1973 to 30 percent in 1985. In 1986 the world price dropped below $10 per barrel, although it has recovered somewhat since then.

The cartel is now trying to reassert its power to fix the world price and will probably succeed in doing so once the current excess of inventories has been worked off. OPEC, however, is not likely to return to the go-for-broke tactics that led to its recent downfall. The cartel's steady performance of the 1970s offers a better example.

The importing countries now have an opportunity to reconsider their oil policies. The experience of the past thirteen years should have taught them to

153

rely primarily on market forces. Competition, in fact, has become much more effective in the oil market in recent years. The introduction of futures trading in crude and refined products has been an especially valuable development.

In the United States the most urgent task for national security is to establish adequate spare capacity in the domestic industry to reduce our vulnerability to economic and political pressures. In view of our rather limited prospects for new discoveries, this goal is more desirable than keeping up domestic output. A variable tariff, designed to guarantee a minimum price for domestic producers without imposing undue burdens on consumers, appears to hold the most promise. Although a fixed tariff could be used to capture some of OPEC's monopoly profits, it would further worsen the allocation of resources, which has already been seriously impaired by the cartel.

Only a few years ago the words "energy crisis" were heard every day. Most people believed that the days of cheap oil were gone forever, while the president of the United States described the efforts allegedly needed to secure our energy as the "moral equivalent of war." Now the same media that spread this hysteria are full of sad stories about the plight of producers at home and abroad who can no longer sell their oil at the prices to which they had become accustomed. After reaching a high of some $35 per barrel at the beginning of the 1980s, the world price of crude[1] plunged to around $7 in the early summer of 1986; it has recovered to around $16 more recently.[2] In real terms the current price is less than one-half its level of five years earlier, although it is still more than twice what it was fifteen years ago.

How did these drastic changes come about? Was the recent downturn just a fluke, soon to be reversed by the increasing tightness of supplies so widely forecast until recently? Alternatively, was the experience from 1973 to 1981 merely a bubble that was finally deflated by overwhelming market forces? And what, under either explanation, are the consequences for the U.S. and the world economy? To what extent can these consequences be influenced by policy? These are the main questions to be addressed in this essay.

Historical Background

A thumbnail history of the world oil market may be helpful in understanding recent developments. Until the end of World War II a handful of countries accounted for nearly all the world's output. The largest among these was the United States, which remained a net exporter until the 1950s. The quarter of a century after 1945 was a period of massive discoveries in many parts of the world, notably the Arab countries on the Persian Gulf, several countries in Africa, the

North Sea, Alaska, and certain new oil provinces in the Soviet Union.

As a result, the trend in world oil prices was downward in real terms, with four important consequences.

• Consumption, which has a low price elasticity in the short run but a much larger one in the long run, grew rapidly, with considerable substitution of oil for coal.

• In the late 1950s the United States adopted import quotas to protect its domestic industry and to reduce its vulnerability to politically inspired interruptions in imports. Combined with the already existing system of market demand prorationing, the quotas served to keep the crude price in the United States above its equivalent in the world market.

• With a view to safeguarding their royalties, a number of third world oil producers set up the Organization of Petroleum Exporting Countries (OPEC) in 1960. Together these countries accounted for more than half of global output by the early 1970s.

• Finally, the major oil companies (particularly the group then known as the "seven sisters") lost their dominance over the market outside the United States. The main reasons for this development were expropriations by host countries, large discoveries by companies outside the group, and adverse antitrust actions. In the Teheran agreement of 1971 the majors in effect recognized the power of OPEC to determine crude prices.

In early 1973 the United States abandoned the quota system, which had become an impediment when domestic consumption rose steadily at the same time that domestic output declined from the peak of 10 million barrels per day (Mb/d) reached in 1970. One of the assumptions underlying quotas had been that the permitted imports would come from nearby sources such as Canada and Venezuela. When the gap between consumption and domestic output widened sharply, it became necessary to draw on more distant sources, including the countries in the Persian Gulf. Until then these countries had sold most of their oil to Europe and Japan. When the United States also became a buyer, the market power of the Persian Gulf nations increased considerably.

The macroeconomic background of the first oil shock is also important. The 1960s had been a period of unprecedented growth in the world economy. Since in the long run oil consumption, aside from the effect of price changes, tends to be proportional to income, this growth had a powerful effect on the world oil market. By the end of the decade, inflation, especially in the United States, started to accelerate, and one of its first victims was the Bretton Woods system of fixed exchange rates. Not only did the dollar, in terms of which world oil prices are expressed, begin to depreciate, but the initial efforts by various countries to keep their currencies from appreciating greatly also increased world liquidity. This (and not, as is often believed, the first oil shock itself) was the origin of the Great Inflation of the 1970s. The inflationary pressures first became manifest in commodities other than oil, such as grains and sugar. The principal reason why these pressures did not show up more quickly in petroleum prices appears to have been the weakness of competition in the oil market, in which there was as yet no futures trading and relatively little spot trading by independent dealers. Nevertheless the inflationary influence was ready to assert itself.

The First Oil Shock and Its Effects

Such was the situation in the early 1970s that made the first oil shock possible. The immediate occasion for that unexpected event was political, namely an embargo proclaimed by the Arab producers against the United States and Holland because of their alleged support for Israel in the 1973 war. The embargo accomplished nothing in the political sphere, but its economic effects were spectacular. The spot market in petroleum came to life, with some cargoes trading as high as $17 per barrel compared with the prevailing "official" price of about $2.50. This appears to have convinced OPEC that a concerted curtailment of oil supplies could be extremely profitable. At the end of 1973 the members agreed not to export crude at less than the equivalent of $10 per barrel. No formal output quotas were set; instead, frequent consultations among the members were to prevent excess supplies from undermining the cartel price (see figure 5–1).

Whatever their feelings about the new price may have been, the major oil companies were no longer in a position to influence it. The consuming countries were equally powerless. Most of them permitted the higher price of crude to be reflected in product prices. The United States, however, maintained price controls, which had the unfortunate effect of delaying and limiting the necessary adjustments in domestic consumption and production. In the years immediately following the first oil shock American petroleum output continued to decline, consumption remained high, and imports soared. Although there was much talk about conservation and alternative energy sources, the price increases that would have led most rapidly to these goals were not permitted.

OPEC, meanwhile, managed to keep the cartel price more or less constant in inflation-adjusted dollars. This apparent stability masked

FIGURE 5–1
WORLD OIL PRODUCTION, 1973–1985

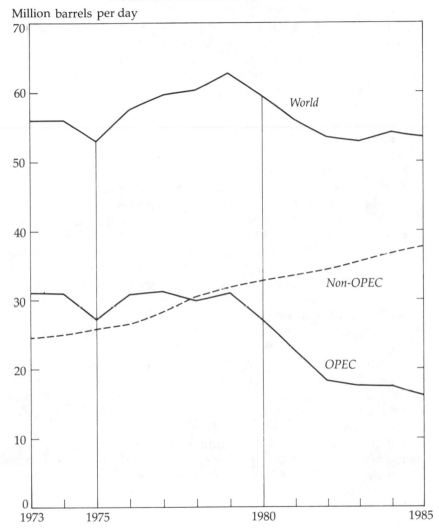

Million barrels per day

SOURCE: U.S. Energy Information Administration, *International Petroleum Statistics Report*, July 25, 1986.

a growing discord among the members over the appropriate pricing policy. Saudi Arabia with its enormous reserves and small population is naturally concerned about the long-run danger of pricing oil out of the energy markets. It has usually been supported in this postion by its neighbors, Kuwait and the United Arab Emirates. The other members of OPEC have generally taken a much shorter view.

In the middle 1970s the market could probably have borne an even higher price than OPEC had set, but Saudi Arabia prevented this by expanding its output. At one point it temporarily surpassed the United States by producing more than 10 million barrels per day. It had, in effect, become the swing producer within OPEC, adjusting its output to maintain the cartel price. The risk inherent in this role was that it would weaken the commitment of other members to the cartel's goals. These other members came to believe that they could produce as much as they liked since the Saudis would adjust their output as needed. When this risk became a reality in 1977, Saudi Arabia was driven to use the ultimate weapon of any cartel leader: it set its own export price below the cartel price. The resulting two-price pattern lasted only until the second oil shock, which (for reasons discussed below) Saudi Arabia could not or would not prevent.

The value of oil in international trade is by far the largest of any commodity. The sharp and sudden price increase therefore had significant macroeconomic effects, though in retrospect they appear less serious than was thought at the time. The combined current account surplus of the OPEC countries increased from $4 billion in 1973 to $65 billion in 1974, and the current account of the oil-importing nations deteriorated correspondingly.[3] The OPEC surplus resulted from the members' inability to increase their imports in line with their exports at short notice and was therefore essentially transitional. Moreover, this surplus remained in the international banking system, where it was available to finance the oil importers' deficits. The contemporary worries about "recycling the petrodollars" were therefore largely misplaced. As a matter of policy the cartel members did not sell crude on credit, but the net effect was much the same as if they had done so.[4]

Rightly or wrongly, however, many importing countries reacted to their external deficits (and to the continuing inflation) by restrictive domestic policies. It may well be argued that after the strong growth of the preceding period a worldwide slowdown was inevitable, but these policies helped aggravate the slowdown into a severe recession during the middle 1970s. The recession had no permanent effect on inflation, which resumed its acceleration soon afterwards.

As far as the oil market was concerned, the recession was useful in reducing the demand. The supply situation in the non-OPEC world also showed the first signs of improvement. Overriding the objections of environmentalists, the U.S. Congress acted to ensure construction of the Alaska pipeline. Its completion in 1977 helped reverse the downward trend in domestic supply. The first oil from the North Sea was produced in 1975, and that area gradually became a sufficiently large source of crude to turn Britain and Norway into net exporters. The Soviet Union and Mexico also brought their large discoveries into production. In many parts of the world—the OPEC countries were a significant exception—exploration moved into high gear.

The Second Oil Shock

Given enough time the developments just described would conceivably have forced the cartel to lower its price. Before this could happen, however, another political event provided unexpected support to those who believed the price was bound to rise indefinitely.[5] The overthrow of the shah of Iran in 1979 had a drastic effect on the cartel's second largest producer; output was reduced from 5.2 Mb/d in 1978 to 1.7 Mb/d in 1980 and even less in 1981. The religious fundamentalists who assumed power abhorred the modernization plans pursued by the shah and saw no need for the oil revenue with which those plans were to be financed. Saudi Arabia soon abandoned the attempt to make up the resulting shortfall in supply, a major change in policy to be discussed further. All OPEC members ultimately agreed on a new price of about $33 per barrel, in line with the spot market at that time.[6]

Further alarm was caused by the outbreak of war between Iran and Iraq, which had replaced Iran as number two in the OPEC hierarchy. Both countries attacked each other's oilfields and export facilities. Since Iran had already curtailed its production, the effect there was minor, but Iraq's output fell from 2.5 Mb/d in 1979 to 1.0 Mb/d in 1981. Although not participating directly, other countries in the Persian Gulf (including Saudi Arabia) became involved in this war by their support for Iraq, thus creating a potentially explosive situation. It did not take much imagination to paint the world oil outlook in dark colors.

Yet it is clear in retrospect that the market was not as vulnerable as it seemed. To be sure, an extension of the Iran-Iraq hostilities to the Western Gulf would have had dire consequences; the industrial nations might have been forced to safeguard the oilfields in that area by military intervention. Fortunately the war did not spread, perhaps because of a reinforced naval presence by the United States and some of its allies or because Iran had enough trouble dealing with its much smaller neighbor. There was some interference with shipping in the Persian Gulf, but by and large the oil kept flowing. In fact Iran had to increase its oil exports to pay for the war, and Iraq found ways of resuming some of its exports.

Indeed it is indicative of the underlying weakness in the world market that the eruption of the Iran-Iraq war did not lead to a third oil shock. The nominal price remained very high in the early 1980s, but it did not keep up with inflation.[7] In addition there was a partly speculative increase in worldwide inventories, whose liquidation had a dampening effect in subsequent years.

The market's weakness was most evident in the prices of refined products, which are of central importance because crude oil has few uses until it is refined.[8] In the past few years much OPEC crude has been sold on a "netback" basis, according to which the crude price is calculated from the value of the refined products less transportation and refining costs. This practice has tended to make the cartel price for crude less relevant.

OPEC Loses Control

In 1973, the year preceding the first oil shock, OPEC accounted for nearly 56 percent of world crude output.[9] As usual when a cartel is established, its market share dropped, mostly because of a continuing rise in non-OPEC production. The cartel's was still close to one-half when the second oil shock occurred; subsequently it fell steadily to 30 percent in 1985. Moreover, domestic consumption in the member countries has risen, contrary to what happened elsewhere; it doubled between 1975 and 1985. More than 20 percent of OPEC's oil production is now consumed internally, further reducing the cartel's leverage.

In light of these figures it is not surprising that OPEC has lost control over the world market. If a group of suppliers has 56 percent of the market, they can impose a cartel price relatively easily; to do so with less than 30 percent is quite another matter. The question of OPEC policy is so essential to our topic that a brief digression into the relevant microeconomics may be in order.

As pointed out earlier, the demand for oil and other forms of energy is much more price sensitive in the long run than in the short run. The main reason is that oil products can be used only in durable equipment, such as cars and furnaces. The design of the equipment in existence at any time is the main determinant of energy consumption, though use can also be varied to some extent. In an adjustment of energy consumption to a significant change in prices, it is usually optimal to replace the equipment, and that takes time. The short-run effect consists largely of changes in utilization; the long-run effect also reflects changes in equipment.

Much the same is true on the supply side. Oil production from existing fields can be adjusted within limits, but a sustained increase in production calls for exploration and development of new fields, a process that normally extends over several years. In the case of a falling price it may also take a long time before some of the existing wells are abandoned because it no longer pays to maintain them.

The distinction between the short run and the long run is depicted in figure 5–2, where aa' represents the short-run world demand for a commodity and AA' the long-run demand, with aa' steeper than AA'.[10] The suppliers are divided in two parts: a group of producers who have agreed to form a cartel, and all others who will be referred to as the "outside suppliers." The supply curves (bb' for the short run and BB' for the long run) refer only to the outside suppliers; a cartel has no supply curve in the ordinary sense.

The figure represents a competitive equilibrium prior to the actual

FIGURE 5–2
PRICE FIXING BY A CARTEL

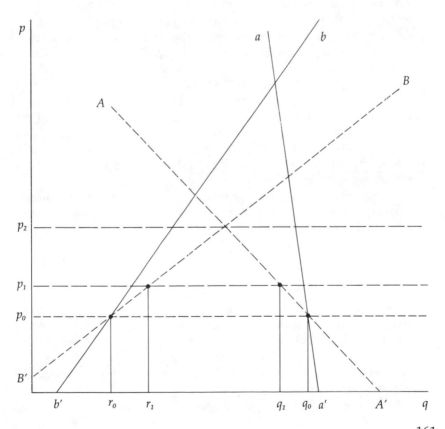

161

implementation of the cartel. Accordingly, the long-run and the short-run supply curves intersect at the precartel price p_0, as do the two demand curves. The quantity sold is q_0, of which r_0 is accounted for by the outside suppliers and s_0 $(= q_0 - r_0)$ by the would-be cartel. To create some resemblance to the oil market at the end of 1973, s_0 is drawn to be larger than r_0.

The question for the cartel is now where to set its price, which in the circumstances will become the market price. Let this price be called p_1, and the corresponding quantities sold q_1 for the total and r_1 and s_1 for the two components. The cartel will presumably set p_1 to maximize its revenue p_1s_1. The location of the maximizing p_1, however, depends on whether the cartel looks at the short run or the long run. It would not be rational to look only at the short run, since this would require frequent reductions of the cartel price as the long run catches up. Cartels generally aim for steady prices in real terms, and OPEC (at least until the second oil shock) was no exception.

Disregarding the cost of production (which is small for most OPEC producers), it may be assumed, therefore, that the cartel will seek to maximize its long-run revenue. In the example this is accomplished by setting p_1 halfway between the horizontal axis (where the price is zero) and p_2, the price at which the entire demand is satisfied by outside suppliers.[11]

There is reason to believe that the leaders of OPEC knew the importance of the long run when they set a price of $10 per barrel at the end of 1973. They could have gone higher, but realized that this would be inconsistent with cartel stability. In fact this price was maintained in real terms until the second oil shock; whether it could have been maintained if the United States had followed less short-sighted energy policies is another matter.

Why then did OPEC change its pricing policy after the revolution in Iran and the start of the war between Iran and Iraq? From a strictly economic point of view the previous strategy with its implicit emphasis on the long run could have been continued because Saudi Arabia and its allies had enough spare capacity to make up for the lower output of the belligerents. The most plausible explanation for the policy change is that the Saudis did not want to antagonize the new regime in Iran, whose influence in other Moslem countries represented a serious threat to the monarchy. In dollar terms Iran received about as much for its sharply reduced production after the second oil shock as it had received before the overthrow of the shah; it would have been a hostile act for the Saudis to upset this agreeable outcome by flooding the market.

Nevertheless OPEC's new policy of charging what the traffic

would bear in the short run carried the seed of its own destruction. The cartel had lost control; it was following the market instead of leading it. Competition finally asserted itself. With its share of the world supply dropping steadily, OPEC was powerless to prevent a gradual decline of the market price that became precipitous in the winter of 1985–1986 and continued into the following summer.

To many observers, and certainly to the public at large, the sharp fall in oil prices was as surprising as the sharp increases of the preceding decade had been. It should be stressed that the recent turbulence in the world oil market cannot be attributed to the much-publicized dissension within OPEC. No doubt the tactics used by Saudi Arabia to get the attention of its fellow members—specifically the increase in its output during the first half of 1986—aggravated the price slump. OPEC's basic problem, however, is not so much internal disagreement as rising outside production and shrinking outside consumption. From reports of recent cartel meetings it appears that most members are well aware of this reality. The price targets that were recently agreed upon are relatively modest. It these targets could be attained, which is by no means certain, the group would in effect be returning to the pricing policy that served it so well from 1974 to 1979.

The cartel has learned two other lessons. One is that the informal supply management of the 1970s, with Saudi Arabia acting as the swing producer, is no longer feasible. Under this mode of operation the kingdom would at times be forced to stop producing altogether, so that it might as well leave OPEC. Although formal production quotas were adopted some years ago, many members chose to ignore them. A binding agreement on more realistic quotas and on stricter enforcement was high on OPEC's agenda; if it had been postponed much longer, the continued existence of the cartel would be in serious doubt.

The other lesson is that OPEC must come to an understanding with at least some of the major outside producers. The admission of additional members would make the setting of output quotas even more difficult, but the group has had some success in getting informal cooperation. Countries such as Mexico, Egypt, and Norway have promised not to undercut OPEC's efforts to reassert its control of the world market. Even the U.S.S.R. has made a token gesture in this direction, but Britain has stuck to its procompetitive policy and the United States has stood aside.[12] In any case a sizable part of the increase in non-OPEC production has come from countries (including the United States) that remain net importers; OPEC can hardly expect to enlist their support.

The Cost and Supply of Oil

To obtain a better perspective on the future of oil prices, let us return for a moment to the theoretical analysis. The two supply curves shown in figure 2 for the outside producers assume competitive behavior on their part, which means that they take the market price as given. The outside supply is therefore determined by the cost of production, which is different in the short run and in the long run.

In the short run (that is, for the already existing oilfields) the marginal cost will typically be close to zero. The oil is normally under pressure and will come to the surface unless it is deliberately shut in. Stripper wells, in which the pressure has declined to the point where the oil must be pumped from the reservoir, are an exception to this statement.[13] A more important exception is provided by fields under secondary recovery, of which there are many in the United States. One analyst puts the average operating cost (which may not be conceptually equal to the short-run marginal cost) for 1984 at $3.87 per barrel in the United States, at $2.12 in the offshore United Kingdom, and at well below $1 in Saudi Arabia.[14]

Even at a very low price the cash flow from the well will be positive, and the operator may well decide to keep it running. Shutting it in may be justified, however, if the operator expects to receive a higher price (properly discounted) in the future. Although the short-run marginal cost is normally zero, this "user cost"[15] is in theory an important determinant of mineral supply. Its practical importance is less clear. In the United States, output in late 1986 was only 1 percent below that of a year earlier, despite a price fall of more than 50 percent. While this small price response is consistent with a short-run marginal cost close to zero, it suggests either that operators paid little attention to user cost—a concept that assumes definite views on future prices—or that they did not expect prices to recover to previous levels.

The effect of a price fall is more pronounced in the longer run because the maintenance and other investments necessary for optimal recovery of the oil in a reservoir will not be justified. When prices are low, therefore, production will decline at a higher rate. The cost of preventing an unduly steep decline of output is part of the long-run marginal cost. Even with optimal maintenance and the adoption of secondary and tertiary recovery, the production from an oilfield will approach zero ultimately, although this may take a very long time.

Exploration serves to replenish and expand the stock of minerals available for extraction. It is often believed that the cost of finding new oilfields is constantly rising, but that is not obvious. The uncertain success of exploration makes it difficult to generalize about the cost of finding oil. Advances in geology and in the technology of extracting oil in difficult environments, such as the deep sea and the Arctic, have played an important role. Some of the largest fields in the world (the Ghawar field in Saudi Arabia is a prime example) were found with minimal effort. On the other side, the vast sums spent on finding oil in the Atlantic off the United States and in the Beaufort Sea have not established any producing fields so far. Moreover, the result of successful exploration cannot be assessed until the necessary development, involving the drilling of additional wells, has been performed. As a rule development is much more expensive than exploration.

The usual measure of success in exploration and development is barrels proved per foot drilled. The cost per foot depends, among other things, on the current activity in exploration and development; drilling rigs, for instance, command much higher rentals when activity is high. Once the cost per foot is known, the cost of finding a barrel of oil in the ground can be found by capitalization as a function of the current interest rate. With this approach the development cost per barrel has been estimated as $9.04 in 1984 in the United States, as $4.43 in the British part of the North Sea, as below $.50 in the Persian Gulf countries, and as $1.81 in Nigeria.[16]

The finiteness of the earth places an upper limit on the global supply of oil, regardless of price. There is little reason to believe, however, that this limit constitutes an effective constraint on exploration in the foreseeable future. In recent decades oil has been found in many areas previously considered nonprospective. In some of these areas the cost of extraction is high, but in others—like southeastern Mexico—it is very low. The principal constraint on exploration since the first oil shock has been OPEC, which has not wanted to undermine its market power by new discoveries in the member countries. Saudi Arabia already has the world's largest proved reserves, but much more could probably be found if the kingdom permitted it. In 1983 Kuwait fortuitously discovered a large oilfield when attempting to augment its domestic gas supply.

Since the United States has been more thoroughly explored than any other country, the prospects are necessarily more limited. At present the largest undeveloped resource is the West Sac deposit in northern Alaska, where oil in place exceeds even Prudhoe Bay. It appears, however, that serious technical problems have to be solved before this deposit can be taken into production, and if it is, additional pipeline capacity may have to be built. At current prices this may not be profitable, but it demonstrates that the United States cannot be written off entirely as a source of future supply. While the level of exploration is very low at present, some recovery is likely when the outlook for prices becomes clearer.

In the unlikely event that conventional crude oil ever runs out, there are still enormous supplies of closely related materials to draw on. These include the Athabasca tar sands in Canada, the Orinoco heavy oils in Venezuela, and the oil shales of the Rocky Mountain area in the United States. Since these are not liquids, they cannot be extracted by drilling wells, but they yield essentially the same refined products as ordinary crude. The Canadian tar sands have been produced for several years; in oil shale a pilot operation in Colorado has been running with government subsidy. Venezuela, a member of OPEC, has been reluctant to open its Pandora's box. Materials of this kind also occur in the Soviet Union and elsewhere.

Most of these oil-bearing solids are high-cost resources and would become reserves only if crude prices rose well above the peak reached a few years ago; some of them are also troublesome from an environmental point of view. Nevertheless their existence in vast quantities, exceeding all known or suspected oil liquids, in effect puts a ceiling on crude prices in the long run. The world price of oil may well reach new highs in the coming decades, but it will not rise without limit.

Competition and Futures Trading

When, for reasons listed earlier, the major companies lost their market power in the 1960s, the alternative entities needed for effective competition were not yet in place. There were only a few independent oil traders and no futures market. After the initial impetus of the 1973 embargo, a competitive spot market in crude and products developed gradually. It is often known as the Rotterdam spot market because of the eminence of that city in transportation and refining; actually it covers much of Europe as well as North America and Southeast Asia, most of the trading being conducted by telex. This market filled the gap created when OPEC assumed control over crude prices without having much involvement in refining and marketing.

The progressive decline of OPEC after the second oil shock made the spot market even more prominent. By the early 1980s oil had become a commodity like copper or soybeans, and like other commodities it provided opportunities for that ultimate embodiment of competition, the futures market. In markets where a few firms are dominant, futures trading is not viable since it requires open entry and public participation. The main economic function of futures trading is in the management of inventories, where it permits price risks to be assumed by those willing to do so in hopes of speculative gain. It thus enables inventory-holding merchants to focus on what they do best, namely merchandizing.

It is no accident that futures trading first emerged in heating oil, a product used mostly for space heating in the northeastern United States. Since in the short run consumption depends primarily on winter temperatures in that area, it is quite risky to hold stocks. The heating oil futures market makes it possible to transfer the risk to those brave enough to take a view on winter weather and other determinants of heating oil prices. After this market proved to be fairly successful, the New York Mercantile Exchange was encouraged to start futures trading in crude oil.

At first crude prices were still under OPEC control and not variable enough to put the new market to the test, but in late 1985 it became clear that the cartel had fumbled and that the price of crude was increasingly governed by market forces. The volume of trading and the open interest[17] expanded rapidly to make crude futures a rival to such long-established markets as those for grains. Initially the futures had for the most part followed the spot market; gradually the price came to be effectively determined by futures trading, as is the case in other commodities. There is also a futures market in gasoline now, and in London futures contracts in gas oil (similar to heating oil) are actively traded.

Entry into a futures market is easy; all one has to do is to find a broker and make a modest security deposit known as margin. Futures trading serves to enlarge the number of individuals whose expectations determine prices. This is socially useful when the price prospects in a market are very uncertain, as is now the case in petroleum. It may seem that outsiders are necessarily less knowledgeable than insiders, but that is only true in the short run. An analysis of pronouncements by oil industry leaders over the past fifteen years would probably show that they were no better at predicting prices two or three years ahead than were people outside the industry. Since spot and futures prices tend to be highly correlated, the expectations expressed in futures prices also affect the spot price. Hedging (that is, arbitrage between the cash and futures markets) helps determine the size of inventories: the higher futures prices are in relation to the spot price, the more profitable it is to hold stocks.

The establishment of futures trading in crude and in products reflected the trend toward competition and has in turn reinforced that trend. This does not mean that the market is now fully competitive. OPEC is still very much alive, and much of the speculation in futures involves guessing what OPEC will do. Moreover, participation in futures trading is still incomplete. As far as is known, OPEC members do not trade in futures, and the major oil companies also appear to be standing aside.[18] Nevertheless the futures markets are now large enough to facilitate the holding of large commercial inventories, and these inventories in turn circumscribe OPEC's power to raise prices.

While futures trading tends to improve the short-run performance of a commodity market, it does not provide much help in long-term investments, such as those necessary to open a new oilfield. This is so because the trading is concentrated in nearby contracts (those calling for delivery within the next few months). In fact, crude futures contracts for delivery more than about nine months ahead are not traded at all. In due course, the crude futures market will possibly expand enough to permit trading in more distant contracts, which would make it more attractive to producers.[19]

In November 1986 the New York Mercantile Exchange started trading in options on crude futures contracts. These differ from the futures themselves in that the owner of an option is not obliged to exercise it, whereas the parties to a futures contract must either take or make delivery of the underlying commodity when the contract expires. The buyer of an option, therefore, has no more at risk than the amount for which the option was originally purchased, while his or her potential profit is theoretically unlimited. The introduction of options is likely to increase public participation, thus making the futures market still more representative of current expectations.

The Outlook

The main conclusion from the preceding analysis is that, barring major political upheavals and ignoring short-term irregularities, the world price of oil is not likely to go much above $20 per barrel in the next few years (through 1990, for example). Indeed, OPEC may need patience in raising the price to its present target of about $18 from the level of around $12 in the fall of 1986. The large inventories still overhanging the market will have to be reduced before a significant price increase can be made to stick.

The underlying price trend during the remainder of this decade, however, is likely to be upward as long as OPEC holds together. Non-OPEC production from existing fields will probably decline, since some of the investments necessary to maintain the present rate of output will not be justified at current prices. Some discoveries already made will not be taken into production, and the slowdown in exploration will reduce the number of new discoveries. These effects will be especially marked in the United States, where oil production may decline by about 25 percent, or more than 2 Mb/d, between 1986 and 1990.

Consumption, in contrast, is likely to turn around in the next few years as the depressing effect of earlier high prices gradually disappears. These past prices still have a depressant effect on demand because of adjustment lags. In the United States, for instance, automobiles have become much more fuel efficient, partly as a result of government regulation. In fact, cars purchased now consume only about half the gasoline per mile as the old cars they replace. Similarly, the substitution of natural gas for oil products in space heating will not soon be reversed. In electricity generation oil is continuing to lose ground to nuclear power, especially outside the United States. Even more important, world GNP is growing at a modest but sustainable rate, and that also stimulates oil demand.

The anticipated changes in production and consumption will lead to an increase in oil imports in the industrial countries and in many developed countries. Toward the end of the decade U.S. oil imports, including refined products, may rise from the current rate of about 6 Mb/d to exceed the peak rate of 10 Mb/d reached briefly in the middle 1970s. Less than half our consumption would then come from domestic sources.

Around 1990, therefore, the world oil market may again be under OPEC control. This does not necessarily imply a third oil shock, since the cartel is now presumably more aware of the dangers of short-run revenue maximization to cartel stability. If so, OPEC is likely to choose a gradual firming of the world price in real terms during the 1990s; if not, the boom-bust cycle of 1979–1986 may be repeated.

Obviously there are major risks in any such forecast. The principal economic uncertainty lies in production; thus some industry sources have predicted a U.S. output as low as 5 Mb/d by 1990. There may also be unpleasant surprises in foreign non-OPEC production; the long-predicted but as yet unrealized decline of North Sea output, for instance, may be steeper than now seems likely. As for consumption, another accident of the Chernobyl type could have a disastrous effect on nuclear power everywhere and force electricity producers to turn to oil. Although it is easier to think of bad news than of good news in this area, the possibility that OPEC will break up cannot be entirely overlooked, and a major discovery in non-OPEC territory is also conceivable.

The principal political uncertainty affecting the world price of crude is the outcome of the war between Iraq and Iran. More than six years after Iraq's initial attack, Iran clearly has the upper hand, especially on the ground. It took Iran several years to translate its numerical superiority into territorial gains, but Iraq is still much stronger in the air. Iraq is supported financially by Saudi Arabia and other Arab nations; it has also been tacitly favored by the West and by the Soviet Union, which facilitates its access to foreign equipment and supplies. Iran has recently managed to improve its external relations somewhat, but it continues to have difficulty in finding supplies.[20] Attempts at a peaceful settlement of the war have come up against Iran's insistence on removing the Iraqi leader, Saddam Hussein. There now appear to be three scenarios:

1. Iran's long-threatened "final offensive" is successful and leads to the installation of a puppet government in Baghdad.

2. Following less catastrophic military reverses, Saddam Hussein is overthrown by an Iraqi group acceptable to Iran; in a negotiated settlement Iraq remains independent.

3. The war continues without either side gaining a decisive advantage; Saddam Hussein remains in power. This scenario includes the possibility that growing popular dissatisfaction in Iran forces the fundamentalist regime to be more receptive to peace initiatives.

As far as oil supply is concerned, the second scenario is the most appealing though not necessarily the most probable. Under that scenario both Iran and Iraq would be able to restore oil exports to more normal levels, and Iraq at least would have strong incentives to do so in order to finance reconstruction from war damage. OPEC, of course, might try to offset the increased output of the former belligerents by reducing output elsewhere, but recent experience suggests that would be very difficult.

The first scenario, by contrast, would have very adverse effects on world oil supplies since Iran would have no interest in restoring, or even maintaining, Iraqi production. Moreover, the prestige of a military victory would raise Iran's standing in the entire Middle East and in OPEC; it might also endanger the pro-Western regimes in several Arab countries, including not only Saudi Arabia and Kuwait but Egypt and Jordan as well. Indeed, the implications of the first scenario are so disturbing that the West will probably do everything, short of military intervention, to prevent it from being realized. Taking all this into account, the first scenario may be judged less likely than the third, at least for the next few years.

The Iraq-Iran conflict is not the only source of political risk. Although the tension between Israel and its Arab neighbors is less acute than ten or fifteen years ago, no comprehensive peace settlement is in sight. The situation in Lebanon remains volatile. Another Arab-Israeli war cannot be ruled out, and the first oil shock has shown how disruptive it could be to the oil market.

To sum up, the supply-demand balance remains relatively favorable to consumers over the next few years; the market will gradually tighten, however, and around 1990 OPEC may again be firmly in the saddle. Although this forecast appears to be close to the consensus, the economic and political uncertainties inherent in it are large. Most of these uncertainties suggest higher prices, except if OPEC disintegrates or a peace settlement between Iraq and Iran is negotiated. It is against this background that policy options will be discussed.

The Role of Government

Government intervention in the oil market has a long history, particularly in the United States. Although its achievements are mixed at best, such intervention will no doubt continue for the following reasons:

1. Oil is one of the very few commodities that truly affects national security. The United States, which depends on imports for a large part of its consumption, is vulnerable to supply interruptions; moreover, the threat of interruption can be used to influence our foreign policy. This argument also applies to other oil-importing countries.

2. Governments are involved in the production process because they own the areas where exploration and extraction take place, and sometimes the deposits themselves. Even without government ownership, licensing is often needed for environmental reasons.

3. When oil transactions are a large factor in the balance of payments, they may be of special concern to macroeconomic policy.

4. Minerals, including oil, require special tax treatment because of depletion, a phenomenon rarely encountered in other goods and services. Exploration, especially when it is unsuccessful, also presents peculiar tax problems.

5. The existence of a foreign cartel casts doubt on the competitive assumptions under which government abstention is optimal.

6. The domestic oil industry may have enough political power to enlist government aid in accomplishing its economic objectives.

Because it is impossible to go into all these considerations here, the focus, rather, will be on the foreign trade regime applied to oil. Before this topic is discussed, the Strategic Petroleum Reserve (SPR) should be briefly mentioned because it bears directly on points 1 and 5 listed above. The SPR continues to be filled at a fairly steady rate to its target level of ninety days' imports; the target is likely to increase in volume over time because imports are likely to rise. The SPR represents a large investment, and a sizable capital loss has already been incurred on the oil that was bought at high prices. Nevertheless, the filling should go on because the long-term world oil outlook is far from reassuring. The oil put into the SPR should come from foreign sources to conserve domestic reserves; use of the SPR as a support program for domestic producers would be contrary to its national security objective.

The Strategic Petroleum Reserve is our first line of defense against attempted blackmail by oil-producing countries, a risk that has not vanished. It would not be realistic to rely entirely on private inventories; as the earlier discussion of futures trading showed, private traders are inevitably more concerned with short-term price fluctuations than with long-term political risks. More thought is needed, however, on the method of making the SPR available in case of an emergency; market forces should be engaged as much as possible.

It is more difficult to be positive about another element of current oil policy, the International Energy Agency (IEA). Its main purpose is to reallocate oil supplies among the member countries in case of a supply interruption. The IEA institutionalizes earlier sharing agreements among the industrial countries that were of some value during the 1973–1974 embargo against the United States and the Netherlands. At that time the spot market was still in its infancy, but at present it would seem that supplies could be at least as efficiently reallocated by the market as by the IEA. In principle, the agency could be useful as a vehicle for a common policy of the oil-importing countries with respect to OPEC; no such policy has emerged, however.[21]

Alternative Trade Policies

Turning now to the foreign trade regime, we will examine four possibilities: import quotas, a fixed tariff, a variable tariff, and free trade.

Import Quotas. Mandatory import quotas were in force from 1959 to 1973. Licenses to import, known as "tickets," were provided without charge to refiners who could use them or sell them. The government did not collect any revenue; yet consumers had to pay much more than the prevailing world price. Apart from its manifest inequity, which could have been corrected by auctioning the tickets instead of giving them away, this system actually worked against the national security interest it was supposed to serve. It stimulated domestic oil extraction to the point where U.S. reserves were being exhausted prematurely; thus it was correctly accused of "draining America first."

Ostensibly justified by national security, the quota system was actually a shortsighted response to the insistence of domestic producers and refiners on protection from low-cost imports. This does not mean that the national security argument itself is invalid; it means, rather, that the argument should not be invoked unless supported by plausible evidence that national security will in fact be enhanced. The effect of the Mandatory Oil Import Program, in the end, was to expose the United States to political pressure and to exploitation by OPEC. The idea of quotas deserves to be buried once and for all.

Fixed Tariff. A fixed tariff (that is, a tariff at a rate that does not change over time) was belatedly adopted by the United States in 1973. It soon became irrelevant to the alleged needs of domestic producers when OPEC solved the problem of low-cost imports with a vengeance. If it had been adopted earlier, a tariff would have had a more positive effect on national security than the quota system actually in force. Since imports would not have been subject to a ceiling, domestic production would not have expanded as much, and the reserves thus kept in the ground would have been available when they were most needed. The adjustments in the world oil market would have been more gradual. Perhaps OPEC would still have had an opportunity to take control of the world price, but the cartel price would probably have been lower.

Since 1973 circumstances have changed so drastically that the case for a fixed tariff (sometimes euphemistically called an "import fee") has to be made on different grounds. It is not enough to point to the difficulties of the domestic industry, manifested by numerous bankruptcies. The industry's problems are attributable to the abnormally high prices of the early 1980s rather than to current prices which, after correcting for inflation, are still twice as high as they were before the first oil shock. The firms that failed had capital losses, not current losses. Acting on the once widespread conviction that oil prices could only go up, they invested and borrowed too much. They, and the banks that financed them, must now pay the normal penalty for their imprudence. It appears that at present prices the bulk of the industry remains profitable in its current operations, though more write-offs of past unsound investments may be expected.

Given the existence of a foreign cartel, the principal argument in favor of a fixed tariff, advanced by Houthakker in 1976 and by Broadman and Hogan ten years later, is that some of the burden could be shifted to OPEC.[22] The federal government would in effect be capturing part of the cartel's monopoly profits. Put briefly, the argument

173

runs as follows. The imposition of a tariff would raise output and lower consumption in this country, thus reducing the demand for imports. Since the United States accounts for a large fraction of OPEC exports, the cartel would find it optimal to set the world price at a lower level than in the absence of a tariff.[23] OPEC would lose revenue because both its price and its exports would be lower. The United States, by contrast, would gain revenue from the tariff on the remaining imports. Thus there would be a transfer from OPEC to the United States.

The net impact of a tariff on American consumers would probably be negative, however. The transfer from OPEC to the United States could be accomplished only if the domestic price (including the tariff) were higher than it would be without a tariff. In other words, the world price would not fall by the full amount of the duty because the United States is not the only oil importer. Although a more detailed quantitative assessment is necessary, it would seem that this adverse effect will not be fully offset by the reduction of nonoil taxes made possible, at least in principle, by the tariff revenue. The main beneficiaries of a U.S. tariff, oddly enough, would be consumers in oil-importing countries that do not impose a tariff: they would gain from the lower world price. If all oil-importing nations imposed the same tariff, OPEC's market power would be effectively destroyed, but that would require an unprecedented degree of international cooperation.[24]

If consumers do not get the benefit of a tariff, who does? Apart from foreign consumers, the benefits would go to the domestic oil industry. The owners of existing wells, in particular, would have a windfall gain; in due course the higher domestic price would enable them to extract more oil from these wells. In addition, some of the benefits would be invested in exploration and other high-cost investments. For essentially geological reasons, the cost of finding and producing oil in the United States has long been rising relative to the rest of the world. The quota system reinforced this tendency; the first and second oil shocks did so more strongly, and a fixed tariff would add further impetus. At some point we must ask ourselves how high the cost of domestic oil should go.

In this connection it is important to realize that the cartel in its heyday created a net loss to the world economy by inducing importing countries, particularly the United States, to substitute their high-cost oil for OPEC's low-cost oil. As far as the efficient allocation of world resources is concerned, a fixed tariff would make a bad situation even worse by encouraging more such substitution. This is the main reason for surmising that American consumers would be net losers under a fixed tariff.

Variable Tariff. Since the effect of a tariff on the domestic price will be very visible, while the net advantage to consumers is uncertain at best, a fixed tariff is likely to be strongly resisted, especially if it is as high as the $10 per barrel proposed by Broadman and Hogan. From this point of view a variable tariff has stronger claims to consideration. With this device the rate of duty is not constant but set daily at the difference (if positive) between a domestic indicator price and the landed price of imports.[25] The effect is to keep the domestic price at or above the indicator price. The domestic market is then effectively insulated from excess supply in the world market. Like a fixed tariff, a variable tariff generates revenue for the government, but at a lower rate; the effect on consumers is correspondingly smaller.

The desirability of a variable tariff hinges on the level of the indicator price. If this price is high relative to the average world price, the duty will usually be positive, and the variable tariff becomes similar to a fixed tariff. Conversely, if the indicator price is low, the duty will be zero most of the time. Although the effect on consumers will then be small, the variable tariff may still be valuable to domestic producers as a "safety net."

Only as a safety net does the variable tariff merit consideration. As long as OPEC is able to set the world price, the domestic industry hardly needs protection. When the cartel loses control, however, the world price may fall precipitously; thus it went briefly below $7 per barrel in 1986. Indeed OPEC might under certain circumstances drive the world price down deliberately to discipline outside suppliers, just as Saudi Arabia did within OPEC on two or three occasions. If very low prices persisted for some time, sizable parts of the American industry might not survive, many wells would be capped, and exploration would come to a virtual halt. Together these developments would make the country more vulnerable to political pressures and to future exploitation by OPEC. It follows that national security considerations may justify a variable levy with a low indicator price.

The purpose of a variable tariff would not be to guarantee comfortable profits to a majority of domestic producers regardless of the world price, as quotas and fixed tariffs tend to do. On the contrary, fluctuating prices can contribute to the health of any industry by weeding out inefficient suppliers when prices are low and attracting new firms when prices are high. Neither would the purpose be to maintain domestic production at a high rate. What matters for national security is not the actual rate of output but the capacity to produce more when needed. Just as the Strategic Petroleum Reserve provides a short-term defense against supply interruptions, spare producing capacity would provide longer-term security. It would

175

constrain OPEC's power to fix prices and the possible desire of some of its members to use oil as a political weapon.

For many years—since about 1970, to be precise—the United States has had little or no spare capacity. Even the Naval Petroleum Reserves, originally intended as spare capacity, are currently being produced flat out, apparently for shortsighted budgetary reasons. The reestablishment of spare capacity, especially in the private sector, deserves high priority in our energy policy. It would require more emphasis on exploration and less on current production; changes in taxation may be needed to provide the necessary incentives. A variable tariff with a low indicator price would give some insurance to the industry against disastrously low prices while permitting adequate variability in prices.

If the concept of a variable tariff is adopted, what would be the optimal indicator price? A precise answer would call for a detailed cost study of the domestic industry and of regional price variations. In the absence of such a study the figure may be tentatively put in the neighborhood of $10 per barrel, with due allowance for grade and location. If a price below that prevailed for some time, a substantial fraction of the nation's wells would probably be abandoned. At the price of around $19 per barrel prevailing in early 1987, the duty would therefore be zero. A similar degree of protection would have to be extended to refined products to prevent circumvention of the duty on crude when it is in force; there is no apparent reason for additional protection of the refining industry.

Free Trade. To those who rightly believe that free trade is the best general prescription for the public interest and for international harmony, any talk of a tariff, whether fixed or variable, is distasteful. The basis for exempting oil from this general rule has already been stated. The mere existence of a foreign cartel is clearly not a sufficient argument against free trade. Such cartels have existed in other commodities, such as coffee and tin, and the United States has at times found it prudent to cooperate with these cartels instead of opposing them with a tariff. This was not just because in these instances there was no significant domestic industry to protect; American consumers, after all, were being harmed.

The critical difference between oil and the cases just mentioned is that in the latter there was no political danger. The politics, if anything, went the other way: the United States saw tolerance of a cartel as a relatively painless way of promoting good relations with the countries involved. Occasional rhetoric aside, OPEC has never shown any serious interest in cooperation with importing countries; from the first oil shock on, it has acted unilaterally. Strictly speaking, even that attitude is not a sufficient reason for departing from free trade, though it comes close. The decisive reason is the demonstrated willingness of leading members to use exports as a means of exercising political pressure. The national security argument is essentially a political argument. It should be added that a variable tariff with a low indicator price would protect our national security with only minimal interference with free trade.

Suppose now that, ignoring these considerations, we maintain an essentially free trade regime in oil. Could any domestic policy measures improve the situation? An increase in the federal excise tax on gasoline and diesel fuel has sometimes been suggested; various European countries took this step when crude prices declined, thus keeping domestic fuel prices more or less unchanged. No doubt a tax increase would have a depressing effect on fuel consumption, especially in the longer run. To that extent it would lessen our dependence on OPEC, though at considerable cost to consumers.

The question is complicated by the Federal Highway Trust Fund, to which revenues from taxes on highway users are dedicated. Many interstate highways need expensive repairs; if current revenues are not enough to finance them, an increase in user taxes would be entirely appropriate. Except as user taxes, however, excise taxes have little merit from an economic point of view. Relatively cheap transportation is an important contributor to the efficiency of the widely dispersed U.S. economy; it should not be lightly interfered with.

Concluding Remarks

The world price of oil has fluctuated more in the past year than at any time since the 1930s. This is not by itself a reason for alarm: such fluctuations are common and salutary in other commodities, and with the advent of competition, oil has become a commodity. Oil, however, differs from most other commodities in at least two respects: it has important national security aspects, and until this year the market was controlled by a cartel. The analysis of this paper suggests that the present respite from high prices is unlikely to last more than a few years.

Although past policies have sometimes been ill conceived, the government does have a role in this area. The Strategic Petroleum Reserve remains necessary as a first line of defense against supply interruption; it should continue to be filled, preferably with foreign oil. Although a fixed tariff could transfer some of OPEC's monopoly profits to the United States, its distributive and allocative effects make it undesirable. A variable tariff on oil, by contrast, deserves considera-tion as a safety net preventing permanent damage to the industry from very low prices. Oil policy should aim at reestablishing spare capacity in the domestic industry, thus creating a second line of defense. These measures could make the United States less depend-ent on whatever OPEC attempts to do in the future.

Notes

1. By "world price" is generally meant the dollar price for Arab Light crude at Ras Tanura, the principal export terminal of Saudi Arabia. Prices elsewhere are mostly higher because of transportation differentials.

2. At current freight rates a world price of $16 is equivalent to about $19 for the standard grade on the New York futures market.

3. According to 1976 estimates of the Bank for International Settlements. It should be borne in mind that there is a large statistical discrepancy in global current-account statistics.

4. The main beneficiaries of this indirect form of financing were the banks. Furthermore, the absence of alternative uses of the OPEC funds was probably the main reason why real interest rates in the 1970s were close to zero and indeed frequently negative.

5. This thesis, according to which the high crude prices of the 1970s were attributable to a scarcity of resources rather than to OPEC, was recently refuted by M.A. Adelman, "Scarcity and World Oil Prices," *Review of Economics, and Statistics* 68, pp. 387–97.

6. With a weighted basket of major currencies the increase was much less since the dollar had declined sharply in the late 1970s.

7. At least not in dollars. The dollar strengthened considerably between 1980 and 1985.

8. Verleger and others have argued that crude prices are determined by prod-uct prices, although this does not mean that the cartelization of crude was without effect. P.K. Verleger, "The Determinants of Official OPEC Crude Prices," *Review of Economics and Statistics* 64, pp. 177–83.

9. The world includes the Communist countries, which should not be left out in a global analysis. Since 1974 the U.S.S.R. has been the world's largest oil producer, with substantial exports to both Western and Eastern Europe. More recently, China has become a net exporter on a modest scale.

10. Straight lines are used for ease of exposition, not because they are realistic. Certain details aside, the argument carries over to more general functions. Income effects are ignored, and the cartel's internal demand is deducted from its output.

11. The particular value of one-half is an artifact of the linearity assumption and has to be modified for differently shaped demand and supply curves.

12. In May 1986 Vice President Bush suddenly went to the Persian Gulf, apparently to convey the U.S. oil industry's concern over low prices. Whether a hint of cooperation by the industry was intended is unclear. When he arrived, Bush learned of strong domestic opposition to any such plan.

13. Absent special tax provisions there would probably be few stripper wells in operation. The high-cost output from these wells would hardly be missed, except perhaps by those who like to think of them as the energy counterpart of the family

farm. As is true in agriculture, the importance of very small operations is political rather than economic; they serve as a pretext for policies that benefit the larger producers.

14. M.A. Adelman, "The Competitive Floor to World Oil Prices," MIT Energy Laboratory, Working Paper no. MIT-EL 86-011WP, 1986.

15. Defined as the expected profit forgone by extracting a barrel from the ground now rather than at some future date.

16. See the working paper by Adelman cited in footnote 14.

17. The number of outstanding commitments to buy or sell; this is the most revealing measure of the importance of a futures market.

18. The absence of really large players is fortunate since futures markets are vulnerable to manipulation. A "corner," in particular, is an attempt to drive up the price by accumulating dominant positions in both the cash and the futures markets. Arab traders took part in the 1979–1980 corner in silver.

19. In the most active of all futures markets, the one in Treasury bonds, contracts for delivery more than two years from the present are traded.

20. The recently revealed U.S. approach to Iran appears to have been a temporary aberration.

21. For a detailed discussion of the IEA, see George Horwich and David Leo Weimer, *Oil Price Shocks, Market Response, and Contingency Planning* (Washington, D.C., 1984).

22. Hendrik S. Houthakker, *The World Price of Oil* (Washington, D.C.: American Enterprise Institute, 1976); and Harry G. Broadman and William W. Hogan, "Oil Tariff Policy in an Uncertain Market," Kennedy School of Government, Harvard University, Discussion Paper E-86-11, 1986.

23. In terms of figure 2, *AA'* would shift to the left and *BB'* to the right.

24. For a quantitative analysis of a tariff imposed jointly by the industrial countries, see Hendrik S. Houthakker and Michael Kennedy, "Long-Range Energy Prospects," *Journal of Energy and Economic Development* 4 (1979).

25. Its prototype is the variable levy on imported farm products, a component of the EEC's agricultural policy. In Europe domestic farm prices are generally well above world prices, but that is not essential to the concept. A variable levy should not be confused with an *ad valorem* tariff, in which the rate of duty is fixed as a percentage of the price.

6

Maintaining Financial Stability: Financial Strains and Public Policy

William S. Haraf

Summary

Over the past decade the U.S. financial system has undergone far-reaching changes as a result of economic conditions, new technology, and market innovations. Legal and regulatory barriers to competition among financial firms have eroded, and new financial products and services have emerged. Accompanying the rapid pace of change have been record numbers of problem and failed bank and thrift firms. This situation has raised concern over the stability of the financial system.

Banks and thrifts have historically been the focus of public policies to maintain financial stability. Federal deposit insurance, the operations of the Federal Reserve as controller of overall liquidity and as lender of last resort, and the examination and supervision apparatus are the principal mechanisms that constitute the federal financial "safety net."

The rationale has been that an unregulated banking system operating without safety net protections would experience some form of market failure, presumably resulting in financial instability. This view is widely held, but supporting analysis and evidence have been challenged in recent years. Today, there is no agreement among economists on the existence or nature of market failure in banking, nor on how regulation might address it. Moreover, the erosion of barriers to competition among financial firms and the increased integration of financial markets have raised new questions regarding both the extensive regulations and the special protections afforded to bank and thrift firms. A rethinking of present safety net policies is now imperative.

The theme of this paper is that in the name of protecting the stability of the financial system, policy has moved too far in the direction of protecting firms from failure and individuals from loss. As a result, serious incentive and equity problems have emerged in the U.S. financial system.

I would like to thank James Barth, Phillip Cagan, Catherine England, Mark Flannery, and Mickey Levy for comments on an earlier draft.

It is well known that the deposit insurance system may not provide sufficient incentives to control risk taking. In recent years these incentive problems have been exacerbated as safety net protections have been extended both explicitly and implicitly. The 1980 increase in the official deposit insurance ceiling, the use of failure resolution techniques that in specific instances have protected large depositors, other creditors, managers, and shareholders of banks and bank holding companies, and decisions to allow insolvent banks and thrifts to remain in operation and to forbear on capital standards have all reduced the force of important market disciplines operating on bank and thrift firms. Over time such policies pose a perverse threat to financial stability as surviving firms are encouraged to take greater risks.

Maintaining financial stability in the new financial environment requires market disciplines. Enforcing greater market discipline demands a set of clearly understood rules for discount window lending and failure management, in which the liquidity of depositor accounts is preserved even if large depositors and other creditors are subject to losses. A workable failure resolution strategy must also be applicable to large as well as small firms. Financial markets will not seriously believe policy makers' announcements to strengthen market discipline by permitting financial firms of all sizes to fail unless a credible plan for failure management is in place.

Accompanying these changes should be a strengthened commitment to prompt closure of firms that are insolvent on a market value basis, since the cost of failures depends significantly on how quickly regulators detect and respond to problem situations. Protecting the interests of the deposit insurance agencies, large depositors, and other creditors also requires greater disclosure, and an end to forbearance on capital requirements.

Banks and thrifts are subject to special regulatory burdens that have hampered their diversification efforts, both geographically and across product lines, and have impeded their response to market changes brought about by changing technology. As a result, regulation may have actually contributed to increased strains in the banking system. A comprehensive approach to redesigning policies to promote financial stability would also address this problem.

The fundamental issue is whether well-managed, well-capitalized firms should be free from most restraints on their activities and markets, on the grounds that this freedom would promote efficiency and adaptability and that sufficient capital would be available to absorb losses and protect the insurance funds. The more bank and thrift regulators rely on market disciplines and prompt closure of firms that are insolvent on a market value basis, the less regulation is needed to protect the insurer against losses.

If the present safety net protections remain in place, pressures for large-scale reregulation of financial markets will inevitably develop. Historical experience has shown, however, that the effect of regulation has often been eroded by competitive pressures for efficiency and innovation. Regulation, rather than restraining potentially risky activities, forces them into new channels. More important, users of financial services have benefited enormously from the ongoing process of financial market restructuring. It is difficult to imagine reregulating in such a way as to preserve these benefits.

Introduction

For the past decade the financial system has been in a state of flux. Volatile economic conditions, significant technological and market innovations, the opening of capital markets worldwide, and new legislation have produced profound changes and a new sophistication.

The segmentation of markets by geographic area, by customer, and by type of product that was encouraged by the legislation of the 1930s is breaking down. Commercial banks, securities firms, insurance and finance companies, and savings and loan associations increasingly find themselves competing for the same business. Moreover, as U.S. and foreign financial firms have expanded their activities in each other's national markets and in the Euromarkets, this competition is taking place in a global arena.

Advances in computer and communications technology have contributed to the increasing sophistication of financial markets by facilitating the collection, organization, and transmission of information. This has led to a broad trend toward the securitization of lending,[1] rapid flows of funds within and across national borders, and a continuing stream of new instruments and techniques for managing cash, funding obligations, and hedging risks. A financial firm's ability to manage risk is now a critical factor in determining its competitive position.

Public policies continue to play an important role in determining the location and type of financial activity through legal and regulatory influences on the scope and cost of operation of financial firms. Among those influences are explicit and implicit financial safeguards afforded by governments. Financial firms within the United States and around the world operate under significant differences in standards of leverage, accounting principles, degree of supervision, and the reach of governmental safety nets.

Commercial banks have been particularly affected by financial innovations and public policies. Banks, for example, are prohibited by law from underwriting most types of securities in the United States. Their share of short- and medium-term business credit and the average quality of their assets have declined in recent years as large prime borrowers, traditionally their strongest customers, have shifted to the

183

securities markets for their funding needs.[2] Many of the largest banks have responded by engaging in underwriting activities overseas and in a wide variety of other capital market activities both in the United States and abroad. Off-balance sheet commitments at the twenty-five largest commercial banks, which five years ago were negligible, equaled $1.5 trillion in mid-1986, well in excess of their deposit liabilities.[3]

Increasing competition and innovation in financial markets have provided users of financial services substantial benefits, but the transition has not been without strains. Banks and thrifts are failing at rates not seen since the 1930s. Many survivors, including some very large ones, are on shaky ground. Over 1,450 commercial banks were officially classified as problem banks by the Federal Deposit Insurance Corporation (FDIC) near the end of 1986, seven times the number so classified in 1980.[4] Approximately one-third of all savings and loans have failed or been merged out of existence over the past five years. Another 250 insolvent savings and loans have been permitted to remain in operation principally because the Federal Savings and Loan Insurance Corporation (FSLIC) does not have the resources to close them, and hundreds more are in jeopardy. The Federal Home Loan Bank Board (FHLBB) estimates that resolving the most pressing cases will require an infusion of $26 billion into the FSLIC fund.[5]

Financial strains within the banking and thrift industries and the enormous changes in financial markets have raised concern over the stability of the financial system. The policy mechanisms for preserving financial stability have three broad elements: (1) the operations of the federal deposit insurance agencies; (2) official arrangements for the regulation and supervision of financial firms; and (3) the operations of the Federal Reserve as controller of overall liquidity and as lender of last resort. Together, these mechanisms constitute the federal financial "safety net."

The safety net was designed to function in an earlier environment in which financial services were provided by specialized firms, with laws and regulations setting the boundaries for their lines of business and other aspects of their activities: banks in commercial lending and deposit taking; securities firms in underwriting, brokering, and trading; and so on. Deposit-taking firms—banks and thrifts—have traditionally been the focus of public policies to maintain financial stability.

Many banks and thrifts depend on, and aggressively advertise, their access to the deposit insurance system. The number that would not survive without it could range into the thousands. Weakened or insolvent banks and thrifts are prominent on the lists of firms paying the highest interest rates in the country. Through deposit brokers and direct advertising, they are able to raise substantial funds nationwide only because the deposit insurance agencies, and ultimately federal taxpayers, stand behind their claims. They pose a continuing threat not only to the deposit insurance funds, but also to healthy, well-capitalized firms that must compete with them for business.

In the 1930s, the proposal to establish the federal deposit insurance system was controversial. Opponents feared that the system would unfairly subsidize unhealthy firms at the expense of healthy ones and that it would encourage excessive risk taking by firms offering insured accounts.[6] For many years, however, deposit insurance was deemed an unqualified success. Today, those earlier concerns are resurfacing. It is widely acknowledged that the system, as now structured, may not provide sufficient incentives to control risk taking by firms funding themselves with insured deposits.

In recent years policy choices and events have extended the level of safety net protections. Legislation passed in 1980 raised the official deposit insurance ceiling from $40,000 to $100,000. A 1982 congressional resolution stated that the full faith and credit of the U.S. Treasury stand behind the deposit insurance funds, reinforcing the idea that taxpayers are ultimately responsible for claims on the insuring agencies. The Continental Illinois Bank bailout gave credence to the view that policy makers would not permit large banks to fail, granting an implicit federal guarantee not only of deposits in excess of $100,000, but also of their extensive nondeposit liabilities, off-balance sheet commitments, and foreign deposits. Since then, competitive equity considerations have compelled the FDIC to adopt a policy of resolving all bank failures in ways that protect large depositors and most general creditors whenever possible. Increasingly, it is planning to provide some protection to managers and stockholders as well, through open-bank assistance plans. Finally, decisions to allow insolvent banks and thrifts to remain in operation and to forbear on capital standards have put taxpayers' funds at greater risk in the operation of depository firms.[7]

Implicit and explicit safety net protections are widely believed to have a pervasive effect on financial markets. Speaking of bond and securities markets, Albert Wojnilower of First Boston Corporation wrote:

> The actual and tacit extensions of official guarantees and insurance have played an important role in attracting all kinds of investors, foreign and domestic. . . . Each default crisis of the past fifteen years or so has led to a broadening of *de jure* or *de facto* official insurance against default and/or illiquidity. A vast range of instruments far beyond anything

ever envisioned is now protected, or deemed by the market to be protected. A partial list of the additions would include most deposits in excess of the Federal $100,000 per account insurance limit, small state-insured deposits, much commercial paper, repurchase agreements against Treasury securities, customers' assets held by stock exchange firms, pension liabilities, and some life insurance liabilities. Add to this the endless expansion and diversification of U.S. Treasury securities and guarantees . . . and it is easy to see why the public assumes that most of its claims are fully insured.[8]

Perceptions such as these, the pace of change in financial markets, the erosion of boundaries, and the proliferation of new instruments and techniques raise important questions about the operation of existing policy mechanisms for preserving financial stability. Is the safety net distorting private risk-bearing decisions? Are risks being concentrated in the banking sector as a result of safety net policies? Is it fair or efficient to have insolvent and nearly insolvent firms propped up by government guarantees competing for business with healthy, well-capitalized financial firms? Is the extension of financial protections solving today's problems at the expense of tomorrow's?

Definitive answers to these questions are difficult to obtain, but critically important. In this paper, I examine U.S. policies designed to maintain financial stability. I argue that, in attempting to maintain the stability of the financial system, policy has moved too far in the direction of protecting firms from failure and individuals from loss. This has led to the erosion of important market disciplines with the potential for distorting risk-return trade-offs economywide.

Antecedents of Financial Strains

Several factors have contributed to strains in the banking and thrift industries.

Volatile credit markets and macroeconomic conditions have played a significant role. The surge of inflation in the 1970s combined with low real interest rates encouraged debt-financed speculation in land, housing, and commodities. The disinflation of the 1980s meant that many such gambles did not pay off. Many of today's problems in financial markets are the result of this cycle of inflation and disinflation and the accompanying volatility of interest rates and real returns. Five years ago discussion among economists of the costs of inflation and disinflation focused primarily on the business cycle costs. The costs of adjustment in capital and financial markets are apparently higher and much longer lived than most economists anticipated: we are still suffering the aftereffects of the acceleration of inflation in the 1970s.

Some observers have blamed financial deregulation for rising failure rates, but it is important to be clear about how deregulation may have contributed. Without interest rate deregulation in 1980, banks and thrifts would have been unable to compete with money market mutual funds and other similar financial innovations. Since then, *de jure* deregulation of activities and products has been limited. A substantial body of restrictions on the products, activities, and geographic markets of depository firms still remains as a heritage of Depression-era legislation. These restrictions have inhibited diversification across regions and products and limited the ability of depository firms to respond to changing market conditions and technology. As a result, they have quite probably contributed to strains in the banking and thrift industries.

As financial markets have opened, however, some previously protected firms were exposed to competition for the first time. In 1980, there were approximately 20,000 banks and thrifts in operation in the United States. Not all of them possessed the management expertise to survive in a more complex, competitive, and volatile marketplace. Studies of troubled and failed banks and thrifts in the 1980s have concluded that most problems have not been caused by newly acquired powers, but by economic conditions, inadequate diversification, excessive exposure to interest-rate risk, poor management, and fraud.[9]

Role of Increased Risk Taking. It is now well known that the deposit insurance system as it is currently structured may not provide sufficient incentives to control risk taking.[10] There is an important moral hazard problem at work. Banks and thrifts can acquire insured deposits at interest rates comparable to those on other risk-free investments. In addition, deposit insurance premiums are a flat percentage of total deposits, regardless of the riskiness of a firm's assets. Because neither depositors nor the insuring agencies are compensated for risk bearing, all the financial rewards for bearing risk go to the firm's owners. This provides an incentive for banks and thrifts to take on more risk than they would otherwise, either by acquiring riskier assets or by increasing leverage. The problem is most serious when regulators allow a firm to remain in operation after its economic net worth has been exhausted. Then, managers and owners have little or nothing to lose by gambling in an effort to restore solvency. The irony is that these incentive problems may be undermining the goal of financial stability that deposit insurance was designed to maintain.

Although the proximate causes of the rising number of failed and problem banks and thrifts in recent years may be macroeconomic or regional or may be traceable industry shocks, the incentive problems from deposit insurance may discourage managers from adopting financial structures that reduce their exposure to such shocks.[11] Regulators are under the greatest pressure to forbear when problems are widespread, either regionally, throughout the economy, or in some specific sector. Recently, regulators adopted forbearance policies designed to ease pressure on agricultural and energy lenders; earlier forbearance was applied to banks lending to third world governments and to savings and loans with negative interest rate spreads. Forbearance in these instances, however, discourages costly diversification and hedging activities, making the system more vulnerable to future shocks.[12]

The incentives that encourage individual managers to take additional risks can spill over to the entire market. If depositors believe that all federally insured deposits are equally secure against default, the choice of where to place their funds is properly based solely on yield. In a competitive market, pressures on banks and thrifts to take greater credit risks in order to match the yields being offered by those with risky portfolios may be powerful. A recent study by the FHLBB concluded that weakened and insolvent thrifts paying high interest rates on deposit accounts have raised the cost of funds for the thrift industry as a whole by $4 billion in 1986.[13]

Although it is difficult to quantify the effect of the deposit insurance system on risk taking, it is apparently not just a theoretical problem. FDIC Chairman William Seidman recently noted, "Increased risk-taking is becoming an increasingly prominent feature of some banks' activities."[14] One recent empirical study concluded that managerial decisions to accept more risk have played an important role in explaining rising bank failures and that the banking system as a whole is more exposed to risk.[15] The study attributed the change to an increased capacity to respond to risk incentives in an environment in which interest rates are deregulated and funds can be moved quickly and easily.

Why Have Banks and Bank Depositors Been Subject to Special Treatment?

"Financial stability" is an often-expressed goal of public policy, but the term is not unambiguous. Implicit in the structure of safety net policies is a definition based on the performance of a specific set of financial firms, namely banks.[16] The historical rationale has been that an unregulated banking system operating without safety net protections would be characterized by some form of market failure, presumably resulting in financial instability. This view is widely held, but supporting analysis and evidence have been challenged in recent years. It is fair to say there is no agreement among economists today on the existence or nature of market failure in banking nor on how regulation might address it.[17]

Although banks have been deemed "special" for a variety of reasons, the inherent specialness of banking in today's financial markets is being called into question. Close substitutes for virtually all bank products and services are also provided by nonbanking firms with substantially less regulation and, so far, without adverse consequences for financial stability. At the same time, the nature of banking is changing rapidly. Off-balance sheet commitments at the largest commercial banks are now well in excess of their deposit liabilities. U.S. bank holding companies are market leaders in underwriting and distributing securities in the Euromarkets and in many local capital markets around the world. Affording special protection to banks in today's financial system will not protect all deposit instruments, and protecting all deposit instruments will not protect banks.

Although the inherent specialness of banking is in doubt, it is clear that banks are subject to special regulatory burdens that have hampered their ability to adapt to change. Over the years, many financial innovations have occurred in response to profit opportunities created by legal and regulatory constraints on prices and activities of regulated firms. Regulated firms are also often competitively disadvantaged in reacting to changing market conditions and technology.[18]

Payments System and Monetary Policy. One reason banks are said to be special derives from their key roles in the payments system and in the transmission of monetary policy. These roles, however, do not justify extensive explicit and implicit guarantees of all types and maturities of *bank deposits*, since it is not clear that such guarantees efficiently reduce payments risks or facilitate monetary policy.[19]

Hundreds of billions of dollars in government securities are transacted each day. Reliable functioning of that market may be at least as essential for monetary policy and financial stability as the operations of banks. Over the past decade, failures of government securities dealers have caused investors to lose approximately $900 million.[20] Yet, in contrast to its views on bank safety, the Federal Reserve has traditionally been cautious in its approach to regulating securities dealers. The 1985 Federal Reserve Bank of New York *Annual Report* recognized the trade-off posed by regulation:

Both the United States Treasury and the Federal Reserve have strong direct interests in maintaining an efficient, well-functioning government securities market. To this end, *any regulatory framework should be limited and tailored to address the specific areas of weakness. Any rule-making should be restrained. . . .* The core of the market . . . should not be disrupted by restrictions aimed at the market periphery. [italics added]

The Government Securities Act of 1986, signed into law on October 2, reflects this cautious philosophy. One can only speculate as to why attitudes toward the regulation of government securities dealers stand in such sharp contrast to those on banking regulation. It is fair to say, however, that if the same principles were applied, banking regulation would be considerably more restrained, and regulators would have exhibited greater tolerance toward bank failures and large depositor losses.

The Problem of Bank Runs. Perhaps the most common argument used to justify the banking focus of the financial safety net is that banks are subject to contagious runs. Although the failure of a single bank may cause losses or inconvenience for its customers, employees, and owners, in that respect it is no different from the failure of any other firm of comparable size. If, however, a bank failure alarms the depositors of other, healthy banks and leads them to withdraw deposits, healthy banks may be forced to sell illiquid assets at fire sale prices to meet depositor demands. The resulting losses could lead to a chain reaction of failures and a contraction of the money stock.

The basic concern is that market participants will be unable to discriminate between troubled borrowers and sound borrowers, so that runs on individual banks will be transformed into runs on the banking system. As Paul Volcker put it: "The failure of a few important institutions—unless handled expeditiously and effectively—could raise unwarranted concerns about other, basically sound banks, and lead to a contagious and spreading loss of confidence."[21]

Much of the concern about financial panics is based on the experience from 1929 to 1933, but this period was highly unusual. Studies of U.S. and British monetary history suggest several important conclusions. First, widespread panics have been rare. Many periods in history had high rates of bank failures that were not accompanied by financial panics. Second, financial panics occurred either in the absence of a lender-of-last-resort mechanism, or as a result of a failure by the central bank to fulfill the lender-of-last-resort function. Third, panics were generally short-lived and did not generally precipitate economic downturns, although they often accompanied them.[22]

Moreover, a review of the evidence on depositor losses from bank failures prior to establishment of the FDIC shows that the risks to depositors may have been exaggerated. From 1865 through 1933, commercial banks were estimated by the FDIC to have experienced losses of $12.3 billion. Of this amount, $2.2 billion (18 percent) was borne by depositors. As a percentage of total deposits in the banking system, total depositor losses were 0.21 percent. Most of the depositor losses occurred between 1930 and 1933. In the sixty-five years between 1865 and 1929, depositor losses were only 0.08 percent of total deposits. Even in the 1920s, when banks were failing at an average rate of 500 per year, depositor losses amounted to just 0.14 percent of total bank deposits. These losses appear small in comparison with losses borne by bond holders from price movements or defaults.[23]

Discussions of the costs and risks of bank runs sometimes blur an important distinction: that between runs on individual banks suspected of problems and contagious runs on sound banks. A recent thorough review of historical evidence on bank runs concluded that the danger to the banking system from runs on individual banks may be overemphasized.[24]

In principle, deposit withdrawals from problem banks can be part of a healthy market adjustment process in which problem firms are forced to shrink in size. Bank runs, however, can occur suddenly with the potential for quickly exacerbating a troubled bank's problems. The assistance provided to Continental Illinois Corporation, for example, was precipitated by a run on the bank during which it lost more than $20 billion of deposits in two months. More recently, the First National Bank of Oklahoma City lost 22 percent of its total deposits in the six months before its failure in July 1986.[25]

The rapidity with which a run can take place when a bank's problems become known is a form of business risk that is characteristic of banking. It does not, by itself, justify public intervention. Firms in other lines of business learn to adapt their policies to the risks they face. Banks are not unusual in this respect. Fear of loss of depositor confidence, a potentially important and desirable constraint on risk taking by bank managers, can be a powerful force for conservatism.

Moreover, a basically sound bank experiencing a run should be able to replace lost deposits in private markets. The $20 billion run on Continental Bank was prompted by depositor fears well grounded in reality: the bank faced the prospect of loan losses well in excess of its net worth. About the same time as the Continental run, another large bank, Manufacturers Hanover Trust, was beset by speculation over

191

the quality of its loan portfolio. The bank managed to convince the market that its position was sound, and it averted a run without FDIC or Federal Reserve assistance.[26] Private efforts to stem deposit drains through consortia of banks were not uncommon before the establishment of the Federal Reserve.[27]

Pervasive Effects of Banks Failures. Another argument for affording special treatment to banks, offered recently by Paul Volcker, is that bank failures can have pervasive effects on the economy:

> A sudden failure of one institution, particularly one of substantial size, can interrupt a long chain of payments and dramatically and unexpectedly affect other unrelated institutions, some of whom may not even have a business relationship with the institution in difficulty and have themselves been well managed and sound. While secondary and tertiary effects are, of course present in some degree in the failure of any business firm, the effects are never so potentially contagious or so disruptive as when the stability of the banking system or the payments mechanism is suddenly called into question.[28]

Clearly, the failure of a large nonbank financial firm could potentially be quite disruptive as well. Banks are not unusual in that respect. Moreover, if large bank customers were exposed to greater risk, they would, of necessity, alter their banking relationships so as to reduce their exposure to bank failures. According to Mr. Volcker's argument, the distinguishing characteristic of a banking failure is that it may call into question the stability of the banking system or the payments mechanism. It is the responsibility of the Federal Reserve, however, in its role as lender of last resort and as provider of liquidity to the financial system, to ensure that this does not take place.

Origins of the Deposit Insurance System. The deposit insurance system was established in a crisis atmosphere in 1933 following severe problems in the financial system and the deepest contraction in economic activity in U.S. history. At the time, the contraction had convinced many people that unregulated and competitive financial markets posed serious risks to economic stability. Reflecting that attitude, the U.S. government embarked on a far-reaching program of government involvement in the financial sector. The establishment of the deposit insurance system was, without question, one of the most significant steps adopted. A review of legislative history indicates two goals: the protection of small depositors and the preservation of financial stability.[29]

Economists continue to disagree about the conditions initiating the "great contraction." Few, however, disagree that the failure of the Federal Reserve to supply additional liquidity to the economy in the face of a large increase in the demand for currency significantly contributed to the severity of the crisis. Institutional reform in 1933 was not achieved by imposing some form of precommitment to serve as lender of last resort on the Federal Reserve. Instead, the deposit insurance system was established as a redundant mechanism to preserve stability, reducing the need for the central bank to serve as lender of last resort.

The insuring agencies, however, are not well equipped for this role, since they do not have the resources to underwrite the losses from a wave of bank failures resulting from a bank panic. In its 1957 report, the FDIC noted that had the FDIC been functioning according to modern rules beginning in the 1920s, it would have run out of its own funds and its borrowing authority by 1930, long before the worst of the banking crisis.[30] Clearly, only the central bank can prevent panics from taking hold by satisfying the increased demand for liquidity associated with financial distress.

In retrospect, the establishment of the deposit insurance system may not have been the best solution to the crisis of the 1930s. Much of the regulation since then has not been designed to preserve financial stability, or to serve some other public purpose, but to protect the insurance funds. Capital regulation, controls over bank liquidity, the examination and supervision apparatus, limits on various forms of bank expansion, and limits on bank chartering have left a legacy of attendant efficiency costs. Access to deposit insurance establishes a continuing legitimacy for further regulatory intervention.

The Erosion of Market Discipline in Banking

Over time, certain policies of the deposit-insuring agencies and other regulators, including policies toward failure resolution, capital standards, and disclosure regulation, have eroded important market disciplines operating on banks and thrifts.

Failure Resolution Techniques. Large depositors have not been an effective source of market discipline on bank behavior, particularly for the largest banks. Over the past twenty years, the majority of bank failures, and practically all large bank failures, have been handled through purchase and assumption transactions (P&As), in which the regulators arrange for a failing bank to be acquired by a healthy one in exchange for compensation by the insuring agencies. In such transac-

193

tions, large deposits are protected in full, and, in most cases, general creditors as well.[31]

In a payoff, the other traditional method for resolving failures, only *insured* depositors are paid by the FDIC. Uninsured depositors, the FDIC (standing in place of the insured depositors), and other general creditors are paid *pro rata* from the proceeds of receivership collections. Since liquidations can take years to complete, this approach can tie up large deposits for long periods and could be disruptive to financial markets if the failed bank is large.

Prompted by concerns over a lack of market discipline from large depositors, early in 1984 the FDIC experimented with a third technique for failure resolution, the modified payoff, on eight relatively small commercial banks. In a modified payoff, the FDIC transfers only insured accounts and some assets to a healthy bank as in a P&A, but not the claims of uninsured depositors and other general creditors. Instead, these parties are immediately paid the FDIC's estimate of the amount they would be entitled to upon liquidation of the bank's assets. If their claims are underestimated, the FDIC stands ready to make additional payments to them later. The principal immediate advantage of the modified payoff is that the disruptive effects of a conventional payoff are minimized, since uninsured depositors have prompt access to at least a portion of their funds.

The experiment with modified payoffs ended abruptly when the Continental Bank crisis began. Bank regulators feared that a modified payoff of Continental could prove highly disruptive and would be difficult or impossible to execute. Since no other bank was willing to participate in a purchase and assumption transaction, the FDIC provided Continental with "direct assistance," rather than liquidate it.[32] There is evidence that shareholders of other large commercial banks received a significant windfall gain from the bailout of Continental.[33] Apparently, the market's belief that a large bank would not be permitted to fail was strengthened by this incident, with significant benefit to shareholders.

The rescue of Continental Bank subjected bank regulators to criticism for treating large and small banks differently. Their policies, it was said, were encouraging a "flight to size," rather than a "flight to quality," and excessive concentration of deposits in the very largest banks. In response to these pressures, William Seidman, the chairman of the FDIC, announced in March 1986 that to maintain equality of treatment for banks of all sizes, the FDIC would undertake P&As whenever feasible.[34] In other words, Seidman instituted a policy of *de facto* 100 percent coverage for all depositors when feasible.

Since then, however, widespread bank problems and depressed

local conditions in agricultural and energy states have made suitable P&A partners for failing banks difficult to find. These problems have been compounded by laws and regulations limiting interstate and interindustry acquisitions. To maintain *de facto* 100 percent coverage for depositors, the FDIC recently announced that open-bank assistance plans will be used more frequently, "where it is cost effective and beneficial to the stability of the system."[35] This type of assistance not only protects depositors, it generally provides management, creditors, and shareholders of a failing bank and its holding company with significant protections as well.[36]

A principal reason for this change in policy according to Seidman was that, "unlike past experience, many of today's failures largely result from severe economic conditions—not incompetent or dishonest management."[37] There are good reasons to question this rationale. Individuals and firms in other lines of business are not protected from the consequences of economic conditions. Owners and managers of nonbanking firms have suffered substantial losses as a result of the same economic conditions facing banks.

More important, these failure-resolution techniques erode important market disciplines. Even if they are cheaper on a case-by-case basis, a policy of using them consistently may raise the cost of failure resolution in the long run, since surviving firms are encouraged to take more risk. As Edward Kane puts it:

> An agency's decision not to enforce its de jure limitations on coverage in particular cases has long-run and system-wide costs that may outweigh the immediate economization of agency resources reputed to occur. It is myopic to calculate the cost of handling an individual insolvency as if the costs of resolving future insolvencies that matter are only those that occur in the very short-run. Subsidies designed to arrest the cumulative short-run spread of current losses to a few other institutions undermine longer-run market sanctions against risk-bearing for all clients. Such a policy lowers the effective cost of deposit institution risk-bearing in ways that threaten to encourage surviving institutions to take even bolder risks in the future.[38]

Capital Regulation, Accounting Rules, and the Timing of Closure. The well-known Modigliani-Miller theorem states that, in the absence of market imperfections such as taxes and bankruptcy costs, a firm's overall cost of capital is independent of its capital structure or debt-equity mix. In such an idealized world, a firm could not lower its overall cost of capital by increasing leverage, since as debt holders bear more risk, they will demand a risk premium to compensate. Clearly, this proposition does not apply to banks, since insured depositors do not demand risk premiums. Other things equal, a bank can lower its funding costs by substituting deposits for equity.

This produces a natural conflict between banks and regulators over the amount of equity to hold. As a guarantor of bank debt, the government will be concerned, like any private lender, with the value and quality of bank assets relative to deposits and thus with a bank's equity capital. From the perspective of bank owners, additional equity capital raises costs and increases the value of the depositors' and other creditors' claims at the expense of equity holders.[39]

Before the establishment of the FDIC, bank capital ratios were more than twice as high as they are today. The average exceeded 30 percent in the second half of the nineteenth century.[40] Bank capital ratios fell sharply following the introduction of deposit insurance in 1933. They recovered somewhat in the early 1950s when capital regulation was first pursued. Since then, capital ratios have declined steadily as the degree of deposit protection has grown. Today, equity constitutes only about 5 percent of the total sources of funds for banks and even less for thrifts. By comparison, consumer finance companies, which also borrow to fund loans, operate with a 15 percent capital ratio.[41]

Capital requirements, in principle, protect the deposit-insuring agencies, large depositors, and other creditors of banks and thrifts from losses.[42] This protection, however, has been less valuable in practice than in theory for several reasons. For one, accounting measures of capital are based primarily on historical cost and therefore do not reflect material changes in a firm's condition as market values change. Moreover, such measures can be manipulated to meet capital requirements or to preserve the appearance of solvency.[43] Experience has shown that the market values of a firm's assets and liabilities can differ substantially from their book values, so that book measures of capital do not always provide a meaningful criterion for solvency. In the absence of meaningful measures of capital and insolvency, firms can continue to accumulate losses well after the market value of their capital has fallen below zero.

In addition, regulators have historically given troubled banks and thrifts an opportunity to regain their financial health, virtually ensuring that when failure occurs, net worth is negative. This type of forbearance has taken place informally by temporizing before closing insolvent firms and formally through relaxations of accounting rules and capital standards when large numbers of firms are troubled.[44]

High interest rates in the early 1980s, for example, produced

massive losses at many thrifts heavily invested in fixed-rate mortgages. Hundreds of them were permitted to remain in operation even
though the market value of their net worth was significantly negative.
To bolster reported net worth, the FHLBB adopted more lenient
accounting standards, and thrifts were allowed to count the insuring
agencies' own promissory notes as part of net worth. As of June 1986,
using the liberal accounting rules allowed by the FHLBB, 190 savings
and loans with negative net worth continue to operate. If the same
accounting standards as applied to banks were used, 456 operating
savings and loans would show negative net worth.[45]

Similarly, in March 1986 federal bank regulators adopted a plan
permitting banks with loans concentrated in agriculture and energy
industries to use more permissive accounting rules for restructured
loans and to operate under relaxed capital standards.[46] In addition to
exacerbating the perverse incentives for risk taking by insolvent or
nearly insolvent firms discussed earlier, this has also reduced the
incentives of managers and owners to seek private market solutions to
their capitalization problems.

As depositor protections have expanded over the years, market
discipline from general creditors, equity holders, and managers has
become increasingly important. Nonetheless, regulator forbearance
on capital standards and the timing of closure, combined with current
failure resolution techniques, has reduced the force of market disciplines coming from these other sources as well. The result has been a
steady and significant erosion of market disciplines operating on
banks and thrifts.

Disclosure Regulation. Depository firms may be unique in being
prohibited by federal agencies from disclosing material financial information; yet disclosure is crucial for market discipline to work. Over
the years since the advent of deposit insurance, regulators have
developed a penchant for secrecy in the handling of problem cases.
Although it is probably true that secrecy has enabled supervisors to
work out some problems that might otherwise have resulted in bank
failures, it is doubtful that the public has been well served over time
by secretive policies.[47]

The question is whether, in the long run, market discipline in an
environment of fuller disclosure would be more effective in reducing
failures by restraining risk taking than the secretive handling of
problems as they arise. The answer clearly depends on how well
depositors would use such information. The cost of mistakes by
depositors is probably not great. If the general public's perception of
the solvency of a bank is incorrect, the bank may be able to replace lost

deposits in private markets. If not, the Federal Reserve can lend on good collateral so that the bank's assets will not have to be sold at fire sale prices. If, however, a firm is insolvent, there may be advantages to having it closed quickly, rather than attempting to conceal the insolvency from the public in the hope that the situation might turn around.[48]

Paul Volcker, however, believes additional disclosure is undesirable. In a letter to Senator Jake Garn, he wrote: "Public disclosure, under certain circumstances, could do irreparable harm to the bank, frustrate regulatory action designed to rehabilitate the bank and, therefore, may not be in the public interest."[49]

Volcker's comments clearly indicate that what is at stake is not the stability of the financial system, but the survival of threatened banks. A policy of nondisclosure that protects a bank from a run based on material information regarding the bank's condition may also harm uninsured depositors and other creditors in the event the bank fails. Volcker's interest in "rehabilitating" private financial firms has little to do with preserving financial stability.

Time Inconsistency and Policy-Maker Incentives

From time to time bank regulators have emphasized the value of market discipline, but when a large financial firm is in trouble, or when financial problems are widespread within a region or industry, they have proven reluctant to incur the short-run disruptions and criticism that result from imposing losses on large numbers of depositors and other bank creditors. In times of trouble, the long-term benefits of improved private incentives to control risk bearing may seem theoretical and far removed to someone with a short term in office.

The temptation of policy makers to forsake the best long-term policies in order to achieve short-run benefits is a policy dilemma that appears in many different contexts. In the economics literature this dilemma is known as the time inconsistency problem.[50] It arises, for example, in setting policy toward hostage negotiations, taxation of capital, property rights over inventions, and control of aggregate demand and the price level. Time inconsistency is not simply a problem of shortsightedness on the part of governments. It involves a dynamic in which a policy is adopted treating private sector expectations as given, without recognizing the effect of that policy on future expectations and future policy.

Implementing the best long-run policy generally involves some form of precommitment, or policy rule, preventing policy makers from doing what is best, treating private expectations as given. The classic gold standard, patent laws, balanced budget rules, and an explicit policy of never negotiating for hostages are examples of rules designed to minimize the influence of short-run pressures on national policies. Such mechanisms may produce short-run problems, but they also constrain decision making in ways that may be beneficial over time.

There is an element of the time inconsistency problem in policy toward bank failures and market discipline. In essence, bank regulators would like market participants to believe they are at risk. This raises the cost of funds to banks perceived to be risky and provides an incentive for bank managers to adopt prudent policies. At the same time, regulators have sought to avoid the disruptive effects of outright failures, particularly when more than a few firms are involved. They would like to protect against disruptive events without announcing a policy of avoiding disruptive conditions.

If the time inconsistency problem correctly characterizes an important aspect of safety net policy, then the rising rate of bank and thrift problems has deeper roots than a succession of transient shocks and policy errors. It arises because public policy toward problem and failing firms has encouraged risk taking by surviving firms. Improving this situation may require the adoption of policy rules that prevent regulators from engaging in expedient policies with long-term costs.

Maintaining Financial Stability

The tremendous changes that have occured in financial markets and the erosion of important market disciplines have made a reconsideration of financial safety net policies imperative. This section presents some proposals for improving safety net policies.[51]

The special protections that banks and thrifts have been afforded under present safety net policies extend beyond deposits under $100,000 to include, in specific instances, large depositors, other creditors, managers, and shareholders of banks and bank holding companies. As banking firms expand their nontraditional products and activities, a broader range of activities and instruments implicitly fall under the federal safety net. At the same time, nonbanking firms are playing an increasingly important role in financial markets. The erosion of traditional barriers and the increased integration of financial markets have rendered the special protections afforded to banks and thrifts increasingly less useful and possibly perverse for maintaining financial stability. New actors, new instruments, and new financing techniques potentially expose the financial system to forms of risk that are imperfectly understood but that are also clearly beyond the capacity and reach of the deposit insurance system.

Maintaining financial stability in the new financial environment requires market disciplines. Enforcing greater market discipline requires shifting responsibility for stabilizing the financial system toward the Federal Reserve and away from the deposit-insuring agencies. If some unforeseen event causes a number of financial firms to fail, the deposit insurance system will not be capable of preventing a financial crisis. The Federal Reserve must act to limit failures to insolvent firms by supplying liquidity to the market so that solvent but illiquid firms can continue to operate.

Over the years, the major events requiring the attention of the Federal Reserve and the insuring agencies have been handled on an *ad hoc* basis. The Continental Illinois experience, for example, illustrated that bank regulators apparently lacked a clear policy for dealing with the failure of a large bank. The absence of precommitment to clearly understood policies unnecessarily heightens uncertainty. Yet, uncertainty about the response of authorities to financial shocks has triggered financial crises in the past.[52]

Experts disagree over the consequences that might have occurred if regulators had permitted Continental Bank to fail. Some believe the failure of such a large bank would have been extremely disruptive, given market expectations at the time, and that the stability of the financial system would have been at risk. Others believe Continental's failure would not have posed such risks, if handled properly by regulators.[53]

The disruptive effects of a failure of a large financial firm or of other financial shocks can be minimized by announcing well in advance, and then implementing, a set of clearly understood rules for discount window lending and failure management, in which the liquidity of depositor accounts is preserved even if depositors are subject to losses. Financial markets will not seriously believe policy makers' announcements to strengthen market discipline by permitting financial firms of all sizes to fail unless a credible plan for failure management is in place.

Economists continue to value the rules Walter Bagehot established for central bank policy in the nineteenth century.[54] Bagehot's study of financial history led him to conclude that failures do not have systemic effects if preannounced rules to prevent panic are followed. He proposed that the central bank lend freely on collateral that is marketable in the ordinary course of business when there is no panic. He also argued that the central bank should not restrict its lending to paper eligible for discount in normal periods but should lend freely at a discount rate above the market rate for such lending in order to discourage borrowing by those who can accommodate themselves in private markets, and to eliminate subsidies to those with access to the discount window.

A set of clearly established rules patterned along Bagehot's lines continues to have considerable merit. The lender-of-last-resort function, however, can be characterized as a form of insurance that may generate its own moral hazard. If lending takes place too freely, firms will have increased incentives to select financial structures that could compromise their own liquidity and solvency. The purpose of discount window lending is to prevent problems at a single firm or group of firms from degenerating into a run on the banking system. It should not serve as a backstop credit facility in normal times, nor should it protect large depositors, stockholders, and managers from loss.[55] Open market operations—Federal Reserve purchases of government securities in the marketplace—can also serve this purpose by providing liquidity to the financial system in a way that does not allocate reserves among particular users. In that respect, it may be a superior instrument of monetary policy when markets are scrambling for liquidity.

With these changes in central bank policy, the deposit insurance system can return to the role of providing limited deposit guarantees. To restore market discipline by depositors at banks and thrifts of all sizes, the deposit-insuring agencies should develop a workable failure resolution strategy that can be applied to large as well as small firms and that exposes large depositors and other creditors to losses. George Kaufman has proposed the "modified trusteeship," a version of the modified payoff discussed earlier in the section "The Erosion of Market Discipline in Banking," which is designed to minimize the disruptive effects of a large bank payoff. In such an arrangement, the deposit insurer would temporarily operate a failed firm, preserving the liquidity of depositor accounts, until a permanent resolution is achieved. If the firm had negative net worth when taken over, the value of all uninsured deposits and other liabilities would be written down by the appropriate *pro rata* amount.[56]

In view of the time inconsistency problem discussed in the section "Time Inconsistency and Policy-Maker Incentives," statutory limits on the ability of regulators to rescue large depositors, other creditors, managers, and shareholders of banks and thrifts may be desirable. The goal of protecting small depositors could be managed with a maximum coverage level under the current $100,000 deposit insurance limit. Nonetheless, a substantial part of the problem would be solved by simply enforcing the $100,000 limit in all cases.

As Edward Kane recently noted, individuals and firms routinely select insurance policies against other risks that include deductibles, coinsurance elements, and other limitations on coverage. Their choice to bear some risk is presumably an informed response to the high marginal cost of complete coverage. It seems unlikely that these same parties would knowingly pay the full cost of virtually perfect guarantees on their deposit accounts.[57]

A policy of strictly enforced limits on deposit insurance coverage would be a significant departure from present practices. Markets will need time to adjust to these new rules, since banking and correspondent relationships are likely to undergo significant changes as diversification becomes more important in reducing exposure. Legislation could specify a phase-in period during which deposits above the coverage limit could receive partial coverage. For example, the insuring agencies might adopt a policy of paying depositors with deposits above the coverage limit no more than 95 percent of par value unless it expects to recover that amount or more upon merger or liquidation of a failing firm. In subsequent years, this partial coverage for large deposits could decline, say, by five percentage points per year.

Accompanying these changes in coverage limits and methods for failure resolution should be a strengthened commitment to prompt closure of firms that are market-value insolvent, since the cost of failures depends significantly on how quickly regulators detect and respond to problem situations. Although there are important practical difficulties associated with fully implementing a market-value accounting system, the potential distortions of a firm's condition under present accounting standards are great enough that proposals to move toward market-value accounting deserve careful attention.[58] In addition, protecting the interests of the deposit insurance agencies, large depositors, and other creditors requires greater disclosure and an end to capital forbearance policies.

In recent years a number of deposit insurance reform proposals have been suggested, including risk-based deposit insurance premiums and risk-based capital requirements. Although proposals along these lines deserve study, the potential improvements from them are swamped by the gross distortions associated with current failure resolution, capital, and disclosure policies. For example, risk-based deposit insurance premiums could, in principle, create a better incentive structure for banking firms. Implementing a truly effective system, however, poses great difficulties associated with properly measuring risk, determining an appropriate schedule of premiums, and establishing a frequency of review that balances considerations of timeliness and cost.[59]

Finally, as noted earlier, certain banking and thrift regulations have hampered firms in their diversification efforts, both geographically and across product lines, and have impeded their response to market changes brought about by technologically induced declines in information and transactions costs. Consequently, regulation may have actually contributed to increased risks to the banking system. A comprehensive approach to redesigning policies to promote financial stability would also address this problem.

The fundamental issue is whether well-managed, well-capitalized firms should be free from most restraints on their activities and markets, on the grounds that this freedom would promote efficiency and adaptability, and that sufficient capital would be available to absorb losses and protect the insurance funds. The more bank and thrift regulators rely on market discipline and prompt closure of firms that are insolvent on a market-value basis, the less regulation is needed to protect the insurer against losses.

Conclusions

The federal financial safety net was intended to support a stable financial structure, not to protect individuals and firms from losses. The threat of a financial crisis should not preclude the failure of mismanaged firms regardless of their size. In recent years, serious incentive and equity problems have emerged in the U.S. financial system largely as a result of policies established in the name of protecting financial stability. As Anna Schwartz put it, "the inefficient are sustained in their misuse of resources because of the imagined hardship that would be imposed on the efficient."[60]

Recommendations for sweeping reforms are unlikely to be taken seriously so long as the present system operates reasonably well. The risk that it will not, however, is significant. If and when a crisis develops, what happens will depend critically on the options that have been explored and have become intellectually respectable. Market-oriented solutions must be available. Decades of academic argument in favor of eliminating Regulation Q had little or no effect until a crisis made changes inevitable. At that point, the existence of that body of literature made interest rate deregulation a realistic option.[61]

If we are fortunate enough to avoid a major financial crisis, and if current policies remain in place, the hidden costs and inequities from present policies will be more difficult to correct. But as private firms gain experience operating under an expanded safety net, correcting such problems will become increasingly important.

If the present safety net protections remain in place, pressures for large-scale reregulation of financial markets will inevitably develop. It may be impossible, however, to regulate the overall risk exposure of financial firms with traditional regulatory techniques. Historical experience shows that the effect of regulation has often been eroded by competitive pressures for efficiency and innovation. As a result, regulation, rather than restraining potentially risky activities, forces them into new channels.

More important, users of financial services have benefited enormously from the ongoing process of financial market restructuring. The range of choices for borrowers and lenders is expanding, many burdensome inefficiencies are being eliminated, and the costs of financial services are falling for many customers. It is difficult to imagine reregulating in such a way as to preserve these benefits.

Notes

1. Securitization refers to a shift in commercial lending from direct loans through intermediaries toward tradable instruments such as commercial paper.

2. A Bank for International Settlements study group examining innovation in financial markets concluded that large international banks worldwide have lost comparative advantage to international securities markets as a channel for credit for large high-grade borrowers. See Bank for International Settlements, *Recent Innovations in International Banking* (Basle, Switzerland: Bank for International Settlements, 1986).

3. Off-balance sheet activities include standby letters of credit, interest rate swaps, and commitments to extend credit and to buy and sell foreign exchange or futures contracts. Banks have been required to report such activity in quarterly call reports to the FDIC since September 1983.

4. "FDIC Chief Warns about Mounting Debt," *Washington Post*, November 12, 1986.

5. See James Barth, R. Dan Brumbaugh, Jr., and Daniel Sauerhaft, "Failure Costs of Government-Regulated Financial Firms: The Case of Thrift Institutions," Federal Home Loan Bank Board Working Paper No. 123 (Washington, D.C.: 1986); and "FSLIC May Be $26 Billion Short," *Washington Post*, September 23, 1986.

6. See Federal Deposit Insurance Corporation, *The Federal Deposit Insurance Corporation: The First Fifty Years* (Washington, D.C.: Federal Deposit Insurance Corporation, 1984).

7. These changes are discussed in greater detail in the section "The Erosion of Market Discipline in Banking."

8. Albert Wojnilower, "Financial Change in the United States" (Paper presented at the Conference on the Origins and Diffusion of Financial Innovation, Florence, Italy, 1985), pp. 19–20.

9. See, for example, George Benston and George Kaufman, "Risks and Failures in Banking: Overview, History, and Evaluation," in George Kaufman and Roger Kormendi, eds., *Deregulating Financial Services: Public Policy in Flux* (Cambridge, Mass.: Ballinger Press, 1986); James Barth, R. Dan Brumbaugh Jr., Daniel Sauerhaft, and George Wang, "Thrift Institution Failures: Causes and Policy Issues," *Bank Structure and Competition* (Chicago: Federal Reserve Bank of Chicago, 1985);

and George Benston, *An Analysis of the Causes of Savings and Loan Association Failures* (New York: Solomon Brothers Center for the Study of Financial Institutions Monograph Series in Finance and Economics, 1985).

10. For a comprehensive discussion of this topic, see Edward Kane, *The Gathering Crisis in Federal Deposit Insurance* (Cambridge, Mass: M.I.T. Press, 1985).

11. Of course, geographic restrictions on banks and thrifts have raised the cost of diversification as well.

12. Thrift firms are again reverting to the practice of funding substantial long-term, fixed-rate mortgages with shorter-term deposits, increasing their exposure to interest rate risk in the process. Fixed-rate mortgages as a percentage of total loans originated by thrifts exceeded 70 percent in the middle of 1986, up from 45 percent two years earlier. Over 80 percent of these are being held by the industry. See "Thrifts Are Forced to Revert to Fixed-Rate Mortgages," *Wall Street Journal*, October 15, 1986.

13. "S&Ls: Bank Board Chief Says Management Consignments Drive Up Costs of Funds," *Daily Report for Executives*, September 29, 1986.

14. "FDIC Cracking Down on Bank Fraud, Preparing Red Flag List For Examiners," *Washington Financial Reports*, June 2, 1986, p. 917.

15. Eugenie D. Short, Gerald P. O'Driscoll, and Franklin D. Berger, "Recent Bank Failures: Determinants and Consequences," *Bank Structure and Competition*, (Chicago: Federal Reserve Bank of Chicago, 1985).

16. The term "banks" is used here generically for depository firms.

17. An article that has fostered substantial debate is by E. Gerald Corrigan, "Are Banks Special?" Federal Reserve Bank of Minneapolis *Annual Report*, 1982. Several of the articles in the conference volume *The Search for Financial Stability: The Past Fifty Years* (San Francisco: Federal Reserve Bank of San Francisco, 1985), debate aspects and implications of bank specialness. See also, Richard Aspinwall, "On the Specialness of Banking," *Issues in Bank Regulation* (Autumn 1983), pp. 16–20.

18. Money market mutual funds, for example, originally emerged as a way to circumvent interest rate ceilings on deposit accounts. The expansion of the Euromarkets was initially encouraged by restrictions that inhibited domestic expansion by U.S. banking firms, as well as by regulations and taxes that increased the profitability of booking transactions overseas.

19. A variety of deposit insurance reform proposals have focused on limiting deposit insurance to transactions accounts to address this rationale for deposit insurance. See John Kareken, "Ensuring Financial Stability," in *The Search for Financial Stability*, for this argument and a proposal to split banks into payments services and lending components, with the "payments" bank holding 100 percent reserves of Treasury securities.

20. "Government Securities Bill Advances," *Washington Post* October 7, 1986.

21. U.S. Congress, Senate, Committee on Banking, 99th Congress, 2d session, February 1986.

22. See Benston and Kaufman, "Risk and Failures in Banking"; Arthur Rolnick and Warren Weber, "New Evidence on the Free Banking Era," *American Economic Review* (December 1983), pp. 1080–91; Anna Schwartz, "Real and Pseudo Financial Crises," pp. 11–31; and Michael Bordo, "Financial Crises, Banking Crises, Stock Market Crashes and the Money Supply," pp. 190–248 in Forrest Capie and Geoffrey Wood, eds., *Financial Crises and the World Banking Sytem* (London: Macmillan, 1985); and Phillip Cagan, *Determinants and Effects of Changes in the Stock of Money 1875–1960* (Washington, D.C.: National Bureau of Economic Research, 1965).

23. From the 1940 FDIC *Annual Report*.

24. George Benston, Robert Eisenbeis, Paul Horvitz, Edward Kane, and George

Kaufman, *Perspectives on a Safe and Sound Banking System* (Cambridge, Mass: M.I.T. Press, 1986).

25. "First Oklahoma Bank Unit Fails; FDIC Steps In," *Wall Street Journal*, July 15, 1986.

26. "Large Banks Are Hit by New Set of Rumors, and Stock Prices Fall," *Wall Street Journal*, May 25, 1984.

27. See, for example, Milton Friedman and Anna Schwartz, *A Monetary History of the United States, 1876–1960* (Princeton: Princeton University Press, 1963), chap. 4.

28. U.S. Congress, House of Representatives, Subcommittee on Commerce, Consumer, and Monetary Affairs of the Committee on Government Operations, 99th Congress, 2d session, June 11, 1986.

29. See The Working Group of the Cabinet Council on Economic Affairs, *Recommendations for Change in the Federal Deposit Insurance System* (Washington, D.C.: 1985).

30. From the 1957 FDIC *Annual Report*.

31. The FDIC has sought legislation to establish a depositor preference statute that would allow it to conduct P&A transactions without protecting general creditors.

32. Authority for the type of assistance provided to Continental Bank was granted to the FDIC in 1950. By law, the FDIC can provide funds to a bank in danger of failing if the bank is deemed "essential" to its community by bank regulators. For a detailed account see Irvine H. Sprague, *Bailout: An Insider's Account of Bank Failures and Rescues* (New York: Basic Books, 1986).

33. John M. Harris, James R. Scott, and Joseph F. Sinkey, "Evidence of Market Perceptions of a More Favorable Regulatory Environment for Large U.S. Banks/Bank Holding Companies" (Athens, Ga.: University of Georgia, 1986), unpublished.

34. William Seidman's testimony before the Senate Banking Committee appeared in *The American Banker*, March 20, 1986. See also, William Seidman, "Deposit Insurance Reform FDIC Style," *The BottomLine*, May 1986.

35. This authority was granted to the FDIC under the 1982 Garn–St Germain Act.

36. Open-bank assistance was arranged for a bank owned by BancOklahoma Corp. "FDIC to Inject Funds into Troubled Oklahoma Bank," *Washington Financial Reports*, August 25, 1986.

37. "FDIC Reconsiders Policy on Open Bank Aid, Will Not Require Wipeout of Shareholders," *Washington Financial Reports*, September 22, 1986.

38. See Kane, *The Gathering Crisis*, pp. 49–50.

39. See, for example, Fischer Black, Merton Miller, and Richard Posner, "An Approach to the Regulation of Bank Holding Companies," *Journal of Business*, no. 3 (1978), pp. 379–412.

40. The capital ratio refers to the ratio of equity capital to total assets. Data are from Benston and Kaufman, "Risk and Failures," p. 71.

41. Federal Reserve Bank of San Francisco *Weekly Letter* June 20, 1986.

42. Capital requirements for commercial banks were recently increased from 5.5 percent to 6 percent. Currently, savings and loans face a 3 percent capital requirement, but an FHLBB ruling will require them to increase capital gradually to 6 percent within six to twelve years depending on industry profitability.

43. For example, a firm can increase its reported net worth by selling assets whose prices have risen above acquisition cost, while retaining assets whose prices have fallen. See John Forde, "Seafirst and Schwab Sales Could Bolster BankAmer-

ica, But the Quick Fix Could Be Costly Over Long Haul," *American Banker*, August 11, 1986; also "Continental's Blow to a Safer Banking System," *Fortune*, June 11, 1984.

44. See, for example, Barth et al., "Failure Costs of Government Regulated Financial Firms."

45. The data are from the FHLBB.

46. Monica Langley, "Regulators to Ease Accounting Rules for Certain Loans," *Wall Street Journal*, March 12, 1986.

47. Several researchers have analyzed motives for central bank secrecy and ambiguity. See, for example, Marvin Goodfriend, "Monetary Mystique: Secrecy and Central Banking," *Journal of Monetary Economics* (January 1986), pp. 63–92.

48. For a fuller discussion of this line of argument, see chapter 7 of Benston et al., *Perspectives on Safe and Sound Banking*.

49. Quoted in *Washington Weekly Report*, Independent Bankers Association, July 26, 1985.

50. For a discussion, see Finn E. Kydland and Edward C. Prescott, "Rules Rather than Discretion: The Inconsistency of Optimal Plans," *Journal of Political Economy* (June 1977), pp. 473–91; and R.E. Lucas, Jr., "Principles of Fiscal and Monetary Policy," *Journal of Monetary Economics* (January 1986).

51. Policy recommendations similar to those discussed in this section have appeared elsewhere. See Kane, *The Gathering Crisis*; Benston et al., *Perspectives on Safe and Sound Banking*; and Allan Meltzer, "Financial Failures and Financial Policies," in George G. Kaufman and Roger C. Kormendi, eds., *Deregulating Financial Services*, chapter 3.

52. Schwartz, "Real and Pseudo Financial Crises."

53. See Burt Solomon, "A Burst of Bailouts," *National Journal*, September 27, 1986, pp. 2315–2317 for a sampling of opinion among financial economists and regulators on this question.

54. See Meltzer, "Financial Failures"; and Hugh Rockoff, "Walter Bagehot and the Theory of Central Banking"; Schwartz, "Real and Pseudo Financial Crises"; and Meltzer's comment on Schwartz in *Financial Crises and the World Financial System*.

55. Between the contraction of the 1930s and 1980, only one major bank run occurred. In 1974 Franklin National Bank lost $1.7 billion in deposits prior to its failure. There was little evidence of contagion effects at the time, but the Federal Reserve, fearing a systemic problem, lent freely to the bank at low interest rates for several months after the bank could have been declared insolvent. This gave uninsured depositors the opportunity to withdraw their funds, since the bank's problems were widely known. For an account, see Joseph Sinkey, *Problem and Failed Institutions in the Commercial Banking Industry* (Greenwich, Conn.: JAI Press, 1979), chapter 6.

56. This proposal is discussed in chapter 4 of *Perspectives on Safe and Sound Banking*.

57. This argument is made by Edward Kane in "No Room for Weak Links in the Chain of Deposit Insurance Reform" (Berkeley: University of California, National Center on Financial Services, 1986), p. 21.

58. For a more complete discussion of the benefits and problems associated with implementing a market-value accounting system, see David Lereah, "Current Value Accounting: Feasibility for Financial Institutions," in *Bank Structure and Competition* (Chicago: Federal Reserve Bank of Chicago, forthcoming).

59. For a recent literature survey, see Arthur Murton, "A Survey of the Issues and the Literature Concerning Risk-Related Deposit Insurance," *Banking and Eco-*

nomic Review (September/October 1986), pp. 11–20.

60. Schwartz, "Real and Pseudo Financial Crises," p. 27.

61. Milton Friedman and Anna Schwartz make this argument in "Has Government Any Role in Money?" *Journal of Monetary Economics* (January 1986).

7

The Influence of Employment Shifts and New Job Opportunities on the Growth and Distribution of Real Wages

Marvin H. Kosters and Murray N. Ross

Summary

Growth in real wages has been significantly slower since the early 1970s than during the preceding two decades, and various measures of real economic well-being, though showing quite different patterns of growth, show significantly smaller increases than earlier. This phenomenon is generally discussed in connection with the slowdown in productivity growth.

The slowdown in real pay per hour of work has been widely distributed across industries and classes of workers. That is, adjustments to reflect a wide range of measurable changes in characteristics of workers and in the economy do not, taken together, account for a significant component of the actual change in the trend of real hourly pay.

Careful analysis of available data and their interpretation is an essential starting point for placing in perspective what has happened to real economic well-being. Taking inflation into account is obviously necessary, but choosing an appropriate price index to adjust for inflation is also essential for a realistic appraisal of how workers have fared. Because of the way they were measured in the consumer price index, the effects of high inflation and interest rates on housing costs and thus on the purchasing power of the average consumer were exaggerated before 1983. The change in measurement introduced meant that the earlier overstatement in the index was not reversed by the subsequent decline in interest rates. Using the personal consumption expenditures deflator avoids this problem and provides a more realistic picture of real economic well-being.

Real compensation per hour provides the most comprehensive and direct measure of pay per hour of work. Measures of earnings and income for families or individuals reflect changes in labor force status and hours of work as well as many other factors only loosely related to workers' earning power. Compensation per hour is more comprehensive than average hourly earnings because it includes nonwage benefits in addition to wages and salaries. According to this measure, real pay per hour of work has continued to rise but at an average rate of only about three-fourths of 1 percent per year since 1972, down from almost 2½ percent in the preceding twenty years.

Because nonwage benefits have increased relative to wages and salaries, real average hourly earnings have increased less rapidly, and their growth has slowed more than that of hourly compensation. Only small effects on average hourly earnings can be traced to shifts in employment shares among industries, changing patterns of hours of work, the growing share of the work force made up of women, and changes in the age and schooling of workers. Shifts in employment away from manufacturing and other goods-producing industries toward services have had small negative effects on the average, but their contribution to slower real wage growth has been negligible. The combined effect of these changes makes no contribution to explaining the slowdown in the growth of real wages since the early 1970s.

Changes in industry employment patterns, particularly a decline in some basic industries and strong growth in services, have frequently been regarded as a source not only of slower real wage growth but also of increased wage dispersion. Measures of income distribution showing a smaller concentration of families and other income-receiving units in the middle-income range have been put forward to support this view. Average wages for industries have also become more widely dispersed. When employment shares are taken into account, however, dispersion in industry average wages has been essentially stable in recent years. More important, the underlying distribution of wages for individual jobs has shown a trend toward smaller dispersion, so that changes in overall income distribution apparently reflect primarily changes in working and living arrangements.

Demographic changes in the work force and changes in the industrial structure of the economy have not resulted in more widely dispersed hourly earnings. Moreover, their effects on average real wages have been small and largely offsetting, so that the slowdown in real wage growth cannot be attributed to them. Although these results leave the slowdown unexplained, they are evidence of the futility of policies that would impede further adjustments in industry structure or partially reverse those that have occurred in an effort to increase real wage growth. Protectionist international trade policies and domestic industrial policy have virtually no potential for raising real wage growth but would almost certainly create inefficiency and raise costs to consumers. The risks of policies intended to protect particularly "good jobs" are that real wage growth would be further retarded for workers already employed and fewer jobs would be available for those who are not.

The U.S. economy has been credited with a remarkably favorable record of job creation. During the four years after the recession in 1982, civilian employment rose by 10 million workers, and employment has increased by about 21 million workers during the past decade. The ratio of employment to population has recently reached record highs of over 61 percent. This experience appears especially favorable when compared with that of the industrial countries of Western Europe, where little job growth has occurred in recent years.

This favorable record for the number of job opportunities generated in the U.S. economy has, however, been accompanied by concerns about what has happened to the quality of jobs and whether forces may have been at work that made new job opportunities less desirable than the jobs they replaced. Perceptions about trends in the quality of jobs have in turn been influenced by factors such as the widely publicized trend toward services and the difficulties experienced by firms in goods-producing industries faced with strong international trade competition.

Concern about the quality of jobs has arisen in part because employment growth has been disproportionately concentrated in services, where average wages are lower than in goods-producing industries. One question this has raised is whether the growing service employment share might be contributing importantly to lower wages—or at least to slower growth in average wages. A second and related question is whether the distribution of wages in new jobs is too uneven to maintain a strong middle-income group in economic terms or a large middle class in broader social terms.

We address these questions concerning job quality first by examining several measures of real earnings and incomes to assess recent trends. We then analyze the influence of changes in industry employment and hours shares, of increased female employment, and of age and schooling on wage trends. Finally we discuss trends in the distribution of incomes and wages and the policy implications of the analysis.

Trends in Real Wages and Incomes

It is generally recognized that rising inflation outpaced wage increases for the typical worker in the late 1970s and that the marked reduction in inflation that has been achieved since the beginning of the 1980s was a major factor in improving real wage trends. Short-term developments of this kind, some of which may mark important turning points, are way stations on a longer-term path. Longer-term trends provide a different and valuable perspective on how the typical

211

worker has fared—a perspective less likely to be dominated by temporary and possibly reversible changes. The underlying factors that influence the direction and pace of growth in real wages are often obscured by short-term developments.

Several kinds of measures are available to examine trends in real earnings and incomes. Four of these—gross average hourly earnings, average hourly compensation, mean family income, and personal income per capita—are charted in figure 7–1. Each is adjusted for inflation (by conventionally used price indexes), and all are normalized to a common 1977 base. Annual average rates of change for each of these series are reported in table 7–1 for selected subperiods. The differences in the growth paths of these series arise from differences in the underlying data and in what they are intended to measure. Despite these important differences (discussed in detail below), two generalizations can be made at the outset.

The first is that virtually every measure of real wages or incomes shows a noticeably slower rate of growth since the early 1970s than during the preceding two decades.[1] This phenomenon is widely recognized and is frequently discussed in connection with a closely

TABLE 7–1

ANNUAL RATES OF CHANGE IN ALTERNATIVE MEASURES OF REAL
ECONOMIC WELL-BEING, SELECTED PERIODS, 1952–1985
(percent)

	Average Hourly Earnings (CPI)	Compensation per Hour (CPI)	Mean Family Income (CPI)	Personal Income per Capita (PCE)
1952–1972	2.20	2.70	2.97	2.47
1952–1964	2.40	3.02	2.90	1.78
1964–1972	1.90	2.20	3.09	3.52
1972–1985	−0.80	0.21	0.11	1.66

NOTE: Each series has been adjusted for inflation by the price deflator conventionally employed in official publications: consumer price index (CPI) or personal consumption expenditures deflator (PCE), as indicated.

SOURCES: For earnings data: *Economic Report of the President*, 1986, tables B-41 and B-43; Bureau of the Census, *Money Income of Households, Families, and Persons in the United States: 1984*, Series P-60, no. 151, table 12; and U.S. Department of Commerce, *Survey of Current Business* (various issues), table 7.6. For price data: *Economic Report of the President*, 1986, tables B-3 and B-55; and *Survey of Current Business*, table 7-11.

FIGURE 7–1

ALTERNATIVE MEASURES OF REAL ECONOMIC WELL-BEING, ADJUSTED FOR INFLATION BY CONVENTIONAL PRICE INDEXES, 1952–1985
(1977 = 100)

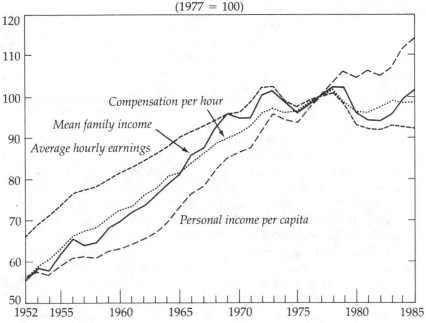

NOTE: The earnings series have been adjusted for inflation by the price deflators employed in official publications and normalized to a common 1977 basis to facilitate comparison. For gross average hourly earnings, compensation per hour, and mean family income, the deflator used is the consumer price index. The personal income per capita series is adjusted by the personal consumption expenditures deflator. See the text for an explanation of conceptual and coverage differences among the series.

SOURCES: Same as table 7–1.

related concept, the slowdown in productivity growth. The fact that a slowdown occurred is well known, but despite careful and detailed analytical efforts, the factors contributing to the slowdown in productivity growth—and in real wages—remain poorly understood.[2]

The second generalization is that differences in trends shown by these conventional measures have been much more pronounced in recent years than earlier in the period and cyclical influences have become more apparent. Consequently, different measures provide considerably different perspectives on what has happened on average to people's economic well-being. These differences have increased the

213

importance of distinguishing carefully between measurement concepts, reconciling differences where possible, and examining possible sources of the growing disparity.

Some of the most significant ways in which the trends charted in figure 7–1 differ are the following. First, two of the measures are expressed per hour, the other two per capita and per family. Second, three of the measures are adjusted for inflation by the consumer price index (CPI) while the fourth (personal income per capita) uses the personal consumption expenditures (PCE) deflator. Third, the underlying wage and income data are collected in surveys that are (at least to a large extent) independent. Finally, the earnings and income concepts vary in their coverage.

The two most closely comparable series are gross earnings per hour and compensation per hour. The main conceptual difference is that, in addition to wage earnings, compensation per hour includes nonwage benefits, such as employer contributions to social security and health and pension benefit plans, vacation and holiday pay, and the like. The increased importance of nonwage benefits in relation to wages and salaries accounts for the steeper trend of compensation per hour than of average hourly earnings. Note also that the average hourly earnings series covers only production and nonsupervisory workers in private nonfarm employment while the hourly compensation series covers all employees in that sector.[3]

Personal income per capita includes several components of income in addition to labor compensation: the imputed rental value of owner-occupied housing; income from rental properties, dividends, and interest; and cash and noncash income from such government programs as unemployment compensation, food stamps, and social security retirement and disability payments. Because income in this series is measured per capita, it also reflects such factors as changes in labor force participation rates, the fraction of the working-age population employed, and changes in the working-age population as a fraction of the total. Finally, this series is the only one charted that uses the PCE deflator to adjust for inflation.

Mean family income is derived from data collected in the Current Population Survey. The income concept used is quite comprehensive, as it is for the per capita personal income series; but noncash income is excluded, and cash income tends to be underreported. Adjustment for inflation by using the CPI is a major feature differentiating the mean family income series from the per capita income series. Since this is the only series charted that is not expressed per capita or per hour, it movement in relation to the others is affected by marriage, divorce, the establishment of separate households, and the prevalence of families with more than one earner.[4]

These data raise the question whether the typical worker or family has made any significant real economic gains during the past ten or fifteen years. With the exception of the per capita income series, all these measures reach peaks either in 1972–1973 or in 1978. The continuing increase in real per capita income reflects in part the bulge in the working-age population and the rising fraction employed. Another very significant difference in the real per capita income series is that the price deflator used to adjust for inflation is the CPI for all except this series. This difference contributes to the more rapid growth in real per capita income at the end of the 1970s and suggests a need to consider how inflation should appropriately be taken into account.

The effect of different price deflators is shown in figure 7–2 for

FIGURE 7–2

REAL AVERAGE HOURLY EARNINGS, ADJUSTED FOR INFLATION BY
ALTERNATIVE PRICE INDEXES, 1952–1985
(1977 = 100)

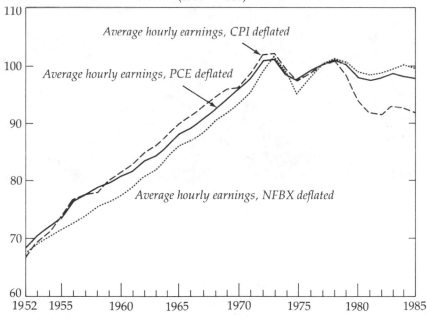

NOTE: NFBX is the implicit price deflator for the nonfarm business sector, excluding housing.

SOURCES: Same as table 7–1.

average hourly earnings, one of the series charted in figure 7–1 and the series analyzed in detail later in this chapter. The inflation adjustment that produces the most pronounced decline from peaks in 1972–1973 and 1978 is that based on the CPI. The major reason for the disparate movement of the CPI in relation to the other deflators since the late 1970s is the treatment of prices for owner-occupied housing, particularly the mortgage interest rate component. When interest rates soared from 5 percent in 1976 to 14 percent in 1981 for short-term Treasury bills (with the prime rate rising above 20 percent), the resulting increase in mortgage interest rates produced a sharp rise in the CPI even though only a small fraction of houses were financed at those high rates. These developments led to the introduction into the CPI of a rental-equivalence price measure for owner-occupied housing beginning in 1983. The net result was a surge in the CPI when

FIGURE 7–3

REAL AVERAGE HOURLY EARNINGS AND COMPENSATION PER HOUR, ADJUSTED FOR INFLATION BY A COMMON PRICE INDEX (THE PCE DEFLATOR), 1952–1985

(1977 = 100)

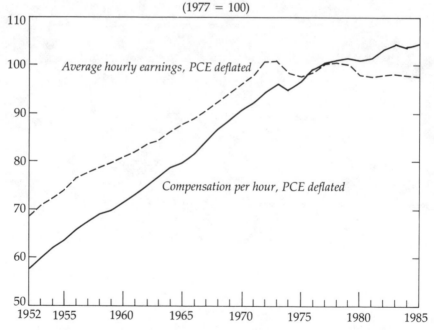

NOTE: See the text for a discussion of conceptual differences between the two series.

SOURCES: Same as table 7–1.

interest rates soared that was not offset by the subsequent decline in interest rates, which came after the new, less interest-rate-sensitive measure of housing costs was incorporated.

If the rental-equivalence measure had been used in the CPI for the decade before 1983, increases in the CPI during that period would have closely paralleled increases in the PCE deflator.[5] Consequently, we use the PCE deflator to adjust for inflation to avoid the distortion that arises from the change in the earlier flawed treatment of housing costs in the CPI. We regard the PCE deflator as the preferred measure of how the typical family was affected by inflation, and we view income and pay adjusted by it as providing a more realistic measure of economic well-being. As shown in figure 7–2, real gross average hourly earnings in 1985 stood at 97.6 percent of their value in 1977 under the PCE-based adjustment for inflation and at 92 percent under the CPI adjustment.

Inflation adjustments based on the CPI and the PCE deflator both take inflation into account on the basis of what households consume. An alternative adjustment would take into account the prices of what workers produce. The third measure charted in figure 7–2 uses the nonfarm business deflator (excluding housing), a price index that corresponds closely in its sectoral coverage to average hourly earnings.

Differences in annual rates of change attributable to the use of different deflators are shown in table 7–2. For the period as a whole, the overall increase in real wages under all three measures was closely comparable between 1952 and 1972. Since 1972, however, prices of goods and services produced in the nonfarm business sector have increased slightly less rapidly than prices of goods and services consumed by the typical household. That is, an hour of work has resulted in slightly better performance when measured by output produced than by the consumption goods that could be purchased by the wages paid. Since the divergence between growth in real average hourly earnings after 1972 as adjusted by the PCE deflator and by the private nonfarm deflator has been fairly small, however, only a small component of the slowdown in growth for private nonfarm workers has apparently been attributable to developments outside that sector.[6]

It is noteworthy that even after the distorting effects of housing prices are removed by using the PCE deflator to adjust for inflation, real average hourly earnings in 1985 remain below levels reached earlier. Does this mean that the real economic well-being of the average worker has declined? How can this be reconciled with the rise in labor productivity in the nonfarm business sector of about four percentage points since 1977? Part of the answer lies in the distinction

217

TABLE 7-2

THE EFFECT OF ALTERNATIVE PRICE DEFLATORS ON MEASURES OF REAL HOURLY PAY, SELECTED PERIODS, 1952–1985

(annual percentage rate of change)

	Average Hourly Earnings (CPI)	Average Hourly Earnings (PCE)	Average Hourly Earnings (NFBX)	Compensation per Hour (PCE)
1952–1972	2.20	1.98	1.99	2.40
1952–1964	2.40	1.94	1.89	2.57
1964–1972	1.90	2.04	2.13	2.34
1972–1985	−0.80	−0.24	0.05	0.77

NOTE: Changes in each series are expressed as compound average annual percentage rates. Each series has been adjusted for inflation by the price deflator indicated: consumer price index (CPI), personal consumption expenditures deflator (PCE), and the implicit price deflator for the nonfarm business sector, excluding housing (NFBX).

SOURCES: Same as table 7-1.

noted earlier between hourly compensation and hourly wages and salaries. The costs of nonwage supplements included in compensation per hour rose from about 6 percent of wage and salary payments in 1952 to nearly 14 percent in 1972 and 21 percent in 1985. Part of this increase is accounted for by the fact that more real benefits are provided and part by increases in their prices in relation to consumption items as a whole. The rising relative costs of health plans and the rise in social security tax rates are examples of the relative price effect, although real benefits provided under health plans have also been expanded.

Real compensation per hour is charted in figure 7-3 along with real gross average hourly earnings. To facilitate comparison, both are adjusted for inflation by the PCE deflator. These measures show that nonwage supplements have increased more rapidly than wages, especially since 1972 (see table 7-2). Compensation per hour is the more comprehensive measure of economic rewards for work, both for the employed workers it covers and for their pay, and it shows continued gradual improvement in recent years. Nevertheless, even for this preferred measure—compensation per hour adjusted by the PCE deflator—the rate of improvement has fallen sharply since the early 1970s.

The real value of economic rewards for an hour of work has continued to rise, but in recent years it has been rising more slowly. The main counterpart of what workers are paid is what they produce —in other words, worker productivity, or output per hour of work. That is, the amount of real goods and services that workers can buy in return for an hour of work—assuming a fairly constant fraction of national output devoted to investment, a share in taxes to pay for government operations, and abstracting from borrowing or lending abroad—is basically set by the amount of real goods and services produced on the average by an hour of work. Within this framework what happens to real pay per hour can be viewed as essentially equivalent to what happens to labor productivity. Real average hourly earnings constitute a large, but gradually declining, share of real pay or compensation per hour.

Sectoral and Labor Force Changes

The slowdown in real wage growth since the early 1970s has been accompanied by changes in industry employment patterns and in the demographic characteristics of the labor force. Although the effects of such changes can be analyzed, the factors underlying many of them are more fundamental. That is, changes in industry structure and demographic composition of employment should be viewed as outcomes produced by the interaction of supply, cost, and demand patterns with relative wages and prices, not as the causal factors themselves. Nevertheless, it is worthwhile to examine the quantitative significance of relations between these factors and real earnings and whether their influence has changed over time.

The continuing shift toward employment in services (and away from manufacturing and other goods-producing industries) has received a great deal of public attention. Data on the magnitude of the shift and on average wages in the two broad sectors are reported in table 7–3. As these data show, employment in the services sector has increased from about 50 percent of the total to 70 percent during the past thirty five years. Most of this growth has been in private sector services. The lower average hourly earnings in services than in goods-producing industries has led some observers to suggest that employment shifts among industries may have contributed significantly to slower growth in wages.[7]

The most important demographic change in the labor force is the growing fraction of the work force made up of women. Rising labor force participation of women and declining labor force participation of men have been persistent trends for at least a generation. Since 1950

219

TABLE 7–3

EMPLOYMENT AND WAGES IN GOODS- AND SERVICES-PRODUCING
INDUSTRIES, 1950–1985

	Employment (millions of workers)			Employment Shares (percent)		Average Hourly Earnings (dollars per hour)		Ratio of Goods to Services
	Goods (total)	Goods (mfg.)	Services (total)	Goods	Services	Goods	Services	
1950	18.5	15.2	20.7	47.2	52.8	1.51	—	—
1955	20.5	16.9	23.2	46.9	53.1	1.95	—	—
1960	20.4	16.8	25.4	44.6	55.4	2.39	—	—
1965	21.9	18.1	28.8	43.3	56.7	2.79	2.23	0.80
1970	23.6	19.4	34.7	40.4	59.6	3.67	2.95	0.80
1975	22.6	18.3	39.7	36.3	63.7	5.27	4.14	0.79
1980	25.7	20.3	48.5	34.6	65.4	7.82	6.06	0.77
1985	24.9	19.1	56.3	30.7	69.3	10.16	7.89	0.78

NOTE: Employment data are for all employees on private nonagricultural payrolls. Average hourly earnings are for production and nonsupervisory workers on private nonagricultural payrolls. (Inclusion of government employees in the services-producing category would raise the services share of total payroll employment from 63.9 percent in 1965 to 74.5 percent in 1985, with the goods-producing share reduced correspondingly.) As noted in the text, payroll data do not cover the entire employed population. Data from the household survey, however, show very similar trends. See, for example, Ronald E. Kutscher and Valerie A. Personick, "Deindustrialization and the Shift to Services," *Monthly Labor Review* (June 1986).

SOURCE: Bureau of Labor Statistics, *Employment and Earnings*, diskette data files.

the rate for women has risen from 35 percent to 55 percent, while the rate for men has declined from 86 percent to 76 percent. As shown in table 7–4, the female share of employment has increased from about 35 percent to 45 percent since 1965. Although men still make up about 55 percent of the work force, during the past twenty years about six of ten new workers have been women, and this ratio is expected to continue during the decade ahead.[8] This growing female share of employment has affected the trend in average hourly earnings because of the lower wages earned by women.

Changes in the age composition of the labor force and in years of schooling have also been large and potentially significant for wage trends. As a result of the baby boom during the first two decades after

TABLE 7–4

WOMEN'S SHARE OF CIVILIAN
NONAGRICULTURAL EMPLOYMENT, 1955–1985
(percent)

	Household Survey Data	Establishment Survey Data
1955	33.1	—
1960	34.6	—
1965	35.9	32.9
1970	38.7	35.6
1975	40.5	38.1
1980	43.2	41.0
1985	44.8	44.1

NOTE: The data on the female employment share from the establishment survey exclude public employment.

SOURCES: Bureau of Labor Statistics, *Handbook of Labor Statistics* (June 1985), tables 1, 66, 68; *Employment and Earnings* (March 1986), table 1; and *Supplement to Employment and Earnings* (June 1986).

World War II, a disproportionately large fraction of the labor force from the mid-1960s until about 1980 was made up of teen-age workers. The teen-age bulge has tapered off during the 1980s, but the composition of the labor force is now heavily weighted toward young workers. The reduction in average age would by itself tend to reduce wages.

Years of schooling completed by young workers have generally been increasing, so that an unusually large share of the labor force is made up of workers entering their prime earning years with more years of schooling on the average than those leaving the work force through retirement.[9] Since wages generally increase with years of schooling, the changes in age and schooling have had partially offsetting effects on wages.

Part-time work increased in importance during the 1950s and 1960s. Since then, however, the part-time share of the work force has apparently stabilized, as shown in table 7–5. Less than 15 percent of the work force has in recent years been engaged in voluntary regular part-time work. Most of the variation in part-time work for economic reasons is apparently associated with the business cycle; this component of the work force has moved closely in parallel with the unem-

TABLE 7–5

DISTRIBUTION OF WAGE AND SALARY WORKERS AT WORK IN
NONAGRICULTURAL INDUSTRIES, BY FULL- AND PART-TIME STATUS,
MAY 1955–MAY 1985
(percent)

	Full-Time Schedule	Part-Time Schedule		
		Total	Economic reasons	Usual and voluntary
1955	88.1	11.9	3.4	8.5
1960	85.1	14.9	4.1	10.7
1965	84.7	15.3	2.8	12.5
1970	83.0	17.0	2.7	14.3
1975	81.3	18.7	4.3	14.4
1980	81.2	18.8	4.4	14.4
1985	81.7	18.3	5.2	13.1

NOTE: Workers on full-time schedules (thirty-five hours or more) include those working full time in the preceding week and those who usually work full time but who worked part time (one to thirty-five hours of work) in the preceding week because of illness, vacation, weather, or other reasons.

SOURCES: William V. Deuterman, Jr., and Scott Campbell Brown, "Voluntary Part-Time Workers: A Growing Part of the Labor Force," *Monthly Labor Review* (June 1978), p. 5, table 1; and *Employment and Earnings* (June 1978 – June 1986), tables A-28 and A-29.

ployment rate. Since part-time work is concentrated among young workers and students enrolled in school, the changes in the share of part-time work may be largely attributable to changes in the age structure of the labor force.[10] Changes in the part-time share have been quite small since the mid-1960s, however, and hence are not likely to be an important source of changes in average wages.

The two kinds of changes whose effects can be examined most directly using the data available are the changing industry employment shares and the rising female employment share. Average wages differ among industries and between women and men, although in both cases wages of individual workers are widely dispersed and the distributions of individual wages accordingly show a great deal of overlap. We first analyze the effects of these changes on overall average wage trends by examining the quantitative significance of compositional shifts in employment by industry and by sex and then take into account the effects of age and schooling.

Sources of Average Hourly Earnings Changes. The average hourly earnings series is essentially a weighted average of industry wages, with numbers of employees and average weekly hours by industry incorporated as weights. To the extent that adequate detailed data are available, changes in the index can be related to a particular kind of change by examining how such a change, taken by itself, has affected the average. The factors analyzed are industry employment changes, industry hours changes, and changes in the female share of employment. A detailed technical description of the method is contained in the appendix. This section describes the analysis and interprets the results.

The data. The gross average hourly earnings series is based on data from the establishment survey, which assembles reports from individual firms. These data contain information by industry on total employment and on production and nonsupervisory workers. Average hourly earnings and average weekly hours are also available, but only for production and nonsupervisory workers. Although analysis that is necessarily restricted to a fraction of the work force because of the data available has certain limitations, the effects of shifts in employment shares between the component of the work force covered by our analysis and the rest of the economy should be mitigated by the stability of the shares.[11] In addition, separate employment totals are available by industry for male and female workers. These data, available directly from the establishment survey, need to be supplemented by data on male and female hours from the household survey and by data from other sources for hourly earnings of women relative to those of men.[12]

Since women earn lower average wages than men, changes in the fraction of the work force made up of women cause changes in the overall average even if hourly earnings within each group remain unchanged. Some factors that contribute to lower wages for women have been identified, but the underlying reasons are not completely understood.[13] For purposes of this analysis the method we use is to put aside these important questions about the underlying sources of wage differences and to work with the observed differentials. That is, we use estimates of actual wage differences to make the adjustments necessary to distinguish between changes in the overall average attributable to changes in industry employment shares and changes attributable to the changing male-female employment composition.

Estimates of the ratio of female to male wages are available from several sources. The estimates most applicable to our analysis are wage rates from broad aggregates, without adjustment for differences between male and female workers in age, schooling, work experience, or other factors. Data from the Current Population Survey for private sector hourly-wage workers, a sample that corresponds closely to the workers covered in our analysis, show a ratio of female to male median hourly earnings of 0.623 for 1977.[14]

This estimate for a broad aggregate should not be used as an estimate of the ratio for each industry, however, because the distribution of male and female employment among industries is uneven, the female employment share generally being larger in industries with lower than average wages. Wage ratios within each industry must accordingly be larger, on the average, than the observed aggregate female-male wage ratio.

By using an iterative procedure to estimate within-industry ratios consistent with the aggregate ratio of 0.623 for 1977 (which we treat as the base year), we obtained an estimate of 0.7 for the average ratio within industries. This estimate, which we assumed to be constant across industries and over time, also generated a gradually rising aggregate female-male average hourly earnings ratio roughly consistent in its magnitude with observed aggregate trends.

The method of decomposition. Four sources of change in average hourly earnings were distinguished in our analysis. Three of these are estimated as quantity changes—in industry average hours of work, in numbers of employees, and in the female share of total working hours. The other component is estimated as a value change—in the average real wage paid in each industry. The real average hourly earnings measure we use is obtained by adjusting for inflation by the PCE deflator, and all changes are measured by using 1977 as the base year.

1. The effect of *employment share changes among industries* is estimated by weighting actual industry average hourly earnings in the base year (1977) by the share of total employment in each industry in each year. Since average weekly hours of work differ among industries and have changed over time, base period hours in each industry are used to avoid picking up effects of hours changes along with those of employment changes. That is, the effects of changing employment shares are estimated by a method that treats hours of work as if they were not affected by changing employment shares among industries. Since only employment shares are permitted to change as annual computations are made, the resulting estimate can be regarded as a "pure" employment effect.[15]

2. The effect of *changes in industry hours* is estimated by using base period industry wages and industry employment to compute the

effects of changes in average hours of work in each industry and in overall average hours of work. A method similar to that used for calculating the effects of changing employment shares is used to avoid intermingling the effects of changes in industry hours and employment shares. That is, to examine the effects of hours changes, employment and wages are held constant, just as hours and wages are held constant to examine the effects of employment changes.

3. Changes in overall average hourly earnings that can be attributed to the *rising female share of employment* are calculated by using the estimate of the ratio of the average hourly earnings of women to those of men in each industry described earlier. Although the actual ratio of female to male wages undoubtedly varies somewhat among industries, the consistency of the computed aggregate ratio with estimates from other sources indicates that this procedure produces a reasonable approximation.

4. The remaining source of change in overall average hourly earnings is *changes in real average hourly earnings in each industry* for the typical male and female worker. Changes in this component can occur for many reasons. Since this series is adjusted for inflation by the PCE deflator, movements in it in relation to the private nonfarm deflator (measuring the real value of goods produced and shown in figure 7–2) are one factor influencing this residual term. Since hourly earnings constitute a declining fraction of total compensation per hour, the real average hourly earnings series also reflects changes in the quantities and in the prices of nonwage benefits in relation to wages (shown in figure 7–3).

This residual change in average hourly earnings is essentially a measure of the growth in productivity or output per hour, after taking into account the effects of changes in industry employment and hours shares and in female employment shares by industry. Changes in measured output per hour reflect not only such factors as capital per worker and the technology it incorporates but also changes in the characteristics of the labor inputs themselves, such as age and schooling. After discussing the estimated effects of the three sources of change outlined above, we will briefly discuss the estimated influence of age and schooling on the fourth, residual component of changes in average hourly earnings.

Estimates of effects. Cumulative changes in real average hourly earnings and in the components of the series are shown in table 7–6. During the entire 1964–1985 period average hourly earnings (in 1977 dollars) increased by ninety cents, with all but two cents of the increase taking place before 1972. In the absence of changes attributed

TABLE 7–6

CHANGES IN REAL AVERAGE HOURLY EARNINGS AND COMPONENTS OF
ACTUAL CHANGES ATTRIBUTABLE TO SELECTED SOURCES, 1964–1985
(1977 dollars)

			Change Attributed to		
	Total *Change*	Industry employment shares	Industry average weekly hours	Female and male employment shares	Industry wages (residual)
1964–1985	0.90	−0.22	0.08	−0.14	1.18
1964–1972	0.88	−0.07	0.03	−0.05	0.97
1972–1985	0.02	−0.15	0.05	−0.09	0.21

NOTE: Real average earnings here and in table 7–7 is the composite series for
our industry-by-industry analysis, which is closely comparable but not identical to the BLS series deflated by the PCE deflator. See the appendix for a
description of the data sources and calculations.

to the first three components, the overall increase would have been
about one-third larger, and there would have been a noticeable increase (21 cents) in average hourly earnings from 1972 to 1985. Nevertheless, a pronounced slowdown from the rate of increase before 1972
would have taken place even in the absence of the other changes.

Changes in industry employment shares reduced average hourly
earnings by twenty-two cents over the entire period. About two-
thirds of this reduction occurred after 1972. The reduction was slightly
more than a penny per year in the latter part of the period and slightly
less than a penny earlier.

The effect of changes in industry employment shares was offset in
part by changes in industry hours. That is, although the shift in
industry employment was toward industries with lower average
hourly earnings, the shift in hours shares toward relatively low-wage
industries was smaller because the decline in industry hours of work
was smaller for relatively high-wage industries. For the period as a
whole, about one-third of the negative effect on average hourly earnings of shifting employment shares was offset by changes among
industries in average weekly hours that raised overall average wages.
Taken together, changes in industry employment and hours shares
reduced real average hourly earnings by fourteen cents over the entire
period, or about two-thirds of a penny per year.

Women's growing share of employment had the expected negative effect on average hourly earnings. The combination of rising female employment shares and differentially lower estimated average wages reduced average hourly earnings by fourteen cents for the period as a whole. The estimated effects have been gradual and persistent, but the smooth pattern may be partly attributable to the assumed stable ratio of female to male wages within each industry. The effect of the rising female employment share on average hourly earnings is about two-thirds the size of the component attributable to employment shifts and is coincidentally identical with the net effect of changes in employment and hours shares taken together.

The most striking feature of these estimates of cumulative changes in average hourly earnings and their sources is the size of the residual. That is, only a small fraction of the overall change in average hourly earnings is attributable to changes in employment and hours shares and to women's rising share of employment. Moreover, most of the slowdown in real wage increases since the early 1970s is attributable to sources other than these changes.[16] After adjustment for these changes, the residual wage increase during the period before 1972 was about 12 cents per year and 1.6 cents per year after 1972.

The large size of the residual compared with the three other components is clearly evident in figure 7–4, showing year-to-year changes in each of these four components of average hourly earnings. These year-to-year changes also show the influence of the business cycle on the effects of shifts in employment shares and on the residual measuring industry changes in real wages. Despite the pronounced cyclical patterns since the early 1970s, both the slower increase in real average hourly earnings and the relatively small persistent effects of changes in employment, hours, and female worker shares stand out in these yearly changes. Although employment shifts contribute importantly to annual changes in some years, they make only a small contribution to the overall slowdown in the growth of average hourly earnings.[17]

Effects of age and schooling. By far the most important component of real wages for the overall real wage trend and for the change in that trend since the early 1970s is the fourth, or residual, term in our decomposition. Since the sex composition of the work force is the only demographic factor that has been taken explicitly into account, all other demographic factors are reflected in this term. The most important general, earnings-related characteristics whose influence can be explored are age and schooling. Although detailed industry-level data that would permit their influence to be taken into account directly are not readily available, it is useful to consider how large the effects of

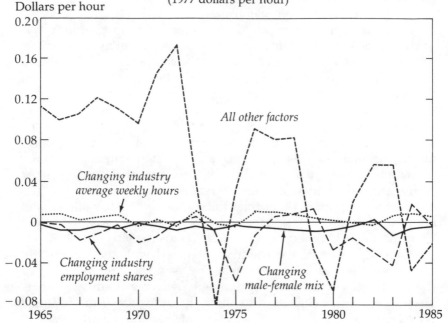

FIGURE 7–4
COMPONENTS OF ANNUAL CHANGES IN REAL AVERAGE
HOURLY EARNINGS
(1977 dollars per hour)

Dollars per hour

All other factors

*Changing industry
average weekly hours*

*Changing industry
employment shares*

*Changing
male-female mix*

NOTE: Figure shows change from the preceding year attributable to the factors indicated. The decomposition of changes in average hourly earnings is described in the text; the precise formulas are contained in the appendix.
SOURCES: Authors' calculations using Bureau of Labor Statistics data.

changes in age and schooling of the workforce might be and whether they might help to explain observed changes in the growth trend of real wages.

Estimates of age-earnings profiles generally show an increase in wage rates with each additional year of age up to a peak that is reached at some time during the middle to late forties and a subsequent gradual decline.[18] The increase in earnings associated with age is generally interpreted as the contribution to increased earning capacity of work experience and on-the-job training. Since measures of central tendency of the age distribution are below estimated earnings peaks, a decrease in the average age of the work force resulting from

228

the large influx of young workers during the past twenty years would be expected to have reduced average hourly earnings.

The estimated mean age of civilian workers declined from 40.6 years in 1964 to 38.9 in 1972 and 37.5 in 1985.[19] These data indicate that the changing age composition of the work force could by itself be expected to reduce average hourly earnings throughout the period and by about the same amount in each subperiod. The probable order of magnitude can be estimated by using conventional earnings functions that incorporate age and age squared as variables. We estimate that the decrease in the average age of the work force from 1964 to 1972 and from 1972 to 1985 led to implied reductions in average hourly earnings of about 1.3 percent, or six to seven cents, in each period.[20] These data indicate that the magnitude of age effects on earnings has been quite small and similar in each subperiod.

Since average years of schooling have increased during the past twenty years and wages generally increase with years of schooling, average hourly earnings have presumably been raised by schooling effects. Estimated average years of schooling of employed workers increased from 10.8 years in 1964 to 11.5 years in 1972 and 12.6 years in 1985.[21] Using these estimates of years of schooling as a guide and applying an estimated effect of 6 percent per additional year of schooling (derived in the same way as that for age), we find that the increase of seven-tenths of a year between 1964 and 1972 would have produced an increase in hourly earnings of 4 percent. The increase of 1.1 years of schooling from 1972 to 1985 would have produced the correspondingly larger effect of about 6 percent. According to these estimates, average real wages would have been raised by seventeen cents in the period before 1972 and by thirty-three cents subsequently because of the rise in years of schooling. The order of magnitude of schooling effects is considerably larger than that of age effects, although the two work in opposite directions.[22]

The adjustments that should be made to the estimated residuals reported in table 7–6 to reflect the effects of changes in age and schooling are summarized in table 7–7. Since the estimated effects of age are about the same size for each of the subperiods, the age adjustment would by itself simply increase the amount of real wage growth in each period to be attributed to other sources of productivity growth. Increased schooling has been one of these other sources of productivity growth, however, and its effects have been larger than those for age. Moreover, the schooling adjustment is about twice as large for the period since 1972, because the increase in schooling has proceeded at about the same pace while the decline in average age has tapered off.

TABLE 7–7

EFFECTS OF CHANGING AGE AND SCHOOLING ON
REAL AVERAGE HOURLY EARNINGS, 1964–1985
(1977 dollars)

	Total Change in Real Average Hourly Earnings	Change Attributed to				
		Combined industry-related effects (from table 7–6)	Residual (from table 7–6)	Changes in age	Changes in years of schooling	Adjusted residual
1964–1985	0.90	−0.28	1.18	−0.13	0.50	0.81
1964–1972	0.88	−0.09	0.97	−0.06	0.17	0.86
1972–1985	0.02	−0.19	0.21	−0.07	0.33	−0.05

NOTE: The combined industry-related effects are the net effects of the first three components of change reported in table 7–6—changes attributable to changes in industry employment shares, industry average weekly hours, and female employment shares. The residual (from table 7–6) represents industry real wage changes, after adjustment of actual changes to reflect the net effect of these three components of change. See the appendix for a description of the data sources and calculations.

Because the adjustment to real wage changes attributable to schooling increases is larger than that attributable to age and larger since 1972 than before, the adjusted residual shows an even more pronounced decline than before adjustment for age and schooling. Thus for the period from 1964 to 1972 the eighty-six-cent increase in real industry wages should be attributed to sources of productivity growth other than those for which adjustments have already been made. In the period from 1972 to 1985, however, the adjusted residual for real industry wages declined by five cents. Thus the adjusted residual, taking age and schooling changes into account, shows a slightly more pronounced growth slowdown than actual real wages before these adjustments are made. The combined influence of all the factors influencing productivity for which we have made adjustments is to leave the slowdown in real wage growth substantially unchanged. On the basis of this analysis the slowdown remains unexplained, but the evidence indicates that it is not attributable to any significant extent to factors such as changing industry employment shares.

Distributional Changes

Changes in employment patterns can be expected to affect not only the level but also the distribution of earnings and income. These effects are related, and analyses of changing industry and occupational employment patterns have sometimes focused on their distributional impact. Income and earnings distributions have also been examined directly to determine what changes have occurred. Some of the evidence shows a reduction in concentration of workers or families near the center of income distributions in recent years, a trend that has been popularized as a shrinkage of the middle class.[23]

Especially in popular discussion, the net shift of jobs toward services has been linked to a decline in middle-income workers and families. Jobs in the more rapidly expanding services sector are viewed as worse jobs in terms of average pay. Moreover, jobs in services are often characterized as more sharply bifurcated into highly paid professional jobs and low-paid menial jobs.[24] Some of this discussion has relied heavily on anecdotes instead of on systematic and comprehensive analysis.

Analyses of the effects of employment shifts among industries have shown a drift toward industries that pay lower average wages. The effects, however, have been small, and they have been occurring throughout most of the postwar period.[25] Contrary to the estimated effects of employment shifts among industries, however, analyses of employment shifts among occupations have shown a drift toward occupations with higher weekly earnings. The evidence from occupation-based studies of wage distribution changes indicates that the fraction of employment accounted for by the middle-income third of occupations has remained about the same from 1973 to 1985.[26] The middle-income share has varied over the cycle, however, and the share of employment in occupations with higher earnings has increased.

It is worth noting that earnings distributions *within* occupations have apparently drifted toward larger employment shares in the lower-paid third of these distributions. That is, changes in employment distributions within occupations have moved in the opposite direction from changes among occupations in their effects on earnings distributions for workers as a whole. Similar offsetting movements may be occurring within industries. Consequently, estimates of the effects on overall average wages or earnings derived from occupation or industry averages cannot provide definitive evidence on whether shifts in employment shares are resulting in jobs with better or worse average pay than earlier patterns.

231

Evidence that is in some respects more direct in terms of incomes actually realized can also be cited that lends support to the possibility of increased inequality and a decline in the share of income accruing to middle-income families. The distribution of money income of families shows a small decline in the share going to the middle fifth, from 17.7 in 1964 to 17.0 percent in 1984.[27] Instead of a flattening of the middle of the distribution, however, the decline for the middle fifth was apparently part of a broader shift in income shares toward the upper part of the distribution. The share of the lowest and second lowest fifths also declined during this period.

These data for families do not, however, mean that similar trends are occurring for individual workers. The main reason for differences between distributions for individual workers and for families is the trend toward more workers per family. Income distribution trends for unrelated individuals, for example, show a rising share of income for the middle fifth as well as for the lower two fifths, in contrast to the trends for families. Data for 1984 for twenty-one income classes show that, for all except the very bottom and top classes, the number of earners per family rises without interruption, from an average of 0.61 to 2.41, as family income increases. Data on the trend in married-couple families with two of more earners show a rise from 55 percent in 1967 to 61 percent in 1984.[28] Taken together, these data indicate that the growing prevalence of more than one earner per family has had a very important influence on trends in the income distribution for families. The rise in multiple-earner families has raised money incomes for these families and thereby increased the share of income that accrues to the upper part of the distribution.

Evidence from industry average hourly earnings data has also been presented that shows increased dispersion in wages.[29] When industry averages are used to compute coefficients of variation in wages without taking into account differences among industries in numbers of employees, the results show increasing dispersion in recent years both in the manufacturing sector and for private nonfarm industries as a whole. When comparable measures of dispersion are computed using employment weights to take differences in industry size into account, however, it appears that there has been little change in dispersion (see figure 7–5). Since the primary welfare significance of these dispersion measures is how members of the work force are affected, not the behavior of industry averages as such, weighted measures of dispersion are more relevant than measures that do not take employment differences into account.

From the point of view of the kinds of job opportunities available to workers, measures of dispersion for individual workers are more

FIGURE 7–5

COEFFICIENTS OF VARIATION IN INDUSTRY AVERAGE HOURLY EARNINGS, 1972–1985

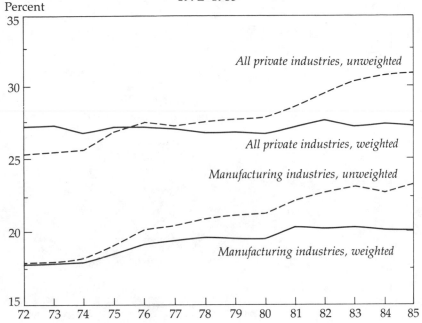

NOTE: Weighted coefficients of variation were calculated for industry observations weighted by shares of total industry hours. The underlying data are industry averages for hourly earnings of all production and nonsupervisory workers.

SOURCE: Authors' calculations using Bureau of Labor Statistics establishment data.

relevant than weighted industry averages. Although coefficients of variation for individual workers naturally show wider dispersion than those for industry averages, the dispersion of average hourly earnings for individual workers has clearly declined in recent years (figure 7–6).[30] These data for individual workers cover the same industry sectors as the data for industry averages. Their coverage is somewhat narrower in that only full-time workers are included but broader in that all full-time workers are included, not just the production and nonsupervisory workers who make up the industry averages.

In the data on dispersion in wages and incomes and related data on trends for middle-income workers and families, a number of

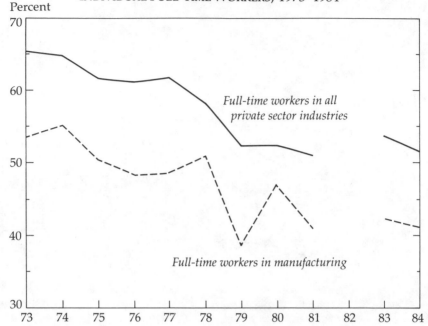

FIGURE 7–6
COEFFICIENTS OF VARIATION IN USUAL HOURLY EARNINGS OF
INDIVIDUAL FULL-TIME WORKERS, 1973–1984

Full-time workers in all
private sector industries

Full-time workers in manufacturing

NOTE: Although data for 1982 are available, they were not included in the analysis in which these results were generated because union status is not available for 1982.

SOURCE: Authors' calculations using Bureau of Labor Statistics household survey data.

crosscurrents are apparently at work. In some instances evidence from different sources seems to point in opposite directions. A careful and detailed reconciliation of trends that appear to be moving in different directions would be very valuable for improving our understanding of the sources and consequences of change. Nevertheless, we can summarize the evidence by sketching out the main elements for reconciling divergent trends.

Data on incomes realized by families tend to show a small increase in dispersion, with lower- and middle-income groups faring less well than those above the middle of the distribution. Evidence for somewhat more homogeneous groups, such as year-round, full-time workers, also seems to show some trend toward more dispersion. Data on average hourly earnings for individual workers, however, show declining dispersion in recent years.[31]

The increased dispersion for some groups, such as families, which is occurring despite declining wage dispersion, may reflect an increase in diversity in working and living arrangements. Differences in hours of work, multiple job holding, job sharing, part-year work, and other adaptations of jobs to suit the interests of workers may increasingly influence annual earnings and money incomes. Differences in living arrangements are influenced by divorce, deferral or avoidance of marriage, and establishment of separate households by single persons. Increased diversity from sources such as these should lead us to expect increased diversity in economic outcomes unless offsetting tendencies are at work.

The role of individual choice, at least at any point in time, is likely to be much more important for working and living arrangements than for wage rates. That is, the distribution of wage rates can be viewed as a menu of opportunities available to workers, given their interests and qualifications. Incomes, however, reflect individual choices of many kinds, within the framework of a range of job opportunities available. Increased dispersion in income, for groups where this has occurred, cannot be attributed to a range of job opportunities more dispersed or less attractive according to the evidence on the hourly earnings paid for such jobs.

The distinction between the roles of choices and of opportunities as they affect economic outcomes is also important for policy. Public attitudes might reasonably show more concern about trends that are mainly attributable to deteriorating opportunities than about those attributable to choices people make concerning their working and living arrangements as these affect their incomes. Moreover, the underlying sources of change are important in considering policies to influence trends that may be an object of public concern. For example, policies intended to influence industrial structure or other broad characteristics of economic activity can be expected to prove ineffectual as well as inefficient in affecting trends that are primarily influenced by individual choices rather than by opportunities among which choices are made.

Conclusions

The main factors influencing measures of economic well-being for most working-age families are employment status, rate of pay, and purchasing power (or prices). Although employment growth has been strong in recent years, rates of pay, adjusted for inflation, have increased less rapidly since the early 1970s than previously. The most useful broad measure of the average real rate of pay, compensation per hour adjusted by the PCE deflator, has increased at an annual rate of about three-fourths of 1 percent since 1972, much less than the 2½ percent rate during the preceding two decades. Although this slowdown in real wage growth was a key element in attaining the rapid employment growth that occurred, the reasons why underlying productivity growth has slowed so much remain unclear.

Among the particularly noteworthy changes since 1972 are those in inflation rates, relative energy prices, international trade patterns, and technology. These changes, some of which have been reversed, may have been important in inducing slower real wage gains. Changes that have persisted, and whose effects can be examined fairly directly, include changes in industry employment shares (often summarized as the shift to services) and a rise in women's share of employment. These changes and changes in age and schooling have not, on the basis of this analysis, contributed importantly to slower average real wage increases. Moreover, these and other changes have not brought about a widening spread in hourly rates of pay. Although some measures show increased dispersion in income and earnings, this increased diversity of outcomes apparently reflects primarily working and living choices rather than a widening distribution of rates of pay for the job opportunities generated in the economy.

Although the evidence is persuasive that real increases in hourly pay have been less rapid and more variable over business cycles in recent years, the slowdown is apparently not attributable to any significant extent to processes such as changes in the industrial structure of the economy. It is consequently unlikely that efforts to modify or redirect industry output and employment patterns through domestic industrial policy or protectionist international trade policies could make any significant contribution to achieving more rapid real wage gains. The main dangers of policies intended to inhibit changes induced by market forces or to maintain particular industry patterns are that the costs and inefficiency that they generate would further slow real wage growth and would also jeopardize continued strong growth in employment opportunities.

Appendix

The change in aggregate average hourly earnings (W) between a given year (t) and a base year (0) can be written as several components that are industry summations of the following form:

- changes in industry employment shares ($e_t - e_0$), evaluated at base year wages and with hours taken into account to hold their overall level constant
- changes in the ratio of industry average weekly hours to overall average weekly hours ($r_t - r_0$), evaluated at base year wages with employment shares held constant
- changes in the relative industry hours shares of male and female employees ($m_t - m_0$), evaluated at a constant male wage premium and base year industry hours shares
- changes in industry wages ($w_t - w_0$), holding industry hours shares and employment for both males and females constant at base year levels
- interaction terms that measure second-order effects (because they are of negligible magnitude, they have been included in the residual with changes in industry wages)

The results of this decomposition are presented in tables 7–6 and 7–7 and figure 7–4 in the text.

Indexing individual industries with the subscript i and letting the superscripts m and f denote terms applicable to males and females, respectively, we write the decomposition formally as

$$
\begin{aligned}
W_t - W_0 &= \sum_i (e'_{it} - e_{i0})\, r_{i0} w_{i0} & \text{(term 1)} \\
&+ \sum_i (r_{it} - r'_{i0})\, e_{it} w_{i0} & \text{(term 2)} \\
&+ \sum_i (m_{it} - m_{i0})\, (w^m_{i0} - w^f_{i0})\, h_{i0} & \text{(term 3)} \\
&+ \sum_i (w^m_{it} - w^m_{i0})\, [m_{i0} + d_{it}(1 - m_{i0})] & \text{(term 4)} \\
&+ \text{Interaction terms}
\end{aligned}
$$

where

e_{it} = the ratio of production and nonsupervisory employment in industry i (E_{it}) to total production and nonsupervisory employment (E_t)

r_{it} = the ratio of average weekly hours of production and nonsupervisory workers in industry i ($\bar{h}_{it}$) to average weekly hours of all production and nonsupervisory workers ($\bar{h}_t$)

h_{it} = the ratio of total industry hours of production and nonsupervisory workers in industry i (H_{it}) to aggregate hours (H_t)

m_{it} = the ratio of total industry hours of male production and nonsupervisory workers in industry i (H^m_{it}) to total industry hours (H_{it})

w_{it} = industry average hourly earnings of production and nonsupervisory workers, adjusted to constant 1977 dollars by the personal consumption expenditures deflator

d_{it} = the ratio of female to male average hourly earnings

237

The base year used for all measures is 1977.

The terms e'_{it} and r'_{i0} in terms 1 and 2 were incorporated to distinguish between changes in aggregate average weekly hours ($\overline{h}_t$) computationally related to changes in employment shares (e_{it}) from those due to changes in industry-specific average weekly hours ($\overline{h}_{it}$). Overall average weekly hours of all workers have declined over time. Calculations involving employment changes, when evaluated at base period industry average hours, would show a decline in total hours of work because of the direct computational link between increasing industry employment shares and relatively low average weekly hours in the same industries. If no adjustment were made to take this computational effect into account, the absolute values of both term 1 and term 2 would be larger than their values when overall hours are held constant.

The adjustment was made by calculating a measure of aggregate average weekly hours that reflects changes due solely to changing employment shares and using this measure to scale the current year employment shares in terms 1 and 2. This was done by defining

$$e'_{it} = e_{it}\,\overline{h}_{i0}$$
$$r'_{i0} = (\overline{h}_{i0}/h'_t)$$
$$\text{where } h'_t = \sum e_{it}\overline{h}'_{i0})$$

Much of the information necessary to evaluate these terms is available directly from the Bureau of Labor Statistics (BLS) establishment survey: industry production and nonsupervisory employment, average weekly hours, and average hourly earnings. The data cover fifty-six two-digit standard industrial classification (SIC) industries for the period 1972 to 1985 and nine one-digit industries for the period 1964 to 1971. Information from the Current Population Survey (CPS) was used to supplement the establishment data.

For production and nonsupervisory workers, male employment shares were estimated by multiplying production and nonsupervisory employment for each industry by the male employment share for all employees, with data on the male and female shares of total employment available directly from the establishment data.

To calculate the male share of industry hours (m_{it}), it was necessary to estimate the average weekly hours of male workers ($\overline{h}^m_{it}$). This was done by calculating the ratio of female to male average weekly hours for nine major industry groups with CPS data and assigning the ratios to the two-digit industries within each group. These ratios, combined with information on the average weekly hours of work and the male share of industry employment, allow calculation of values of

$\bar{h}_{it}^m$ that are consistent with the establishment data. These calculations are

$$\bar{h}_{it}^m = \bar{h}_{it}/[a_{it} + (1 - a_{it}) k_{it}]$$

where a_{it} is the ratio of male to total production and nonsupervisory employment in industry i (estimated from establishment data), and k_{it} is the ratio of female to male average weekly hours (estimated from CPS data); and

$$m_{it} = (E_{it}^m - h_{it}^m)/H_{it}$$

Given the estimated male hours share and the ratio of female to male average hourly earnings, d_{it} (discussed below), calculation of the average hourly earnings of males in each industry (w_{it}^m) is as follows:

$$w_{it}^m = w_{it}/[m_{it} + (1 - m_{it})d_{it}]$$

Data on industry-specific female-male wage ratios are unavailable. In the absence of such data, we assumed a constant ratio across industries and years. The ratio was estimated by using an iterative procedure to generate a set of industry-specific male and female wages that, when appropriately weighted, would yield an aggregate female-male wage ratio consistent with published estimates. (Because the distribution of male and female workers among industries differs, with females tending to be employed in lower-wage industries, assigning the observed aggregate wage ratio to each industry yields an implicit aggregate ratio smaller than the actual ratio.)

For consistency, the year 1977 was chosen as a reference point. According to data from the CPS, the aggregate female-male wage ratio for hourly wage and salary workers in that year was 0.623. To achieve that aggregate ratio, a ratio of 0.7 was assigned to each industry in the nine- and fifty-six-industry samples. That is, $d_{it} = 0.7$ for each i and t.

Notes

1. Although average hourly earnings and compensation per hour show increases that appear roughly linear for most of the twenty years before 1972, it should be noted that a linear increase in an index drawn on this scale implies a declining percentage rate of increase.

2. A number of comprehensive and authoritative analyses of changes in productivity growth have been carried out by Edward F. Denison. See, for example, his *Accounting for Slower Economic Growth* (Washington, D.C.: Brookings Institution, 1979) and *Trends in American Economic Growth, 1929–1982* (Washington, D.C.: Brookings Institution, 1985). See also J. R. Norsworthy, Michael R. Harper, and Kent Kunze, "The Slowdown in Productivity Growth: Analysis of Some Contributing Factors," *Brookings Papers on Economic Activity*, no. 2 (1979), pp. 387–421; and the papers on productivity by Edward F. Denison, William Fellner, John W.

Kendrick, and Herbert Stein in William Fellner, ed., *Contemporary Economic Problems, 1979* (Washington, D.C.: American Enterprise Institute, 1979).

3. The two series also differ in the underlying source data used to compile them. The average hourly earnings series is derived from the survey of business establishments of the Bureau of Labor Statistics (BLS). The compensation per hour series, though published by the BLS, is derived from estimates made by the Bureau of Economic Analysis (BEA) as part of the national income accounts. The data underlying the BEA estimates of wages, salaries, and nonwage benefits are obtained independently of the BLS establishment surveys.

Although the two series differ in their coverage, data from the employment cost index indicate that the growth rate of total compensation in relation to the growth rate of wages and salaries has been approximately equal for production and nonproduction workers since these data became available for both. That is, both groups of workers have apparently experienced comparable growth in nonwage benefits in relation to wages and salaries.

4. A careful reconciliation and analysis of trends in real per capita and mean family incomes can be found in Paul Ryscavage, "Reconciling Divergent Trends in Real Income," *Monthly Labor Review* (July 1986), pp. 24–29.

5. A comparison of inflation rates in the late 1970s as measured by the CPI for all urban consumers and by the experimental version (incorporating a rental-equivalence housing price measure and introduced in January 1983) is given in *Economic Report of the President*, 1983, table B-56. See also John C. Weicher, "Mismeasuring Poverty and Progress," in Douglas Besharov and John C. Weicher, eds., *The New Meaning of Poverty* (American Enterprise Institute, forthcoming).

6. It should be recognized, of course, that interactions between sectors can also influence productivity and real earnings growth. For example, the expansion of government regulatory requirements in the 1970s, intended to further goals such as pollution abatement, has increased resource requirements for achieving a given level of measured output. See Edward F. Denison, "Effects of Selected Changes in the Institutional and Human Environment upon Output per Unit of Input," *Survey of Current Business* (January 1978), pp. 21–44. Another example is the massive increase in the price of imported oil, which created incentives in the domestic private nonfarm sector for devoting far more resources per unit of output to exploration and production of additional oil and natural gas.

7. See, for example, Bob Kuttner, "The Declining Middle," *Atlantic Monthly* (July 1983), pp. 60–72; and Industrial Union Department, AFL-CIO, "Deindustrialization and the Two-Tier Society" (1984). This idea was an important theme in Barry Bluestone and Bennett Harrison, *The Deindustrialization of America* (New York: Basic Books, 1984).

8. Howard N. Fullerton, Jr., "The 1995 Labor Force: BLS' Latest Projections," *Monthly Labor Review* (November 1985), pp. 17–25.

9. U.S. Department of Education, Office of Educational Improvement, *Digest of Educational Statistics, 1985–86*, table 10.

10. See William V. Deuterman, Jr., and Scott Campbell Brown, "Voluntary Part-Time Workers: A Growing Part of the Labor Force," *Monthly Labor Review* (June 1978), pp. 3–10. By the time this article was written, the growth in part-time work had leveled off.

11. Production and nonsupervisory workers account for slightly more than 80 percent of all private nonfarm workers, a share that has declined only slightly over time. The detailed data available since 1972 for fifty-six industries account for almost 55 percent of total civilian employment, a share that has been stable over time.

12. Detailed data on many two-digit industries in the services-producing sector have been published only since 1972. For the period 1964–1971, our analysis is based on data covering one-digit industries. The series for both periods were then spliced (with appropriate adjustments) to generate a single series spanning the entire period. Although the level of aggregation can have an important effect (because of movements among two-digit industries but within one-digit industries), the loss of industry information is offset somewhat by the additional coverage of the broader industry series.

13. A number of studies examining the sources of wage differences between men and women have been undertaken. See, for example, Welch Associates, "Comparable Worth: An Analysis of Issues, Evidence, and Impacts," prepared for the California Chamber of Commerce, January 1985; and June O'Neill, "The Trend in the Male/Female Wage Gap in the United States," *Journal of Labor Economics* (January 1985), pp. S91–S116.

14. Bureau of Labor Statistics, *Labor Force Statistics Derived from the Current Population Survey: A Databook* (1982), table C-20. Much of the available information on female-male wage ratios pertains to weekly earnings, but because of differences between women and men in weekly hours worked, these ratios are inappropriate in an analysis of changes in average hourly earnings. Ratios of weekly earnings adjusted for differences in hours tend, however, to show a similar pattern. See, for example, O'Neill, "The Trend in the Wage Gap," table 4.

15. The exact formulas used to compute the effects of employment shifts, changes in average weekly hours, and the growth in the female employment share are presented in the appendix.

16. The fact that the unexplained residual is large in relation to the fraction of the change that can be explained by changes in employment, hours, and demographic characteristics is consistent with Denison's characterization of the sources of the decline in productivity as a "mystery." See Denison, *Accounting for Slower Economic Growth*, p. 4.

17. This is in sharp contrast to the view expressed in a recent AFL-CIO report that employment shifts from goods- to services-producing industries are probably the single most important factor explaining the decline in real wage growth. See Industrial Union Department, AFL-CIO, "The Polarization of America: The Loss of Good Jobs, Falling Incomes, and Rising Inequality" (1986), p. 17.

18. A discussion of the age-earnings profiles implied by standard estimated earnings functions is contained in Marvin H. Kosters and Murray N. Ross, "Union/Nonunion Wage Differentials: Their Magnitude and Trends (1973–1984)," American Enterprise Institute, November 1985, pp. 34–35.

19. These estimates were computed from data on the age distribution of employed civilians in Bureau of Labor Statistics, *Handbook of Labor Statistics* (June 1985), table 15, assuming an even distribution of workers within age intervals.

20. Our estimates of the effect of a changing age distribution on average hourly earnings are obtained by substituting the mean age (and its square) of the work force in each year into an estimated earnings equation and computing the implied percentage difference in wages. The percentage difference is then applied to the actual average hourly earnings series to obtain a measure of dollars per hour.

21. Estimates of the average years of schooling were computed from Bureau of Labor Statistics, *Handbook of Labor Statistics* (June 1985), table 61, assuming an even distribution of individuals within educational attainment categories.

22. These estimates are closely comparable in magnitude to those in Denison's studies despite differences in the underlying methods and data. See, for example, *Trends in American Economic Growth*, tables 8–1 and 8–3.

241

23. McKinley L. Blackburn and David E. Bloom conclude their study, for example, by noting: "Yes the middle class still cuts itself a large slice of the American pie, but the country has moved in the direction of becoming a nation of 'haves' and 'have nots,' with less in between" ("What Is Happening to the Middle Class?" *American Demographics*, January 1985, p. 25). But see also Sar A. Levitan and Peter E. Carlson, "Middle-Class Shrinkage?" *Across the Board* (October 1984), pp. 55–59.

24. See Kuttner, "The Declining Middle," and Bennett Harrison, Chris Tilly, and Barry Bluestone, "Wage Inequality Takes a Great U-Turn," *Challenge* (March/April 1986), pp. 26–32.

25. As noted in table 7–5, the negative effect of changing employment is small compared with the effect of changes in industry wage levels. Similar results are obtained in Marvin H. Kosters, "Job Changes and Displaced Workers: An Examination of Employment Adjustment Experience," in Philip Cagan, ed., *Essays in Contemporary Economic Problems, 1986: The Impact of the Reagan Program* (Washington, D.C.: American Enterprise Institute, 1986), table 9–3. The analysis there, however, focused solely on employment changes and did not take interindustry differences in average weekly hours into account.

26. See, for example, Neal H. Rosenthal, "The Shrinking Middle Class: Myth or Reality?" *Monthly Labor Review* (March 1985), pp. 3–10; and Patrick J. McMahon and John H. Tschetter, "The Declining Middle Class: A Further Analysis," *Monthly Labor Review* (September 1986), pp. 22–27.

27. U.S. Department of Commerce, Bureau of the Census, *Money Income of Households, Families, and Persons in the United States: 1984*, Series P-60, no. 151, table 12.

28. Bureau of Labor Statistics, *Handbook of Labor Statistics* (June 1985), table 58.

29. See, for example, Colin Lawrence and Robert Z. Lawrence, "Manufacturing Wage Dispersion: An End Game Interpretation," *Brookings Papers on Economic Activity*, no. 1 (1985), pp. 47–116. Lawrence and Lawrence begin their study by noting, "Over the past fifteen years there has been an extraordinary increase in the dispersion of wages among manufacturing industries in the United States." See also Organization for Economic Cooperation and Development, *Employment Outlook* (September 1985), chart 15.

30. Kosters and Ross, "Union/Nonunion Wage Differentials," table 21.

31. The evidence from a number of analyses of wage and income dispersion is summarized in Richard B. Freeman, "Factor Prices, Employment, and Inequality in a Decentralized Labor Market" (Corporation for Enterprise Development, Study no. 85/229).

8

The Domestic Budget
after Gramm-Rudman
—and after Reagan

John C. Weicher

Summary

Despite the Gramm-Rudman-Hollings (GRH) deficit reduction process, total nominal and real domestic expenditures were not reduced in 1986, and they will not be reduced in 1987. On the domestic side of the federal budget (excluding defense, international affairs, and interest), GRH was essentially an agreement that, if cuts were unavoidable, they would not fall on social security or programs for the poor, which neither President Ronald Reagan nor Congress was proposing to cut seriously anyway. It reflected a continuation of the budget policy of recent years.

The 1986 outcome and the current outlook for 1987 increase the likelihood of further and more rapid real growth in the domestic budget, if not during the rest of the president's term, then after 1988. Higher outlays can automatically be expected in the largest budget categories, and the last Congress acted to expand some programs for the poor; the current Congress is likely to expand them further. More generally, congressional willingness to control spending has been diminishing in the past few years.

During President Reagan's administration, however, the growth in the domestic budget has been dramatically reduced. It remains low by historical standards for 1986 and probably 1987; in fact, the 1986 growth rate was lower than the average for the president's first term. Increasingly it seems likely that the Reagan presidency will appear in the budget annals as a period of a sharp but temporary cut in the growth of outlays.

While aggregate expenditures have continued to grow, a remarkable reallocation has taken place within the budget. This may turn out to be an enduring legacy of the Reagan presidency.

• Social security and Medicare have continued to grow despite almost annual cuts in the latter; they now amount to nearly half the domestic budget.

243

• *Real growth has also occurred, at a slower rate, in federal civilian and military retirement outlays.*

• *After significant cuts at the beginning of President Reagan's first term, expenditures on programs for the poor have begun to grow again, albeit more slowly than in earlier decades. The ratio of federal "safety net" outlays to the number of poor people reached a record high in 1985 and has surely continued to increase since then.*

• *At the same time, a number of programs have sustained large reductions in real terms, including in particular most of the grants to state and local governments.*

Two conclusions are suggested by these changes: the domestic budget is increasingly a budget for the elderly and the poor; and the president's New Federalism, buried without ceremony in 1982, now seems to be alive and increasingly viable. An informal redistribution of responsibilities between levels of government may be occurring on terms less fiscally favorable to state and local governments than the president proposed five years ago.

The Overall Domestic Budget

The political debate over the domestic budget during President Reagan's second term has obscured the nature of his achievement. He has not been able to cut the budget in real terms, but he has been able to cut its growth rate sharply. Table 8–1 shows the change. From 1980 to 1985, outlays increased by about 7.5 percent, or $34 billion, measured in 1982 dollars. This compares with 25 percent, or $94 billion, over the previous five years, and 60 percent, or $137 billion, in the five years before that. In both the 1960s and the 1970s, the real domestic budget doubled. Nothing like that will happen in the 1980s. After six years real outlays are only about 8.1 percent higher than at the beginning of the decade. Faster growth is likely for the rest of the 1980s, but it seems clear that real growth will be lower than in any postwar decade.

Measured as a share of the gross national product, the domestic budget grew steadily from about 4½ to more than 14 percent between the end of the Korean War and the 1980 election. It peaked at 14.6 percent in 1982 as a result of the recession and has since declined.

Figure 8–1 shows the year-by-year percentage changes in real domestic expenditures since 1950.[1] This form of presentation tends to give an exaggerated impression of policy changes: a decline in the growth rate appears as a downward movement in the figure. But it brings out the difference between the Reagan administration and earlier decades. The low domestic budget growth rate of the 1950s was really the net result of two divergent trends: a dramatic decline in domestic outlays by more than a third during the Korean War, fol-

TABLE 8–1
DOMESTIC BUDGET, 1950–1986

Year	Current Dollars (billions)	Constant (1982) Dollars (billions)	Share of Total Federal Budget (percent)	Share of GNP (percent)
1950	19.4	81.0	49.2	6.73
1955	18.6	68.5	28.4	4.58
1960	34.1	110.4	36.9	6.63
1965	53.7	159.0	46.0	7.62
1970	95.2	226.8	49.4	9.38
1975	215.5	363.4	64.9	13.38
1980	391.7	457.1	66.3	14.34
1985	548.0	491.4	57.9	13.71
1986	566.3	494.2	57.2	13.43[a]

NOTE: Excludes national defense, international affairs, and net interest paid.
a. Estimated.
SOURCES: U.S. Office of Management and Budget, *Historical Tables, Budget of the United States Government, Fiscal Year 1987*, and *Budget of the United States Government, Fiscal Year 1988, Supplement*.

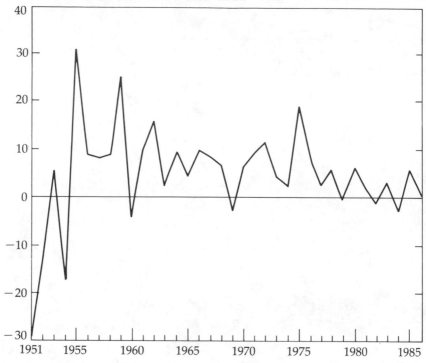

FIGURE 8–1
ANNUAL PERCENTAGE CHANGES IN THE REAL DOMESTIC BUDGET,
1951–1986

NOTE: Domestic budget excludes national defense and net interest, including on-budget and off-budget. Transition quarter omitted between fiscal years 1976 and 1977.
SOURCE: U.S. Office of Management and Budget, *Historical Tables, Budget of the United States Government, Fiscal Year 1987.*

lowed by an equally dramatic increase that continued past the end of the decade and indeed for more than twenty years. (Domestic policy in the 1960s was very different from the 1950s, as the figure shows; outlays did not decline during the Vietnam War.) Between the end of the Korean War and 1980, the *average* real annual growth rate was about 8 percent; few years saw increases of less than 3 percent, and those years were widely scattered. Since 1980 the *highest* annual growth rate has been less than 6 percent; in all other years the rate has been less than 3 percent. Some deceleration is evident during the administration of President Jimmy Carter, but the 2.7 percent average annual growth rate during his term was double the rate under President Reagan.

In his second term the president has had a more ambitious objective, annually proposing substantial budget reductions in nominal as well as real terms. He has been conspicuously unsuccessful in this effort. The pattern for fiscal year 1986 (shown in the left-hand panel of table 8–2) is remarkable. At the time the fiscal 1986 budget was prepared, outlays for fiscal year 1985 were projected to be $555 billion. With no changes in policy, they were expected to rise by $10 billion, or about 1.8 percent, measured in current dollars. (In constant dollars, the current services projection constituted a decline of 1.5 percent.) The president proposed to cut $38 billion. Congress rejected his budget out of hand, but six months later, after the congressional budget resolution and just before the start of the 1986 fiscal year, the president still hoped to cut outlays by $34 billion.[2] When he submitted his fiscal 1987 budget six months later still (and four months into fiscal year 1986), the projected savings had shrunk to $11 billion. By then, however, GRH had been enacted, and under its provisions some $6 billion was sequestered to help meet the 1986 deficit target of $171 billion. As the last line of the panel shows, it did not help. The domestic budget for fiscal 1986 was actually $1 billion *higher* than the original current services estimate and $18 billion (3.3 percent) above outlays for 1985. Meanwhile, the deficit for the year turned out to be $221 billion. In the aggregate the president could not cut the domestic budget (although he could hold down its growth), and the sequestration left no trace.

This does not augur well for the president's 1987 budget. Its progress is shown in the right-hand panel of table 8–2. The current services estimate of $575 billion is based on the February 1986 projection of the 1986 budget, which was $554 billion. The president then hoped to hold outlays for fiscal year 1987 to $545 billion. During 1986 this became increasingly unrealistic, although the president's estimate was not changed much until Congress passed the budget in the fall, rejecting the president's cuts and raising outlays some $7 billion above the current services level. The experience of previous years suggests that a further increase is likely during the remainder of the fiscal year.

These patterns have discouraging implications for the 1988 deficit. To meet the GRH targets, the president is proposing to reduce the deficit from $173 to $107 billion in a year. About $9 billion of the overall deficit reduction is supposed to come from lower domestic outlays. This certainly seems dubious. Continuation of current policy would result in a $25 billion increase in the domestic budget, implying

TABLE 8–2
Projected and Actual Domestic Budget Outlays, Fiscal Years 1986 and 1987
(billions of current dollars)

Panel A: Fiscal Year 1986

1985 estimated outlays (February 1985)	555.2
1986 current services (February 1985)	565.1
1986 Reagan proposal (February 1985)	527.2
1986 midsession review (August 1985)	531.2
Estimate in FY 1987 budget (February 1986)	554.3
1987 midsession review (August 1986)	568.8
Actual outlays (January 1987)	566.3

Panel B: Fiscal Year 1987

1986 estimated outlays (February 1986)	554.3
1987 current services (February 1986)	574.7
1987 Reagan proposal (February 1986)	545.2
1987 midsession review (August 1986)	538.2
Estimate in FY 1988 budget (February 1987)	581.3

Sources: U.S. Office of Management and Budget, *Budget of the United States Government*, Fiscal Years 1986, 1987, and 1988; U.S. Office of Management and Budget, "1986 Mid-Session Review of the 1986 Budget," August 30, 1985; and U.S. Office of Management and Budget, "Mid-Session Review of the 1987 Budget," August 6, 1986.

that the deficit would be $142 billion. Since most policy changes result in more money being spent, the deficit will probably be larger.

Reallocation within the Domestic Budget: New Priorities

Clearly the president has been unable to achieve his overall domestic budget objectives so far in his second term. Nonetheless, total outlays tell only half the story. He has won approval of substantial reductions in a number of individual categories and programs and fundamental structural changes in at least a few major programs. This was true in fiscal year 1986; it is truer still for the full Reagan presidency to date. Indeed, the 1986 and likely 1987 budget outcomes, including GRH, can best be understood as continuations of the policy established earlier in the decade.

The 1986 Budget by Category. The fiscal 1986 budget illustrates the pattern in detail. The aggregate increase in outlays above the current services level was the net result of very large increases in a few programs offset by smaller reductions in a number of others. The president did not want the increases; he did want many of the cuts.

By far the largest increase came in farm price supports. Outlays for agriculture turned out to be $13 billion, or almost 75 percent, above the current services level (and almost $20 billion above the president's budget). Agriculture has been a continuing policy problem throughout the 1980s, and the Reagan administration has been unable to limit the cost of farm programs.[3]

The second largest increase, $2.3 billion, occurred for the two federal deposit insurance funds, the Federal Deposit Insurance Corporation (FDIC) for banks and the Federal Savings and Loan Insurance Corporation (FSLIC) for savings and loan associations. These funds consist of premiums paid by the financial institutions; they incur outlays when individual institutions fail or weak institutions are merged with stronger ones. Normally their receipts exceed their outlays; in the 1980s, however, a number of banks have found themselves with bad energy, farm, or international loans, and a number of thrift institutions have made bad real estate loans or investments. The premiums and outlays of these funds are counted as part of the federal budget, and therefore the outlays count against the GRH deficit reduction targets. This is a case where GRH could have unanticipated and undesirable consequences: minimizing FDIC or FSLIC outlays in the short run may exacerbate the problems of the banking system, with adverse effects for the economy and even for federal revenues in future years that would more than offset an increase of a few billion dollars in the deficit for 1986 or 1987.

It is tempting to hope that these unforeseen expenditures may prove to be temporary. That might happen, but there always seem to be unforeseen expenditures somewhere in the budget, and these particular categories do not look encouraging. Agricultural outlays are in fact projected to fall over the next few years by both the Office of Management and Budget and the Congressional Budget Office, but the experience of the past few years (discussed in the next section of this paper) suggests skepticism; subsidies have been rising steadily for a decade. FDIC and FSLIC expenses are much more likely to rise than to fall; the projected cost of closing failed savings and loan associations is far in excess of the FSLIC's assets, although it may be possible to keep the costs out of the federal budget. A bill to recapitalize that fund failed at the end of the last Congress; some action will be required early in the present one.[4]

The fact that over $15 billion above the current services level was spent for farm subsidies and insured deposits necessarily implies that $10 billion was cut from current services elsewhere in the budget. These cuts were less noticeable; they were spread over many programs, and they occurred for a number of reasons. Some were "technical"; that is, the number of participants in a program or the rate of expenditure turned out to be lower than the estimate in the budget. Social security is a good example; outlays were $3.4 billion less than projected (over 1.5 percent), even though the program was unchanged, because fewer persons than expected applied for benefits. (Technical factors can also bring about higher outlays; most of the increase in farm price supports above the budget projection resulted from crop underestimates.)

Some savings occurred because economic conditions improved. Because inflation was slightly lower than projected, there was a $150 million reduction in food stamps. (In 1987 savings from lower inflation are likely to be much larger, over $4 billion, thanks to the oil price decline.)[5] The unexpected decline in interest rates contributed to a $1.5 billion reduction in outlays by the Rural Electrification Administration. Expenditures in any year are largely the result of previous credit commitments at interest rates determined at the time of the commitment; when rates fall, rural electric and telephone cooperatives may decide not to take up the commitment, so that loans (and therefore expenditures) by the federal government are lower.

An easy $1.5 billion was saved simply by postponing purchases for the strategic petroleum reserve. This is another instance where GRH may have perverse incentives. If there is any reason to have a strategic petroleum reserve, it is more sensible to buy more oil when prices are low, not less.

But there were real policy changes as well. Budget authority for the Farmers Home Administration's rural housing subsidy programs was reduced by $1.3 billion, or 30 percent, and outlays fell by $1.2 billion. There were reductions in a wide variety of programs in the category of community and regional development: $124 million, or 28 percent, for urban development action grants; $42 million, or 26 percent, for the Appalachian Regional Commission and other regional commissions; and so on. These added up to $1.0 billion, about 13 percent, for the category as a whole. Some $100 million, or 10 percent, was taken from the Amtrak subsidy. These are programs that the president has tried to terminate. He has not been able to, but Congress has grudgingly cut their budgets from year to year. Congress did eliminate the Synfuels Corporation, saving $200 million in fiscal year 1986. In addition, there was no federal pay raise; it was sequestered under GRH. This saved $1.3 billion. Finally, Medicare outlays were $1.1 billion lower, about 1.5 percent, because of a combination of technical, economic, and policy changes, including in the latter some of the changes sought by the administration.

Because the changes are scattered across so many budget categories, it is hard to calculate how much of the reduction reflects specific requests by the president. The reductions were nowhere near what he requested, but they were not negligible. Moreover, if farm subsidies had not risen so much more rapidly than anyone anticipated, he would probably have achieved at least a small cut in real terms, though not in nominal dollars. Decisions were made to cut many programs, both before and as part of GRH, before the magnitude of farm price supports for the year became clear.

From 1980 through Gramm-Rudman-Hollings. The 1986 budget outcome is consistent with the trends that have been established during the 1980s, up to and including the provisions of GRH. In this decade the domestic budget has increasingly become a budget for the elderly and the poor. Table 8–3 breaks the domestic budget into seven categories and shows each as a share of the total. The categories are programs for the poor, other grants to state and local governments, programs for the elderly (mainly social security and Medicare), federal retirement, unemployment compensation, farm price supports, and everything else, termed "other government" for convenience and again excluding net interest, defense, and international affairs.

As the table shows, the trend in the overall domestic budget

251

TABLE 8–3
DOMESTIC BUDGET COMPONENTS, 1965–1986
(percentage of domestic budget)

Year	Safety Net Programs	Other Grants to State and Local Governments	Federal Retirement	Programs for the Elderly	Unemployment Compensation	Farm Price Supports	Other Government
1965	10.0	15.8	5.3	43.9	4.8	6.6	13.5
1970	10.6	18.0	5.8	47.1	3.5	4.8	10.3
1975	11.8	16.2	6.1	43.5	6.2	1.0	15.1
1980	12.8	15.0	6.8	44.4	4.6	1.9	14.5
1986	14.1	10.2	7.3	52.8	3.1	5.2	7.3

SOURCE: Same as table 8–1.

results from widely divergent trends in particular functions. Programs for the elderly are continuing to grow; programs for the poor are growing more slowly but certainly holding their own; grants to state and local governments and the "other government" category are dropping sharply. Most of the 1986 cuts mentioned at the end of the preceding section fit into these last two categories.

The share of the domestic budget accounted for by programs for the elderly has increased by over eight percentage points in the past six years; they now constitute more than half the domestic budget. All the increase is accounted for by social security and Medicare, which by themselves now amount to 47 percent of the domestic budget, compared with 38 percent six years ago. The Medicare increase is the more striking since it has come from a much lower base; it continues and accentuates the trend of the preceding fifteen years. The social security increase is a departure from previous patterns; its share had been roughly stable. Both are likely to continue growing over the next five years and beyond.

Programs for the poor have been increasing slightly, though erratically, as a share of the domestic budget in the past six years. They have been doing so since the creation of the Great Society. This category is harder to predict, but several straws in the wind point to renewed growth, perhaps accelerating in the next administration.

Agricultural price supports and unemployment compensation are shown separately because they respond to special circumstances. The latter is highly cyclical; otherwise it shows no apparent trend.[6] Farm price supports gradually declined from the early 1960s until 1973, then dropped abruptly from 2.8 to 0.9 percent of the budget in one year. They remained at about that level through 1976, three exceptionally prosperous years for American agriculture. Since then they have generally increased from year to year, with especially large rises in most years during the 1980s.

That leaves two categories that have shown pronounced declines: grants to state and local governments and all other domestic outlays. Both have dropped sharply since 1980.

Table 8–3 is perhaps an unusual way to conceptualize the domestic budget. Since the total increased by over 8 percent from 1980 to 1986 in real terms, a declining share need not imply declining real expenditures. Table 8–4 presents the same information in the more familiar form of constant dollars, using 1982 as the base. Grants to state and local governments and other government outlays again show large declines, the latter by 50 percent. In both cases the past six years have seen a marked departure from previous years. Unemployment compensation has been coming down since the end of the last

TABLE 8–4

DOMESTIC BUDGET COMPONENTS, 1965–1986

(billions of 1982 dollars)

Year	Safety Net Programs	Other Grants to State and Local Governments	Federal Retirement	Programs for the Elderly	Unemployment Compensation	Farm Price Supports	Other Government
1965	16.0	25.1	8.5	69.9	7.6	10.5	21.5
1970	24.0	40.9	13.2	106.8	8.0	10.9	22.9
1975	43.0	58.6	22.3	158.1	22.7	3.6	55.0
1980	58.5	68.5	31.0	203.0	21.0	8.7	66.5
1986	69.5	50.4	36.1	261.0	15.5	25.8	35.9

SOURCE: Same as table 8–1.

recession. The other categories have all increased in real terms. The 200 percent rise in farm price supports should not obscure the growing importance of programs for the elderly and the poor. The increase in programs for the poor is much smaller, but all have risen.

These tables provide an incomplete picture of the changes in the total federal budget. Net interest and defense, the two large omitted categories, both rose sharply during the 1980s; so the domestic budget declined as a share of the total. Before 1980 the reverse was true. Defense outlays dropped by $100 billion in 1982 dollars, or 40 percent, between their Vietnam War peak in 1968 and 1976; then they rose modestly by $10 billion, or 6 percent, through 1980. Since then defense spending has increased by $74 billion, or 45 percent, but it is still lower than it was in 1968. Despite their limitations, the tables may be useful as indicating which budget categories expanded as defense outlays were cut after 1968 and which were squeezed the most by the increases in interest and defense and the 1981 tax cut.[7]

As a share of GNP (table 8-5), the domestic budget has declined slightly since 1980 but is still larger than in any year before 1976. The same two categories show declines, while programs for the elderly, the poor, and farmers have increased. The safety net increase, however, is very slight.

GRH is fully consistent with these trends. It was essentially an agreement between the president and Congress that, if spending cuts were necessary, they would be shared between defense, which the president did not want to cut and Congress did, and those domestic programs that Congress did not want to cut and the president did. But domestic programs that neither wanted to cut, or to cut much, were exempted. Most notably, these domestic programs were social security and the safety net programs for the poor. These have been largely left alone, especially since 1982. No change in social security has received serious attention since the bipartisan national commission's recommendations were enacted in 1982, except for the Senate's brief consideration of cutting the cost-of-living adjustment in 1985. For the past four years the president has proposed essentially the same minor changes in most safety net programs—particularly minor when compared with his proposals in the rest of the domestic budget—and Congress has consistently rejected them. These categories constitute almost half the domestic budget excluding interest on the debt and over two-thirds of the domestic spending exempt from GRH.

At the other extreme the programs subject to the full brunt of GRH include many that the president has tried to cut or eliminate altogether, with mixed success. Grants to state and local governments (excluding benefit programs for the poor that are administered by the

TABLE 8–5
DOMESTIC BUDGET COMPONENTS, 1965–1986
(percentage of GNP)

Year	Safety Net Programs	Other Grants to State and Local Governments	Federal Retirement	Programs for the Elderly	Unemployment Compensation	Farm Price Supports	Other Government	Total
1965	0.8	1.2	0.4	3.4	0.4	0.5	1.0	7.6
1970	1.0	1.7	0.6	4.4	0.3	0.5	0.9	9.4
1975	1.6	2.2	0.8	5.9	0.8	0.1	2.0	13.5
1980	1.8	2.2	1.0	6.4	0.7	0.3	2.1	14.3
1986	1.9	1.3	1.0	7.1	0.4	0.7	1.0	13.4

SOURCE: Same as table 8–1.

lower levels of government) have been a particular battleground; so have economic development, farm price supports, Amtrak, and guaranteed student loans, among others. If GRH had come into play for fiscal 1987, they would have been cut, not as much as the president has requested but still significantly. Of course, many more programs would also have been cut that have not been at issue, including basic functions of government such as the administration of justice and public goods such as the Weather Bureau. The much-publicized cutback in Library of Congress hours in early 1986, as part of the overall fiscal 1986 sequestration of $11.7 billion, is probably the best-known example.

An intermediate category of programs have been controversial but face only limited reductions under GRH. This category comprises Medicare and federal retirement programs; it constitutes a quarter of the domestic budget, and Medicare alone accounts for half of it. In recent years the president has proposed significant reductions and even structural changes, with partial success. Automatic cuts under GRH are limited for these programs. Only cost-of-living adjustments for retirees could be cut, for example. Cutting them is part, but only part, of the changes that the president has been seeking. For Medicare the maximum cut would be about the same as the president's proposal. The savings would take a different form, but they would be larger and closer to his original budget than he has been able to achieve in recent years.

The terms of GRH on the domestic side are thus the terms set in previous budget proposals by the president: not much change in programs for the poor and social security but reductions in many other areas. This is roughly what happened in fiscal year 1986 and seems to be happening in 1987.

Recent Trends in Major Categories and Programs

Programs for the Elderly. Benefits for the elderly have continued to grow in the 1980s. Outlays rose by 25 percent in real dollars between 1980 and 1985, about the same as in the preceding five years. Their share of the domestic budget has risen by eight percentage points, after fluctuating around 45 percent since the mid-1960s.

Social security and Medicare constitute almost 90 percent of this category and account for nearly all the growth. They are, of course, the two largest social welfare programs in the United States, but they are treated here separately from the safety net programs because neither is limited to the poor and both provide benefits to many older people who are well above the poverty line. Although there is a concentration of the elderly between about 75 percent and 150 percent of the poverty line, the real incomes of the elderly have been increasing steadily for many years, and they now make up a disproportionately small share of the poor.

Close to half the elderly households receiving social security are above the poverty line without counting their benefits. Another 35 to 40 percent are lifted out of poverty by social security. About 15 percent of beneficiaries are poor.[8] Over 85 percent of Medicare beneficiaries are above the poverty line; about half have incomes at least twice that high.[9]

Both social security and Medicare are partly insurance programs but partly also income transfers. Social security benefits are far in excess of past contributions by most current recipients, even including the employers' contributions. These benefits are simply a transfer from current workers to the elderly. Moreover, they go largely untaxed, while payments under private pension plans in excess of the employee's contribution are included in taxable income. Medicare also involves transfers. In the medical insurance program (as opposed to hospital insurance), premiums cover a declining share of program costs, down from 50 percent when the program started to 25 percent today, with the remainder coming from general federal tax revenues.

Social security has been left severely alone since President Reagan's first budget proposals.[10] In 1981 he asked for $6 billion in annual benefit reductions, and Congress approved $4 billion; but the changes did not affect the core of the program. Later in 1981, when Health and Human Services Secretary Richard Schweiker proposed to save $9 billion annually by reducing benefits for early retirees, the Senate quickly and unanimously voted a resolution of disapproval, and the administration disavowed the plan. After that it avoided social security. The threat of a fiscal crisis for the system was left to a bipartisan national commission. Its recommendations, enacted in 1983, reduced outlays by about $4.6 billion annually and raised revenues by $5.4 billion. There have been no benefit reductions since.

Last year the law was changed to make the program more generous, despite the deficit. Benefits are now adjusted each year by the change in the consumer price index, regardless of its magnitude; previously the adjustment occurred only if the inflation rate was above 3 percent. The change was precipitated when the inflation rate in 1986 fell below 3 percent, so that there would have been no increase for 1987. GRH simply continues the policy of protecting social security beneficiaries.

Unlike social security, Medicare has been the subject of annual administration proposals to reduce benefits, by an average of about $2 billion per year. This figure is not precise, because some of the same proposals have been reoffered and changes approved in one year will generate further savings in later years; but the issue has been raised each year, and Congress has acted several times. The program changes approved by Congress, however, typically differ from those proposed by the president. The president has asked for a gradual increase in the medical insurance premium, to cover about 35 percent of costs eventually and an increase in the annual deductible, now set at $75. Congress has been unwilling to impose costs directly on beneficiaries. It last approved an increase in deductibles in 1981, and the 1987 budget reconciliation bill included an increase in outlays in order to limit future increases in the hospital deductible. Congress has been willing to approve some of the president's proposals to cut payments to doctors, hospitals, and other providers of medical services. Under GRH the maximum cut would have been larger than Congress has approved in recent years.

Both programs will continue to grow as a share of the domestic budget in the foreseeable future. The economic assumptions used by the social security trustees imply increased outlays of 30 to 45 percent from 1986 to 1991 in nominal terms.[11] Most of the increase is due to inflation. Real increases are projected at 12 to 15 percent, or about $22 to $28 billion in 1986 dollars.

Medicare is currently projected to grow still faster, by 50 to 75 percent in current dollars between 1986 and 1991. In real terms the increase would be between 30 and 45 percent, or $8 to $13 billion in 1982 dollars. The increase is larger partly because medical costs have outpaced prices generally and are assumed to continue doing so in the future. In the light of past experience, the size of this increase is more uncertain; Congress has been willing to cut benefits in recent years and may do so again. Nonetheless, Medicare is likely to continue growing faster than the domestic budget as a whole.

Federal Civilian and Military Retirement. Pensions for retired federal civilian workers and military personnel currently amount to about $35 billion in 1982 dollars, or 7 percent of the domestic budget. They have continued to grow in response to past increases in federal employment, though more slowly during the Reagan administration than previously.

Both programs are more generous than most private pensions, and the administration has tried to modify them. It has had little success with respect to current employees. In 1986, however, Congress did approve new, somewhat less generous retirement systems for new federal civilian and military workers.

The civilian system is the larger one and is projected to grow more rapidly in the next few years. It encourages early retirement, paying full benefits to persons with thirty years' service at age fifty-five and to those with twenty years' service at age sixty. Benefits are based on the three highest earning years and, like social security, are indexed to the consumer price index. The federal system also differs from private pensions in that about 60 percent of its cost is paid by taxpayers through direct appropriations. Only about 40 percent is paid into a retirement fund by federal workers and the government during the workers' years of employment.

The Reagan administration has been proposing to modify this system since 1983. The most important proposal in its fiscal year 1987 budget would have increased contributions by employees and reduced the system's demands on general tax revenue. This would have increased retirement fund receipts by about $900 million. It has also wanted to change the cost-of-living adjustment (COLA) formula and the earnings base and raise the retirement age for full benefits. Congress has been willing to eliminate COLAs from year to year but not to approve structural changes. The 1986 adjustment was omitted under GRH a year ago; the 1987 adjustment was also subject to sequestration. The current level of benefits is exempt.

The Federal Employees Retirement System established last year is more like a private pension plan. It includes some of the features sought by the administration but applies only to employees hired in 1984 and later years. It was necessitated by the social security reforms of 1983, which placed new federal workers under social security. The system provides additional pension benefits, including both a required defined benefit and a voluntary plan for additional contributions by workers. The benefit formula is less generous than the old system, and the COLA is less complete. But early retirement with full benefits is still available, at age fifty-six or (after the year 2027) age fifty-seven, and benefits are still based on the highest three years' earnings.

The employee's share of the cost will be higher under the new system, about 31 percent rather than 22 percent.[12] Measured as a share of payroll, the new system will cost 23 percent, less than the 25 percent of the old system but more than the 20 percent that the Reagan administration wanted.[13]

The military retirement system is similar. Current servicemen can retire after twenty years with benefits equal to 50 percent of the average for the three highest years' earnings, indexed to the consumer price index. The early retirement provision has been much criticized; it allows servicemen to start new careers at about age forty, with substantial pensions. This has finally been changed in the Military Retirement Reform Act of 1986. Those entering the armed services in the future will receive lower benefits than current servicemen unless they retire with at least thirty years' service. The COLA will be the same as under the new civilian system.[14] These changes do not affect current servicemen; the only changes for them will be in COLAs. As with the civil service system, GRH affects only COLAs; they were omitted in 1986 and subject to sequestration in 1987.

The new retirement systems can be seen as partial victories for the administration. They incorporate some of the changes for future employees that it has proposed for current workers. They have some effect on the current budget, but nearly all the savings will come in the future, mainly in the far distant future.

Poverty Programs. The long-term growth in expenditures on programs for the poor shown in table 8–3 masks a decline early in President Reagan's first term. This is brought out in table 8–6, showing recent real outlays year by year. The pattern is a result of changes in the political strength of the president and his opponents and changes in his program.

The president's first budget proposal included real reductions in the safety net programs (a phrase coined by the administration at the

TABLE 8–6
REAL EXPENDITURES ON SAFETY NET PROGRAMS, 1965–1986
(1982 dollars)

Year	Outlays (billions)	Outlays per Poor Person
1965	16.0	481
1970	24.0	947
1975	43.0	1,660
1980	58.5	1,995
1981	62.7	1,970
1982	59.6	1,733
1983	64.3	1,811
1984	64.9	1,925
1985	66.8	2,018
1986	69.5	n.a.

n.a. = not available.
SOURCE: U.S. Office of Management and Budget, *Historical Tables, Budget of the United States Government, Fiscal Year 1987;* and U.S. Bureau of the Census, *Money and Poverty Status of Families and Persons in the United States: 1985,* Current Population Reports, Series P-60, no. 154, August 1986.

same time). The proposed cuts amounted to about 9 percent from 1981 to 1982. For later years the president proposed to hold real outlays constant at the 1982 level. This was a marked departure from both President Carter's last budget and the trend of the previous twenty years, during which real outlays had quintupled.

Congress was unwilling to go this far; it gave the president only about half the cuts he asked for. The changes were extensive enough to reduce real outlays in 1982 despite the recession, an unusual occurrence. Since then, however, real safety net outlays have been rising. As the recession continued, Congress was unwilling to approve any further cuts, and the results of the 1982 election strengthened the opposition. During 1982 and 1983 the president was unable to win approval of the other half of his original program or any further changes. In 1984 he essentially stopped trying. His last three budgets have proposed mostly minor changes. Many would not affect the poor, such as limiting eligibility for school lunch subsidies to children from families with incomes below 130 percent of the poverty line (instead of the present 185 percent) and imposing stiffer penalties for errors on the state and local governments that actually administer many of these programs. Congress has steadily rejected these changes. His major accomplishment has been to change subsidized housing policy from building expensive projects for the poor to relying on the existing stock of decent privately owned housing, reversing half a century of public policy. This extraordinary achievement, ironically, will have very little effect on the budget during his presidency, although it has already reduced long-term outlays by over $100 billion, compared with the programs of the Carter administration.[15]

Medicaid remains at issue. It has grown more rapidly than most programs for the poor; controlling its costs has proved elusive. In 1981 the president achieved a temporary three-year reduction in the federal matching rate for state outlays, saving about $500 million per year; since it expired, he has regularly proposed a cap on federal payments that would reduce outlays by about $1 billion annually. But Congress has been unwilling to renew the 1981 limit or to enact a cap.

Medicaid is one example of programs in which little-noticed changes resulted in higher outlays. The matching rate reduction was one of the two largest dollar changes that Congress approved in 1981. The other was a decision to raise the share of subsidized housing tenants' incomes that must be paid as rent from 25 to 30 percent over five years. In 1984 Congress tried to reverse that policy, and the administration ultimately compromised on a formula that effectively offset about a quarter of the increase. Thus the largest 1981 changes have proved at least in part to be temporary.

In addition, Congress has enacted a number of smaller policy changes that raise expenditures and has considered others. In 1985 it extended Medicaid to all pregnant women and infants below state income limits, whether or not they live with the father; historically Medicaid has been available only to low-income families without fathers, in conjunction with Aid to Families with Dependent Children (AFDC). In 1986 Congress further extended coverage to all pregnant women and infants below the poverty line, which is above the income limits for Medicaid in every state. One of the last issues to be resolved in the fiscal 1987 appropriation bill was whether states should be required to include families with unemployed fathers (the AFDC-UP program); coverage has been optional. The administration opposed the change, and Congress ultimately decided against it, but the issue is sure to recur. These changes indicate a renewed willingness to help the poor. In the future, real outlays are likely to continue rising.

Perhaps the best simple measure of federal policy is the ratio of real outlays on programs for the poor to the number of poor people. This is shown in the last column of table 8–6. The ratio rose steadily until 1980. The early Reagan years show a small decline, the combined effect of the program changes and the recession. Since 1982 the ratio has been rising again; in 1985 it reached a new high.

The ratio does not measure benefits actually going to the poor, since many programs are open to persons above the poverty line. One goal of administration policy in this area has been to focus programs more narrowly on the poorest people. Income limits were lowered in 1981 for food stamps, subsidized housing, and AFDC, although the AFDC limit was raised again in the next Congress. The AFDC rules determine eligibility for Medicaid as well except for the elderly.[16] The policy has apparently been successful. A larger share of the benefits is actually going to the poor. In 1980, for example, less than half the in-kind benefits (housing, food and nutrition programs, and Medicaid) went to people below the poverty line; since 1982 the share has been more than 50 percent.[17] This means that the ratio in the table understates the size of the safety net after 1981 relative to its size in earlier years.

GRH essentially ratified the outcome of the past three years. It explicitly exempted all safety net programs except subsidized housing. Even most housing outlays were protected, since they are commitments made in prior years and therefore also exempt. Only public housing operating subsidies and budget authority for additional subsidized housing were subject to sequestration. This meant that if the president were unsuccessful in persuading Congress to limit Medicaid directly, he could not achieve that goal through GRH. But he might be able to reduce the number of incremental subsidized housing units and thus hold down future outlays slightly. By agreeing to exempt the low-income programs, the president was in effect giving up the possibility of a small reduction in Medicaid; in return he was avoiding a storm of protest about "fairness."

Grants to State and Local Governments. Grants show the same pattern as programs for the poor: a decline early in the Reagan administration, followed by an increase. But the magnitudes are far different. As shown in table 8–7, real outlays for grants began to decline in the middle of the Carter administration. This was itself unusual but nothing compared with what followed. During the first two Reagan years, real outlays fell by over a quarter and budget authority by almost one-third. Budget authority then rose sharply from 1982 to 1983 and has been roughly constant since. Since outlays have lagged behind authority, some further growth is in prospect. But

TABLE 8–7
GRANTS TO STATE AND LOCAL GOVERNMENTS, 1965–1986
(billions of 1982 dollars)

Year	Outlays	Budget Authority
1965	25.1	n.a.
1970	40.9	n.a.
1975	58.6	83.5
1977	70.2	79.0
1978	75.7	65.7
1979	71.9	73.8
1980	68.5	65.8
1981	61.4	54.9
1982	50.3	45.7
1983	48.9	54.6
1984	49.3	52.5
1985	50.8	53.5
1986	50.4	49.2

n.a. = not available.
NOTE: Excludes payments to individuals, which are primarily safety net programs.
SOURCES: U.S. Office of Management and Budget, *Historical Tables, Budget of the United States Government, Fiscal Year 1987*; and U.S. Office of Management and Budget, *Budget of the United States Government*, Special Analysis H, various years.

both authority and outlays are still much lower than they were before 1980.

The president was able to persuade Congress to approve over four-fifths of his proposed changes in 1981. In the process he cut back or eliminated most of the major grant programs enacted during the administrations of his four predecessors, back to Lyndon Johnson. Again, however, he had little success thereafter. Congress rejected any further reductions in 1982 and instead voted for about a 25 percent increase. More than a third was for highways and mass transit, financed by the increase in the federal gasoline tax voted after the 1982 election, but Congress also increased grants to a greater or lesser extent in almost every category. Many of those that were cut most sharply in 1981 received large increases in the next year and a half, among them social services and transit.

Since 1983 the president has continually proposed substantial cuts and program terminations; Congress has voted smaller cuts and killed very few programs. There has been no consensus. Fiscal year 1986 is a good example. The president wanted to end more than a dozen grant programs and reduce budget authority by $12 billion, almost 20 percent in nominal dollars. Congress voted to terminate only one program—general revenue sharing—and cut $3 billion, about 5 percent. It sharply cut some programs, such as urban development action grants and community services block grants, but it also increased aid to education. For 1987 the president asked Congress again to terminate many of these programs, and Congress again refused, but it cut budget authority by a further $1 billion.

Education, Training, Employment, and Social Services. The functional budget category of education, training, employment, and social services exemplifies the changes in grants. Except for higher education, nearly every program in this category is a grant. Most of them could also be included in an extended definition of the safety net; they are intended either to help poor people directly or to provide services to them so that they can become more productive. They do not give assistance directly to the poor, however, but rather pay other people, such as teachers or social workers, to provide services, and they are not as narrowly directed to the lowest-income households.

Real outlays in this category are shown in table 8–8. They grew rapidly up to 1980. President Reagan asked for a 25 percent cut, amounting to $8.5 billion, and Congress approved two-thirds of it, $5.5 billion.

The biggest change came in job training programs. Congress first eliminated public service employment, the largest program under the

TABLE 8–8
REAL OUTLAYS ON EDUCATION, TRAINING, EMPLOYMENT, AND
SOCIAL SERVICES, 1965–1986
(billions of 1982 dollars)

Year	Outlays
1965	6.3
1970	20.6
1975	27.0
1980	37.2
1981	35.9
1982	27.0
1983	25.6
1984	25.6
1985	26.3
1986	26.7

SOURCE: Same as Table 8–1.

Comprehensive Employment and Training Act (CETA), and then repealed CETA entirely and replaced it with the Job Training Partnership Act (JTPA). Public service employment had been widely criticized for simply enabling local governments to rehire laid-off municipal workers instead of providing training in the form of temporary public service jobs for economically disadvantaged persons, its original purpose. Most of the funds in the other CETA programs were spent for administrative costs and payments to enrollees rather than for training. The new law required 70 percent of the funds to be spent on training, with a more restrictive definition of training than under CETA. Total outlays were cut in half in two years, a reduction of $4.9 billion.

The details of these changes are less important in the present context than the fact that the administration has made them stick. Measured in current dollars, budget outlays in 1985 were slightly below the 1982 level, which is true of only one other grant category, and half the 1980 figure, which is unique. (In constant dollars outlays dropped by 60 percent in five years.) The fiscal 1987 reconciliation increased budget authority by about 5 percent, but still left it far below the Carter years.

By contrast, other programs were less drastically changed in 1981 and have gradually regained at least their nominal pre-Reagan funding levels. The major social services programs were combined into one block grant and cut 20 percent, from $3.0 to $2.4 billion, for fiscal year 1982, but Congress restored half the cut the next fiscal year as part of the Emergency Jobs Bill. Funding has been maintained at that nominal level since then, so that real outlays are declining at the inflation rate.

A number of elementary and secondary education programs were incorporated into two block grants, and total outlays were cut by about $1 billion, from $8 to $7 billion, between 1980 and 1982. No other major structural changes were made, however, and since 1982 both nominal and real budget authority have increased. Since aid to education is funded a year in advance, to enable local school districts to plan their budgets, outlay changes lag by a year. Real outlays rose in 1985 for the first time since 1980. They are still only about two-thirds of their 1980 level, but the trend is up.

Whatever happens to funding for these programs in the next two years, it now seems likely that they will remain in existence in about their present form. A future administration would be able to expand them without difficulty if it wanted to and to fund very nearly the same range of activities that were funded under President Carter. It could not easily, however, go back to CETA.

A New "New Federalism"? The changes in the grant programs may be indications of a nascent rearrangement of functional responsibilities between different levels of government that looks strinkingly similar to President Reagan's 1982 New Federalism. The federal government is gradually providing more money for welfare programs and at the same time reducing real expenditures for many programs that generate mainly local benefits, leaving the states and localities to fund them.

The lower levels of government have apparently been able to absorb the grant reductions without fiscal hardship. State and local governments were able to raise taxes toward the end of the 1981–1982 recession. The new taxes contributed to the large surpluses that quickly developed in the course of the economic recovery. In 1984 the surplus was almost $20 billion. Since then it has declined, to about $7 billion in 1986, a little more than 1 percent of state and local government revenues.[18]

This is an evolution in the direction of the president's 1982 proposal. He wanted to turn some forty federal programs over to the states, in the areas of health, education, transportation, community development, and social services—essentially the grant programs that have been cut in real terms and that are subject to GRH. He also offered to create a $28 billion trust fund for the states to support the programs for four years. At the end of that time states would have to terminate the programs or fund them themselves.

As policy has developed over the past four years, the states are providing a gradually increasing share of funding for many of these programs without getting the $28 billion trust fund.

- As federal operating subsidies for mass transit have been cut, state subsidies have increased by the same share of operating costs.
- Federal funding for social services was cut sharply under the new block grant, but states have taken advantage of a new option to transfer funds from other block grants, and localities have also increased their support; overall social services spending is increasing in nominal terms, though declining slightly in real dollars.
- Total spending for elementary and secondary education has reached a new high while federal support has fallen.

This pattern has led some analysts to conclude that the states should have considered the 1982 proposal more seriously and should try to negotiate a comparable package.[19]

President Reagan also originally wanted to turn AFDC and food stamps over to the states, in return for federal government assumption of the full costs of Medicaid. This proposal was modified in the course of 1982 to keep food stamps and the child nutrition programs at the federal level. AFDC would then have been the only major program for the poor left to the states. There is less evidence of any rearrangement along these lines, although policy since 1982 has moved slightly in the direction of greater federal responsibility for the safety net.

It would be ironic if the states found themselves with the responsibility for programs that they originally refused to accept, on less favorable terms than originally offered, as a result of the federal budget process. Most of the programs that would be forced on them do seem appropriately to belong with the states or localities. Community development, economic development, and mass transit benefit the locality; they may provide useful infrastructure, but the rest of the country gains little from them. Education is much more important from a national standpoint, but it has long been regarded as a local and state responsibility. The rationale for funding social services and job training at lower levels of government is more problematic. They are intended to increase the well-being of the poor, and the states where they may be most useful are likely also to be the states least able to afford them; but local governments may be in a better position to provide specific training in cooperation with potential employers.

Conclusion

Ronald Reagan is turning out to be an unusual president. He came into office intending to reduce the size and burden of the federal government. With regard to the domestic budget, he achieved a partial but still substantial victory. Although he has not been able to cut the budget, despite public concern over the deficit and despite the GRH deficit reduction legislation, he has been able to cut the rate of growth. The increase so far in the 1980s is much less than the growth in the 1960s and 1970s and even smaller than in the 1950s.

This remarkable achievement may well prove only temporary. The largest and most rapidly growing domestic programs in the 1980s have been social security and Medicare. They are projected to continue growing at a somewhat lower rate in the 1990s. Federal civilian and military retirement benefits are also expected to continue growing; the new retirement systems will reduce the growth rate only gradually. Congress could, of course, choose to change any of these programs to reduce their cost, but Medicare is the only likely instance. Congress has refused to make structural changes in the current federal retirement systems, and it has refused to change social security in any way whatsoever since 1983. On the assumption that current policies continue—that is, Medicare benefits are cut from year to year about as much as in recent years while social security and federal retirement programs are left unchanged—real outlays for these programs will be about 15 to 20 percent higher in 1990 than they were in 1985. That would be modestly less than their growth rate in the first half of the decade.

Slower growth in these programs would probably not be enough to hold down the overall rate of increase in the domestic budget, however. In other areas Congress seems likely to take actions that will increase the budget. Increasingly it wants to spend more on programs for the poor. Agricultural subsidies have been notoriously unpredictable in recent years, but they have been growing rapidly for a decade. Grants to state and local governments were cut sharply in the early 1980s; they have not increased much since then, but any further cuts are unlikely. If there is a modest reduction in the growth rate of retirement programs, it will probably be more than offset by greater growth in the rest of the domestic budget. Overall, greater growth in domestic spending seems assured.

The likelihood of growth is enhanced by the nature of the budget changes that have occurred. The president has wanted to terminate many programs—over forty in 1986 alone. Congress has been willing to terminate very few—only one in 1986. The president has had some notable achievements: he has restructured subsidized housing, job training, and federal civilian and military retirement and has achieved smaller but still significant structural changes in some other programs.[20] He has ended general revenue sharing (the one program actually eliminated in 1986). For the most part, however, Congress has only cut outlays, by substantial amounts in some programs and at least modest amounts in many programs. The programs remain. It will be relatively easy for a new president to expand them again.

This means among other things that the GRH targets are likely to become increasingly irrelevant. The required reduction to a $154 billion deficit in fiscal year 1987 will not be reached; current estimates are over $170 billion. The $118 billion target for fiscal year 1988—cutting the deficit by about 50 percent, more than $100 billion in two years—seems utopian. If the present deficit is to be reduced, it will have to be through revenue growth, from either economic growth or an increase in taxes. But neither the economic recovery after 1982 nor the tax increases between 1982 and 1984 have resulted in lower deficits.

This is not meant to minimize the changes in the Reagan years. There has been a real realignment of domestic budget priorities, toward programs for the elderly and the poor and away from grants to state and local governments and a broad range of general and special-purpose activities. That reallocation seems likely to last. Moreover, future budget growth will probably be nowhere near the growth of the 1960s and 1970s. The Congressional Budget Office estimates growth of 10 to 15 percent in real domestic outlays for the full decade of the 1980s.[21] That is a base-line figure, assuming no changes in current policies. It will probably prove to be a lower bound; it includes a 15 percent decline in farm price supports, for example. But any plausible adjustment still implies a sharp deceleration in domestic expenditures. And other factors should restrain the budget. The tax reform passed in 1986 will make future tax increases more obvious and therefore more difficult politically; the continuing large budget deficits will put downward pressure on federal spending.

Even with these considerations, however, the low growth rate is unlikely to persist after President Reagan leaves office. Unlike most of his predecessors and probably unlike his successor as well, he began with plans to cut the size of the government, not with proposals for new programs to solve various problems. Any new president of either party is likely to have at least a few new proposals, perhaps a good many, if only to distinguish himself or herself from President Reagan. In the category of programs for the poor, for example, a liberal president and Congress may respond to current concerns about hunger and homelessness; a new conservative administration may be motivated by the "feminization of poverty" to expand child support enforcement programs. The budget would grow in either event. On the chart of domestic spending, therefore, the Reagan years are likely to look like a pause in the growth rate but not the beginning of a reversal.

Notes

1. The definition of the domestic budget in figure 8–1 differs slightly from that used in the rest of this paper. The figure includes international affairs; elsewhere that category is excluded. The latter seems more appropriate, but the differences in domestic budget levels and changes are slight.

2. The budget proposals and projections for the next fiscal year in table 8–2 are based on estimates of outlays for the current fiscal year, and those estimates change during the year. During calendar year 1985 the estimates for fiscal year 1985 declined. The February estimate of $555 billion, shown in the table, was reduced to $552 billion by August; actual outlays for 1985 turned out to be $548 billion. Thus the president could reasonably anticipate some outlay reduction for fiscal year 1986 as 1985 unfolded. For this reason, the actual outlays for fiscal years 1985 and 1986 in table 8–1 are not the same as the projected outlays for those years shown in the first line of table 8–2.

3. Bruce L. Gardner, "Farm Policy and the Farm Problem," in Phillip Cagan, ed., *Essays in Contemporary Economic Problems, 1986: The Impact of the Reagan Program* (Washington, D.C.: American Enterprise Institute, 1986), pp. 223–46.

4. For a more extensive discussion of the insurance funds' problems, see the paper by William S. Haraf, "Maintaining Financial Stability: The Financial Safety Net and Public Policy," chapter 6 in this volume.

5. Office of Management and Budget, "Mid-Session Review of the 1987 Budget," August 6, 1986, p. 11.

6. This pattern is not clear from the five-year intervals in the table; some of the years were recession years, and others were not.

7. Expenditures on programs for the poor *have* declined as a share of the total federal budget during the Reagan administration, but this is the only sense in which they have fallen. The same thing is true of every major category except farm price supports and Medicare, owing to the rapid growth in interest and defense; even social security is down slightly.

8. The numbers in the text are not precise, because the data on households raised above poverty by social security do not separately identify elderly-headed households with three or more people. In 1983, 16 percent of the elderly households receiving social security were poor (U.S. Bureau of the Census, *Characteristics of the Population below the Poverty Level: 1983*, Current Population Reports, Series P-60, no.138, February 1985, table 34). Between 37 and 42 percent were raised above poverty by social security (U.S. Bureau of the Census, *Estimates of Poverty Including the Value of Noncash Benefits: 1983*, Technical Paper 52, August 1984, table 4). These figures imply that between 42 and 47 percent would have been above the poverty line even if they had received no social security. The incidence of poverty among elderly social security beneficiaries has been declining, and the proportion who do not need social security to avoid poverty has been increasing.

271

9. U.S. Bureau of the Census, *Characteristics of Households and Persons Receiving Selected Noncash Benefits: 1984,* Current Population Reports, Series P-60, no. 150, November 1985, table 12.

10. For a more detailed discussion of the Reagan administration's proposals and the policy outcomes in both social security and Medicare, see John C. Weicher, "Accounting for the Deficit," in Phillip Cagan, ed., *Essays in Contemporary Economic Problems, 1985: The Economy in Deficit* (Washington, D.C.: American Enterprise Institute, 1985), pp. 5–31, esp. pp. 20–21.

11. David Koitz, "Social Security: Its Funding Outlook and Significance for Government Finance," Congressional Research Service, June 1, 1986; and "Memorandum" from Steven F. McKay, Office of the Actuary, Social Security Administration, April 1, 1986.

12. Civil Service Retirement Team, "A Retirement Plan for Federal Workers Covered by Social Security: An Analysis of the Federal Employees Retirement System (P.L. 99-335)," Congressional Research Service, July 21, 1986.

13. "New Federal Retirement Plan Wins Approval from Congress," *Congressional Quarterly,* May 24, 1986, pp. 1201–3.

14. Robert L. Goldich, "Military Retirement: Major Legislative Issues," Congressional Research Service, August 7, 1986.

15. Low-income projects have traditionally been financed in the same way as private housing, with long-term contracts. Outlays in any one year therefore consist almost entirely of bond or mortgage payments for projects built in the past, and major policy changes today have little effect on current outlays. The president has not quite ended all subsidized housing production, but he has been able to persuade Congress to terminate the main new construction program (Section 8). In 1983 he also won a temporary halt in new public housing. He almost repeated the latter success in 1986; both houses of Congress passed appropriation bills without funds for new projects, but the reconciliation bill included money for 2,500 new or rebuilt units. For a more extensive discussion of low-income-housing policy, see John C. Weicher, "Halfway to a Housing Allowance?" in John C. Weicher, ed., *Maintaining the Safety Net: Income Redistribution Programs in the Reagan Administration* (Washington, D.C.: American Enterprise Institute, 1984), pp. 92–118.

16. These changes are discussed in more detail in John C. Weicher, "The Safety Net after Three Years," in Weicher, *Maintaining the Safety Net,* pp. 1–19, esp. pp. 13–14. A full description of program eligibility limits and other rules appears in Vee Burke, *Cash and Noncash Benefits for Persons with Limited Income: Eligibility Rules, Recipient and Expenditure Data, FY 1983–1985,* Congressional Research Service, September 30, 1986.

17. Detailed calculations of benefits going to the poor and going to reduce poverty for the years 1979 to 1984 appear in John C. Weicher, "The Reagan Domestic Budget Cuts: Proposals, Outcomes, and Effects," in Cagan, *Contemporary Economic Problems, 1986,* pp. 7–44, esp. pp. 19–23. Similar calculations for 1985 are consistent with those reported in the paper.

18. These surpluses exclude the surpluses of state and local social insurance funds. Sara Johnson, "State and Local Government," *Review of the U.S. Economy* (January 1987), pp. 43–47.

19. Claude Barfield, "National Urban Policy, New Federalism, and the Gramm-Rudman-Hollings Act" (Paper presented at the Conference on Urban Policy, Boulder, Colorado, June 1986).

20. There were fundamental changes in other programs; those listed in the text have the largest budget implications. AFDC, for example, was redesigned to exclude most of the working poor. See Edward D. Berkowitz, "Changing the

Meaning of Welfare Reform," in Weicher, *Maintaining the Safety Net*, pp. 23–42.

21. Congressional Budget Office, *The Economic and Budget Outlook: Fiscal Years 1988–1992*, January 1987, chap. 2, pp.55–64. The CBO base line covers the years from 1985 to 1990; these projections have been combined with the record of 1980 to 1985 to construct the estimate in the text.

9

The New Tax Law

Eugene Steuerle

Summary

Despite some problems and needless complications, the Tax Reform Act of 1986 constitutes a major step forward in tax and economic policy. Tax rates are reduced significantly. Poor and lower-income workers receive significant tax reductions and improved work incentives. The returns to different types of assets are taxed on a much more equal basis, and the allocation of assets in the economy should improve. Barriers to entry to new businesses are partially removed, and all business, both established and new, should thereby be made more competitive. Through the lowering of tax rates, the elimination of negative tax rates on certain equity investments, and the imposition of various limits on loss deductions, investment in more productive assets is encouraged. Investment in assets expected to be unproductive should be virtually eliminated. Interest rates will be less distorted by taxes, and monetary policy will need to be less concerned with differences between before-tax and after-tax rates of interest, especially in periods of inflation. In general, taxation should have less influence on decision making.

Difficulties still remain. The tax act fails to lower tax rates to the extent that would have been possible if Congress had been willing to deal with many individual preferences, especially fringe benefits, transfer payments, and state and local tax deductions. Tax rates for various forms of capital investment still vary significantly with the rate of inflation. The double taxation of corporate income is not addressed, and comprehensive approaches to pension, international, and estate taxation were not attempted. Fortunately , lower rates of taxation still lessen the effective cost of many of the distortions left in the system.

Although the fear of a drop in investment spending is exaggerated, the cost of capital is raised slightly, and the opportunity to lower that cost was forgone. This lost opportunity resulted primarily from effective trades of accelerated deductions or loans from the government for indexation of depreciation allowances. In several cases more than income is put in the tax base, thus creating exactly the same kinds of distortions that are caused by preferences: the differential taxation of different sources of income. Finally, a number of backdoor approaches to policy are needlessly complex and in some cases reduce the efficiency of economic activity. Although these additional

275

burdens are not trivial and should have been avoided, they do not compare in size or importance with the benefits that should be generated through this tax reform package.

The Tax Reform Act of 1986 is one of the most sweeping changes in the tax code in this century. Certainly it involves the largest reshuffling of incentives and priorities ever achieved in a (roughly) revenue-neutral act. Its economic effects, however, are only beginning to be understood. This chapter provides an initial assessment of what was achieved, what was not done, and what new problems have been created.

What Was Accomplished?

The tax reform process took almost three years. It was never directed to short-term goals; rather, it was aimed primarily at correcting some of the long-term distortions created by the tax laws. Although tax reform could also have been used to deal with many of the shorter-run contingencies or problems in the economy, the speed of the political process would have made that objective difficult to attain.

The basic purpose of any tax system—indeed, the very reason for its existence—is to raise revenues. It is only reasonable to require that the system also create minimal distortions and inefficiencies in the long run. Despite the slowness of the political process—often yesterday's problems, not today's, were being solved—tax policy in recent decades had been used increasingly as a short-term economic tool. Overemphasis on this one aspect of tax policy prevented policy makers from dealing with longer-run issues and deflected attention from the basic purpose of taxation. Eventually the longer-run issues and the social costs related to their neglect began to outweigh any benefits that might have been achieved by setting up a patchwork of incentives to meet short-term objectives.

In my view, the gains from this round of tax reform are considerable, but at the same time the number of failures and new problems are not trivial. This first section focuses on the positive aspects, while later sections focus on the failures.

Reduced Taxation and Improved Incentives for Lower-Income Workers. Tax reform succeeded in reducing the taxation of poor and lower-income taxpayers, particularly those who work. It achieved this goal primarily through three changes: increases in the personal exemption to $2,000 by 1989 (from $1,070 in 1986); increases in the standard deduction (for a married couple, from $3,660 in 1986 to $5,000 by 1988); and significant expansion, as well as indexing for inflation, of the earned income tax credit (EITC). By 1988 the expansion and the indexing together will raise the maximum credit to about $870 (from $550 in 1986), and the credit will not be completely phased out until income exceeds about $18,500.

The first two of these provisions raise the tax-exempt income—the income at which individuals begin to pay income tax—to about the poverty threshold for households of almost all sizes. At low incomes above poverty, the average tax decrease is also significant, primarily because these two provisions considerably reduce the amount of income subject to taxation.

The change in the EITC can be viewed as offsetting most social security taxes on the first $5,700 of wages. In 1989 about $4 billion in additional outlays or reduced tax collections will be used up by the EITC. The maximum credit is raised but only to the real amount that applied in 1975, the first year that the credit was available. Because of the increase in the incomes at which the credit begins to be phased out, however, at least now it is available for full-time workers at minimum and slightly higher wages. Under old law the credit was completely or substantially phased out for such workers, making it principally a credit for part-time or part-year workers.

The net effect of these changes should be to increase the incentive to work, especially for those who have a discrete choice between working and not working. As workers move into the phase-out range of the EITC, however, their combined direct marginal tax rates, including state income tax rates, rise as high as 45 percent. Ten percentage points of this total are contributed by the EITC phase-out alone, fifteen percentage points by social security taxes (including the employer's share), fifteen percentage points by federal income taxation, and about five percentage points by state income taxation in a typical state. In the EITC phase-out range, marginal rates are actually higher under the new law than before, so that here the marginal incentive to undertake more work is reduced.

Few base-broadening reforms apply at low incomes, but one change—full taxation of unemployment insurance—complements the tax reductions applying to low-income persons. Under old tax law, priority in taxation was given to low-income unemployed persons over low-income workers. Under the Tax Reform Act of 1986, poor workers not only pay significantly less tax but pay no higher tax than unemployed persons with the same amount of income. Although many unemployed persons may not pay any more tax than formerly —other increased benefits may offset the loss of nontaxation of unemployment insurance—their *relative* incentive to work will still be improved. Lower rates of tax on earned income plus higher or more nearly equal rates of tax on unemployment income thus complement each other in improving work incentives. The trade-off of lower tax rates and a broader base, of course, is the essence of tax reform.

Some comparisons give an idea of the magnitude of the changes in the taxation of poor and low-income workers. For a married couple with two dependents the tax threshold is about $7,980 for 1986 but rises to $12,800 by 1988 under the new law. The tax threshold will thus be just above the estimated poverty threshold of $12,135 for the same year. If the EITC is included in the calculations, the changes are more significant. The average tax rate (income taxes, less EITC, divided by income) at the poverty threshold drops from 3.3 percent in 1986 to − 5.3 percent in 1988. Thus the EITC offsets some social security tax, as well as income tax, at poverty-level incomes.

At low incomes above the poverty threshold, the changes are still significant but less dramatic. From a historical perspective the 1986 tax act only partially offsets a continuing trend to raise taxes on low-income workers. Federal income tax rates on a family of four at half the median income, for instance, were zero until 1960. Inflation and real growth then began to push the family at that income into positive tax brackets, and previous tax reforms were insufficient to compensate for the increase. By 1985 the average tax rate reached 6.5 percent. Under the tax act the average rate drops initially to about 5.0 percent but then rises again toward 5.5 percent by the end of the decade. Persons with this income have no earned income credits available to offset social security taxes. The combined employer-employee social security tax rates were set at 4.0 percent in 1955, 9.6 percent in 1969, 13.4 percent in 1984, and 15.3 percent for 1990. At one-half the median income, in fact, the drop in income taxes from 1986 to 1990 (− 1.0 percent of income) will just offset the social security tax increases (+ 1.0 percent of income) over the same period.[1]

Improvements in the Allocation of Assets. One major benefit of the tax act will be a significant improvement in the allocation of assets and investment within the economy. The government will greatly reduce its role in directing which industries and which business activities should be favored and which should be penalized. Effective tax rates will be made more equal among assets.

Table 9–1 presents estimates of effective marginal tax rates by asset type and by broad categories of assets. These calculations take into account both corporate and personal taxes.[2] Before the Tax Reform Act of 1986, the differences in effective rates were greater among equipment, structures, and inventory than among different types of equipment or different types of structures. Much, but not all, of the variance in effective rates can be attributed to the investment tax credit, which was made available to equipment but not structures and was not adjusted according to the economic depreciation rate or life of the asset. Most types of equipment are shown to have tax rates of about 7 percent before 1986; under inflation assumptions lower than the 4 percent used in the table, the effective tax rate becomes negative. Structures averaged about a 38 percent tax rate before tax reform and inventories about 58 percent.

Under the final act passed by Congress, the differences in effective rates are considerably narrowed. There are fewer distinctions among types of equipment or between structures and equipment. Tax rates on investments in structures are approximately 39 percent and on equipment about 38 percent. The tax rate on inventories will also be reduced and made closer to returns on other assets.

Not shown in the table is another form of equalization of effective tax rates that is important to the economy but difficult to measure under traditional procedures. Economists have long recognized that investments take place not just in physical assets but in research, better management, and human capital. Payments for these intangible forms of capital are difficult to calculate separately from other wage payments. In the case of invention and ideas, the common concept of "investment" may be inadequate to describe, much less measure, a process that may involve little in the way of monetary investment in either labor or capital in the traditional sense.

Many of the most dynamic companies in an economy essentially pay the statutory tax rate on the returns to their ideas and advances in knowledge and procedures. That is, such advances are often associated with very high rates of return to the companies that succeed. In part, the high rate of return is related to the risk of the ventures. These high rates of return cannot be offset by investment credits or other preferences that are associated only with gross purchases of physical assets. Nor does expensing, or immediate write-off, of wage payments really result in a much lower rate of tax, both because the riskier investments tend to generate a higher rate of return and because the tax law grants very imperfect loss offsets.

Thus under the old law the innovative and dynamic firm often paid tax at a statutory corporate rate of 46 percent to subsidize the firm that was effectively paying a zero tax rate on many of its purchases of equipment. Under the new law the dynamic firm pays the statutory corporate tax rate of 34 percent rather than 46 percent, while the less innovative firm, whose profits come mainly from further investment

TABLE 9–1
TOTAL EFFECTIVE TAX RATES ON CORPORATE INVESTMENT BY BROAD ASSET TYPE AND BY INDUSTRY
(percent)

	Old Law	Treasury[a]	Administration[a]	House	Senate	New Law
Total	38	34	30	40	39	41
By broad asset type						
Equipment and structures	29	33	25	38	37	39
Equipment	11	33	24	39	34	38
Structures	38	33	26	37	38	39
Inventories	58	35	44	47	47	48
By specific asset type						
Equipment						
Automobiles	7	34	26	45	40	46
Office and computing equipment	8	35	26	41	42	42
Trucks, buses, and trailers	8	34	25	39	39	41
Aircraft	7	34	25	45	36	41
Construction machinery	7	33	24	33	35	35
Mining and oilfield machinery	7	32	24	41	34	40
Service industry machinery	7	32	24	38	34	40
Tractors	7	32	23	41	34	38
Instruments	13	31	22	42	34	39
Other equipment	7	37	26	42	33	38
General industrial equipment	12	32	23	40	32	37

Metalworking machinery	7	31	22	38	30	35
Electric transmission equipment	25	37	25	45	39	44
Communications equipment	7	34	24	29	30	30
Other electrical equipment	7	34	24	38	30	35
Furniture and fixtures	7	33	23	38	30	34
Special industrial equipment	7	32	22	36	29	33
Agricultural equipment	6	31	22	36	28	33
Fabricated metal products	19	31	21	35	32	40
Engines and Turbines	32	34	24	44	42	46
Ships and boats	6	34	23	39	35	42
Railroad equipment	27	32	22	35	33	29
Structures						
Mining oil and gas	16	28	10	11	19	20
Other	48	39	34	44	45	46
Industrial structures	44	36	31	41	43	43
Public utility structures	28	31	18	36	34	37
Commercial structures	41	34	29	38	40	41
Farm structures	42	34	29	38	40	41

NOTE: Calculations assume a 4 percent inflation rate and separate marginal tax rates for corporations, interest income, dividend income, and capital gains. Only effective tax rates on corporate investments are shown here, but the effective tax rates include both corporate and personal taxes. Investment is financed one-third by debt.

a. Calculations for Treasury and administration proposals assume that taxation of dividends on existing shares does raise overall effective tax rates on capital.

SOURCE: Jane G. Gravelle, Congressional Research Service.

in known types of equipment, pays close to the same corporate rate.[3]

New Business versus Old Business. Closely related to the discrimination under old law against dynamic and successful firms was a broad discrimination against new firms, as well as against certain older firms that had not been profitable for a number of years. For a given marginal investment, these firms were made to face higher tax rates than most established firms. Thus the new firms had to achieve a higher-than-normal return from an investment to compete.[4] The reduced threat of entry may simultaneously have lessened the efforts of existing firms to take advantage of new technologies and new markets.

Two features of all postwar investment incentives were that they were available only as tax reductions and were available almost immediately, either at the time of investment or soon thereafter. These features implied that any tax saving would be received mainly by firms with enough outside income to make full use of the credits and accelerated deductions. The new firm can seldom make use of such incentives because the new equipment cannot be expected to return enough output in so short a period to create either sufficient taxable income to offset the accelerated deductions or sufficient tax liability to offset credits against tax. Some existing firms are also effectively in the same situation when existing lines of business generate inadequate taxable income to allow full use of incentives for marginal investments. (Previous years' income must also be insufficient to allow carry-back of current-year tax losses and credits.) This, by the way, helps explain why some companies in basic industries supported a tax reform that eliminated the investment tax credit: they felt they were at a competitive disadvantage with respect to new investment, and they already had a large carry-over of unused investment credits from previous years. Potential new firms, of course, are almost totally unrepresented in the political process simply because they do not yet exist.

As an example of the discrimination under the old law, at a zero inflation rate an asset generates (on an undiscounted basis) output valued at about 31 percent of the initial price over a 2½-year period if it depreciates at 10 percent per year and yields about a 4 percent real return over and above depreciation. Yet under old law tax deductions and credits could offset income equal to 80 percent of the purchase price over the same period. Since the income from the asset is less than half (31/80) the allowed offsets, only the established firm with existing flows of taxable income could make full use of the deductions and credits.

The new law reduces some of the disparities between new and established firms. Deductions in the first two and one-half years now offset income only up to 56 percent of the purchase price. Thus, although the discrimination against new business will not be eliminated, it will be considerably lessened. Most of the change between the two laws is due to the repeal of the investment tax credit. The greater leveling of tax rates faced by new and old businesses should enhance productivity, in part by making potential domestic new businesses a more likely source of competition with established businesses.

Investment in More Productive Assets. Perhaps the major improvement in the tax bill is brought about by a significant restoration of the market incentive to invest in the most productive assets. This restoration is dramatized by the virtual removal—without a significant increase in the inflation rate—of any incentive to invest in unproductive assets. An unproductive asset is one that returns to the economy less in value than the resources used to build or make it, that is, one with a negative before-tax rate of return. I have argued elsewhere that an important cause of the stagnation and lack of productivity increases in the 1970s and early 1980s was the interaction of inflation and the tax system.[5] During that period labor increased significantly in supply, and percentages of national income spent on capital investment remained about at historical levels. These facts strongly suggest that the lesser growth in the economy was due more to the use made of labor and capital than to the total supply of those factors. Capital was not being put to its best use, and the tax system, combined with inflation, often induced investment in assets that provided a negative return to the economy. Here it will be shown how that problem is greatly reduced when both inflation and tax rates are lowered.

Investment in assets with less than maximum productivity is encouraged whenever some assets are tax favored. At the extreme, investment in unproductive assets can actually become profitable when one of two conditions holds: the effective tax rate on equity-financed investments is negative, or the after-tax real interest rate is negative.[6] In the latter case it is through leveraging—borrowing (or selling short a tax-disfavored asset) to purchase another asset that is relatively tax preferred—that the taxpayer can make an after-tax profit even when the asset itself produces a negative rate of return.

The 1986 tax act takes two very important steps that considerably reduce the probability that the conditions necessary for unproductive investment will hold. First, it eliminates the investment credit. As long as the investor writes off no more than the real cost, acceleration of depreciation allowances can never result in a negative tax rate on equity investments in depreciable assets. To see this, note that expensing is equivalent under most conditions to a zero tax rate. Any acceleration less than expensing requires that the purchase price be written off over a period of time rather than immediately and therefore results in a positive tax rate.

Second, the tax act lowers the marginal tax rate. This normally makes the tax consequences of any miscalculation of income less important. In the case of interest, the failure to index (in both old and new law) means that the subsidy given to borrowing (or overtaxation of interest paid) is equal to the tax rate times the inflationary component of the interest rate. That subsidy declines when either the tax rate or the inflation rate decreases.

It is apparent that negative after-tax interest rates can induce investment in unproductive capital. When borrowing takes place, the investor must receive a return from the investment that is greater than or equal to the after-tax interest rate. If the after-tax real interest rate is positive and real, the after-tax return from the investment (calculated without regard to the borrowing) must also be positive in real terms, for it must be great enough to pay the after-tax interest rate. When, however, the after-tax interest rate is negative in real terms, the investor may profit from investment in an unproductive asset, that is, one with a negative real rate of return.

While it is true that investors should still invest in assets with the highest rates of return, different assets have different amounts of risk. With a negative after-tax interest rate, investment in assets with little perceived or actual risk may become competitive on a risk-adjusted basis. For instance, if commodities are expected without much risk to increase in price with inflation, some saving may be diverted to the wasteful storage of commodities. The corporate manager may also be induced to invest in riskless assets that almost surely would not have been purchased if the after-tax interest rate were positive.

For the interest rate to be positive and real for most business investors, it must be at least twice the rate of inflation when the tax rate is 50 percent but only one and one-half times the inflation rate when the tax rate is 33 percent.[7] At an inflation rate of 10 percent, for example, the interest rate must be 20 percent or more to prevent the taxpayer with a tax rate of 50 percent from investing in unproductive assets and activities. At an interest cost of exactly 20 percent, the tax deduction pays for one-half the interest rate, or ten percentage points of cost, and inflation covers the remaining ten percentage points. Correspondingly, the required interest rate is only 15 percent at a tax rate of 33 percent. Similarly, at an inflation rate of 4 percent, the required interest rate falls one-quarter, from 8 percent to 6 percent, when the tax rate falls from 50 percent to 33 percent.

Not only does the interest rate required to prevent investment in unproductive assets fall, but the new tax rates most likely reduce the interest rate as well. Starting at a given before-tax interest rate, lower tax rates initially increase the after-tax interest rate. As a result, the demand curve for borrowing (with respect to the before-tax rate) should initially fall, and the supply curve of saving in interest-bearing assets should initially rise. Both movements tend to reduce the market interest rate.

Some Further Implications. Our recent economic experience provides a major lesson for economic policy makers: when negative after-tax interest rates or negative tax rates for a significant portion of taxpayers are allowed to persist for extended periods of time, investment will be diverted toward less productive activities, the rate of growth of the economy will be slowed, and productivity increases will be moderated. Because these conditions are more likely to hold in an inflationary economy, sluggish growth can be seen as resulting from the interaction of the tax system with inflation.

Because the misallocation of investment is caused both by inflation and by tax policy, the implications extend beyond tax policy. For instance, in the late 1970s high inflation and high tax rates essentially left monetary policy in a dilemma. If monetary authorities attempted to tackle the problem alone and raise interest rates high enough to make after-tax rates of return positive for most taxpayers, this policy hit especially hard those sectors for which cash flow was crucial. Potential new homeowners and new car purchasers were deterred by increases in nominal interest rates. New business formation was also discouraged by high inflation-induced interest rates both because cash flow from economically sound investments was far from sufficient to pay interest costs and because the tax system favored old over new business. When the monetary authorities lowered interest rates, however, taxpayers were given added incentive to invest in unproductive capital. In some cases borrowing to stockpile commodities even became profitable, and price inflation was further encouraged. In addition, low and negative after-tax interest rates stimulated the private demand for loans.

We are less likely to be confronted with the same set of problems in the near future. Changes in nominal interest rates should translate more readily into changes in real after-tax interest rates even for taxpayers in the top bracket.

Of course, it is not simply lower and more nearly equal tax rates that bring about this result. Lower inflation helps greatly. The combined effect may be clarified by a simple example. At a 50 percent tax rate and a 7 percent inflation rate, it requires an 18 percent interest rate to reach an after-tax rate of return of 2 percent. At a 33 percent tax rate and an inflation rate of 3 percent, the same after-tax rate of return can be attained with a nominal interest rate of 7.5 percent (see figure 9–1). Thus tax reform adds significantly to the downward pressure on interest rates and will affect the extent to which changes in the monetary policy and inflation translate into changes in after-tax interest rates.

Tax Shelters. Tax shelters in the past often involved investment in unproductive assets but tended to be concentrated in the individual sector rather than the corporate sector. Individuals were able to take negative statements of taxable income from one business and use them to offset wage and salary income as well as capital income from other businesses and partnerships. Because interest payments are

FIGURE 9–1

INTEREST RATES NECESSARY TO PREVENT UNPRODUCTIVE INVESTMENT

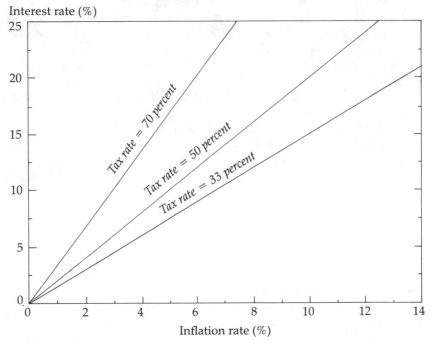

Interest rate (%)

Inflation rate (%)

SOURCE: Author

indexed for neither tax accounting nor financial accounting purposes, the overstatement of real interest was a desirable feature of an individual shelter. It presented problems, however, for a corporation attempting to report maximum income to shareholders.[8] Moreover, when corporations generate negative statements of taxable income, they are often unable to take immediate advantage of available deductions and credits.

Tax shelters grew rapidly in the 1970s and 1980s, not only because direct new investment increased but also because corporations began to sell off hundreds of billions of dollars of assets to various kinds of partnerships. In what I have labeled the disincorporation of America, whole sectors of the economy sold off their assets and then leased them back from syndicated partnerships. This option, by the way, was less readily available to corporations holding assets, such as plants, that tend not to be divisible and packageable to separate groups of investors.

As indicated above, when the tax rate on the investment asset was negative or the after-tax interest rate was negative, the investor could generate a positive after-tax return even when the return to the economy or the before-tax rate of return was negative. Since tax shelters leveraged tax advantages by both borrowing and purchasing assets that benefited from credits and early write-offs of expenses, the required before-tax return was often negative. Indeed, the attraction of some shelters was that the value of the tax deductions themselves purported almost to pay for the cost of the investment.

The Tax Reform Act should significantly reduce the amount of money flowing into such shelters by reducing tax rates and by making the effective tax rate positive for equity investments in various assets. In addition, the act attacks shelters by limiting deductions from passive investments, by restricting investment interest payments in excess of investment income, and by deferring many deductions through minimum tax rules.[9] Although these approaches are cumbersome and inefficient, as discussed later, they too should reduce the flow of money into shelter investments. In many ways individuals are treated more like corporations under the act: where taxable income from a designated group of investment assets (that is, all passive income for the individual, all income within the corporation for the corporation) is negative, deductions cannot be used fully (or must be carried over) until such time as enough positive taxable income is generated from investments within the same group.

Reduced Influence of Taxes on Consumers' and Producers' Choices. Another important and related benefit of tax reform is that taxes should have less effect on the decision making of both business managers and individual investors. The Tax Reform Act of 1986 eliminated a number of special preferences, deductions, and exclusions but retained many others. Nonetheless, the lower rate of taxation means that the value of deductions is calculated at a maximum rate of 28 or 33 percent for individuals and 34 percent for corporations. Thus, even when choices are made between nontaxable and taxable items, the tax consequences of alternative consumption or production patterns will be reduced.

In some areas the reduction in the tax rate should help lessen excessive, tax-induced demands for products or activities. For instance, the reduced value of the employer exclusion of health insurance costs should moderately restrain increases in health care expenditures and costs. The rate reduction also lowers the inherent subsidy to borrowing and may have significant long-run implications for debt-equity ratios in the private sector as a whole. For upper-income taxpayers the reduced incentive to invest in preferred assets extends to such items as vacation homes. The imputed rental value and capital gains remain nontaxable or deferred, and the purchase can still be financed with significant borrowing, but lower tax rates increase the relative value of alternative taxable investments and reduce the value of the interest deduction.

In choosing among financial assets, taxpayers are more likely to invest directly in equities or savings accounts. Under prereform law, the large potential tax saving from various portfolio strategies subsidized and supported the use of numerous agents and transactions. While there is no good estimate of the attrition of saving due to these additional transactions costs, the amount was probably substantial. For instance, many tax shelters provided ultimate investors with 80 percent or less of the dollars originally saved. As tax savings fall in relation to transactions costs, taxpayers are more likely to avoid those additional costs by channeling saving more directly into investment, through either purchases of stock or use of a single financial intermediary such as a bank.

What Was Neglected?

The amount of change introduced by the tax reform is significant by almost any standard. Hundreds of billions of dollars of tax liability are switched, not so much from one group of taxpayers to others as from some kinds of activities to others. The drop in the top tax rates—from 46 percent to 34 percent for corporations and from 50 percent to 33 percent or 28 percent for individuals—has for many symbolized the extent of these changes.

Nonetheless, many "tax reform" items did not make it through the process. Where such issues were neglected, differences in taxation remain. These will continue to induce taxpayers to produce and consume inefficiently.

Base Broadening for Individuals. Certainly one of the major failures of this tax reform is that the amount of base broadening for individuals, though significant, was still fairly limited. Failure to expand the tax base means higher remaining tax rates and greater welfare losses arising from tax-created distinctions among economic activities. Individual base broadening was limited partly because of undue attention to the top rate of tax rather than to the marginal rates faced by all taxpayers.

Some of the rate reduction for individuals is financed by increases in tax payments by corporations. The most significant changes in the individual tax base are the full taxation of capital gains, the elimination of the two-earner deduction, the reduction in the availability of individual retirement accounts at upper income levels, the repeal of income averaging, and the elimination of the sales tax deduction. Other lesser but important changes include an extension to all income levels of the taxation of unemployment insurance, a floor on miscellaneous deductions, an increase in the floor on medical contributions, and elimination of the small dividend exclusion and the political contributions credit.

Outside of the capital gains exclusion, however, most of the major preferences granted to individuals in the old tax law are untouched or touched only slightly. Nontaxable compensation provided in the form of health and life insurance is still available to employees, while other fringe benefit exclusions—for educational assistance, legal service plans, and dependent care assistance—are actually extended. Except for the small change in the taxation of unemployment compensation, most transfer payments—workers' compensation, most social security retirement and disability benefits, veterans' compensation—remain largely untaxed, often without regard to the needs or income of the recipient.[10] Deductions of state and local income taxes and of real estate and personal property taxes remain. Because nontaxable fringe benefits, nontaxable transfer payments, and deductions of state and local taxes constitute such a large portion of the total tax benefits granted to individuals, it is fair to say that the amount of individual base broadening is limited.

Whether to treat the full taxation of capital gains as a broadening of the base is not clear. As will be discussed later, the failure to index in many cases brought into the tax base more than complete taxation of the related income. Of more relevance here, the discretionary nature of the capital gains tax means that any increase in tax rates may be offset by a lower rate of realization of such gains. By some estimates net taxes on capital gains will actually go down. Other estimates predict a small increase, but all conclude that a higher rate means fewer realizations.[11] Thus, even though these estimates are subject to much debate, it is clear that the extent of any capital gains base broadening is limited because the tax is discretionary and can be avoided.

At the same time, full taxation of capital gains will help deter a common form of tax arbitrage—borrowing to purchase capital assets and profiting simply from the tax differential. Legal experts also argue that the capital gains exclusion has caused much of the complexity in taxation. The exclusion requires taxpayers to distinguish between long-term and short-term gains and between capital income and ordinary income. It also requires the Internal Revenue Service to frame recapture rules to prevent the benefits of the exclusion from going to taxpayers who already take advantage of accelerated depreciation or other tax deferrals. In effect, all these rules try to prevent situations in which the taxpayer deducts $100 of "ordinary" expense today and then excludes some portion of $100 of "capital" income tomorrow.

Some elements of tax reform should not be put in the category of base broadening. The so-called phase-outs of "the benefits of the bottom brackets" and of the personal exemption are simply disguised rate increases. In addition, elimination of income averaging implies an increase in rates and no expansion of the tax base, although this change is justified partly on grounds of simplification and partly because the old law did not target well those persons deemed most deserving of averaging provisions.

Indexing to Account for Inflation. Congress also declined to deal with the problems of inflation and of indexing the measure of income to account for that inflation. Accordingly, changes in the inflation rate will continue to play havoc with the effective tax rate that applies to different forms of investment income.

In the case of depreciation allowances, the failure to index the basis of the assets means that less than 100 percent of the real value of an investment can be depreciated. To compensate for this deficiency, depreciation allowances continue to be accelerated, in many cases about as fast as under old tax law. The overstatement of the depreciation in the early years then compensates, at least on a present-value basis, for most of the understatement in the later years of the investment.

At least three major difficulties are caused by the failure to index depreciation allowances. First, the effective value of the depreciation allowances varies widely with the rate of inflation. A decline in inflation can lead to increased incentives to invest, and a rise significantly decreases the value of the depreciation allowances. Second, in using acceleration to compensate for the failure to index, the new law continues to favor old business over new enterprise, though not as much as current law. Many start-up firms still will not be able to make full use of the initial tax incentive, and the competitiveness of established domestic business can still be expected to suffer. Third, because both financial accounting and tax accounting fail to index, many decision makers—investors, union negotiators, and firm managers— may continue to be misled by inappropriate calculations of income. The tendency to overstate income in the later years of an investment, for instance, can easily lead to such miscalculations as excess demands for wage increases in declining industries and understatements of the true cost of providing energy to utility regulators.[12]

Failure to index for capital gains implies that the tax base will often be more than capital income. The expansion of the tax base beyond economic income (or the double taxation of certain kinds of income) causes the same problems as limitation of the tax base through exclusions from taxation of certain forms of income. That is, many, if not most, of the economic, legal, and accounting problems associated with income taxation are caused by the differential taxation of different kinds of income. The capital gains tax change moves too far in one direction rather than trying to strike a balance.

Because of the discretionary nature of capital gains taxation, the net effect of this change on the cost of capital or on effective tax rates is minimal. Taxpayers will offset much of the increase simply by realizing fewer gains. Deferral of tax will reduce tax rates significantly, and, of course, exclusion of gains at death will continue to leave a large portion of capital gains untaxed. Overtaxation will occur mainly for those taxpayers who sell assets after short holding periods.

Even if the capital gains changes involve no increase in effective tax rates on capital income and do not change aggregate saving in the economy, they are still distortionary. First, the relative amount of capital invested in shorter-term, risky projects will be reduced. Second, the lock-in effect on portfolios will be increased. The economy will suffer to the extent that markets are made less liquid and saving is deterred from moving to the highest and best use.

Finally, the failure to index implies that the rates of return on different types of investment continue to differ, as inflation has differential effects on different types of investment and forms of financing. John Makin and Michael Allison, for instance, estimate that with inflation indexing, the present value of welfare in the economy could be improved by several hundred billion dollars. Of course, the higher the rate of inflation, the greater the gains from indexing. (The present-value estimates include not only gains in the current year but also the discounted value of gains in future years.) These gains derive from the reduced disparities in the taxation of different sources of income, as well as from the tendency of a fully indexed system to avoid increases in taxes on capital at higher inflation rates.[13]

Other Neglected Issues. Despite the comprehensiveness of the Tax Reform Act, it failed to deal with a large number of relevant tax issues. Although it made some pension changes, notably with respect to individual retirement accounts, 401 (k) rules, and the integration of private pension plans with social security, pension policy was never examined in a comprehensive way. There was never a thorough examination, for instance, of whether current policy is optimally designed to encourage saving. Estate taxation and capital gains at death were also never studied in depth. The combination of the minimum tax on gifts of appreciated property and the complete exclusion from taxation of gains at death may unnecessarily encourage the retention of capital gain property rather than its donation to charity. Although many scattered international tax issues were raised in the tax reform process, the provisions finally enacted were for the most part not based on any rigorous or thorough analysis of international tax issues. Indeed, congressional action in the international area seems to have been driven primarily by a desire to reach a predetermined revenue goal.

To maintain a number of existing preferences, integration of corporate and individual income taxes was quickly abandoned after the original Treasury proposal.[14] Remaining in the new tax system, therefore, are many of the problems associated with taxing corporate income twice, at both the corporate and the individual levels: the encouragement of debt rather than equity financing; legal problems associated with distinguishing between dividends and interest; and the encouragement of noncorporate over corporate ownership. Similarly, problems remain in measuring the tax base of partners in noncorporate business where rights of ownership, as well as types and timing of income payments, are difficult to value and separate among the various partners.

Finally, corporate and individual tax rates are left far apart. Under the old law individual rates were often higher than corporate rates, thus encouraging the taking of deductions (such as tax shelter expenses) in the individual sector. Now that top individual rates are lower than corporate rates, even without taking into account the double taxation of dividends, incentives are reversed. Deductions are now more valuable in the corporate sector. For instance, the after-tax interest rate will be lower for the corporate investor facing a 34 percent interest rate than for the noncorporate investor facing a 28 percent rate. At the same time, equity investments are given greater incentive than ever to be held in the individual sector, since taxable receipts from equity investments are always most valuable when taxed at the lowest rate. Some corporations are again beginning to disincorporate, only this time the corporations involved are those holding fixed investments with generous yields. When the corporate rate was much lower than the individual rate, disincorporation took place mainly among corporations holding preferential assets or assets that could be highly leveraged to produce large deductions and negative statements of taxable income. (See the discussion above of tax shelters.)

New Problems

An Increase in the Cost of Capital. As tax reform worked its way through the political process, the effective tax rate on returns from capital investment was needlessly increased. Both table 9-1 and table 9-2, derived under slightly different estimating assumptions, show a higher effective tax rate on capital under the 1986 law than under old law. The original Treasury proposal and the administration proposal (sometimes referred to as Treasury II) were criticized by some for their changes in effective tax rates and the cost of capital. Under either estimating procedure in the two tables, however, the administration proposal actually lowered the total effective tax rate. The lower rates on structures and inventories more than compensated for a higher rate on equipment. The original Treasury proposal also lowered effective tax rates in table 9-1.

Perhaps the principal difference in the estimating procedures in the two tables is the assumption with regard to the importance of dividends. Table 9-2 essentially assumes that a lowering of the tax rate on dividends has no effect on total tax rates on capital income; table 9-1 makes the opposite assumption. If the former assumption, or "new" view of dividend taxation, were replaced by the "old" view, table 9-2 would also show a reduction in effective tax rates under the original Treasury proposal.[15]

TABLE 9–2
Total Effective Tax Rates on Corporate Investment, by Broad Asset Type at Different Rates of Inflation
(percent)

	Old Law	Treasury[a]	Administration[a]	House	Senate	New Law
			0% Inflation			
Total	35	43	37	40	38	39
By asset type						
Equipment	−15	41	28	33	26	29
Structures	36	46	40	37	39	39
Public utilities	26	44	31	39	35	39
Inventories	50	43	42	44	43	44
Land	52	45	44	46	45	46
Addendum: residential structures plus land	21	25	25	22	21	21
			4% Inflation			
Total	37	44	36	42	41	42
By asset type						
Equipment	5	41	27	41	33	37
Structures	42	46	38	41	44	44
Public utilities	33	44	30	43	40	44
Inventories	48	43	41	42	43	43

			8% Inflation		
Land	50	46	43	45	45	46
Addendum: residential structures plus land	19	21	24	20	20	20
Total	38	44	34	43	43	44
By asset type						
Equipment	17	41	24	44	38	43
Structures	44	47	36	42	47	47
Public utilities	36	44	28	44	43	47
Inventories	45	43	38	41	43	43
Land	47	46	41	43	45	46
Addendum: residential structures plus land	17	16	23	19	19	19

NOTES: Calculations assume separate marginal rates of tax for corporations, interest income, dividend income, and capital gains. Corporations finance 33.7 percent by debt. Only effective tax rates on corporate investments are shown here, but the effective tax rates include both personal and corporate taxes. Addendum item is not part of total.

a. Dividend relief in Treasury and administration proposals is here treated as influencing effective tax rates only through issuance of new shares. Under the "old view" that taxation of dividends on existing shares matters, at 4 percent inflation the effective tax rate falls in moving from current law to the Treasury proposal.

SOURCE: Yolanda K. Henderson, "Lessons from Federal Reform of Business Taxes," *New England Economic Review* (November/December 1986), plus unpublished data.

A common perception is that business was successful in negotiating with Congress to lower effective tax rates on capital. The perception is wrong. Certainly some compromises helped certain kinds of investment. For instance, equipment does fare better under the Senate bill than under the House bill. To achieve this gain, however, negotiators implicitly accepted an increase in the effective tax rate on many types of structures, inventories, and the returns to invention and "ideas."

In addition, among the important compromises made along the way to a final tax act was abandonment of a number of means of lowering the cost of capital, the most important of which was the indexing of depreciation allowances. The revenue pickup from these changes allowed some acceleration of depreciation allowances for equipment and retention of some early write-offs for intangible drilling costs and expenses of long-term contracts. Although these trade-offs were supposedly designed to improve the overall cost of capital, they actually did the opposite.

One way to explain this surprising outcome is as follows. Through retention of some initial deductions and slight acceleration of depreciation allowances, certain capital expenditures, especially equipment purchases, were given slightly better treatment than they might otherwise have obtained. Acceleration of deductions and depreciation allowances, however, is equivalent to an increase in loans from the government (a tax deferral), albeit at a zero interest rate. Those loans are repaid through a reduction in deductions or depreciation allowed in later years. Per dollar of cost under the accounting system used for tax reform—revenue estimates are made for only five years—loans reduce the cost of capital much less than direct grants or other forms of relief that do not later get "recaptured" or repaid. Thus, when revenue-neutral exchanges were made in the corporate and business sector, they tended to be of a kind that exchanged direct tax decreases for loans.

As a result of these compromises, the cost of capital and effective tax rates were in my view raised needlessly over old law (again, see tables 9–1 and 9–2). If indexing of depreciation allowances or, to a lesser extent, some small investment credit had been retained, the revenues so used would have been much more valuable in lowering the cost of capital than the slight accelerations of deductions that were put in as substitutes. The preferences given or retained were not the most "revenue-efficient" means of reducing the cost of capital.

The Shift in Tax Burdens from Individuals to Corporations. While tables 9–1 and 9–2 show a slight increase of 9 to 13 percent in the effective tax rates for capital investment, the tax burdens of corporations are increased by a much larger percentage over the estimating period. A corresponding fear is that this change in revenues will reduce capital investment. Economic analysis, however, emphasizes that it is the total tax burden on investment over time, not the corporate tax burden at a particular time, that is most important for long-term investment policy. Therefore, the shift in timing of payments may be relatively unimportant if the cost of capital is little changed. Similarly, total taxation of capital income includes both corporate and individual taxation. To the extent that individual tax reductions compensate for corporate tax increases, the shift in which sector withholds the payments for the government should make little difference.

To be sure, any shift contains some elements of disruption and therefore of transition cost. Traditional macroeconomic analysis, however, has tended not to attribute much effect to revenue-neutral acts. Some econometric models do predict that money in different sectors will be treated differently, that is, individuals will consume and corporations will save (and somehow the increased consumption will not lead to increased investment). This conclusion is certainly debatable. Even if it is true, the amount of the shift in tax burdens from corporations to individuals is on the order of about one-half of 1 percent of GNP. Sensitivity analyses tend to show that typical changes in other variables—exchange rates, growth of the money supply, or total taxes in relation to expenditures—outweigh even over the short run the effects of this kind of revenue-neutral tax change.

In summary, some transition costs are bound to be associated with any shift in incentives and tax burdens. Moreover, there is a slight increase in the cost of capital, and, according to some estimates, a higher cost of capital eventually leads to a smaller capital stock. Nonetheless, the amount of change in the cost of capital is moderate, and there is almost no change in broader macrovariables such as total tax collections. Tax reform, therefore, is not likely to have a large effect on aggregate demand, investment, or consumption. That result should not be surprising for a process that was designed mainly to deal with the composition, not the aggregate size, of tax burdens.

Inclusion of More Than Income in the Tax Base. Many of the problems in the tax system are caused by the differential taxation of income. The differentials not only result in inefficient portfolio shifts but, especially when leveraged, can lead to such difficulties as investment in unproductive capital. Tax differentials, however, can be caused not just by granting preferential treatment to some types of income. They can be created equally well by the penalization or overtaxation of certain sources of income. As the tax reform process evolved, the desire to keep down the top rate for both individuals and corporations generated pressure not only to expand the tax base to include all income but to go beyond that tax base to add items that would not, under most theories, be considered items or flows that should be treated as income or taxed at all.

First, the failure to index depreciation and capital gains means that more than 100 percent of the returns from some depreciable and capital assets will be taxed.

Second, one of the largest revenue raisers in the minimum tax is the taxation of book income until 1989 and of the accounting measure of earnings and profits (E & P) after 1989. (More precisely, half the excess of book income or E & P over a measure of alternative minimum taxable income—AMTI—must be added to the AMTI tax base.) Both book income and E & P tend to overstate income because of their failure to adjust for inflation. In addition, the former measure of financial income is especially arbitrary because accountants can choose among accounting methods; in effect, they can choose among various tax bases.

Third, the final tax bill, unlike Treasury I, eliminates income averaging. Although the current averaging provision was poorly targeted and might justifiably be pared for certain groups, some taxpayers still bear higher-than-average tax burdens because of the annual period used for income tax accounting.

Fourth, almost entirely for revenue reasons, Congress either changed or failed to adjust a number of small provisions. Moving expenses typically exceed the amount that will now be deductible. Reasonable costs of child care, treated conceptually as a cost of working, are nonetheless still not to be fully deductible for many middle- and upper-income taxpayers (a credit, rather than a deduction, is allowed). Only those miscellaneous expenses of work and asset management in excess of 2 percent of adjusted gross income will be deductible. While some floor was justifiable on grounds of simplification, a 2 percent floor is higher than necessary on administrative grounds and hits especially hard at those who have much higher-than-normal expenses of this kind.

Backdoor Complications. Political constraints on direct means of base broadening meant that more and more of the revenues necessary to finance rate reduction would come in through the back door. Backdoor increases in taxes are those that are designed to be complicated —the complication being a way of befuddling opponents, making costs difficult to calculate, and otherwise hiding what is taking place. Backdoor approaches are often necessary to ensure that certain distributional, equity, or appearance goals are met but without defining a single tax base correctly. Because of the additional effort necessary to come in through the back door, the tax code is almost inevitably made more complex.

Many of these backdoor approaches expand the tax base beyond a realistic measure of income or ability to pay. Some ways in which the tax base includes more than simply income and in which appropriate deductions are disallowed have already been mentioned.

One of the more significant backdoor proposals is the new alternative minimum tax. Among the additions to the minimum tax base are excess depreciation, certain benefits from acceleration of deductions under long-term contracts, certain mining and development costs expensed for purposes of the regular tax, the excess of bad debt deductions over deductions taken on the basis of actual experience, some amount of book income, untaxed appreciation on charitable contributions, and deductions for passive losses.

For several reasons it is difficult to assess the full effects of the minimum tax. First, there are ways to avoid the tax. Since the minimum tax is assessed only when it is higher than the regular tax, a corporation with many preferences can avoid a minimum tax by merging with a corporation with significant regular tax liability and few preferences. Second, some amounts of tax—such as that associated with the accounting measure of book income—are optional. Third, many who owe minimum tax will probably fail to pay it. It would be too burdensome to require all taxpayers to report both a regular tax base and a minimum tax base. Many of those who fail to report a minimum tax base, however, will probably owe minimum tax. The history of error rates in previous minimum taxes is not hopeful.[16]

The new tax code also makes crucial the definition of "passive activities." Such activities "include trade or business activities in which the taxpayer does not materially participate (for example, a limited partnership interest in an activity) and rental activities."[17] Deductions from passive activities, to the extent that they exceed income from such activities, generally must be deferred until receipts exceed deductions or the assets are sold. The definition of a passive activity becomes critical, since material participation can convert passive losses into active ones. In effect, the limit on passive losses does not prevent the sheltering of income within a given business but greatly reduces the marketing of such shelters to wage earners and salaried professionals.

Various forms of interest payments also face different limits. Much interest is paid by active businesses and remains deductible. Other interest is paid by passive businesses, where the amount of current deduction will depend on the net amount of income declared. Personal interest payments on automobile loans and credit card balances (for personal expenditures, somehow separated) are not deductible. Mortgage interest is deductible, but only for first and second residences of a taxpayer. Mortgage interest on these homes is, however, not deductible to the extent that the mortgage debt exceeds the original purchase price of the residences plus the cost of major improvements (defined essentially as capital improvements). An exception to the exception is provided if the excess mortgage debt is incurred for educational or medical purposes.

It is easy to assess these various backdoor approaches as more costly than a better designed tax system. It is also clear that many needless complications are added to the tax code. Countless disputes can be expected to arise, especially for businesses and individuals with significant income from business activity subject to possible minimum taxes and passive loss rules. Since interest deductions could be affected by one of several limits, the rules must be "stacked" to allow the taxpayer to figure out which one, if any, becomes binding before the others. The phase-outs of the personal exemption and lower rate bracket add lines to the tax forms.

For total economic activity, at least compared with current law, the costs are less clear. Where the minimum tax base includes more than economic income, as in the case of depreciation under the minimum tax, efficient behavior is certainly deterred. The rules separating various kinds of interest and trying to trace them from one asset to another also somewhat reduce the liquidity of financial markets and at least raise administrative costs. Competitive problems can be expected to arise when some persons borrow at substantially different after-tax rates from others engaged in the same economic activity.

Much of the deterred activity, however, is likely to fall in categories of unproductive investments in the economy. For instance, the greatest effect of the passive loss rules is probably on those "tax shelters" that were generating large statements of negative taxable income. To avoid some of the added complications, taxpayers are likely to channel saving more directly to corporations or through traditional financial intermediaries. Moreover, corporations have always been limited to taking losses only against income, so that "passive" individual investors are put on a footing similar to corporate investors.

Conclusion

Throughout the tax reform debate, public expectations and the political process seemed to demand that four conditions be met if any final act was to be labeled "reform." First, taxation of the poor was to be significantly reduced or eliminated. Second, the top rate of taxation was to be lowered to 35 percent or less for both individuals and corporations. Third, some of the disparities in the treatment of different kinds of capital income were to be eliminated. Fourth, tax shelters were to be curtailed.

All four of these objectives are met in the final tax act. At the same time other gains for the economy are generated. New businesses are made more competitive with old business. Investment in unproductive capital is no longer encouraged. Interest rates have probably been reduced. Finally, the lower rate of taxation means that existing preferences cause less distortion simply because they are now less valuable.

At the same time the final tax act reflects neglect of other possible objectives of tax reform and, in some cases, deforms rather than reforms. Much individual base broadening is avoided because reductions in rates other than the top rate never received much attention. The calculation of business income is made more complicated, rather than simplified, as much direct base broadening is cast aside in favor of minimum taxes, limits on passive losses, and interest limits of several kinds. The tax base is expanded in some cases to include more than income, and double taxation of corporate income continues to cause distortions.

Some of the problems created by the tax act are important enough that they will have to be addressed at some future time. Despite these limitations, the act should both improve the efficiency of investment and consumption choices within the economy and restore public confidence in the equity of the tax system. In effect, for once we may indeed have "reformed" the tax system.

Notes

1. Further details are provided in Eugene Steuerle and Paul Wilson, "The Taxation of Poor and Low Income Workers," in Jack A. Meyer, ed., *Papers Prepared for the Project on the Welfare of Families* (Washington, D.C.: American Horizons, forthcoming).

2. The marginal rates used are effectively averaged across individuals by weighting each taxpayer according to the amount of interest, dividends, or capital gains received. Different marginal rates are used for capital gains, interest, dividends, and so forth. A constant debt-equity ratio for corporate investments is also assumed. For further details, see Jane G. Gravelle, "A Comparative Analysis of

Five Tax Proposals: Effects of Business Income Tax Provisions," Report No. 84-832 E, December 27, 1984, and "Effective Tax Rates in the Major Tax Revision Plans: Updated Tables Including the Senate Finance Committee Proposal," Report 86-691 E, May 16, 1986 (Washington, D.C.: Congressional Research Service).

3. Charles R. Hulten and James W. Robertson make essentially the same argument in their finding that high-technology industries in manufacturing experienced an appreciably higher average effective tax rate during the 1970s than other manufacturing industries. See Charles R. Hulten and James W. Robertson, "The Taxation of High Technology Industries," *National Tax Journal*, vol. 37 (September 1984), pp. 327–46.

4. See Eugene Steuerle, "Building New Wealth by Preserving Old Wealth: Savings and Investment Tax Incentives in the Post War Era," *National Tax Journal* (September 1983), pp. 307–19.

5. See Eugene Steuerle, *Taxes, Loans, and Inflation* (Washington, D.C.: Brookings Institution, 1985).

6. In a pure capital market where assets can be sold short (so that, in effect, lending can take place at the rate of return for those assets), problems are caused not only when tax rates are negative but when they are greater than 100 percent. Thus, in the case of interest payments, a tax rate of more than 100 percent can convert a positive before-tax rate into a negative after-tax rate.

7. If n = the inflation rate, i = the nominal interest rate, and t = the tax rate, the after-tax interest rate is negative whenever $i - ti - n$ is less than zero or i is less than $n/(1 - t)$.

8. The expansion of tax shelters is reflected in partnership data. By 1983 over 64 percent of high-income taxpayers (those with total positive income greater than $250,000) reported some amount of partnership loss. Net partnership losses reported by individuals reporting losses grew from $1.4 billion in 1965 to $28.3 billion in 1982. See Susan Nelson, "Taxes Paid by High-Income Taxpayers and the Growth of Partnerships," *Statistics of Income Bulletin*, vol. 5 (Fall 1985), pp. 55–60; and Lowell Dworin, "An Analysis of Partnership Activity, 1981–83," *Statistics of Income Bulletin*, vol. 5 (Spring 1986), pp. 63–74.

9. An investment is passive if the taxpayer does not materially participate in the conduct of the activity. Limited partnerships are presumed to be passive, as are most rental activities. Most activities in which the taxpayer provides substantial services are not defined as passive.

10. Up to one-half of social security benefits are taxable for higher income recipients. Still, the bulk of social security payments remains nontaxable.

11. The debate on the relationship between tax rates and capital gains realizations has not been settled. See Martin S. Feldstein, Joel Slemrod, and Shlomo Yitzhaki, "The Effects of Taxation on the Selling of Corporate Stock and the Realization of Capital Gains," *Quarterly Journal of Economics* (June 1980), pp. 777–91; Gerald E. Auten and Charles T. Clotfelter, "Permanent versus Transitory Tax Effects and the Realization of Capital Gains," *Quarterly Journal of Economics* (November 1982), pp. 613–32; Joseph Minarik, "The Effects of Taxation on the Selling of Corporate Stock and the Realization of Capital Gains: Comment," *Quarterly Journal of Economics* (February 1984), pp. 93–110; Office of Tax Analysis, Department of the Treasury, *Capital Gains Tax Reductions of 1978* (Washington, D.C., 1985); and Lawrence B. Lindsey, "Capital Gains Rates, Realizations, and Revenues," in Martin S. Feldstein, ed., *The Effects of Taxation on Capital Formation* (Chicago: University of Chicago Press, forthcoming).

12. Some economists believe or at least assume that financial accounting is irrelevant and that economic actors either see through all veils or at least act

accordingly. The argument in the text, however, assumes that information is costly to gather and that inaccurate information does indeed lead to inefficient decision making.

13. See Michael T. Allison and John H. Makin, "Evaluating Welfare Gains from Tax Reform," American Enterprise Institute Fiscal Policy Studies Occasional Paper No. 10, forthcoming. Their estimates actually compare the new tax law with the original Treasury Department proposal but relate much of the gain in welfare to the indexing provisions of that proposal. At 4 percent inflation, the present value of welfare gains in 1973 dollars is $131 billion for the new tax law and $393 billion for the Treasury proposal. At 7 percent inflation, the corresponding numbers are $63 billion and $505 billion. Because the laws are constant in the model, most of the relative gains as inflation increases from 4 percent to 7 percent are due to inflation indexing under the Treasury proposal.

14. A corporate deduction, rising eventually to 50 percent of dividends paid out of previously taxed earnings, was proposed in Treasury I.

15. See Don Fullerton and Yolanda Henderson, "The Impact of Fundamental Tax Reform on the Allocation of Resources," American Enterprise Institute Fiscal Policy Studies Occasional Paper No. 8, April 1986. Using basically the same model as table 9–1 but assuming the old view of dividend taxes, the authors find a decrease in effective tax rates.

16. Even the much simpler alternative minimum tax in prior law resulted in understatement of tax on at last 32.6 percent of returns. See Internal Revenue Service, "Taxpayer Compliance Measurement Program for 1982 Returns," table 10.

17. Joint Committee on Taxation, "Summary of the Conference Agreement on H.R. 3838 (Tax Reform Act of 1986)," 1986, p. 17.

10
Are There Lessons for the United States in the Japanese Tax System?

John H. Makin and John B. Shoven

Summary

This paper compares the tax treatment of income from new investment under U.S. and Japanese tax law in existence before 1987. We find that Japanese investors have two main advantages over American investors. First, the exemption from tax of much household interest income provides corporations, which are able to deduct interest expense, with a considerable advantage from highly leveraged, debt-financed investment. Second, investors have benefited from the relative stability of the Japanese tax system over the past thirty years. Although between 1955 and 1981 the basic corporate tax rate varied from 36.75 percent to 42 percent, its structure was largely maintained. Tax treatment of individuals, especially with respect to provisions governing investment income, has also been quite stable.

Until recently, the advantage to debt-financed investment in Japan has been enhanced by the relatively closed nature of the financial system. Corporations have tended to maintain close relationships with a single bank, which in turn has become involved in management of the company or companies to which it provides credit. This close relationship has permitted debt-to-equity ratios that are high by U.S. standards, thereby further enhancing the advantage to debt-financed investment.

As a counterpart to its stability over the years, the Japanese tax system has made limited use of targeted investment incentives such as accelerated depreciation, investment tax credits, and research and development (R&D) credits. Such incentives are used selectively in a way that allows them to affect the targeted investments while limiting revenue loss. Further, the incentives are usually in place only temporarily and, as in the case of R&D credits, are applicable only to incremental R&D expenditures. This method, while minimizing revenue loss, also discriminates in favor of rapidly growing R&D-intensive firms.

Our comparison of the U.S. and Japanese tax systems reveals a distinction between taxes on corporations and investment incentives. Japan's corporate tax raises about 30 percent of national tax receipts, three times the U.S. level. Investment incentives, however, in the form of light taxation of debt-fi-

nanced capital incomes, are strong. The combination of full deductibility of interest on corporate debt (as in the United States) and light taxation of personal interest income, capital gains, and some dividends (the reverse of that in the United States) allow Japanese investors to capture a higher fraction of gross earnings from investment than do U.S. investors.

The U.S. tax system would be best advised to adopt the saving incentives and the stability that characterize the Japanese tax system. An opportunity to strengthen saving incentives by indexing interest income and expense for tax purposes did not survive the political process that produced the Tax Reform Act of 1986. Nevertheless, the sharply lower marginal tax rates do help reduce the incentive to use debt, while they enhance the attractiveness of normal saving by virtue of the lower tax rate on interest income.

It is interesting, if not ironic, to note that the passage of the Tax Reform Act of 1986 in the United States has accelerated Prime Minister Nakasone's drive for "tax reform" in Japan. Unlike the situation in the United States, this would be Japan's first major tax reform since the initial drafting of its postwar tax system by a team of U.S. experts in the early 1950s. Proposed changes in the Japanese tax system include a cut in personal tax rates, an end to tax-free interest on savings, introduction of a consumption-style value-added or national sales tax, and the phasing in of a broad capital gains tax on securities transactions for individuals.

The purpose of the national sales tax or value-added tax is to improve compliance among farmers and smaller businesses, which are said to evade much of their tax liability. It would also offset the reduction in saving incentives implied by an end to the tax exemption for interest income.

We hope that while Japan moves toward the base-broadening, rate-lowering pattern of tax reform in the United States neither it nor the United States will engage in a round of internationally motivated tax reforms either annually or even biennially.

Lower tax rates and the attendant reduction in the value of tax preferences will help to stabilize tax systems, especially in the United States. It remains to be seen whether the United States will be content to leave the new tax system alone for at least five years while investors and households become accustomed to its new set of incentives. At the same time it will be interesting to watch the tax reform movement in Japan and other industrial countries that seems to have been set in motion by the U.S. example. In view of the frequent adulation expressed for the Japanese tax system during the American debate on the subject, it is perhaps ironic that tax reform in the United States appears to be influencing the Japanese to adopt a more American-style tax system.

Introduction

The United States has been actively "reforming" its federal tax system for most of this decade. At the beginning of the Reagan presidency the influential supply-side economists argued that the tax system was stifling the incentives to work and save in our economy. The result was the Economic Recovery Tax Act of 1981 (ERTA). It liberalized depreciation schedules and the investment tax credit (ITC), lowered capital gains tax rates, and made individual retirement accounts widely available, among other things. It promised a sharp decrease in the tax bills of corporations and provided incentives for saving, investment, and economic growth. This bill was followed in one year by another major tax bill, the Tax Equity and Fiscal Responsibility Act (TEFRA) of 1982. The 1982 bill rolled back the liberalized depreciation allowances that had just been enacted as part of the 1981 bill and increased corporate taxes.

Since 1984, the government has been considering truly sweeping tax changes. The Tax Reform Act enacted in the fall of 1986 would increase taxes on corporations, eliminate the investment tax credit, raise capital gains rates, and restrict individual retirement accounts. In all of these areas the Tax Reform Act of 1986 reverses the direction of the 1981 bill. Without too much difficulty, one could get the impression that we, as a country, are not certain about the direction in which we should change our tax system. It is also quite likely that the lack of a stable tax environment has caused investors to refrain from the type of long-term commitments required in making major capital outlays.

Another significant aspect of the economy of the 1980s has been the growing openness of the U.S. economy and its change from a supplier of funds to world capital markets to an international borrower. Widespread concern has been expressed about the ability of American firms to compete in world markets. Much of the international competitiveness issue focuses on our relationship to one of our major trading partners and the second biggest economy in the world, Japan. In general, the economic performance of Japan has been the envy of the rest of the world. Its growth rates continue to lead the developed countries. Despite a large national government deficit, at least until 1986, the Japanese have been able to finance robust investment in their economy internally and even export financial capital. And they seem to have prospered with both the rise and the fall of OPEC.

In this paper we examine the Japanese tax system and ask whether it contributed to Japan's remarkable economic performance. Are there lessons in the design of the Japanese tax system for the United States? How do the Japanese treat such items as depreciation, ITCs, individual retirement accounts, and capital gains? And, perhaps most important, how heavily do the Japanese tax the return to corporate investments relative to the United States? It should be admitted at the outset that many important differences exist between the two countries other than the design of their tax systems. Although we believe that it is instructive to examine whether the Japanese tax system has contributed to Japan's successes, one can never pin down the causal links with certainty. We enter this research knowing that we will not be able to prove conclusively the effects of the design of the Japanese tax system on Japan's performance but believing that observation of how such a successful economy finances its public sector can teach us much.

The second section of the paper briefly outlines the Japanese tax system, particularly the treatment of income from capital. The third section then describes an approach to measuring the effect of the tax system on investment incentives. In the fourth section, we compare saving and investment incentives in the United States and Japan. A key issue, which is not fully agreed upon in the literature, is whether Japan taxes capital income heavily or lightly. We attempt to answer this question by examining both their corporate and their individual tax systems. Section five concludes the paper by discussing the lessons the United States can learn from the Japanese example. A number of issues relevant to the U.S. debate receive attention, including capital gains, the research and development credit, the taxation of old capital versus new investments, individual retirement accounts, and the treatment of debt versus equity finance.

Summary of Tax Differences

The taxation of capital income in Japan is quite different from that in the United States. First, the corporate tax raises a lot of revenue, around 30 percent of national tax receipts, in comparison with about 10 percent for corporate tax here. Of course, more small businesses tend to be incorporated in Japan. In fact, all companies engaged in profit-making activities are subject to the corporation tax, including partnerships and sole proprietorships. The corporate tax rate structure is also fairly high. One recent study calculated the marginal corporation tax rate on an additional unit of profit in Japan at 52.6 percent in 1980, taking into account the national, prefecture, and local taxes.[1] This slightly exceeds the same tax rate calculated for the United States for the same year, which came to 49.5 percent. These facts make Japan appear to place a high tax on capital income, and, in fact, the Federation for Economic Organization (Keidanren) claims that Japan's real rate of corporate taxation is the highest in the world. Although this claim could easily be disputed, that is not the relevant number for determining the effect of the tax system on investment incentives. Investment incentives depend on what fraction of the gross earnings of the investment investors can hope to capture. While Japan does apply high marginal tax rates to corporate equity capital, a great deal of investment is debt financed, and personal capital income is extremely lightly taxed. Some forms of the return to capital, namely debt, are deductible for corporations and very lightly taxed for individuals. This opens up the possibility that capital income may be taxed lightly in Japan, despite the high corporate tax rate. It also means that a firm has some choice about whether to pay corporate or personal taxes on the return from capital when it determines its financial structure. This choice is also available in the United States.

Japan's financial system itself enhances the advantage of a high degree of leverage. Businesses can carry very high debt, by American standards, because typically these businesses have a close working relationship with a bank. Many Japanese firms deal almost exclusively with a single bank that has a quasi-managerial role because of its large stake in its highly leveraged client company. The banks are, in turn, highly leveraged by American standards. The close relationship between the large "city" banks and the Bank of Japan makes this possible. In both cases, between firms and banks and between "city" banks and the Bank of Japan, the vulnerability to large, rigid cash flow requirements that the leverage would normally engender is mitigated by a close and integral working relationship. The tax advantage to debt finance is increased by these unique relationships in the financial sector without a significant element of additional risk, save any risks or encumbrances that businesses may associate with having banks involved in management.

The general outline of the corporate income tax in Japan is not very different from that in the United States. As in our country, the tax base is corporate profits or the excess of gross revenue over total costs. Included in costs are the interest payments on debt obligations (both bonds and bank loans). In other words, interest expenses are deductible as in the United States. The corporate tax is approximately a flat-rate system (also as in the United States) with slightly lower rates applying only to very small corporations.

The two countries differ significantly in their approach to the taxation of dividends. The United States has what is sometimes referred to as a "classical system" with completely separate methods of personal and corporate taxation. No real attempt has been made to integrate the two tax programs even partially. As a result, dividends are taxed twice. In the United States, the current maximum federal tax rate on corporate earnings paid out as dividends is 73 percent. This can be seen by noting that a corporation earning an extra dollar will owe an extra $.46 on its corporation income tax. If the remaining $.54 is paid out as a dividend and the recipient is in the maximum personal income tax bracket, then the net after tax received by the investor will amount to $.27. The total federal government collections out of this extra dollar of earning would thus amount to $.73.

Even with the 1986 tax reform plan, the federal government would take up to $.52 out of a dollar of equity earnings paid out as dividends. First, it would collect $.34 from the corporation income tax and then 28 percent of the remaining $.66 from personal taxes. (For taxpayers in the 33 percent bracket, the federal government takes 56 percent out of equity earnings paid as dividends.)

In Japan, several features of both the corporate and the personal income tax systems offset the double taxation of dividends. First, the corporation income tax rate is lower for earnings paid out as dividends. In 1984, the rate for retained earnings was 43.3 percent, while that for earnings paid out as dividends was 33.3 percent. Second, the investor is given a tax credit of 10 percent of dividends received to be applied against his or her personal tax liability. Third, dividends can be taxed separately from other income at the option of the taxpayer, with the maximum rate applying to separately taxed dividends being 35 percent. This compares with a maximum rate on ordinary income of 70 percent. And finally, taxation for intercorporate dividends is completely exempted, in contrast to the 85 percent exclusion for these flows offered in the United States. These features add up to a rather substantial program of relief from the double taxation of dividends in Japan, although several European countries have gone farther in completely eliminating the double taxation problem.

Capital gains also receive special tax treatment in Japan—they are largely untaxed. In the United States capital gains have received preferential treatment, being taxed at a maximum rate of 20 percent. (Under the new 1986 tax law, capital gains are taxed as ordinary income.) The result, since both corporations and their lenders have the same incentive (not to pay or receive dividends), has been cash retention and heavy reliance on internal financing. For less dynamic managements, excessive cash buildup and the advantages to debt finance mentioned above have resulted in takeovers financed by junk bonds.

Dividends for noncorporate shareholders are taxed more lightly in Japan than in the United States in view of the 10 percent dividend tax credit, the lower corporate tax rate for earnings paid out as dividends, and the lower maximum tax rate on dividends. Still, since capital gains escape taxation for most individuals, they are more attractive than dividends. As stock ownership by households rises, the favorable treatment of capital gains in Japan becomes increasingly significant.

The complete exemption from taxation of intercorporate dividends effectively eliminated double taxation of dividends in Japan until the 1980s, since most corporate shares were held by corporations. Therefore, the preference for capital gains so characteristic of the United States has not been operative in Japan until very recently, as individual ownership of shares has risen. In 1986 consideration is being given to taxing capital gains for individuals just as their participation in the ownership of shares has increased. Discussion is also under way to restrict tax-free interest earnings for households. Both measures would raise the effective tax rate on income from capital unless accompanied by some offsetting measures.

Japan has not adopted anything similar to the Accelerated Cost Recovery System (ACRS) of depreciation and, in general, uses lifetimes longer than those in use in the United States. The Japanese system does permit the double-declining balance method of depreciation, however, and also allows some additional acceleration of deductions in particular industries or for particular investments. For example, machinery or equipment to prevent environmental damage is given a 25 percent first year write-off. Investments in particularly depressed areas of the country are allowed more rapid depreciation. In all, more than thirty categories of investments qualify for extra acceleration in depreciation deductions. This amounts to part of the Japanese industrial policy.

Inventory accounting is quite similar to that in the United States. Firms have the choice of first in/first out (FIFO) or last in/first out (LIFO) accounting or of several average-cost techniques. Most firms use one of the average-cost techniques to determine the cost of goods sold. The key difference between FIFO and LIFO is in the way they interact with inflation. FIFO reflects the nominal appreciation of inventoried stocks as an addition to profit and thus produces higher income figures and higher tax bills at higher rates of inflation. LIFO defers the gain on inventoried stocks until such stocks are liquidated. Under the average methods, the effect of inflation on the bottom line and the tax bill falls somewhere between the effects of LIFO and FIFO.

The use of the investment tax credit is fairly minor in Japan. A 7 percent credit and a 30 percent first-year depreciation are allowed for certain equipment for the efficient use of energy. There are the same allowances for investments in robotics and other automation techniques in small and medium-sized enterprises. And there is a credit for 20 percent of the amount by which R&D expenses exceed their maximum level since 1966. The beauty of this last feature is that it operates at the margin only. Only extra R&D investments qualify. This is obviously a feature of the law that favors rapidly expanding firms relative to others. In general, though, the ITC is not so widely used. Instead, its use is highly targeted and again is part of the industrial policy of the government.

Limited use of accelerated cost recovery systems and investment tax credits in Japan may result from consistently low inflation. Without indexation, steady high inflation, such as occurred during the 1970s in the United States, tends to raise the tax burden on income from capital. ACRS and ITC, together with low capital gains tax rates, have been employed to try *ex post* to reduce such "capital bracket creep." Of course, such measures are not as effective as long-run investment incentives signaling stable and predictable prospective tax burdens on income from capital. In Japan, consistent monetary policy and stable prices, save for the year after the 1974 oil shock, have encouraged stable tax policy and thereby long-run capital formation more effectively than have *ex post* corrective measures like ACRS and ITC in the United States.

The Japanese personal income tax differs from the U.S. system in a number of ways. It is based on the individual rather than on the household. The rate structure is steeply progressive, going from 10.5 percent to 70 percent. There are rather generous personal exemptions and standard deductions. The largest difference between the tax systems of the two countries, however, is probably in the taxation of personal capital income. We have already mentioned that dividends carry a 10 percent credit with them and can be taxed separately at the taxpayer's option. Also, as already mentioned, there is no capital gains tax on securities in Japan. This means that the peak tax rate on retained earnings nationally is 43.3 percent (collected by the corporate tax). The appreciation due to retained earnings is not taxed. In the United States, retained earnings currently face a marginal corporate tax of 46 percent. This may be lowered by tax reforms now being discussed. In addition, to the extent that retained earnings raise share values, they ultimately result in a capital gains tax obligation. The peak effective rate on capital gains is now 20 percent, but the basis is not adjusted for inflation. The rate on real capital gains can easily exceed 20 percent and, in some circumstances, can exceed even 100 percent. The 1986 tax reform act increased the maximum capital gains rate to 33 percent. The fact that the capital gains tax can be deferred until the capital gain is realized reduces it somewhat.

Perhaps the most important way the Japanese tax law affects investment incentives is the provision for nontaxable accounts similar to our individual retirement accounts. Each individual is allowed to have four such accounts for different purposes. First, interest accruing in postal saving accounts is tax free on the first 3 million yen of principal. As a result, one can have up to about $17,500 in this type of account and enjoy tax-free returns. Second, one can also have a "small saving tax exemption" account, which can include bank deposits, bonds and debentures, or mutual funds. The limit is again 3 million yen. Third, one can earn tax-free interest on central and local government bonds, again up to 3 million yen in principal. Finally, one can set up an account for pension and home equity saving that can have a balance up to 5 million yen. These four types of accounts allow an individual to shelter about $82,500 from taxation. A family of four could legally accumulate $330,000 in them and, because the accounts are completely unregistered, it is possible to have more of these accounts than allowed in the law. There is considerable evidence of widespread abuse of these accounts, and yet there has been a great deal of political resistance to requiring them to be registered. They are a very important feature of the Japanese capital markets. It is estimated that about 70 percent of the ownership of debt and equity capital uses these tax-free accumulation vehicles. They dwarf the similar individual retirement accounts in the United States.

Interest income not sheltered with the tax-free saving accounts is eligible for separate taxation in a manner similar to dividends. Ordinary deposits can be taxed at a separate rate of 20 percent at the taxpayer's option. Time deposits and similar accounts can be taxed separately at a rate of 35 percent. Because of these features, interest income is never subject to the high rates on ordinary income that go up to 70 percent.

The combination of no capital gains tax on securities, large opportunities for tax-free saving accounts, separate taxation of dividends and interest, and a 10 percent tax credit on dividends received results in very low taxation of personal capital income. According to one estimate, the average marginal tax rate applying to personal interest income in Japan in 1980 was 12 percent.[2] Another study estimated the average marginal rate applying to interest income in the United States for that year was 28 percent.[3] While Japan has a zero capital gains tax, the United States has an effective rate of 14 percent and might raise it. The effect of these differences on the tax wedge between what the investor receives and what the investment earns is apparent in the results of work presented in the section on effective marginal tax rates on investment.

Beyond a collection of features that imply low taxation of personal capital income, the Japanese tax system has been remarkably stable in the postwar period since its introduction in 1950, based on the recommendations of Carl Shoup. The major modifications have been aimed at steady reduction of tax burdens on income from capital. In 1952 the tax on retained profits of corporations was abolished. In 1953 taxation of capital gains and net worth was abolished, and special depreciation measures were introduced.

The 1960s saw the introduction of regular long-run tax planning by a tax commission first established for this purpose in 1956. The long-run burden of taxes as a share of national income was limited to 20 percent. The revenue bonus from the period of rapid growth was divided between tax reduction and increased public expenditure so that the public sector did not simply grow as revenues permitted. This planning followed naturally as part of an annual review of the tax code conducted each November as the federal government prepared the budget for the fiscal year, beginning April 1. In 1966 a large-scale tax reduction was effected to coincide with the first postwar issuance of government bonds (deficit finance).

During the 1970s a decision to enhance social overhead capital, expansion of a system of social insurance, and the severe recession after the 1974 oil crisis led to issuance of deficit-financing bonds and construction bonds. These deficits raised Japan's deficit and debt-to-GNP ratios to levels that at times exceeded those of the United States in the 1980s. As a result, growth of government spending was curtailed until deficits as a share of GNP fell to below 1 percent in 1985.

Relative to U.S. fiscal policy, Japanese policy has been a model of gradual change based on long-range planning. The tax system has generally been viewed as a means to finance a consciously selected level of expenditure in a way consistent with long-run capital formation. Revenue bonuses of the 1960s were directed partly to tax reduction by design. Revenue shortfalls of the 1970s and 1980s have led to programs of predictable and consistent expenditure reduction. While Japanese tax planners at the Ministry of Finance recognize the need for investment incentives, their strategy has been to offer investors a stable prospective tax burden on income from capital based on highly leveraged debt-financed investment. The supply-side notion that simply cutting tax rates is a sufficient means to raise revenue appears to have gained few adherents in the world's fastest-growing major industrial economy.

The Investment Tax Wedge Model

In this section we present a brief description of the King-Fullerton[3] investment tax wedge model. This model generates the results from the Shoven-Tachibanaki study, which we report in the next section.[4] The model is fundamentally quite simple. It says that if an investment earns a gross-of-tax rate of return p and if the owners of that investment earn s after taxes, then the government's take or the tax wedge is obviously

$$w = p - s$$

The effective tax rate is defined as

$$t = \frac{w}{p} = \frac{p - s}{p}$$

The usual technique in the literature has been to assume a figure for p, often 10 percent, and to apply all applicable taxes carefully to arrive at s, w, and t. Such considerations as capital gains taxes, ITCs, inventory accounting, inflation, R&D credits, and the like need to be taken into account. The size of the tax wedge depends on many considerations, including the nature of the investment, the industry in which it occurs, the means of financing, and the type of investor providing the funds. The tax laws discriminate so much along these dimensions that King and Fullerton and Shoven and Tachibanaki calculate the tax wedge and the effective marginal tax rate for eighty-one different combinations of asset types, industries, sources of finance, and ownership categories. The three alternatives examined in each of the four categories are shown in table 10–1.

The procedure of choosing a particular gross-of-tax rate of return (p) for each of the eighty-one combinations and calculating the resulting ultimate after-tax return of the investor is not the only one available. After all, one would not actually expect all investments to have the same gross-of-tax rate of return (especially if they are taxed differently), but this procedure does give a meaningful measure of the effective participation of the government in the investments return. An alternative approach, not reported here, would be to assume all investments generate the same after-tax rate of return, s, and calculate the required gross return to cover all related tax obligations. The two measures, while conceptually different, yield similar results.

Effective Marginal Tax Rates on Investment in Japan and the United States

Using the technique just described for eighty-one combinations of investors, investments, industries, and means of finance, we calcu-

315

TABLE 10–1
TYPES OF INVESTMENTS EXAMINED IN THE CALCULATIONS

Asset Types	Sources of finance
Machinery	Debt
Buildings	New share issues
Inventories	Retained earnings
Industries	Ownership categories
Manufacturing	Households
Other (construction, transporta-	Tax exempt
tion, communications, and	Insurance companies
utilities)	
Commerce	

SOURCE: Authors.

lated the results displayed in table 10–2 for Japan in 1980. The effective marginal tax rate figures are computed for four rates of inflation: 0, 5, 10, and 9 percent (9 percent is the actual average rate of inflation for the 1970s for Japan). The figures in each row refer to the average marginal tax wedge for twenty-seven different combinations of investment flows. For example, the number for "machinery" with 9 percent inflation is 8.3 percent. This is the average marginal tax wedge for machinery investments in three different industries, using three sources of finance, and for three different classes of owners. Similarly, the number for debt (− 59.7 percent) is the average for three types of debt-financed assets in three industries with three different classes of owners.

The table highlights a number of facts about the Japanese tax system. First, there is an enormous difference between the taxation of debt and equity capital. At 9 percent inflation, debt-financed capital is heavily subsidized, whereas equity capital is highly taxed. The reason for this is that corporations pay tax on equity capital, whereas interest is deductible. Individuals pay only light tax on both equity capital and interest, although equity is again somewhat more heavily taxed. Higher rates of inflation just increase the advantage of debt, since the ability to deduct from a high-rate tax and be subject only to a low-rate personal tax offers an arbitrage possibility. The Japanese government is actually subsidizing debt capital, and to an even greater extent if inflation bloats nominal interest payments. The estimates of the tax rates by asset type and by industry show relatively even taxation. Tax-exempt investors, primarily pension funds, are not really tax exempt in Japan. The assets of pension funds are subject to a separate

TABLE 10–2
EFFECTIVE MARGINAL TAX RATES IN JAPAN, 1980
(percent)

Type of Investment	Inflation Rate			
	0	5%	10%	9% (actual)
Asset				
Machinery	19.3	14.8	6.3	8.3
Buildings	23.4	15.0	1.5	4.4
Inventories	34.1	15.0	−4.3	−0.4
Industry				
Manufacturing	25.9	18.8	8.3	10.6
Other industry	20.4	6.3	−11.5	−7.7
Commerce	30.0	16.8	1.8	4.9
Source of finance				
Debt	−0.9	−32.0	−67.0	−59.7
New share issues	48.6	57.5	64.4	63.1
Retained earnings	47.6	54.9	59.7	58.9
Owner				
Households	23.1	11.5	−3.2	−0.0
Tax-exempt institutions	24.9	14.7	1.6	4.4
Insurance companies	35.8	31.7	23.8	25.6
Overall	25.3	15.0	1.5	4.4

SOURCE: Authors.

low-rate tax, resulting in the tax wedge being somewhat larger than for households.

The corresponding numbers for the United States in 1980, taken from King-Fullerton, are shown in table 10–3. Perhaps the most important comparison is that at the actual decade-long average rate of inflation, the United States had an average tax wedge on incremental investments of 37 percent, whereas Japan had a 4 percent rate. This means that investors in Japan reaped 96 percent of the return that their investments produced, while their American counterparts captured only 63 percent of the gross return on an incremental U.S. investment. The variation in the effective marginal tax rates across assets and industries is much greater in the United States. The largest difference in tax rates between assets amounts to 8.7 percentage

TABLE 10–3
EFFECTIVE MARGINAL TAX RATES IN THE UNITED STATES, 1980
(percent)

Type of Investment	Inflation Rate		
	0	10%	6.77% (actual)
Asset			
Machinery	3.9	22.8	17.6
Buildings	35.4	41.8	41.1
Inventories	50.9	45.5	47.0
Industry			
Manufacturing	44.2	55.0	52.7
Other industry	24.0	15.8	14.6
Commerce	37.9	37.5	38.2
Source of finance			
Debt	−2.0	−22.2	−16.3
New share issues	61.0	104.6	91.2
Retained earnings	48.4	66.5	62.4
Owner			
Household	44.1	61.9	57.5
Tax-exempt institutions	4.0	−37.3	−21.5
Insurance companies	4.0	44.3	23.4
Overall	32.0	38.4	37.2

SOURCE: Mervyn A. King and Don Fullerton, eds., *The Taxation of Income from Capital: A Comparative Study of the United States, the United Kingdom, Sweden, and West Germany* (Chicago: University of Chicago Press, 1984), p. 244.

points in Japan, whereas the difference goes to almost 30 percentage points in the United States. This is largely because the investment tax credit in the United States applies only to machinery and equipment and not to buildings and inventories.

Like the Japanese system, the U.S. tax system also imposed a negative tax wedge on debt-financed capital. Debt is less subsidized here, however. The tax rate on equity-financed investments was extremely high in both countries, above 60 percent for both retained earnings and new equity in the United States. The reason that debt is more subsidized in Japan is that its personal taxation is much lighter. All of the results of tables 10–2 and 10–3 use weighted averages, where the weights reflect the importance of different investments and financial instruments in the two economies. As we have already noted, Japanese firms use more debt finance and use it more aggressively than their American counterparts. Whereas 20 percent of new investments in manufacturing in the United States were financed with debt instruments, for example, the corresponding figure for Japan is 40 percent. As a result, the overall taxation is lower in Japan not only because debt is treated more favorably, but also because it accounts for a larger fraction of total new investment. Certainly, this kind of tax wedge calculation explains the high debt ratios in Japan, the nature of the Japanese banking system, and the increased popularity of leveraged buyouts in the United States. These financial structures will continue in both countries as long as such a huge tax wedge exists between the treatment of debt and equity capital.

Largely because the Japanese rely more heavily on debt finance, a smaller tax wedge exists between investors and investments. This reliance on debt finance flows through the banking sector, which, as already noted, plays a substantially different role in capital markets in Japan. The key difference is that the banks hold equity as well as debt in their major borrowers and are involved in important managerial decisions. Because of their close involvement in the operations of the firms, the banks are willing to tolerate higher debt levels. The incentive to do this, of course, is imbedded in the structure of the tax laws and in the heretofore unique nature of Japanese capital markets.

As in any calculation of this sort, the results are only as good as the assumptions and the data. We have done some sensitivity analysis to determine whether the lower tax wedge on new investments of the Japanese is fragile or robust to our modeling. One analyst has suggested that the results of the Shoven-Tachibanaki study derived from Japanese measures of the rate of economic depreciation that are too low.[5] The figures they use (and we adopt here) are the best available but do suggest that Japanese machinery and structures are more durable than their American counterparts.[6] For example, the Japanese estimate that the productivity of machinery in utilities, transportation, and communication decays at a 9 percent exponential rate, whereas figures for the United States indicate a 13 percent rate.[7] The difference in manufacturing is even greater. These differences may well reflect reality and result in some measure from our investment tax credit, which rewards relatively frequently replacement investment. Estimating rates of economic depreciation, however, is notoriously treacherous, and the differences could be artificial. To test the claim that Japanese measures of economic depreciation were too low, we recalculated the Japanese effective tax rates, assuming their assets were as short-lived as their U.S. counterparts. The results, shown in table 10–4, support that claim, but, at least at the actual rates of

TABLE 10–4
EFFECTIVE MARGINAL TAX RATES IN JAPAN,
USING U.S. DATA FOR ECONOMIC DEPRECIATION RATE, 1980
(percent)

Type of Investment	Inflation Rate			
	0	5%	10%	9% (actual)
Asset				
Machinery	28.9	29.5	25.3	26.5
Buildings	26.1	18.7	5.8	8.6
Inventories	34.1	15.0	−4.3	−0.4
Industry				
Manufacturing	32.0	27.9	19.8	21.7
Other industry	24.1	12.2	−4.1	−0.6
Commerce	31.8	19.6	5.5	8.4
Source of finance				
Debt	4.9	−23.1	−55.7	−48.9
New share issues	51.8	62.2	70.4	68.9
Retained earnings	51.0	60.0	66.2	65.1
Owner				
Households	27.7	18.4	5.7	8.4
Tax-exempt institutions	29.4	21.5	10.2	12.7
Insurance companies	39.8	37.9	31.8	33.3
Overall	29.8	21.8	10.2	12.7

SOURCE: Authors.

inflation, this result does not affect the qualitative conclusion. Now, instead of yielding a 4 percent rate of tax on Japanese investments, the overall figure comes to 17.3 percent. It is still less than half the U.S. figure. Note that the tax rate on machinery does increase dramatically if the lives are shortened in this manner, however. It is our belief that the Japanese estimates are probably reliable. We take this position partly because it is sensible, given the tax law, for U.S. firms to invest in less durable machinery.

The figures in tables 10–2 through 10–4 also assume that firms use LIFO accounting, an assumption made because FIFO and other techniques increase taxes and are nonoptimal in that sense. This is also consistent with the King-Fullerton study. The approach is to calculate the tax for a given combination of asset, investor, industry, and financial instrument assuming that taxes are minimized along the way. Firms do use inventory techniques that exaggerate profits with inflation, however. Approximately 70 percent of U.S. inventories are carried with FIFO accounting. In Japan about 60 percent use the equivalent of FIFO. If this "voluntary" tax is included in the calculation, then the tax rate is increased with inflation. This consideration alone would raise the Japanese tax rate at the actual inflation rate from 4.4 percent to 17.3 percent as is shown in table 10–5. It also raises the U.S figure from 37.2 percent to 43.2 percent, however. Even with taxes on inflation-produced inventory profits, then, the Japanese tax wedge on new investments is less than half that in the United States. If we take both these factors into account at once—that is, use the U.S.

TABLE 10–5
EFFECTIVE MARGINAL TAX RATES IN JAPAN,
USING JAPANESE DATA FOR ECONOMIC DEPRECIATION RATES, 1980
(percent)

Type of Investment	Inflation Rate			
	0	5%	10%	9% (actual)
Asset				
Machinery	19.3	14.8	6.3	8.3
Buildings	23.4	15.0	1.5	4.4
Inventories	34.1	37.2	40.2	39.6
Industry				
Manufacturing	25.9	23.7	18.2	19.6
Other industry	20.4	13.1	2.0	4.5
Commerce	30.0	29.7	27.6	28.1
Source of finance				
Debt	−0.9	−22.3	−47.7	−42.3
New share issues	48.6	62.3	74.1	71.8
Retained earnings	47.6	60.0	69.9	68.1
Owner				
Households	23.1	18.8	11.5	13.2
Tax-exempt institutions	24.9	21.8	15.9	17.3
Insurance companies	35.8	38.1	37.0	37.4
Overall	25.3	22.1	15.9	17.3

NOTE: Percentage of firms using FIFO equivalent = 60 percent.
SOURCE: Authors.

TABLE 10–6
Effective Marginal Tax Rates in Japan,
Using U.S. Data for Economic Depreciation Rates, 1980
(percent)

Type of Investment	Inflation Rate			
	0	5%	10%	9% (actual)
Asset				
Machinery	28.9	29.5	25.3	26.7
Buildings	26.1	18.7	5.8	8.6
Inventories	34.1	37.2	40.2	39.6
Industry				
Manufacturing	32.0	32.8	29.8	30.6
Other industry	24.1	18.9	9.4	11.5
Commerce	31.8	32.5	31.3	31.6
Source of finance				
Debt	4.9	−13.4	−36.3	−31.5
New share issues	51.8	67.0	80.1	77.6
Retained earnings	51.0	65.1	76.4	74.3
Owner				
Households	27.7	25.8	20.3	21.6
Tax-exempt institutions	29.4	28.6	24.6	25.6
Insurance companies	39.8	44.4	45.0	45.1
Overall	29.8	28.9	24.6	25.6

NOTE: Percentage of firms using FIFO equivalent = 60 percent.
SOURCE: Authors.

depreciation rates and the observed use of FIFO-equivalent inventory accounting—the average tax wedge rises to 25.6 percent for Japan. This result, shown in table 10–6, should be compared with the corresponding U.S. rate of 43.2 percent. So, even in this case the Japanese investor receives a significantly higher fraction of the gross returns of incremental investments than the American investor (74.4 percent versus 56.8 percent).

These sensitivity analyses, we believe, demonstrate that the total Japanese tax system, which allows investors to receive a larger fraction of the return on the real investments they finance, is robust to the assumptions we have had to make. The result is not obvious at a first glance at the Japanese tax law, since Japan has a high corporate tax rate, relatively unaccelerated depreciation, and no investment tax credit. When one examines the personal tax code as well as the corporate one, however, and considers their interaction, the result of the low marginal tax on investments becomes apparent.

While the Japanese tax law has not been changed too dramatically since 1980, the United States has experienced several major tax bills since then and is now considering fundamentally changing the tax system. Naturally, this raises the issue about whether the 1980 results are relevant to the 1985 debate. While it would involve a very significant amount of work to recalculate the results for both countries for 1985, other research on this topic gives a fairly accurate impression of the 1985 numbers. The cost-of-capital approach to calculating tax rates, which we have reported on in this paper for Japan, has been used extensively to examine the U.S. tax system, including the post-1980 tax law developments.

The three papers most relevant for this issue are Don Fullerton and Yolanda Henderson's "Incentive Effects of Taxes on Income from Capital," Don Fullerton's "The Indexation of Interest, Depreciation, and Capital Gains," and Yolanda Henderson's "Tax Reform and Investment Incentives,"[8] because they use an identical approach. Their data sources, however, are somewhat different, and they examine a different and more disaggregated list of industries. The Fullerton-Henderson paper calculates the effects of both the Economic Recovery Tax Act of 1981 and the Tax Equity and Fiscal Responsibility Act of 1982 on the marginal effective tax rate on capital income. The Fullerton paper contains the calculations for the November 1984 Treasury I tax reform proposal, as well as some figures for the administration proposal of May 1985. Finally, the Henderson paper contains figures for the Senate bill of June 1986.

Considering the additional disaggregation and changes in the data sources, the results are quite harmonious with those presented in this paper for the United States for 1980. In the more recent studies by Fullerton and Henderson, the overall tax wedge rate on new investments in the U.S. corporate sector in 1980 was estimated at 35 percent, rather than the 37 percent of the previous study by King and Fullerton. The effect of the 1981 law, with its introduction of ACRS and lower marginal tax rates, was to lower the overall effective marginal tax rate on investments in the corporate sector to 24 percent. TEFRA, however, rolled back the more rapid depreciation that ERTA had promised and also reduced the depreciation basis of depreciable property by half the investment tax credit. The result of these and other provisions of TEFRA was to raise the overall marginal tax rate to 30 percent. By 1985, taking into account the tax changes enacted in

1984 and the lower inflation rate of the economy, Fullerton calculates the effective tax rate as 31 percent. Henderson estimates the effective marginal tax rate for corporate sector investments for 1986 as 37.6 percent. Both the Treasury's November 1984 plan for reform and the administration's 1985 plan would have raised the tax wedge between investors and investments. The Treasury plan—with its Real Cost Recovery System (an attempt to match tax depreciation with economic depreciation), elimination of the investment tax credit, and increase in the capital gains tax—would have raised the overall effective marginal tax rate on corporate investments to 43.1 percent. Fullerton calculates the marginal rate imposed by the administration plan, with its Capital Cost Recovery System and other features, as 34.4 percent. Both the Treasury and the administration plans greatly even out the taxation of assets by type and industry; the Treasury plan, however, would have substantially increased the tax wedge facing new investments, and the administration plan would have left the wedge at essentially its 1980 position. Fullerton and Henderson put the overall wedge applying to corporate investments at 34.5 percent in 1980, while Fullerton (using exactly the same techniques) calculates the figure for the administration proposal as 34.4 percent. Henderson's results show that the Senate bill generates an average marginal effective tax rate of 41 percent on corporate investments but that the variance across asset types is greatly reduced.

Anyone looking at these figures for the recent U.S. tax laws, then, can clearly see that a major reduction in the tax wedge facing corporate capital was put in place in 1981 and that its effects have been eroded with each change since then. The administration plan would have completely eliminated the reduction in the effective marginal tax rate on corporate capital investments. The Ways and Means bill, while not formally evaluated, would certainly make the U.S. tax wedge even larger than would the administration plan. And the Senate bill, closely related to the 1986 tax reform bill in its treatment of income from capital, would result in an effective tax rate almost double the post-ERTA rate.

The changes enacted by the Tax Reform Act of 1986 will provide some test of the effectiveness of incentives like investment tax credits and accelerated depreciation. Removal or alterations of the credits and alteration of depreciation schedules have become the norm in the United States, so the changes in the 1986 Tax Reform Act may have been anticipated to some extent. The impact after the fact may therefore have been muted. On balance, if the 1986 measures are left in place, more economically motivated and less tax-motivated investment will take place in the United States. Overall investment should fall, based only on the slight rise in the overall tax burden on new investment. If, however, allowance is made for the possibility that the lower tax rates and reduced borrowing incentives in the 1986 tax reform bill may reduce nominal and real interest rates, the negative tax impact on investment may be mitigated or eliminated. Careful analysis of effects of the tax changes will be important.

Even though the Japanese tax laws have remained relatively unchanged, Japan has experienced at least as sharp a fall in inflation as has the United States. Because of the two oil shocks and the response of the Japanese to them, inflation was quite high in Japan in the 1970s, even higher than in the United States. The average rate was 9.0 percent. The inflation rate since 1981, however, has been quite low—in the 2–5 percent range. This has had a greater effect on the rate of taxation of capital income than have the relatively minor changes in the tax law. Our calculations of how inflation has affected the results for Japan are shown in table 10–2, and we find that the overall marginal tax rate now ranges from 18 to 22 percent, depending on the actual rate of inflation. If forced to pick a single number, we would focus on 20 percent. While the reduction in inflation has increased the tax wedge in Japan (because lower inflation implies lower nominal interest payments and, therefore, smaller deductions from the corporate tax), the Japanese rate is still substantially lower than ours. We can neither take much of the credit for narrowing the gap (it resulted from the slowing of Japanese inflation) nor expect a further narrowing (since inflation in Japan is now running very low). The 1986 tax reform bill would allow the U.S. government to continue to take at least twice as large a share of the gross return of debt-financed investments as the Japanese government.

Lessons for the United States

We believe that the United States could learn several lessons from the taxation practices of Japan. Most of these lessons suggest ways that our tax system could be improved if it were more like Japan's, but not all. In fact, one major lesson is a tax incentive to be avoided rather than adopted.

Tax Stability. The Japanese tax system has been relatively stable for the past thirty years. Between 1955 and 1981 the basic corporation tax rate varied from 36.75 percent to 42 percent, but its structure was largely maintained. The split rate between dividends and retained earnings was introduced in 1963. Depreciation allowances have remained quite stable. We have already documented some of the principal changes that have taken place in the United States. Depreciation rules change with great frequency, as do the investment tax credit, the treatment of capital gains, and the availability of tax shelters for pensions. We believe that the stability of the Japanese system is, in itself, one of its strengths.

Distinction between Taxes on Corporations and Investment Incentives. Japan's corporate tax raises about 30 percent of national tax receipts, three times the U.S. level. Investment incentives, however, in the form of light taxation of debt-financed capital income are strong. A combination of full deductibility of interest on corporate debt (as in the United States) and light taxation of interest on personal income, capital gains, and some dividends (the reverse of the United States) allows Japanese investors to capture a higher fraction of gross earnings from investment than American investors can capture. The fact that tax treatment of household interest income and expense in Japan exempts most interest income from tax while not allowing deductibility of interest expense—the reverse of treatment in the United States—is more relevant to comparing investment incentives than is the level of corporate taxation. The United States could move in this direction by (1) at least indexing interest income and expense for tax purposes to avoid the borrowing-subsidy-lending tax that causes very high nominal rates; (2) adopting the Japanese practice on interest income and expense; or (3) equivalently, adopting an expenditure-based tax system.

Saving-Investment Incentives. Our fundamental finding is that Japanese investors are allowed to keep a far higher fraction of the return on their investments than are their American counterparts. The single most important feature of the tax law that permits this is Japan's generous tax-sheltered saving plans. The Japanese have far more of their saving in the equivalent of individual retirement accounts.

Equity earnings are also somewhat more lightly taxed in Japan. The relief from the double taxation of dividends and the zero taxation of capital gains in securities largely account for this.

One way in which the United States could move toward the Japanese approach to saving incentives would be to liberalize IRA accounts and adopt a consumption or expenditure tax philosophy. Although this seemed to be the way we were headed in 1981, that no longer appears to be true. While the current tax reform momentum seems to be driven by issues of fairness and simplicity, there is no necessary conflict between these goals and an expenditure-based tax system.

Targeted Investment Incentives. Rather than use accelerated depreciation, investment tax credits, and research and development credits across the board, the Japanese use these tax incentives very selectively. This allows them to affect the investments they desire with a minimum revenue loss. Both generous accelerated depreciation and investment tax credits were made available for energy saving investments in the 1970s, a policy now credited with the economy's successful adjustment to the post-OPEC world price of oil. The two instruments are also used to aid particularly depressed industries and regions of the country. In addition, some technologies identified as particularly promising, such as robotics, receive special tax incentives.

The research and development credit is designed in a particularly clever way so that its major impact falls only on incremental R&D expenditures. The 20 percent credit applies only to the increase in R&D expenditures over and above any preceding year since 1966. This effectively discriminates in favor of rapidly growing R&D-intensive firms. It is a hidden, but well-designed industrial policy.

Tax System Biased toward Debt Financing. A negative lesson, something not to follow, in our opinion, is the design of the Japanese tax system that strongly favors debt financing and that has resulted in the highly leveraged financing of Japanese industry. To deal with the debt ratios they finance, Japanese banks are much more involved in the management of their borrowers than are American banks. Japanese leverage ratios would be too high for U.S. corporations, especially in view of desirable preservation of arms-length transactions between banks and their corporate clients. It is likely that as Japanese financial markets become more international, the intimate relationship between Japanese banks and their corporate clients in Japan will become awkward. Non-Japanese corporate clients will not wish to deal with banks that may be, effectively, part of the management of firms that could be competitors. Japanese banks may adopt international practices, moving toward an arms-length relationship with their corporate clients. The result may be lower leverage ratios in Japan and less advantage to the use of debt finance for Japanese firms.

The Tax Reform Act of 1986 may reduce incentives for debt finance in the United States. The sharp drop in tax rates for both corporations and individuals to 34 and 33 percent respectively reduces the tax advantage of debt finance over equity finance. So does the taxation of capital gains as ordinary income by reducing incentives for retained earnings and thereby for debt-financed leveraged buyouts.

Still, the U.S. tax system is burdened by double taxation of dividends, which will blunt the incentive to switch from debt to equity finance, and by inadequate indexing provisions, which make prospective tax burdens on income from capital both uncertain and positively tied to inflation. It may be that U.S. policy makers could do more to encourage capital formation by adopting the Japanese macro policy combination. This combination consists of a credible monetary policy aimed at price stability, its credibility enhanced by a fiscal policy characterized by expenditure control that has virtually eliminated the budget deficit.

Conclusion

We conclude that the United States can glean several lessons from a study of the Japanese tax system. The Japanese tax regime is marked by its stability, its generous incentives for saving and investment, targeted credits and deductions that are effective at the relevant margin, and a strong preference for debt finance. The United States could benefit from adopting the first three of these attributes and should hesitate to follow the last one. Currently, there is some talk about stabilizing the U.S. tax environment, but movement is away from the Japanese example of saving and investment incentives and targeted tax relief. If the United States is to emulate the stable tax environment of Japan, we shall have to devise a credible means of deficit reduction. The first step should be a fundamental decision about the share of government spending in national income. Once that is set, an adjustment of spending levels may be implied, which in turn should be financed by a tax system with moderate and stable prospective burdens on income from capital.

Notes

1. John B. Shoven and Toshiaki Tachibanaki, "The Taxation of Income from Capital in Japan" (Paper presented at the Center for Economic Policy Research Conference on Government Policy towards Industry in the United States and Japan, Stanford, California, May 2–3, 1985; and at the United States–Japan Productivity Conference of the National Bureau of Economic Research Conference on Research in Income and Wealth, Cambridge, Massachusetts, August 26–28, 1985).
    2. Ibid.
    3. Mervyn A. King and Don Fullerton, eds., *The Taxation of Income from Capital: A Comparative Study of the United States, the United Kingdom, Sweden, and West Germany* (Chicago: University of Chicago Press, 1984).
    4. John B. Shoven and Toshiaki Tachibanaki, "The Taxation of Income from Capital in Japan."
    5. Unpublished comments of Alan Auerbach presented at the Center for Economic Policy Research Conference on Government Policy towards Industry in the United States and Japan, Stanford, California, May 2–3, 1985.

6. M. Kuroda and K. Yoshioka, "Measurement of Services from Capital Stock by Industries and Assets," *Mita Shogaku Kenkyu*, vol. 27, no. 4 (October 1984).

7. Charles R. Hulten and Frank C. Wykoff, "The Measurement of Economic Depreciation," in C. R. Hulten, ed., *Depreciation, Inflation, and the Taxation of Income from Capital* (Washington, D.C.: Urban Institute, 1981).

8. Don Fullerton and Yolanda Kodrzycki Henderson, "Incentive Effects of Taxes on Income from Capital: Alternative Policies in the 1980s," National Bureau of Economic Research, Working Paper no. 1262, January 1984; Don Fullerton, "The Indexation of Interest, Depreciation, and Capital Gains: A Model of Investment Incentives," National Bureau of Economic Research, Working Paper no. 1655, June 1985; and Yolanda K. Henderson, "Tax Reform and Investment Incentives: An Update," *Tax Notes*, June 2, 1986, pp. 931–33.

Bibliography

Aoki, Masahiko. "Shareholders' Non-Unanimity on Investment Financing: Banks Vs. Individual Investors." In *The Economic Analysis of the Japanese Firm*, pp. 193–224. Elsevier Science Publishers B.V. (North-Holland), 1984.

Hatsopoulos, George N. "High Cost of Capital: Handicap of American Industry." Paper presented at the American Business Conference and Thermo Electron Corporation, April 1983.

Makin, John H., Norman Ornstein, and Eugene Steuerle. "The Economics and Politics of Tax Reform: Some Talking Points on the Senate Finance Committee Plan." Paper presented at the American Enterprise Institute for Public Policy Research, Washington, D.C., June 1986.

Tax Bureau, Japan Ministry of Finance. *An Outline of Japanese Taxes, 1984.* Printing Bureau, Ministry of Finance, 1984.

CONTRIBUTORS

Phillip Cagan—*Editor*
Professor of economics, Columbia University; former senior staff economist for the Council of Economic Advisers; visiting scholar at the American Enterprise Institute.

Eduardo Somensatto—*Associate editor*
Consultant, World Bank; former assistant director of Economic Policy Studies, American Enterprise Institute; former lecturer in economics, Georgetown University.

Kenneth M. Brown
Senior economist, Joint Economic Committee of Congress; formerly with the U.S. Department of Commerce; former visiting fellow at the American Enterprise Institute.

Jacob S. Dreyer
Deputy assistant director—fiscal analysis, Congressional Budget Office; former deputy assistant secretary for international economic analysis, Department of the Treasury; former assistant professor of economics, New York University.

Gottfried Haberler
Galen L. Stone Professor of International Trade Emeritus, Harvard University; past president of the American Economic Association and of the International Economic Association. Resident scholar with the American Enterprise Institute.

William S. Haraf
J. E. Lundy Scholar and director of Financial Market Regulation Project at the American Enterprise Institute; former special assistant to the Council of Economic Advisers.

331

Hendrik S. Houthakker

Henry Lee Professor of Economics, Harvard University; former member of the Council of Economic Advisers under presidents Nixon and Johnson; adjunct scholar of the American Enterprise Institute.

Marvin H. Kosters

Director of Economic Policy Studies, American Enterprise Institute.

John H. Makin

Director of Fiscal Policy Studies and resident scholar with the American Enterprise Institute; former professor of economics and director of the Institute for Economic Research, University of Washington.

Murray N. Ross

Research assistant in Economic Policy Studies, American Enterprise Institute.

John B. Shoven

Professor of economics and chairman, Department of Economics, Stanford University; research associate, National Bureau of Economic Research.

Eugene Steuerle

Director of finance and taxation projects with the American Enterprise Institute; former economic staff coordinator in charge of the coordination and design of the Treasury Department's Project on Fundamental Tax Reform.

John C. Weicher

Resident fellow and first scholar named to the F. K. Weyerhaeuser Chair in Public Policy Research at the American Enterprise Institute; former deputy assistant secretary at the U.S. Department of Housing and Urban Development; past president of the American Real Estate and Urban Economics Association.

A NOTE ON THE BOOK

*This book was edited by
Janet Schilling, Trudy Kaplan, and Dana Lane
of the AEI publications staff.
Peg Schreiber designed the cover, and
Hördur Karlsson drew the figures.
The text was set in Palatino,
a typeface designed by Hermann Zapf.
Exspeedite Printing Service, Inc., of Silver Spring, Maryland,
set the type, and Edwards Bros., Inc., of Lillington, North Carolina,
printed and bound the book,
using permanent, acid-free paper made by the Glatfelter Company.*

American Enterprise Institute for Public Policy Research

CONTEMPORARY ECONOMIC PROBLEMS SERIES